Human Relationships

Second Edition

Steve Duck

SAGE Publications
London • Newbury Park • New Delhi

SAGE Publications Ltd
6 Bonhill Street
London EC2A 4PU

SAGE Publications Inc
2455 Teller Road
Newbury Park, California 91320

SAGE Publications India Pvt Ltd
32, M-Block Market
Greater Kailash – I
New Delhi 110 048

British Library Cataloguing in Publication Data

Duck, Steve
 Human relationships. – 2nd ed.
 I. Title
 306.8

 ISBN 0-8039-8380-8
 ISBN 0-8039-8381-6 pbk

Library of Congress catalog card number 91-050649

Typeset by Mayhew Typesetting, Rhayader, Powys
Printed in Great Britain by Dotesios Ltd, Trowbridge

Contents

Acknowledgements   iv

Preface   v

Chapter 1 The Languages of Human Relationships   1

Chapter 2 Social Emotions: Showing Our Feelings about
Other People   32

Chapter 3 Interaction and Daily Life in Long-term
Relationships   67

Chapter 4 Relationships with Relations: Families and
Socialization   103

Chapter 5 Influencing Strangers, Acquaintances and Friends   146

Chapter 6 Staying Healthy . . . with a Little Help from Our
Friends?   174

Chapter 7 Human Relationships Take the Witness-Stand   207

Afterword   241

Appendix: To Help You and Your Instructor   243

References   249

Index of References   275

Subject Index   278

Acknowledgements

I am grateful to many people for their help, both witting and unwitting, in preparing me for the writing of this book. These include: Jesse C. Stickler, Miss Jordan, Miss Burt, Robin Ovens, F.C.G. Langford, John Radford, Michael Booker, Lynda Cox, Mike Gardner, J.C.B. Glover, my late father and my mother, Carole Wade, Brian Little, Chris Spencer, George Kelly, Sanchez and John Davies, Linda Acitelli, Pembroke College (Oxford), Sheri Meserow Scott, Diane Lowenstein-Pattison, Sandra, Christina, Jamie, and Joanna and Ben.

Also, I thank those who helped and supported me during my guest professorship in the University of Connecticut, Storrs, when the first edition was prepared: Carol Masheter, Reuben Baron, Barbara Montgomery, Ross Buck, Bob Ryder, Jeff Fisher, Dave Kenny, Steve Anderson and, above all, Linda Harris who fixed it all up.

I thank also Peter Collett, David Clarke, Jill Crosland, Robert McHenry, and Michael Argyle at Oxford University for their hospitality whilst I was a visiting scholar during the preparation of the first edition of the book.

David Watson, Mark Leary, and Andrew Colman made extensive and careful comments about various drafts of the first edition, and Roz Burnett, Kathryn Dindia, Sue Jones, and Paul Wright made detailed and insightful comments on the draft of the second edition, which did more than anything to improve the final product. Robin Gilmour provided sustained discussion of some of the key ideas in the first edition. Michael Saks, Peter Blanck, and Zick Rubin provided me with extensive advice and guidance for the chapter, new to the second edition, on relationships and the law. Joanna Lawson read several drafts of the whole ms for both editions very thoughtfully and provided many excellent critiques and case examples. I am grateful to them all. I am also grateful to Farrell Burnett, formerly of Sage, whose attentive editing of the first edition contributed substantially to those parts of the book that attracted praise.

Preface

When I finish reading a social science textbook I always regret that I learned so little about much that is a familiar part of the real social life of myself and my students – liking and disliking, falling in and out of love, shyness, jealousy and embarrassment, loneliness, friendship and family, health, everyday concerns about the way that we appear to other people, and our problems and successes in relationships. Why should my students' learning be focussed on what the SS (Schutzstaffel) did during the Second World War, why madmen climb clocktowers in Texas and fire machine guns randomly at people, what attracts us to strangers we know that we'll never see again, how people sell us insurance or encyclopaedias, or what Charlie Brown said about attitude change? While much of this is interesting, it is remote from my life and my students' personal experience.

For this reason, I often feel uncomfortable when I ask my students to rely solely on introductory social science textbooks even when they do, admittedly, an excellent job of reporting current research. What we read in them is interesting but stops short of describing the social processes with which we actually live because the research descriptions are, on their own, incomplete accounts of the living personal experiences of our daily lives. Therefore, my aim is to supplement available introductory texts by covering some important elements of life which they do not.

I focus upon the essence and substructure of interpersonal behaviour, the long-term and the short-term relationships which we have with other people and which so strongly influence our thoughts and behaviour. Most of us realize that we find our major sorrows and joys in personal relationships, that we can achieve our goals more easily with the help of friends, and that our feelings about other people can influence the direction of our lives from time to time. But there is more to it than that – important though those facts are – and the influence of relationships runs deeper through the fabric of social behaviour and interpersonal communication.

Relationships are not just attitudes or feelings about other people, nor are they equivalent to 'cognitive structures', nor some abstraction of thinking about abstract 'social events'. Rather they are real and have real effects on our behaviour and the ways in which we spend our time. Equally, the groups, communities and societies which we talk about in the abstract are actually composed of real people and the personal and social relationships that bind them and bring them together. When we speak or write of 'students' or 'communication scholars' or 'social psychologists' or 'society' we are actually referring to real human beings with real personal ties and real relationships with one another. These relationships affect the ways in which information is transmitted. They exert pressures on individuals to act in certain ways (e.g. in their dress or even their responses to fashionable attitudes) in order to be accepted and liked. They influence the sorts of social behaviour that we choose from our repertoire on a given occasion, for instance whether we treat someone in a special way because we know him or her or merely as 'yet another person in a hurry who is claiming special treatment'.

For these reasons I believe that everyday life and everyday relationships should be the starting points for the exploration of interpersonal behaviour. The first edition of this book started with a chapter on emotions and cognition, because it is often felt that emotion and cognition are the bases of relationships. This second edition argues otherwise and finds the basis of relationships in routine behaviours and everyday communication. Not only relationships but also emotions themselves are based in routine. The parallel existence of relationships and emotions has previously fooled researchers, who failed to see that their data on such things were often correlational and could not establish causality. But even if relationships are based on emotion, they are not based just on the individual's feeling of those emotions but on the communication of those feelings to others, willy-nilly. We could sit and love someone desperately, but if we do not let them know, or if they do not work it out for themselves from our behaviour – in short if the emotion is not communicated to them – then they may as well inhabit a different universe as far as relationshipping is concerned.

Emotions are as much founded in the routine knowledge that we have about our partners and their regular styles of behaviour as they are to be found in our own particular styles of feeling. More than this, however, they are also founded in cultural knowledge, shared and commonly understood language and terminology, and ways of expressing ourselves. Thus a proper starting place for exploration of relationships is not in abstract thought or in emotion but in the cultural basis of knowledge and the ways in which behaviour is systematized as a context for relationships.

With the title that this book has, it is obvious that I will be writing about relationships and their influences, both hidden and declared, on people's social behaviour. But I am not able as many authors before me have been to think of a way of doing this without focussing explicitly on the communication that goes on in relationships. I find it hard to think about 'interaction' in the abstract, or 'social participation' without talk, for example, so I have decided to make communication the topic of the first chapter in this edition of the book. This term is used somewhat loosely and in one form or another we cover many forms of such communication where we see our normal behaviour coming into view. For example, language usage, metaphors, everyday nicknames, coded relational words, everyday speech, friendly chat, gossip, discussing, asking, requesting, offering, persuading, pleading, influencing, arguing, are all familiar ways in which our subjects – human beings just like us – use speech and discourse every day to relate to other people in their interpersonal behaviour. Sadly, especially in present social psychology texts, such crucial timbers of the structure of relationships are virtually ignored and this book intends to repair this ignorance.

Many texts, particularly in social psychology, focus on cognitive processes rather than interactive interpersonal ones and refer obliquely to unspecified 'social processes of interaction'. For me, however, the central element of any such process is communication between people, the words that we say to one another and the ways in which we converse in relationships. Although individual psychological processes like attitude formation or social cognition may be influential in our communications, nevertheless, they, too, are based on words. Talk is *inextricably* linked in to human social interaction and underlies human relationships. To write about relating is actually to imply and assume a continuous and routine basis for interaction, but also to imply a language and communication system that provides that daily basis for our relationships. This system contains the things we say to each other to conduct and maintain the relationship, the terms that we use to describe our relationships or our feelings, the way we comfort a miserable friend, the way we present ourselves, the means or strategies we select to ask someone out on a date, the chosen ways in which we try to persuade someone else into or out of a relationship, or the subtle manner in which we convey our feelings about someone else by our choice of words and names for them.

Therefore, I begin the book with interpersonal communication and go on from there to emotion and the growth of personal relationships, influencing strangers, and social relationships in childhood. I look at the development of courtship, at sexual decision-making in dating, and at the family. I discuss problems in relationships and how to put them right, deal with gossip and persuasion, and apply research on relationships to the psychology of health and to behaviour in the courtroom.

Mainly for the instructor . . . a psychology of human concerns

My argument is that people spend a large part of their time involved in relationships which are underrepresented not only in the introductory textbooks but also in research. My intent is not a non-standard version of the familiar attack on laboratory research, to criticize the old for the sake of it; it is to point in some new directions. The status of laboratory research is prematurely attacked, since we cannot properly claim that it is 'artificial' until we know exactly what daily life is made up of (or unless one relies on intuitions about the value and representativeness of laboratory research that are truly the kind of assumption that laboratory research is itself designed to replace!).

That the typical present-day textbook in the social sciences gives so little space to relationships is surprising, but I believe that it is a reflection of the broad assumption that most average people are leading orderly interesting lives doing important things. We tend to write research articles and textbooks as if everyone spends each day on a jury, making life or death decisions or deriving complex scientomimetic attributions instead of shouting at his or her children or admonishing a spouse for leaving the top off the toothpaste tube.

We are 'nice' to people in all our other assumptions, too: we assume that everyone is good and we 'explain' the bad side. For instance, we assume altruism and spend years 'explaining' bystander apathy; we assume impartiality and 'explain' prejudice; we assume scientific rationality and 'explain' fundamental errors. Overall, our present model of social life is one where essentially nice, inter-changeable, serious-minded, calculating laboratory technicians meet one another for brief periods of time to do significant, positive things in an environment void of context, where today is an exact replica of yesterday and no one has any shopping to do or a summer holiday to plan or a disagreeable colleague.

By contrast, our own daily lives are more likely to consist of quite humdrum experiences with the same people we have known for years, whom we meet for insignificant social, emotional, or relational purposes, in a special context where we have plans about the future. Furthermore, some of these people will be colleagues with whom we have a long-standing relationship, be it friendship, formality, or feud. We often see people squabble and make stupid, irrational mistakes; we have meetings where no one acts like a scientist; and we may deal with deans and tenure committees to whom none of our kindly textbook assumptions can possibly be applied. In short, our real social lives are based on complex but routine relationships which we do not emphasize in the textbooks, and we go around believing 'It's not what you know but who you know' and writing as if we didn't. Relationships run through the fabric of our lives, too, but are regarded as too unimportant or too obvious to write about.

My students were wiser than the textbooks and unashamedly turned their assignments towards this general human concern over relationships. After they had had one whole year of social psychology, I taught them advanced library skills. They were to pick a topic in social psychology and evaluate the important research on it in the last five years, using tools such as *Current Contents* and *SSCI* (see the exercises in the Appendix). I gave them a list of topics derived from the adopted text, but did not restrict them to that list.

Not one of them picked a 'pure' topic. Instead, all chose personally relevant research that, broadly, focussed on relationships. Admittedly shy people researched shyness; students from broken homes followed research on the effects of parental divorce on children; unattractive students wrote about self-fulfilling prophecies and Pygmalion effects. Moreover, the answers invariably were better than those for the usual class assignments and often were thoughtful and even exciting to read. I realized not only how much more effectively students learn from being personally involved but also the great potential for illuminating their personal involvements.

I believe that, for all the preceding obvious and unobvious reasons, everyday relationships are significant subject matter and consequently I have structured this book around the theme of personal relationships. They are simultaneously the most personally important part of most people's lives, a potentially cohesive force in theories of interpersonal behaviour, and a recently booming area of research. Not least of my reasons for taking that position, however, is the belief that social science lacks substance when it addresses only the large-scale societal issues of the day. Social science has a supplementary and equally significant role: to be informative about the familiar; to explain the everyday; and to understand life as it is lived by the individual relating to other people.

CHAPTER 1

The Languages of Human Relationships

Two scholars once wrote that 'We converse our way through life' (Berger & Kellner, 1975), and in the case of human relationships, it is rather clear that this is so. If you were to sit and list the things that you do with friends, one of the top items on the list would surely have to be 'talking'. Talking is fundamental to relationships – whether they are starting, getting better, getting worse, or just carrying on. Also, such talk is one obvious vehicle for creating change in relationships, for expressing emotion, for handling conflict, and for indicating love and affection. We talk to share attitudes; we express love through talk; we talk about our desires, goals and relational fantasies; in short we talk to relate.

There is more to human relationships than talk, though. It is rather *communication* that is the basis for relating in the real world – communication that includes not only talk but 'paralanguage' (such things as tones of voice that communicate emotions or feelings about another person). Indeed there are those who claim that every spoken message contains not one but two elements (Watzlawick et al., 1967): the *content* and a *message about the relationship* between the speaker and the listener. In other words, you can barely open your mouth without indicating how you *feel* about the other person.

An even broader view of communication also includes NVC (i.e. nonverbal communication), the silent messages of touch, smiles, warm and tender eyes, and bodily postures that indicate invitation or approval rather than rejection. Through usage of spacing (closeness or distance, for example), messages of intimacy or dislike can be conveyed, just as they are by words. From the nonverbal accompaniments of speech, human beings tend to deduce important overtones about relationship messages, as when a sensitive comment is made more comforting by a tender touch or a supportive embrace.

If we extend our thinking even further, then sociological context, structural factors and social forces are relevant to human relationships – society forbids us to make love in the street; we often conceal our true emotions in order to be polite; we may exaggerate

or misrepresent expression of our interest in someone or our relational feelings about them, as when we meet boring strangers at
parties or embarrassing relatives at Christmas time. Furthermore,
even the apparently enjoyable news that someone loves us can be a
source of discomfort or displeasure. Since an expression of 'I love
you' can be judged inappropriate if it comes from the 'wrong
person' or at the 'wrong time', it is clear that simply *having*
emotions and simply *expressing* them naked and raw is not all that
we need to understand in learning about human relationships.

In short, human communications about relationships, and also the
emotions that we feel in them, are both affected by a host of intriguing influences that lie some way beneath the surface of social conven-
tions, norms and rules. If we wish to improve relationships and to get
a better understanding of their processes, then we must understand
this Big Picture. If we seek to understand human relationships – and
for all the fact that they may feel cosily familiar, most of us would
like to know more about them – then we have to understand all of
these contexts for the raw expression of raw relational emotions.

Much of our communication in relationships – whether it is
verbal, paralinguistic or nonverbal – is extremely familiar to us. Yet
just as a kid may be able to ride a bicycle without being able to
explain anything about balance or the physics of motion, so too we
may be unaware of the fascinating system of rules and meanings that
underlie such routine behaviour as conversing with friends or such
disruptive experiences as falling in love. In order to comprehend
some of these systems, we need to begin at the beginning and understand the contexts for talk and for inferences about other people.
Then we can go on to explore, in chapter 2, the ways in which
emotions such as love develop in that context.

Contexts for Talk

Silent Language: Nonverbal Communication

Bodies talk. Whenever we sit, stand, walk, position ourselves next
to someone, or look at someone else, we give off messages, some of
which we may not have intended to make public. Equally, we can
learn that someone dislikes us when they have not even said a word,
that he or she is deliberately lying to us, or that a person finds us
sexually attractive. We can do all this by understanding the hidden
languages of social behaviour.

Our human relationships are based not on one language but on two. Whilst spoken language is the one that we recognize more easily, there is an unspoken language, too: the language of nonverbal communication. Nonverbal communication is made up of, for instance, the spacing between people when we interact, the gestures, eye movements and facial expressions that accompany or supplement our speech, and a range of other cues. We hardly ever speak without adding to the message by intimate body language, by frowning or smiling or looking interested, impressed or bored. These messages are at least as powerful as speech itself. If someone spoke to you *saying* that he or she was interested in you but *looked* bored or was reading the newspaper, which would you believe, the verbal or the nonverbal message? However, before we get too carried away with this idea and look at studies that show the effects of combining nonverbal communication and talk, we need to learn a little about each of them on its own.

BOX 1.1 Some points to think about
- *What are the social skills of interpersonal communication and how do our verbal messages combine with the silent, nonverbal messages, like facial expression, to communicate meaning?*
- *Is social behaviour a skill, like riding a bicycle, with certain almost automatic abilities that we have to know how to use properly in order to get along with other people?*
- *How does an apparently 'unrelational' factor, like the usage of space in social interaction or decoration of territory, have any impact on relationships or on 'atmosphere' in interpersonal interaction?*
- *Would you be surprised to find that lonely, depressed, embarrassed or shy people show patterns of nonverbal social behaviour that are inappropriate and socially unskilled? If they do this, what are they doing wrong and why do other people react to them negatively?*
- *How is social skill related to the self-concept or to communication about one's (lack of) comfort in a social setting?*
- *How can we tell when other people are lying? What cues give them away to us?*

The nonverbal context for speech is thus a part of a full system of social communication. It is less susceptible to conscious control than is speech, so we can readily 'leak' our real feelings unintentionally by means of NVC, including the way we manage space in interactions. We can also add important emphasis or context to our words through socially meaningful messages like accent, humorous sarcasm and the twinklings, winks, significant stares, gestures and loudness/softness that are the embroidery on the cloth of common speech. We can also convey relationships in such ways, through formality and informality in messages, or by showing that we like or dislike someone, creating status differences and many ways of show-ing who is in charge. A large number of such messages about status and liking are structured into interactions and a great deal of influence on social encounters is exerted by space and its manage-ment. These factors position people both literally and metaphorically in relationship to one another. Space carries forceful messages about relationships and is a powerful ingredient in the mix of nonverbal and verbal indicators of liking.

Are there social rules about space?

Isn't it interesting that we talk about being 'close' to someone? 'Close' is a word that literally refers to space and to physical distance or nearness, and yet we use it metaphorically to apply to relationships, almost unthinkingly. We can even talk about 'growing further apart' when we mean that our liking for someone is decreas-ing or our relationship with them is getting more difficult. In fact spatial metaphors run through much of our thinking about relation-ships and there is a reason for that: space influences the way in which we relate to others and it communicates messages of power, liking, and attitudes towards others. Just think for a moment about the rich array of metaphorical statements about power and position that are made in spatial terminology. For example, space can be used to provide metaphors about relationships, which can be close or distant. Furthermore, we talk of people being 'high and mighty', they can be 'head and shoulders above the rest', 'the tops', 'way above the competition', 'the greatest'. Good experiences are 'highs' or 'high-points'. We have *high* moral principles and are *above* doing anything mean such as showing *low* cunning.

Spatial metaphors are also used to refer to 'inferiority' (which is derived from the Latin word *inferus*, meaning 'lower'): people are of low status, lowly, lowdown no-goods, beneath (rather than above, beyond, or outside) contempt. A bad experience is a 'downer', and we feel low. In doing something bad, we may be accused of stooping low, or letting others down. When we assert ourselves, on the other hand, we stand up for ourselves or stand up to someone powerful:

we 'walk tall, walk straight and look the whole world in the eye'. In short, our choice of language equates spatial position with moral or social or relational position.

There are quite complex social rules governing the use of space in social situations and movements through space. These work *nonverbally*, by means of bodily cues to do with posture, gesture, orientation (i.e. the way our body is facing) and various other subtleties like eye movements (Patterson, 1988). Unfortunately, the very discussion of it is something that is embarrassing and hard to do. We hardly ever refer directly to someone's nonverbal behaviour and to do so is usually rude or aggressive ('Wipe that smile off your face'. 'Look at me when I'm talking to you', 'Don't stand so close to me'). All the same, competent use of NVC is a prerequisite to relating to other people and there is a dynamic rule system that presumes five basic assumptions: (1) the use of nonverbal cues is identifiable and recognizable; (2) the operation of nonverbal cues is essentially systematic, even if occasionally ambiguous; (3) we all must be able to translate our feelings and intentions into nonverbal messages (i.e. we must be able to '*encode*'): (4) observers must be able to interpret (or '*decode*') it; (5) whether or not we intend it, observers may decode our behaviour systematically and as relationally relevant, even attending to signals that we thought we had successfully concealed.

As Patterson (1988) has shown, nonverbal communication is not only systematic in the above ways but also serves five functions for us, some of which I will explore here. These functions are: (1) to provide information to others about ourselves, especially our feelings or our relational attitudes; (2) to regulate interaction (e.g. by enabling us to see when someone has said all that they intend to say and it is our turn to talk); (3) to express intimacy and emotional closeness in relationships; (4) to attempt social control (e.g. by dominating others); (5) to engage in a service-task function (i.e. to depersonalize certain contacts that would otherwise be 'intimate'. For example, think of the parts of you that physicians can touch but which other people may not – unless they are remarkably close friends).

Territories in space

At first sight 'territory' may not seem relevant to relationships, especially since such a concept is usually thought to be relevant mostly to animals and governments. Some birds fight other birds that come into their 'patch', baboons control space and attack invaders, dogs and cats mark out their territorial boundaries with body products. Second thoughts about space may alert us to echoes of this style of behaviour in human relationships, in general. We use space in a systematic way that has territorial and relational overtones (i.e. we use space as if it is invisibly 'attached' to us or under our control). This occurs both in fixed settings, like offices, and in dynamic settings, during conversations.

BOX 1.2 Division and allocation of space

Families on the beach fill up the available space systematically and when the beach is empty, people space themselves wide apart. As the beach fills up, so the newcomers divide the space up just about equally.

This division and allocation of space are not confined to beaches, however, and you can try it for yourself in the library or cafeteria. Find an empty table of six chairs (3 each side) and position yourself at it. The chances are you will take the middle seat on one of the sides, but if you didn't, move to that seat. The next stranger who arrives is most likely to sit on the opposite side of the table in an end seat; the next one in the remaining end seat of that side of the table. My prediction for you to test out would be that the last seat to be taken will be the one directly opposite the one that you occupied. You could also see if the same prediction works if you sit in other starting positions, or if people arrive in pairs, or if they know some of the occupants of the table.

The study of human spatial behaviour is known as 'proxemics' (Hall, 1966). Space can be differentiated into *intimate* (i.e. from direct contact to around 18 inches [46cm] away from another person – obviously used with someone we know and like); *personal* (from around 18 inches [46cm] to about 4 feet [1.4m] apart usually used when talking to casual friends or acquaintances); *social* (from around 4 feet [1.4m] to around 12 feet [4.2m] apart – usually used for business transactions and impersonal encounters), or *public* (from around 12 feet [4.2m] or more apart – e.g. think how a speaker at public events and formal encounters stands away from the rest of the group or audience).

In different relational settings we are comfortable with different distances; imagine talking to friends, to a teacher, and going to a lecture. Another thing to notice is that, as we get to know someone better, so we indicate this by holding conversations standing at smaller distances from each other. The more intimate we become emotionally, the more intimate we get spatially; we get closer in two senses. So space and human relationships are linked in subtle ways.

As long as we can breathe comfortably and our basic physiological needs are met (e.g. we are not too hot or too cold) then sociocultural and relational rules for distribution of space will be the ones that we follow. These rules have several interesting features; space claims are information about status, ownership, and the social or personal relationship between participants; also, position and relative distance during conversation are important indicators of emotional closeness between the persons.

Claiming space is claiming power

Human beings decorate their rooms, houses and, to some extent, their cars, other possessions and themselves. For instance, furniture in offices is arranged in ways that indicate who owns what, who is superior to whom, and how much of the space is 'public'. Desks and tables can be arranged in such a way that they show power relationships between people, in addition to any reasons to do with lighting or ease of communication. For example, bank managers usually make you sit across the desk from them as a distancing device to indicate their power and emphasize their service role in the relationship. By contrast, counsellors tend to have their desks off to the side, or to sit with nothing between clients and themselves. This removes or reduces both physical and psychological barriers and promotes a less formal and more relaxing relationship.

Furniture can also act as a barrier, which is itself an implicit statement of a social rule indicating who is in charge and how far you can go. For example, receptionists' desks are usually placed in your path and so communicate the existence of the receptionist's power to control your entry further into the office. It is *physically* possible to break the rules, but is a *social* offence. For example, moving your chair round the barrier so that you sit next to the bank manager, moving round to the other side of the table, opening a door marked 'Private', or sitting on a receptionist's desk, all violate a social rule. Such violations would most probably lead to comment or discomfort or possibly to the other person becoming angry. Someone who habitually violates such rules in conducting relationships will obviously be rather difficult to deal with.

Symbolic decoration also indicates ownership of space and so it affirms control and power. The most obvious example is clothing: physically, I could put my hand in your pocket, but socially . . . . Furthermore, if, in a library or refectory, we observe an empty seat with coat hanging over the back, we know it is a symbol: the coat owner is indicating that he or she will return and use the chair. If we see sets of books arranged on library tables in such a way that someone could read them, when no one is in fact doing so, then we would probably go somewhere else to seat ourselves. You might like to consider whether the same sort of principle is implicit in *relational* 'decoration' such as wedding rings.

A further way of claiming space is achieved through *self-extension*. Placing your feet on a coffee table or desk, sprawling across an otherwise empty bench, and leaning across a doorway are all ways of claiming control over the space. Claiming space is claiming power, ownership and, above all, status. The first-class seats on airlines are broader and have more foot-room in front of them rather than merely being more comfortably made. As people are promoted in an organization this is symbolically recognized by the award of larger offices, longer desks, broader areas of carpet, taller chairs and wider blotter pads. Space is a metaphor for status.

Most often, a spatial claim is *horizontal* and concerns the amount of floor space allocated to a person. Status claims, however, are often related to vertical space too, as in 'higher' or 'lower' status. Kings, queens, judges and professors sit on raised platforms. Popes are carried round at shoulder height when they are elected. Equally, temporary changes in status can be acknowledged by height changes, as when a scoring footballer jumps up in the air or is lifted up in triumph by team-mates. More subtly, people sometimes bow or curtsy (thus reducing their height) when they are introduced to someone of much higher status, and in Ancient China people introduced to the emperor had to reduce their height to the extent of hurling themselves to the floor and banging their foreheads on the ground. Nowadays, only assistant professors seeking tenure do this.

Space and conversation

Space matters not only in the structural ways mentioned but also in the dynamic flux of conversations and social encounters (Argyle, 1975). Space claims often control not only the space but the person in it (i.e. they dominate that person by including them in a controlled area). To lean across someone's desk more than about half-way is a threat to them personally. To lean beside someone with your hand on the wall behind his or her shoulder at a party is to 'claim' the person so enclosed: you are telling other people to 'Keep out'. The other person in these circumstances can obviously escape physically by brushing past, but to do so would violate a social rule about the relational 'meaning' of space. It would be rude; it would be hostile; it would be offensive, too. The case is often that of an uninvited man trapping a woman and to 'be rude' is sometimes her only sensible option, either by saying something personal or by calling his attention directly to the violation of the social norm of closeness.

Nonverbal systems of meaning

You may be starting to see a problem here. What exactly is the meaning of proximity and space in social encounters? At some times, proximity (or physical closeness) indicates intimacy, or emotional closeness. We sit next to people that we like and sit closer to those we like more. But at other times closeness can indicate exactly the opposite: invasion and personal threat. When a stranger stands close to us we can experience threat, irritation, fear or even a rise in blood pressure (Clore, 1977).

Both of the same kinds of meaning are attached to eye movements as well as to proximity. Gazing at a person's eyes is often, but not always, an indication of intense liking; we look at a person more often if we like them. Eye contact (i.e. when two people look one another in the eye) indicates interest, liking and acceptance (Argyle & Cook, 1976). Pupil size marginally increases when we see someone or something that we like, and we prefer faces in which the pupils are dilated – presumably because it signals that the face likes us. Thus the eyes convey indications of liking in different ways. As with proximity, however, staring and gazing can also be threatening. An intense stare can be used as a threatening cue both in animals and in humans. The stare is a stimulus to flight, and those who are stared at when they stop at traffic lights will move away faster from the junction when the lights go green (Ellsworth et al., 1972). Thus, as with physical closeness, eye contact can indicate either threat or dominance, as well as liking.

How do people decide which reaction is the right one? The answer is not only that the verbal–nonverbal communication system is a system that helps us to decode people's meaning (see below) but also that the nonverbal communication system is a system within a system. The parts work together to help us to clarify meanings intended in particular cases. For one thing, the individual cues, like proximity, hardly ever happen in isolation. A complex interrelationship exists between space and other nonverbal cues, such as eye movements. The way in which we can learn the full relational message is by attending to the system of cues, not just to one in isolation. We work out relational meaning from eye-contact-plus-context or from proximity-plus-words. When someone stares and smiles, we know we are favoured; if someone stares and frowns, we are in trouble.

If we add two positive messages together, what do we get? For example, does eye contact plus closeness take the intimacy level beyond what people can bear? Argyle & Dean (1965) proposed an equilibrium model, namely, that the intimacy level of an interaction is held steady by a balancing of proximity and eye contact. As proximity increases so eye contact will decrease (unless the two are lovers where the two cues are 'appropriate' together); that way, the total level of signalling for intimacy will stay about right. If proximity decreases then eye contact should increase to maintain the equilibrium of the encounter. This works with other signals for intimacy, too. For example, as an interviewer's questions become more personal, so the interviewee reduces eye contact when giving answers (Carr & Dabbs, 1974).

Nonverbal signals as interaction regulators

The above shows that simple nonverbal cues, such as spatial positioning or eye contact, serve to communicate liking and disliking and attraction to a relationship. Nonverbal communication serves another important function besides acting as an indicator of liking. This second function is to smooth out and 'regulate' social behaviour. Interactions have rules about speakers' turn-taking, for instance, and interactions do not run smoothly if one or both partners violate(s) the rule. Think briefly whether you could state precisely what the rules of social behaviour are. (You could even try to list them for yourself before reading on and then check your list against mine.) Skilful regulation of interpersonal communication is essential to the conduct of human relationships and we all know *how* to do it, but might find it hard to write out. The behaviours that enable it are termed 'social skills' and the teaching of such behaviours is called 'Social Skills Training' or SST for short.

Interactions have to be started, sustained and ended in appropriate ways, and this is usually managed by nonverbal means. Two nonverbal signals are generally used to start typical interactions: one is eye contact (in this case, 'catching someone's eye'); the other is orientation (i.e. we need to face the right way and have our body oriented openly towards the other person). It is inappropriate, rude and extremely difficult to open up a conversation without looking at the person and having them look back. It is also hard to continue an

---

BOX 1.3 Some research findings about space usage

People find it more appropriate to sit opposite others with whom they will have an argument and to sit next to someone with whom they agree (Sommer, 1969; Cook, 1968). Conversely it is 'harder' to disagree with someone sitting next to us.

There are cultural differences in tolerance for closeness in conversation. Watson & Graves (1966) observe that Arabs habitually stand close to partners and touch them during conversation whilst Americans stand further apart. Legend reports that if you put an Arab and an Englishman in a room to stand and converse, you get fascinating results. The comfortable distance for the Arab is too close for the Englishman, who will therefore edge back. This makes things uncomfortably distant for the Arab, who edges forward. But, for the Englishman, this is now too close . . . a slow but definite movement around the room occurs! The same 'dance' can be created when you talk to other people. If you edge slightly forward, they will edge slightly back, and vice versa.

Violent prisoners overreact negatively to spatial invasion (Kane, 1971), particularly to someone entering the 'body buffer zone' that we all perceive around ourselves. Such body buffer zones are the area that we regard as 'ours' immediately around our body. Since the body buffer zones for violent prisoners have been found to be larger than normal ones, they are more easily invaded and violated. That is, normal people have smaller body buffer zones than the violent prisoners did and people can therefore get closer to the normal people without violating the zone. For the violent prisoners, the body buffer zone was larger than normal and so the 'owners' more easily and frequently became upset when other people got physically close. A negative reaction was particularly likely in response to invasion from behind.

---

interaction when one is wrongly oriented; for instance, try sitting back-to-back with a friend and have a cosy chat. You will certainly be physically able to hear what they are chatting about, but you will soon become socially uncomfortable with this form of communication.

A person can decline to engage in a conversation merely by refusing to establish eye contact or orientation. However, eye contact conjoins with many other cues to serve a regulatory function in interactions (Patterson, 1988). Eye contact, gaze, looking and eye movements are associated with 'floor-sharing' (i.e. turn-taking in conversation) and with power and dominance of interactions.

Speakers look at listeners less than listeners look at speakers, but speakers start to signal that they have come to the end of their 'speech' by looking at the listener and establishing eye contact; this lets the listener 'take over the floor', if desired (Kendon, 1967). Socially anxious people tend to avert their eyes too frequently and so disrupt the flow of the interaction by breaking the rules (Patterson, 1988). High power, on the other hand, is associated with high levels of looking at a listener whilst you are talking whereas less powerful or less expert people tend to look only when listening (Dovidio et al., 1988).

Our conversations are also regulated by other factors, some to do with the general rewardingness that is expected in social encounters (Burgoon et al., 1986), and some to do with the general rules about turn-taking (Cappella, 1988). Specifically, we alter our speech patterns and conversational turns as a result of the 'reinforcements' that we receive. Reinforcements here are nonverbal cues that reinforce, encourage or lead us to increase whatever behaviour they positively reinforce or seemingly approve. Several forms of reinforcement for speaking are available. Smiling, nodding and gazing at other persons in an interaction, for instance, are reinforcers that will induce others to continue talking (Argyle, 1967). This can be generalized: the same nonverbal cues will encourage and reinforce quite subtle parts of behaviour. One can induce the production of plural nouns, use of abstract concepts, or particular kinds of topic, each of which can be reinforced and increased by nonverbal encouragements from a listener (Argyle, 1967).

However, there are also social expectations about amount of gaze, and people who do not gaze enough are violating such an expectation. Without such reinforcements, speakers will often stop, under the impression that the listener is bored, is becoming less involved in the conversation or else, perhaps, wants to intervene (Coker & Burgoon, 1987). One way of 'taking the floor' (or getting a word in edgeways) is to stop being reinforcing and to signal one's lack of interest. The listener sends a strong signal by this: 'Please stop talking. It's my turn now.'

Does nonverbal communication show how we really feel?

An important role of nonverbal communication is to convey attitudes (Patterson, 1988). These may be attitudes about self (e.g. conceited, diffident, mousy, shy, humble); attitudes towards the other person (e.g. dominant, submissive, attracted, disliking, hostile, aggressive); or attitudes about the interaction (e.g. affability, comfortableness, relaxation, intimacy, nervousness).

BOX 1.4 Functions of gaze, eye movements and nonverbal communication

Mutual gaze (when two people gaze or stare at one another) is used to signal that two persons wish to 'engage' or start a social encounter (Kendon & Ferber, 1973). It is also used at the correct distance – during the 'salutation' or greeting phase at the start of an encounter. Sometimes if people see each other from too far away, they will move towards one another but will look away (or look down) until they are closer, when they will start mutual gaze again.

Speakers begin long glances at the listener just before the end of an utterance (Kendon, 1967). This seems to signal the end of the utterance so that the listener has a chance to contribute and take over the conversation, if desired.

In couples of equal power, female–female pairs exhibit higher amounts of mutual gaze than either male–male or male–female dyads (Mulac et al., 1987).

Eye contact relates to 'floor-sharing' and the patterning of speech in an encounter (Cappella, 1991); but staring at someone else will cause him or her to make more frequent speech errors (Beattie, 1981).

Gaze and eye contact are reduced when a person is embarrassed or when a partner makes unsuitable self-disclosures to the other person (Edelmann, 1988).

Gaze and eye contact also serve to indicate:
— warmth, interest and involvement in the interaction (Duck, 1991);
— liking for one's conversational partner (Rubin, 1973);
— dominance or threat of the other person (Exline, 1971).

Gotlib & Hooley (1988) discuss various ways in which the nonverbal and other interpersonal communicative behaviours of depressed persons are abnormal and make it difficult for their marital partners to relate to and deal with them.

Some findings on the functions of gaze (BOX 1.4) indicate that we tend to assume nervousness and anxiety just by detecting the presence or absence of certain particular nonverbal behaviours. This is not surprising, given that increased body movement tends to occur in association with speech dysfluencies or errors (Hadar, 1989). Several studies find that such cues are the ones used by police or customs officers in detecting criminality or smuggling (Stiff & Miller, 1984). However, there are many reasons for nervousness apart from criminality (e.g. embarrassment, low self-esteem, shyness).

Let us consider the issue of whether such nonverbal cues actually indicate anxiety, deceit, and the like, or whether people just continue to believe that they do. In a provocative paper, Stiff & Miller (1984) look at the behaviours that people show when they lie and the behaviours that people use to determine when someone else is lying to them. The crucial behaviours that we use are response latency (i.e. the time the person takes before starting to answer a question) and speech errors (i.e. interruptions to the flow of speech). Facial expressions are generally less useful for detecting deception, but they do indicate nervousness.

In a pair of studies where people were filmed telling real lies (i.e. concealing the fact that they had cheated on a test to earn $50), judges relied heavily on the stereotypical vocal and visual cues, but these are not actually related to deception (Stiff & Miller, 1984). Evidently, observers tend (foolishly) to interpret any unsystematic, awkward or nonfluent behaviours as indicating deception, and may sometimes remark on a person's 'smoothness' and fluency as a sign of their plausibility. Obviously this is very relevant to relationships – particularly beginning ones – since people who appear shy or nervous may be distrusted or disliked.

One feature of real lying is that it involves some concentration ('cognitive load'). We do not merely have to say Yes or No to some experimental question that we care nothing about; we are involved, so we experience emotional stress. We also realize that if we are talking to someone we know, then they may know us well enough to know what behaviours of ours give us away – so we pay close attention to our behaviour and try hard to control anything that might 'give us away', or 'leak' our true meaning or feelings or the true state of affairs. The whole experience is therefore arousing for us. In a clever study looking at these factors, Greene et al. (1985) had subjects lie (about where they had been on holiday) to a confederate of the experimenter. That was the easy part; many people can lie that they have been to Puerto Rico, as some of the subjects were asked to do. It's particularly easy if you have been told some time in advance that the question will be asked and what you should say. The difficult part – which the subjects were not actually expecting – was what to do when the confederate became intensely interested in the trip and asked all sorts of details about it. Greene et al. (1985) found that subjects can control leakage of the fact that they are lying up until the point when they suddenly have to think hard and carefully about what they are saying.

These results are interesting in themselves, but let us apply them directly to relationships. They are relevant, for instance, to the ways in which partners in relationships conduct 'secret tests' of the state of the relationship (Baxter & Wilmot, 1984). Bear in mind that we misjudge other people's 'deceptiveness' whilst I discuss these results. Baxter & Wilmot argue that partners are often uncertain about the strength of their relationship yet are reluctant to talk about 'the state of the relationship'; they regard it as a taboo topic. Our usual solution is to apply direct and indirect tests – secret tests – as means of discovering how things stand. Such methods involve, for instance, asking third parties whether your partner has ever talked about the relationship to them. Alternatively one might use trial intimacy moves to see how a partner reacts – and so gives away some indication of intimacy. Obviously, such moves can take the form of increased physical or emotional intimacy, but might be more subtle. For example, a person might use 'public presentation': inviting the partner to visit parents or friends or talking about intentions to have children some day. The real but concealed questions in each case are: how does my partner react, and does he or she accept the increased intimacy or the open commitment? Other methods described by Baxter & Wilmot (1984) are the self-put-down (when you hope the partner will respond to your self-deprecating statement with a supportive, intimate statement) and the jealousy test (when you describe a potential competitor and hope to observe a possessive, committed response by your partner).

Clearly such ploys are a useful test of partner commitment to a relationship only if you can genuinely assess your partner's responses, and when you make the tests you will be carefully reading all the nonverbal signs described thus far. Nonverbal communication can be relevant to the testing of relationships (and hence to their future) as well as to their conduct and regulation. Consider, however, these are precisely the signs that Stiff & Miller's study of deception points out we do not read very intelligently in reality!

Skilful use of nonverbal cues

Nonverbal communication is relevant to relationships in another way also. Some shy or lonely people have been found to have poor NVC skills (Patterson, 1988). They are nervous, embarrassed or socially incompetent and their NVC communicates unflattering attitudes about themselves or their awkward feelings in the encounter. Persistently lonely people have poorly adapted eye movement, smiles, gestures, nods, and the like (Spitzberg & Canary, 1985), but this is often because they have essentially disengaged from the social world and stopped trying. They become passive in encounters and have a poor view of themselves and their own social performance (Vitkus & Horowitz, 1987).

Such poor quality of social skills could take two forms: poor encoding or poor decoding. *Encoding* refers to the ability to put our feelings into practice, to 'do what we mean' (e.g. to act assertively if we want to assert, to look friendly if we feel friendly). Conversely, *decoding* refers to the ability to work out what other people mean, by observing their nonverbal communication and correctly working out their intent. Some people are inept at this. For example, sometimes you may read in the papers that a fight began in a bar because someone was staring 'provocatively' at someone else. Perhaps one was staring inappropriately (poor encoding) or perhaps the other just thought he or she was (poor decoding) or perhaps drink caused their social psychological judgement to decline in accuracy.

People with poor social skills

Many people have poor social skills and poor relationships, and this, in particular, is true of depressives and schizophrenics (Argyle, 1983). Such skills deficits not only are symptoms of their problems but may be partial causes (or, perhaps, may exacerbate and increase their problems). Also, Noller & Gallois (1988) show that partners in distressed marriages are poor at decoding one another's meaning and/or poor at encoding their own feelings, often communicating feelings as negative when they are not intended to be negative.

The list of people who show social skills deficits is lengthy. At the extreme end, patients with schizophrenia are very poor at decoding nonverbal signals (Williams, 1974), as are some violent prisoners (Howells, 1981); and depressed patients (Libet & Lewinsohn, 1973), particularly when describing themselves (Segrin, 1991). In less extreme ways, the same has been found to be true of alcoholics (before they became alcoholics – afterwards they are even harder to relate to, of course; Orford & O'Reilly, 1981) and children who are unpopular at school (Asher & Parker, 1989). By contrast, those who are successful in their careers are better at social skills than those who are failures (Argyle, 1987), and physicians can improve their success in healing patients by improving their social skills (Hays & DiMatteo, 1984). Clearly, then, the importance of such socially skilled communication cannot be underestimated. Although it usually occurs in the context of verbal behaviour too (see following sections), it has been found that nonverbal cues exert 4.3 times more effect than does verbal behaviour on the impressions formed of a speaker (Argyle et al., 1970). Even when such results have been challenged on the grounds that the studies were poorly carried out (Walker & Trimboli, 1989), the dominance of NVC is still accepted. It is important, however, to pay attention to the context in which the cues are shown, which can help other people to see the meaning of the nonverbal behaviour itself.

For these reasons, correction of social skill problems is often attempted in training programmes (Duck, 1991). Such social skills training brings about improved social functioning in relationships and also improves the person's feelings about himself or herself, as BOX 1.5 shows.

BOX 1.5 Social Skills Training (SST)
Some examples of successful social skills training are:

General 'pepping up' of depressives' responsivity in social encounters is shown in several mental health contexts to contribute to patient recovery and improvement (Dunkel-Schetter & Skokan, 1990).

Gotlib & Hooley (1988), however, have shown that individual attention to such things is not enough on its own and that therapy involving interpersonal functioning in marriage (i.e. with the marriage partner) is more successful.

Lonely and shy people can be trained to adopt new styles of social behaviour that enhance the skill of their performance (Jones et al., 1984). Such training can also be directed at conversational turn-taking or topic management and general interpersonal communication competence (Spitzberg & Cupach, 1985).

Nonassertive persons benefit from training related to posture as well as to other behaviours more obviously related to request-making (Wilkinson & Canter, 1982).

Muehlenhard et al. (1986) developed ideas for SST to help women convey their (lack of) interest in dating a particular man and to help men to grasp that meaning.

Curran (1977) successfully trained young people to make dates with members of the opposite sex by use of social skills training and related techniques.

Social skills training can be used to train managers to take the chair effectively at meetings, deal with disruptive employers, and sell products (Rackham & Morgan, 1977).

Speaking up for yourself: using words

It ain't what you say . . .: the role of paralanguage

The ways in which we use words are just as important as the words themselves. If I *shout* 'Fire!!', then it means more than just 'I can see pretty dancing flames': it means there is an emergency. The structure, use and form of language carry messages over and above the content or meaning of the actual words that are spoken. Researchers use the term *paralanguage* to refer to such features of speech as accent, speed, volume, error rate and tone of voice. Rather like space in the paragraphs above, however, paralanguage has meanings in relationships but also occurs within a system of meanings that sometimes clarify what is intended. For instance, persons who shout 'Fire!' in an emergency probably also have some accompanying NVC that indicates at least urgency and possibly even panic which distinguishes them from someone shouting it out as a joke. Also notice that the way a person does the shouting could convey messages about their credibility: someone who screams while looking distraught is likely to be believed; someone who shouts 'Yoo. . .oo. . .oo. . .hooo! . . . . Fi. . .i. . .re!' may be disregarded.

These observations create two issues for us to think about. First, how do people use language so that it conveys messages for (and about) speakers? Second, how does language interface with NVC to affect human relationships? We want to know how accent, speed, volume, error rate, tone of voice and 'speech style' affect the relational impact of messages. We shall see that power is indicated by a communication's tone and shall learn how to structure messages to maximize their persuasiveness. Language style conveys more information than is merely contained in the sentence: different actors can give different character to the same passage of Shakespeare just by speaking it differently.

Accent

An easily observed element of speech is accent. Does this affect evaluation of a speaker? A speaker's accent is evaluated separately from the content of the speech and is probably a more significant influence on the reception of the message (Giles & Powesland, 1975). A person's accent can identify him or her as a member of a certain group or social class and this sets off a number of stereotypes associated in the perceiver's mind with that group. In the UK particularly, not only are people who use 'regional accents' very likely to be regarded as less competent or less intelligent than those who use 'proper speech' ('received pronunciation'), but listeners rapidly identify with speakers through accent. General favourability towards an accent will lead to general favourability towards the person speaking it, at least in the stage of first impressions. Cheyne (1970) found that Scots and English raters both rated a speaker with an English accent as more self-confident, intelligent, ambitious, wealthy and prestigious, good looking and clean. Scots accents were rated by Scots listeners as indicating that the speaker was friendlier, with a better sense of humour, generous and likeable.

Amount of speech

A measure of leadership in small group discussions is the amount of speech: the more often someone 'holds the floor' the more will observers assume that the person was leading the group's activities (Stang, 1973). In Stang's study, subjects listened to tape-recorded group discussions which had been arranged so that one person spoke 50 per cent of the time, another person 33 percent of the time, and a third spoke only 17 percent of the time. The most talkative person was seen as the leader, irrespective of what was said, and the second most frequent contributor was rated the most popular. This is further confirmed and extended by Palmer (1990) who showed that management of 'floor time' (or amount of time spent 'holding the floor' by speaking) is used as an important indication of someone's control of, and contribution to, the conversation. I find this very sad, in that if three physicists in 1900 had sat down to discuss physics and one spoke for only 17 percent of the time saying only '$E = MC^2$', no one would have liked him or followed his lead.

Amount of speech is also affected by communication apprehension and social anxiety (Ayres, 1989), with highly anxious males talking less (and also using smaller amounts of reinforcing head nods) than less anxious subjects. So there is some truth to the common belief that fluency means something about expertise, mastery, competence and truthfulness. From a person's verbal fluency we deduce information about the kind of person that he or she is, how that feels inside, and whether anxiety is felt in the present setting. The other side to this belief is the assumption that people's views of themselves and the kind of person they (think they) are, actually do affect fluency. Competent people simply do speak fluently: they know what they are doing and their fluency is a signal of that. So what about the opposite case, those who are habitually nonfluent? Are we correct to deduce that they see themselves as incompetent, worthless, and of low value? There are people in the world who habitually stammer, just as we all from time to time get thrown off our stride by stress. A large amount of work now relates habitual stammering to identity problems (see BOX 1.6).

BOX 1.6 Speech fluency and dysfluency

Several pieces of work indicate that fluency of speech is taken as a sign that the speaker is competent while dysfluency (or hesitation and stumbling) is taken to show anxiety and tension. Ayres (1989), however, showed that highly apprehensive males tended to be more fluent than non-anxious ones. This is probably because the anxious people tend to withdraw from interpersonal interaction somewhat and to say very little. When they do speak, however, it is probably planned out and hangs together well because they have thought about it and it is important to them!

As an interesting anecdotal example of this, I have a friend who stutters except on subjects where his self-concept is strong or when all the company is very familiar. He is an orthopaedic surgeon and I have never heard him stutter when talking about his area of expertise!

Berger et al. (1989) support this by showing that when a person has to devote a lot of mental energy to planning what they have to say, their verbal fluency goes down dramatically.

Fransella (1972) showed that many stutterers have the notion of their speech difficulty as a key part of their view of themselves and can be cured or helped only by attempts to reformulate their view of themselves. In other words, speech difficulties are not simply mechanical difficulties but involve identity issues also.

Rules about speech

How does language change as a result of the situation or relationship in which the conversation takes place, and what are the influences of language and 'speech style' on social evaluation or on the impressions observers form? Whilst a linguist would be interested in the grammatical rules in a given society (the *langue*), a communication scientist, social psychologist or sociolinguist is more likely to be concerned with the ways in which people use language (the *parole*). Social uses of language do not always follow the strict rules of grammar (e.g. on the radio this morning I heard an interviewee say 'I reckon there's lots of dockers as thinks the same like what I does' – and yet everyone knows roughly what he meant to convey by this).

Language is 'situated' in various ways according to the goals of the interactants. As people's goals change, so does their speech. For instance, in a social setting, conversation is frequent and almost any topic of conversation is permissible in a chat with close friends. By contrast, when concentration is required, it seems perfectly natural that people converse less and speech acts will decline or, at least, that speech will be task-oriented. Similarly, competent university lectures are supposed to contain information about the course, and professors may not normally just show holiday slides and talk about their vacation.

Just as in nonverbal communication, a most significant aspect of verbal communication is an appreciation of the social rules that apply. Actors in a conversation must be polite and recognize when it is appropriate to raise particular topics and when it is not. They must know when to match their speech acts to the rules, since evaluation of their competence depends upon it. Daly et al. (1987) indicate that especially competent conversationalists are excellent at picking up social cues of appropriateness, sensing the hidden messages in others' speech, and noting unspoken power dynamics in conversational settings.

Such sensitivity can apply to issues surrounding the goals of the actors. In task-oriented discussions, people are happy with a language system containing technical, jargon-based forms. By contrast, a conversation between friends is usually not task-oriented but socio-emotionally oriented. Because it is focussed on feelings, 'atmosphere' and informality, a different speech style is appropriate – one where grammatical rules may be broken and where the transfer of information is less significant than is the aim of keeping people happy and relaxed. Of course, such 'atmosphere' is important in human relationships.

Most cultures have two forms of language code available, a so-called *high form* and a *low form*. The high form is formal, planned, careful, precise, complex, full of jargon, and a little pompous. It appears in educational settings, religion, courtrooms, and on official notices: for instance, 'I was proceeding in a northeasterly direction towards my domestic establishment' and 'Kindly extinguish all illumination prior to vacating the premises'. The low form is informal, unplanned, casual, direct and simple. It is the most familiar form of everyday speech. For example, 'I was going home' and 'You guys switch off the lights when you go'.

The two forms are used in different settings in appropriate ways. However, there are occasions when this causes difficulties and we deliberately break the rules to communicate a social message, like a joke or a distancing from someone. An example of the conveyance of social messages through use of codes is use of a high form in a casual setting to deflate someone, for instance when a close friend abruptly addresses you as Ms or Mr and starts to use formal language, the calculated misjudgement of the circumstances conveys a social message over and above the grammatical content. When the message form or structure is made inappropriate to the form or structure of the encounter (e.g. informal language in a formal setting) the social result is negative (for example a judge called by his or her first name by a witness might fine the witness for contempt of court).

One other message is conveyed by differences in use of high and low forms of code, and that is power. Powerful and knowledgeable persons use jargon-based high code, while the rest use low code translations. One reason why do-it-yourself auto repairers are usually 'one down' in going to buy spare parts is because they do not know the proper terminology. Asking for 'one of those round things with the bent bit at one end' is a betrayal of low status in such situations. Use of technical terms is a way of claiming status, particularly if it is done deliberately to someone who does not know the terminology. Car mechanics could perfectly well talk about 'round things with the bent bit at one end', but they do not. Social scientists could write about chatting and conversation, but instead they write about 'socially situated speech acts' and 'interacts'. As Guinan & Scudder (1989) show, clients prefer experts (in this case computer experts) who talk in proper English, and not only do they prefer them, they rate them as more effective and competent! There is justice in the world!

More about content

The content of speech carries two important social messages, one of which is *power* and the other is *relationship* between speaker and listener. Brown (1965) refers to these dimensions as *status* and *solidarity*. These two dimensions are very similar to two 'messages' conveyed by nonverbal cues also: dominance and liking.

Status

Language conveys different power relations in encounters between persons, differences in power over objects (i.e. ownership), and differences in control of the interaction itself. Relative status of participants in an encounter is an ever-present and powerful dimension of the encounter. One immediate way in which people reveal relative status and power is by their title, another is by the form of address used to them. Someone greeted as 'The Most Magnificent Eminence, Child of the Sun God, Father and Mother of the Earth, Bringer of Harvests and Lord of the Seas' will obviously not be given the chipped cup to drink from, whereas 'scumbag' may not be given a cup at all. Yet what is the difference between a chief secretary and an Office Manager or between a 'terrorist' and a 'freedom fighter'? The terms and titles are not innocently neutral, and as airlines and car manufacturers are aware, titles such as Ambassador, Consul, Executive, and Monarch convey status on the user. Titles will attract people to buy status instead of just settling for second-class air tickets or low-range cars. The titles carry social messages and emotional or social meaning. To travel Ambassador Class presumably feels different from merely travelling 'at the front of the plane'.

Particularly important nowadays is the distinction between 'everyone should take his seat' and 'everyone should take his or her seat'. Just as with previously widely used words like 'Negro' or 'queer', the titles and assumptions built into the use of the word 'his' on its own have now become offensive to us. Hyde (1984) shows that the use of the pronoun 'he' or 'his' on its own to cover both sexes, rather than the gender-neutral 'he or she' or 'his or her', significantly influences a whole range of people, from first-graders to college students, to think of males exclusively. Gender-related pronouns also affected the concepts that children formed of a fictitious occupation ('wudgemaker'); in particular the use of the pronoun 'his' dramatically reduced their perception of a woman's competence to do the job. Unger (1986) also notes that qualifiers such as 'woman executive' and 'Lady doctor' are offensive because they tend to *confirm* traditional sexist views of social organization, since they imply that the female is breaking the 'usual' pattern of ownership for titles like 'doctor' and 'executive'. Indeed, there are many differences in meaning between the terms 'girl', 'woman' and 'lady' just as there are between terms like 'boy', 'man' and 'gentleman'.

Recently, important work has also been done on the differences between 'men's' and 'women's' language, for example. This has drawn attention not only to the fact that the male term is often treated as the norm (e.g. the use of 'mankind' to include not only men but also women and children), but also to the fact that male terms are often positive while the female equivalents are not (e.g.

'bachelor' as compared to 'spinster'). Are you, by the way, studying for the degree of Bachelor or Master or Doctor – all male terms originally? As Marshall (1984) further points out, such words as Sir, Master and King convey authority and competence (Master Brewer, master of a skill, for example). By contrast, their parallel female terms (Madam, Mistress, Queen) have acquired debased meanings associated with sexual activity or sexual relationships that are officially 'disapproved' or marginalized by society.

BOX 1.7 Julius Caesar's use of language
The Romans had several styles of address just as we do (see text). When talking to the mass of private citizens in the forum at Rome, orators would address them as 'Quirites' ('Ladies and Gentlemen'); serving legionaries in the field were hailed 'Milites' ('Soldiers'). Once when Caesar's legionaries mutinied, he began his speech to them with 'Quirites' rather than 'Milites', thus implying that they were not acting like trained soldiers but like a crowd of private citizens in Rome. Caesar's own account of this event is that this single word was enough to shame the troops and quell the mutiny.

Relationships between speaker and listener

In some languages (e.g. French, German, Spanish), there are two words that can be translated as 'you' in English, and in times gone by there were also two choices in English (thee/thou, ye/you). The so-called V-form (*vos* in Latin, *vous* in French, *sie* in German, *usted* in Spanish) is actually plural, just as ye/you used to be in English, where the T-form (*tu*, *du*, *thee/thou*) is actually singular. Where the two forms still coexist, intimate friends and relatives are addressed with one pronoun (*tu*, *du*) and the other is used for people whom one does not know or whom one treats with respect and deference (*vous*, *sie*, *usted*). Thus the French say *tu* when talking to a friend, to someone younger or to a person of lower status, but use *vous* for talking to a stranger or a parent-in-law. This choice of just one single word tells everyone about the speaker's familiarity with the other person and communicates something about the closeness or distance of relationship between speaker and addressee.

Brown (1965) notes that a status norm has evolved in countries which still use the two forms of address. The V-form is used to address a person superior to oneself in status. The T-form is reserved for those of status lower than oneself. Persons who are of equal status both use the T-form to each other if they are close personally, but the V-form if they are not. German and French each contain special words (*dusagen*; *Tutoyer*) to describe the switch from one form to another (i.e. to indicate that it is OK to be more intimate). The form of address carries a message about the power relationship between the speakers. The message can be a personal one ('I am superior to you'), a solidarity one ('We are equals'), or a political one ('All persons are equal; there is no hierarchical structure in society'). During the French Revolution the peasant revolutionaries purposely addressed the toppled aristocrats as *tu* in order to reinforce by language the social and political changes that had taken place. It was meant to stress the new-found equality.

In seventeenth-and eighteenth-century England, the Quakers also decided to adopt the style of calling everyone 'thou' in order to indicate the equality of all people. As in present-day French (*tu*) or German (*du*), this pronoun had previously been reserved for use only to close intimates, lower-or equal-status family members, and 'inferiors' like servants, children and pet animals. This style caused considerable amounts of abuse to be heaped on Quakers; indeed in 1714 Thomas Ellwood found that it led to trouble between himself and his father, who evidently felt disrespected: 'But whenever I had occasion to speak to my father . . . my language did [offend him]: for I [did] not say YOU to him but THEE or THOU, as the occasion required, and then he would be sure to fall on me with his fists'!

We may like to believe that such linguistic messages are a thing of the past, but they still survive. We still distinguish respectful forms and informal ones. Do you call your professor Professor Surname, or Chris? What do colleagues call the same person? Do you call your father by a title (dad, father, pop, or even 'sir') or by his first name? What does he call you? Whenever I discuss this with my students in class it is obvious that the difference is a very real one. Those people who use a title would feel uncomfortable using a first name, and vice versa. As with all cases of 'in-law relations', the problem is even more acute for people in deciding how to address the parents of their romantic partner. Think about it.

In some cases a fictitious first name is used when one person does not know the proper name, but does not want to accept a lower status by using a general polite form, like 'sir' or 'madam'. Thus, New York taxi-drivers call male passengers 'Mac', Londoners call men 'John', and many Scotsmen call other men 'Jimmy', and – unfortunately for me – many people in northern England call everyone 'duck'. Interestingly, when talking to other women or when women talk to either sex, a term of endearment is often used in England, such as 'luv' or 'dear', terms otherwise seen to be patronizing, especially if used by men to women. These points and observations may seem quaint and unreal until you actually try to break the rules. Try calling some of your professors by their first names without permission and see what reaction you get. More interestingly, see how it feels to you personally. If you really want an experience then try calling them 'Mac'.

Speech style, power and relationships

Speech style can be classified as powerful or powerless according to its general structure (Lakoff, 1973). Powerless speech uses a high proportion of *intensifiers* (words like very, extremely, absolutely, totally, really); *empty adjectives and adverbs* (wonderful, incredibly, amazingly); *deferential forms* (would you please? may I?); *tag questions* (isn't it? don't you? *n'est ce pas?*); *hedges* or *lack of commitment* (I suppose, I guess, maybe); *gestures* with speech (suggesting lack of emphasis in the speech itself); *intonational patterns* that seem to 'fuss' and 'whine'; *lack of perseverance* during interruptions and *acquiescence in simultaneous speech*. Note that since many of these forms are 'polite' in our culture, polite speech can seem powerless.

Is women's speech generally powerless? Lakoff claims that women's language contains more intensifiers, qualifiers/hedges, and tag questions than does men's speech. This, Lakoff argues, leads to women's speech being seen as less powerful than the speech style typically produced by men. More recently, Mulac et al. (1988) have shown that there are 'gender-linked language effects' ('men's talk and women's talk') but that they show up more in same-sex dyads than in mixed-sex dyads. 'Men's talk' contains more interruptions, directives, and fillers to start a sentence; 'women's talk' contains more questions, intensifying adverbs, and adverbial starts to sentences ('Actually. . .'). However, Mulac (1989) shows that these differences are 'consistent with the appearance, but not necessarily the actual implementation, of power'. For Mulac, the alleged differences in powerfulness are not powerful, in the sense that men and women also wield power in interactions by means other than speech style.

Several pieces of evidence confirm that men actually talk more than women (e.g. Argyle et al., 1968), although this may indicate that men take the floor and do not concede when interrupted by women. It used to be believed that women are more likely than men to be interrupted, and those who interrupt them are more likely to be men than women (McMillan et al., 1977). However, Dindia

(1987) has convincingly shown that when the sex of *partner* is taken into account as well as the sex of the speaker, men do not interrupt more than women and women are not interrupted more than men. Instead, there is a pattern of more opposite-sex interruption, both male–female and female–male, than same-sex interruptions.

Using language to relate to other people

One most intriguing aspect of language is the way in which it can be used to indicate the relationship between the speaker and the listener. We have already learned that power and solidarity can be conveyed by such a simple cue as the choice of pronoun used to address persons (whether the T- or the V-form). There are other ways in which the immediacy of language can indicate closeness, intimacy or acceptance (Mehrabian, 1971). 'Immediacy' refers to the amount of positive feeling or inclusion of the other person in the message and to the amount of distance implied in the message. Consider the differences in 'Ms Jones and I have just been for a walk', 'We two have just been for a walk', and 'Jonesey and I have just been for a walk'. What about 'X is my neighbour' and 'X and I live in the same neighbourhood'? And, what of 'I hope your career is successful' as distinct from 'I hope you are successful'? These different phrasings of the same messages convey different degrees of interest and involvement.

Such messages also help to create and hold together our relationships with other people. We are all sensitive to the different relational messages conveyed by our forms of speech, and we change them as relationships develop. Processes of growth in a relationship are managed through communication; we can indicate to a partner and to the world at large that we have grown closer simply by subtly changing the way in which we address the person (Premo & Stiles, 1983). To become noticeably more immediate is to become noticeably more intimate; to start talking of 'us' is to claim that a relationship exists or is coming into existence; to encourage greater intimacy in language is to instigate greater intimacy in relationship (Morton et al., 1976). It can be a condemnation of a relationship to complain about the language used in it, and vice versa. 'We don't communicate any more' is just such a statement.

Equally, partners develop private languages and personal idioms to personalize their relationship (Hopper et al., 1981). For instance, for some partners the single word 'jellybeans' may be used to mean 'You're talking over my head and I don't understand'. In short, language conveys degrees of intimacy, is a powerful developer and definer of relationships, and is used to indicate many privacies in relationships. It conveys messages by its structure as well as by its content, but it does not do it on its own in the course of normal everyday interactions. It is a part of a system that works together. We can be both verbally immediate and nonverbally intimate, for instance, and this could be important in indicating relational intimacy – it could be problematic if the two 'channels' (verbal and nonverbal) do not match up, as we'll see below.

Switching: the messages of change

An understanding of the role of language style in social relationships leads to our questioning the social functions of 'switching' between styles. What social messages are conveyed by a sudden switch in immediacy or a switch from high to low or from low to high forms of speech? Low form is typically associated with informal, friendly settings whilst a high form goes with formality and emotional distance. A switch from low to high is a distancing strategy that shows disapproval, aloofness, dislike and hostility. By contrast, a high–low switch is an affiliative strategy that indicates liking, approval, and a desire to be less formal and more friendly.

In an influential theory relating speech to social behaviour, Giles (1977; Giles & Powesland, 1975) argues that we 'accommodate' our language (whether language style, speech style, accent, code or content) to our interaction partner if we feel attracted. We play down the distinctiveness of our own individual style of speaking and accommodate, or move towards, that of the other person ('convergence'). For instance, parents frequently accommodate the style of their language and talk 'baby talk' to young children, whilst adults adopt the code form preferred by the powerful actor in a given setting (e.g. they talk formally to their boss).

On the other hand, when we wish to distinguish ourselves from some other person or group, we accentuate differences in our speech style ('divergence'). For instance, French Canadians prefer their politicians to make public speeches in English with a thick French accent, even if they are capable of speaking perfect English (Bourhis & Giles, 1977). Accommodation is a strong indicator of group identification (Giles, 1977). One forceful historical example is from 1973, when Arab oil producers suddenly switched from issuing their decisions about oil prices in English to doing so in Arabic. That was a powerful message to the world, indicating who now had the upper hand and who now had to accommodate to whom.

BOX 1.8   Speech accommodation

Speakers often adapt their speech to be more similar to that of their conversational partner, particularly when they wish to relax that person or ingratiate themselves (Giles et al., 1973).

Such 'convergence' occurs at various linguistic levels, involving speech rate, silences, choice of language (where the speakers are bilingual), regional accents, or vocal intensity and loudness (Giles & Powesland, 1975).

In bilingual Canada, there is a norm that a bilingual salesperson is supposed to converge towards the language chosen by the customer (Scotton & Udry, 1977).

The higher-prestige language is usually adopted in a bilingual community as long as partners like one another (Giles, 1978).

Divergence is equally powerful (Bourhis & Giles, 1977). When speakers dislike their partner or the ethnic group from which he or she comes, they will adopt extremely different speech styles, occasionally refusing to speak in the partner's adopted language (e.g. persisting in speaking Welsh to disliked English weekend-holidaymakers in Wales).

Putting verbal and nonverbal together

So far I have been looking at the components of communication separately as linguistic and nonverbal forms; but obviously, in relationships they occur together most of the time. In real life, they most often go together and amplify one another. When we say angry things we usually look angry; when we say 'I love you' we usually look as if we mean it. Recent work has shown that NVC can also help in the production of speech (Hadar, 1989). This might explain why people gesture vigorously when they are on the telephone and the person at the other end of the line cannot see any of it! However, researchers have been interested for a long time in studying the *relative* importance of language and NVC and this has led them to look at inconsistencies between the two channels. For instance when I say nice things but frown, or when I say 'I'm NOT ANGRY!!!!!', how do observers interpret such inconsistencies?

Facial messages are the most powerful components of such contradictions (Zaidel & Mehrabian, 1969). They are seen as conveying the real messages and as giving the true evaluation of the person. Words, on the other hand, are assumed to relate to the person's acts or deeds. That is, we tend to assume that the facial expression indicates the speaker's evaluation of the person as a person, while the words evaluate the person's behaviour. 'Well done' said with a scowl, for instance, indicates grudging praise for someone who is disliked. Young children have particular difficulty with such inconsistent messages and tend to treat all such messages as if they were negative, whichever channel conveyed the negativity (Bugental et al., 1970). Walker & Trimboli (1989) point out that laboratory or experimental work on such inconsistency very often strips it from all the important embedding context in which it is *always* placed in real life. Such a context, which is created by the human relationships in which the communication occurs, gives people very strong cues about the overall 'meaning' of the inconsistency. While the NV channel is usually seen as the more important ('Actions speak louder than words', after all), the most likely thing is that an observer will work out the 'true meaning' from the context – and that is usually built into the relationship as much as anything.

In sum, the evidence shows the importance of nonverbal cues in social behaviour and the extreme subtlety of some influences upon impressions and social judgements. We know that impression management can depend upon our nonverbal performance, and we have learned that judgements of ingratiation, liking, intention and sincerity can depend on the way we move our eyes or distribute our limbs.

Both ordinary language and the silent language of nonverbal cues convey messages about liking, strength of feelings towards someone, trust, liking, status differences and power. Most of these are relational messages, so in chapter 2 we shall look at the ways in which we express and communicate emotions in relationships, while chapter 3 will look at relationships, their growth, decline and repair.

Summary

Language and nonverbal communication (even down at the level of usage of space) both convey implicit as well as explicit messages about power, control, liking. Every time we speak to someone we can convey messages about how much we like them and what we think is our relationship to them – not just by explicitly saying so in the content of our talk but also by the style of the language we use and the accompanying nonverbal communications we make.

Identity management is achieved by both verbal and nonverbal means, and the form of speech is as important as the minute movements of face, eyes and body that make up the whole nonverbal system. In chapter 6 we shall see that there are some extremely powerful applications of such work in medicine, and in chapter 7 also applications to the law.

Further reading

Burgoon J.K., Buller, D.B. & Woodall, W.G. (1989) *Nonverbal Communication: The Unspoken Dialogue*. Harper & Row: New York.

Duck, S.W. (1991) *Friends, For Life*, revised second edition. Harvester: Hemel Hempstead, UK. [Published in the USA as *Understanding Relationships*. Guilford: New York]

Giles, H. & Powesland, P.F. (1990) *Handbook of Language and Social Behaviour*. Wiley: Chichester, UK.

CHAPTER 2

Social Emotions: Showing Our Feelings about Other People

Emotions are the stuff of which the peaks and troughs of life are made, as when, for example, we feel exhilarated, depressed, shy, lonely, jealous or in love. Those emotions that cause us to focus on other people are particularly powerful (for example, love and jealousy – which some countries accept as legitimate legal justifications for 'crimes of passion'). However, emotions that create and sustain relationships (and make them more interesting!) are not just internal subconscious disturbances that never get out into the real world. Indeed, as cheating lovers may well find, jealousy can be expressed in some intriguing, and occasionally fatal, ways. Therefore the exploration of emotion in relationships should not stop short at the point where the feeling is felt, nor rest satisfied with explanations in terms of the cognitive or social structures that produce it. Rather in this context we must understand the ways in which emotions impact on relationships in their everyday working reality. Such a goal will entail us understanding the ways in which human beings have been socialized to *express* (or limit their expression of) emotions about relationships and relational partners.

Labelling and expressing feelings

First, the strong social imperatives about communication of emotion spoil some people's relationships; relationship problems, like shyness, often show up as unusual or inappropriate ways of communicating feeling. Second, when we report or describe emotions, we frequently edit our accounts of them so that they make sense to other people, not just to ourselves. So we use culturally accepted terminology and reference points, describing emotions in ways that are accepted in our culture as valid ones (for example, 'falling in love' rather than 'bitten by the love god's mosquito').

Usually this also means that we summarize them as future-oriented, enduring or continuous *states* rather than momentary or fleeting micromomentary feelings (Duck & Sants, 1983). For instance, we are more likely to say 'I am in love with you' or 'I will love you for ever' or 'I am friends with you' rather than 'I felt a twinge of love for you at the moment when you looked at me' or 'I felt friendship towards you the moment when you shared that secret with me'.

Summarizing emotions and translating them into the language of enduring states in this way both make it hard to pinpoint the true initial causes of the enduring emotions or long-lasting relationships of love and friendship. Perhaps we can explain it as 'love at first sight', but usually we prefer to look back over a whole range of experiences and events to explain our love for someone. Our accounts usually state publicly that emotions and relationships are on more sound bases than momentary reactions or single causes. We would feel foolish saying that we loved someone only at a particular few seconds a week or merely for the shape of the nose. Our culture prefers to believe that it takes time to fall in love, and that love is a complete emotion constructed from many cues and causes all rolled together. We also suppose that the feeling evolves to envelope us over a period of time.

In more technical language, statements about social emotions use dispositional or continuous language to provide 'summary affect statements' about our partner and these are socially appropriate to the culture in which we happen to find ourselves. They summarize our feelings about someone using culturally approved terminology and accepted explanations for the basis of relationships. They are not simple descriptions of short-term emotional peaks or troughs; they emphasize implicit continuity in relationships and prepare partners and others to expect a certain shape to the future – a future that still has the relationship in it! In fact, as I shall argue here, much of the construction of relationships is based on various ways of manipulating our expectations about the future in this way, since relationships involve unfinished business that continues throughout the life of the relationship itself (Duck, 1990b). Much of the basis of emotion is founded in the organization of routines of behaviour that make up the day-to-day conduct of this unfinished business. In short, social emotions are not just fleeting physiological experiences but are organized, long-term behavioural creations that find their form and shape in the behaviour and routines of everyday conduct of relationships. They are also, as we shall see in considering each of the emotions below, expressed in ways carrying symbolic force in a given society.

As a matter of fact there is some evidence that the symbolic values of emotion and relationships have changed somewhat through history, even in our own culture. In a recent fascinating report, Contarello & Volpato (1991) have explored both the similarities and the differences in literary descriptions of friendship over the last 1000 years. They found that friendship has always involved intimacy, respect and mutual help, plus the likelihood of the friend confronting one's own weaknesses honestly. By contrast, in the passage from the sixteenth to the seventeenth century, friendship went through a profound change, with conflict emerging as a common element. Also although all the texts examined in this study were written by female authors, female friendship was hardly ever mentioned in the early texts!

BOX 2.1 Points to think about
- *Are emotions just how we feel inside or are they tied in to behaviour towards other people in relationships?*
- *Are there different types of love?*
- *Is adult love based on the same mechanisms as is childhood attachment to parents?*
- *What makes people jealous?*
- *How do you recover from an embarrassing predicament?*
- *What is embarrassment anyway?*
- *What is loneliness and how can it be dealt with?*

Love

Although recent researchers have now looked at friendship, including female friendship, quite extensively, they have also looked at the juicier topic of love, and this could be seen as the primary relational emotion. If we were Contarello & Volpato, we'd immediately note that love was not 'big' in marriages in the twelfth century. It was not even expected to be there – at least not in the sense that we expect it to be the basis of marriage nowadays. Marriage, especially between noble persons, was politically arranged and served the needs of strengthening the ties between different groups, families or 'houses'. If the partners liked each other then that was a bonus. All that was necessary was loyalty and fidelity. Nowadays we do things differently, and, in America and the UK, we have a divorce rate approaching 50 per cent!

Love is blamed for a lot of things, from the Trojan War to various crimes of passion that appear in the tabloid newspapers. It is called 'a temporary insanity' (Bierce, *The Devil's Dictionary*: he went on to add that it is 'curable by marriage'). So what is it? Kovecses (1991) notes that we communicate about love in many different ways, using some very obscure and some very complex metaphors and meaning systems. For example, love is often likened to food or eating ('sugar', 'honey', 'feast your eyes upon . . .', 'good enough to eat . . .') but also to consumption of other types ('all aflame with passion . . .', 'burning desire', 's/he sets my heart on fire'). The extensive system of meaning and communication through metaphors and other linguistic devices shows us, through Kovecses's analysis, the power of the system of description. This perhaps points to common threads of experience for us all in trying to understand and communicate our feelings of love to other people. For instance, we can readily understand and sympathize with someone who claims to be displaced (for example, 'head over heels in love') or distracted (for example, 'I'm mad with love for you', 'They are nuts about each other').

Does such a finding of regular and systematic use of specifically vivid metaphors about love indicate that we typically experience it in culturally 'agreed' ways? Marston et al. (1987) looked at the subjective experience of love and the ways in which people communicate about it. From interviews and questionnaire data they found that there are essentially six ways in which people communicate about love (see BOX 2.2). Love is experienced in several different manners (through labels, through physiological arousal, through behaviour and through nonverbal communication). In addition, there is strong coherence between the ways that people experience love and the ways in which they communicate about it (see end of BOX 2.2).

In the recent massive upsurge in work on love, this interesting theme arises in other forms of research on the possibility that there are different sorts of love. There are several approaches to this idea, and I will select two. I will start with the idea that there are different sorts of love that stem originally from the kinds of attachment that we have to love-objects, such as parents in our early years and other adults in our later years. The second idea is that there are basically six styles of loving in adults. The basic idea of the first notion is that, as it were, we learn how to love, how to attach ourselves to other human beings, and how to relate, in our first infant relationships. That learning carries over into later relationships that we form as adults. The basic idea of the second notion is that love, however it originates, is made up of different components felt in different ways and different degrees by different people.

Attachment styles

In 1987, Hazan & Shaver suggested that adult styles of loving may represent processes similar to those found in attachments formed by infants or children to their parents. A considerable amount of work by developmentalists and psychiatrists has indicated that infants develop strong attachment to their mothers in the first few months of infancy, and Ainsworth et al. (1978) claimed to have discovered three styles of attachment that can be reliably distinguished in children and infants. *Secure attachment* is based in a sense of confidence and security in intimacy. By contrast, *anxious/ambivalent attachment* is characterized by dependency, lack of confidence in attachment, and a sense of lack of appreciation by others. Finally, *avoidant attachment* is characterized by lack of acceptance of others, avoidance of closeness and discomfort in intimate situations. Hazan & Shaver argue that these can be extended to patterns of attachment shown by adults. Evidence is beginning to be amassed to support this view in the areas of marital relationships, work, and even alcohol abuse (Hazan, 1987; Shaver & Hazan, 1988; Senchak & Leonard, 1992). Recently, however, Bartholomew (1990) has criticized the original Hazan & Shaver tripartite system and pointed out that the avoidant style of attachment can be broken down into two separate subsets. These are a *fearful avoidant style*, when the person feels a desire to obtain social contact but is fearful of its consequences; and a *dismissive avoidant style*, when the person defensively denies the need for social contact. People who are fearfully avoidant tend to regard themselves as undeserving of the love and support of others. People who are dismissively avoidant view themselves positively but just do not regard the presence and support of other people as necessary. Thus Bartholomew (1990) effectively extends Hazan & Shaver's (1987) three-part system to a four-part one.

Because it represents an attempt to try to tie adult experience to infant and child experience (and so implicitly identifies a common thread running through all human relationships), this approach to attachment is likely to be one that receives a lot of attention in the coming years. Indeed, Newcomb (1990) has argued that there is a fundamental human tendency to associate with others that is based on attachment and can be found all through life in adolescent and young adult relationships as well as in social support, expectancies about others' likelihood of helping one in a crisis and several other examples of human relationships. Also Beinstein Miller (1989) has shown that individuals have a tendency to remember their child-hoods in ways that reflect their adult styles of handling conflict. Clearly, until thoughtful lifelong studies (or at least long-term studies from childhood to adulthood) are done on these issues we shall not be able to determine whether people who are insecure/avoi-dant/secure *remember* their childhoods in characteristic ways or whether people who are insecure etc. *were* insecure etc. in child-hood. I believe that a mixture of the two will prove correct, in that I would expect people to remember childhood in a way that is not entirely distinct from their present patterns of behaviour. This is because these patterns are likely to be induced by memory to some degree (Miell, 1987) or by one's adaptation to such memories (Putallaz et al., 1991). The attachment style approach represents an exciting area for future work.

Are there different types of love?

Another typological approach is based on the idea that we can distinguish different sorts of the same basic emotion that some (Shaver & Hazan, 1988) have tried to show to be related to attach-ment processes. As Davis & Latty-Mann (1987) note, the sort of typology described below strikes a responsive chord for most people. As I consider it, think to yourself whether your experience of love has any similarities to the typology outlined here.

'Love' may not be one emotion but several – or, at least, it may have several components: some good, some bad. You can decide for yourself if they are good or bad, but there are different types. Early theorists, such as Maslow, distinguished B (for Being) love, which he saw as positive and implying independence, from D (for Dependency) love, which he saw as negative and implying neediness. By contrast, another way to look at it is that independence is egotistical and D-love is more proper! Indeed, the latter view is the one that is often taken in Japan, where subser-vience to group needs and requirements is admired over selfish individualism.

Another distinction is between passionate love and companionate love (Berscheid & Walster, 1974): passionate love is the steamy sort that Casanova and Don Juan specialized in, whilst companionate love is the kind that kin and long-term marriage partners may have.

Companionate love is enhanced by an increased sense of commitment whilst passionate love derives primarily from physiological arousal and excitement.

Is love really just either madly passionate or boringly dispassionate? Is this passionate–companionate dichotomy too simple to account for all the feelings that we can have towards a lover? Another proposal (Lee, 1973) suggests that there are six types of love and that persons can mix these together in various ways. The six types are labelled with various Latin and Greek words for types of love: Eros, Ludus, Storge, Pragma, Mania and Agape. Each has a typical character, and a brief explanation may assist in determining the nature of love.

Eros (Romantic love)

Eros, or romantic love, focusses upon beauty and physical attractiveness; it is a sensual love that expects to be returned. People who score highly on Eros typically believe in 'love at first sight' and are particularly sensitive to the physical blemishes of their partner, such as overweight, broken nose, smelly feet or misaligned teeth. They are attracted to partners on the basis of physical attraction, like to kiss and cuddle soon after meeting a new partner and report a definite genital response (lubrication, erection) to the first kiss.

Ludus (Game-playing love)

Ludus love is like a game and is seen as fun, not to be taken seriously. People scoring high on Ludus typically flirt a lot, keep partners guessing about their level of commitment to them and stop a relationship when it stops being fun. They get over love affairs easily and quickly, enjoy teasing their lovers and will often go out with someone even when they know they do not want to get involved.

Storge (Friendship love)

Storgic love is based on caring, not on passion. People scoring high on Storge typically believe that love grows from friendship, that lovers must share similar interests and enjoy the same activities. For Storgic lovers, love grows with respect and concern for the other person. They can put up with long separations without feeling that the relationship is threatend and are not looking for excitement in the relationship, as Ludic lovers are.

Pragma (Logical, shopping-list love)

Pragmatic love is practical and based on the belief that a relationship has to work. People scoring high on Pragma ask themselves whether their lover would make a good parent and they pay thoughtful attention to such things as their partner's future career prospects. Pragmatic lovers take account of their partner's background and characteristics like attitudes, religion, politics and hobbies. Pragmatic lovers are realistic and relatively unromantic.

Mania (Possessive, dependent love)

Manic love is essentially an uncertain and anxious type of love; it is obsessive and possessive and half expects to be thrown aside. Manic lovers get very jealous. People scoring high on Mania typically believe in becoming ill or doing stupid things to regain their partner's attention if ever the partner ignores them or takes them for granted. They also claim that when the relationship gets into trouble, they develop illnesses like stomach upsets.

Agape (All-giving, selfless love)

Agape is selfless and compassionate and generally loves other human beings in an unqualified way, as preached by Gandhi, Buddha and Jesus. In their close relationships, Agapic lovers would claim that they use their strength to help their partner through difficult times and may say that if their partner had a baby with someone else, they would want to help to care for it as if it were their own. Lee (1973) reports that he did not encounter any persons who were perfect examples of Agapic lovers, although many people reported brief Agapic episodes.

If there are these types of love, then do men and women experience them to different extents? Yes. It seems that men are often Erotic and Ludic in their attitudes to love (Hendrick et al., 1984), whilst women are often Pragmatic, Manic and Storgic. In other words, men's love is typically passionate and uncommitted, with an element of game-playing coupled with romance. Women's love is typically practical and caring, with an element of possessiveness. This is not to say that women do not base their love on passion or that men do not care about their lovers. The sexes mix their experience of love in different blends.

Developing love?

So far, we have seen love as a state of feeling, but this can most definitely develop and change (Cunningham & Antill, 1981). One possibility is that falling in love is a transition between different blends of the types of love. For instance, initial attraction to a possible lover might begin as Erotic love, mixed perhaps with Mania (desire for possession) and Ludus (game-playing). As the relationship develops, the lovers might experience greater feelings of Storge (friendship) as they develop caring on top of passion. This may lead them on to question the working of the relationship in the long term, that is, to concern over the partner's potential as a long-term mate, co-parent of the children, and so on – in short, to an assessment of pragmatic concerns. If the partner seems to pass that test, then they might begin to feel Pragma love.

All of this would suggest that married couples would score more highly than other couples on Pragma love, whilst new dates might score more highly on Erotic love; that is, views about the 'right type' of love for different sorts of relationship will vary. As the relationship to a partner develops, so the type of love will also alter.

Another suggestion that follows from this idea is that women (who are generally more Pragmatic in love than men) get to the Pragma stage earlier than men do and will either fall in Pragma love sooner than men will or else decide to get out of the relationship because their partner fails the test of a Pragmatic approach (e.g. fails to show signs of being a good parent). Women get out of relationships earlier than men do (see 'LIFOs' BOX 2.2, p. 43). What remains to be seen is whether women pass through the love stages more quickly than men do, as suggested. What do you think? Different people may have different styles of loving, on top of the general differences between the sexes, so the picture would probably become more complicated, indicating the need for further research.

Up to this point we have seen that there are several ways to experience and express love (Marston et al., 1987), several ways in which adult love/attachment themes relate to other forms of attachment (Hazan & Shaver, 1987), and several ways in which adult love styles appear to be manifested (Hendrick & Hendrick, 1988). Can these positions be reconciled? Are they saying the same thing?

Some attempts have been made to show that the six Lee love styles are not really as distinct a six as they were first thought to be (Davis & Latty-Mann, 1987), while other efforts have shown that the three attachment styles are really four (Bartholomew, 1990). Shaver & Hazan (1988) have claimed that the Lee love styles are really different forms of expression of the three (or four) attachment styles. . . . And so it goes. This reconciliation and differentiation will undoubtedly continue, as they are always a part of the advancing of scholarly knowledge. At this point, it is too early to see how it will all turn out, but I do think that one important point is missing from the psychologists' attempts to identify attitudes and styles of thinking about love, so let's turn to that.

One thing for you to think about is the question of whether love is an attitude, a set of beliefs, a set of communicative devices, or all of these. As Marston et al. (1987) found, I can feel love, think about it, or communicate it. When I feel it, I may think of inventive ways to convey it ('My love is like a red, red rose that's newly sprung in June; My love is like a melody that's sweetly sung in tune. . .'). But there is something equally important: the way in which we express love may be *coloured by the circumstances of the moment*. If we are on a date then we may be interested in openly conveying lust (if we are feeling lucky) or at least strong positive feelings (something like Eros). By contrast, if we are discussing marriage, our minds may turn to the roles involved in long-term commitment (something like Pragma). If we are feeling playful and having a good time, or in a group of friends who can overhear what we are saying, then we may just start teasing (something like Ludus). These could all be different modes of expression of the same single positive attitude toward a partner rather than different types or styles of emotion. Attitudes do not have a single level of intensity or only one mode of expression. As rhetorical theorists note very regularly (Billig, 1987), we express our attitudes and make statements in particular forms as a result of the *audience* to whom we are talking and the *situation* in which we are speaking. 'The attitude' is thus represented by many different forms of expression and is a somewhat amorphous and protean thing. I suspect that researchers of love ought to look less at the presumed single-minded and enduring aspect of the person who feels the love (as psychologists tend to do when they explore love attitudes or love styles). Instead they should pay more attention to the circumstances and rhetorical/social/interpersonal contexts or situations where love is expressed and communicated in everyday life. Although you can feel love without expressing it, the occasions that are most interesting are obviously those where it is not only felt but also expressed. There it carries social and relational consequences and is also constrained by social and relational forces without actually changing its nature.

The behaviour of lovers

Aside from the feelings of love which drive us into relationships, there are behavioural and communicative consequences too (Maxwell, 1985). Love is both a felt emotion and an expression of that feeling in the behaviour through which we communicate to partners – and to the outside world – that we love them. Obviously, partners who are married often choose to wear wedding rings to communicate the fact; dates hold hands and may dress alike or share clothing; partners embrace or put their arms around one another in the street. These indications are slight but well known. They are called 'tie signs' (Goffman, 1959) in that they indicate that two people are 'tied' to one another (cf. the use of symbolic spatial markers discussed in Chapter 1). They show that emotions affect the tiny behaviours of everyday life. Furthermore, lovers sit closer to one another than do 'likers', and they gaze at one another more than do people who are just friends (Rubin, 1973). One part of love, then, is a communicative display of the fact that we love our partner; it not only reassures the partner but tells the outside world. Of course, the sorts of display that we choose on a given occasion are also likely to be influenced by the rhetorical situation, the social context and the interpersonal environments, as discussed above. Presenting a partner with a ring, doing a really big and inconvenient favour, and disrobing are all, in their own ways, capable of conveying a message of love and fondness through behaviour. Nevertheless, each is appropriate only to a particular set of circumstances and would be inappropriate in others.

For this reason, *loving behaviour* itself develops and changes as love attitudes themselves develop. Developing love is not simply an increasingly powerful attitude but is also a changing constellation of behaviours. As Aron et al. (1989) show, the *experience* of falling in love is usually described in terms only of attitudes and feelings, based on other people's personalities or physical characteristics, similarity to oneself or propinquity. There is a strongly reported change in behaviour, as well, such as increased eye contact, physical closeness, and self-disclosure. Beyond this there is a broader change to the structure of everyday life behaviours. For instance, we gradually pay more attention to a new lover and spend less time with old friends; we start to share more activities and adjust our lifestyles as we let our new lover into our lives; we arrange to spend more time with our partner and less with other people (Milardo, 1982; Parks & Adelman, 1983). In short, part of falling in love is an increased binding together of the routines of daily life and a developing

BOX 2.2 Some research findings about love

— Men 'fall in love' at an earlier point in a relationship than women do, but women fall out of love sooner than men do (Walster & Walster, 1978). This has led to men being called 'FILOs' (First In, Last Out) and women 'LIFOs' (Last In, First Out). Research should look at the possibility that men are satisfied that they are 'in love' when they experience mere Ludus, while women wait until they reach the Pragma stage. If this notion is valid, then it 'explains' the difference reported here.

— Aron et al. (1989) compared subjects' reports of falling in love and falling in friendship. Falling in love is characterized by frequent feelings that the other person is like the self, observing the other's desirable characteristics, moderate feelings of similarity, and a sense of 'mystery or magic'. By contrast, falling in friendship is seen as due to similarity and propinquity, with a little less emphasis on the other's desirable characteristics and practically no mention of any magic or mystery.

— Men and women report experiencing the same levels of intensity of love (Rubin, 1973) although their experience is made up of a different mix of love types (Hendrick et al., 1984; described in text here).

— Women say that they have been infatuated more often than men (on average, 5.6 times for women and 4.5 times for men), but both sexes report being in loving relationships about as often – around 1.25 times (Kephart, 1967).

— Marston et al. (1987) found that the subjective experience of love has at least three components:

(1) Relational labels/constructs, like commitment and security;
(2) Physiological labels, such as feelings of nervousness and warmth;
(3) Behaviour and NVC, such as doing things with the other person or ways of looking at one another.

Given that love-smitten subjects conceptualized love in terms of different mixes of these elements, rather than in terms of different strengths of the same mix, as implied by Rubin's approach, Marston et al. found evidence for 6 types of experience of love. These are: collaborative love (supportiveness); active love (joint activities and 'erratic rhythms' such as changes to the pace of daily routines); intuitive love (NVC ability to communicate feelings); committed love (togetherness); traditional romantic love (future commitment and feeling good); expressive love (telling the other person about one's feelings).

routine interdependence. More than this, a big part of it is extending the range of ways in which love can be expressed and communicated.

What happens when you fall in love?

Given that the routines of life are comfortable and important to us, a break with ordinary routines – such as occurs when we fall in love with a new partner – could be a problem. Surely, it is a pleasant experience to be in love and it heightens self-esteem, as leading psychologists have shown (Hendrick & Hendrick, 1988). It also means that we have to restructure our lives, accommodate to the lifestyle of someone else, adopt new routines, and bring our new partner into our own daily pattern of activities.

People who *fall in love frequently* report that it is highly disruptive and that they develop a high level of nervous disorders and skin problems (Kemper & Bologh, 1981). However, when love is going well, people report feeling good both in mind and in body (Hendrick & Hendrick, 1988). Disruption to love is more problematic. People who have never been in love claim that they have a high number of minor bodily disorders like colds and flu, and people who have recently broken up with a partner suffer similar physical disorders too (Kemper & Bologh, 1981). Those whose partners have broken off with them typically report sleep problems, headaches and loss of control of emotions. Those who caused the break-up suffered less, except that females reported stomach upsets.

In summary, love is more than just an attitude or disembodied emotion that we simply feel inside ourselves. It has consequences for our behaviour and for larger aspects of our functioning in social groups. It affects not only our feelings but our actions and the way we communicate. Love can take several forms and exerts an influence on our lives by restructuring our routines. We talk about it in different ways depending on our audience and the situation. Love also exposes us to the need to adjust our behaviour; for example by restricting our romantic activities exclusively to our lovers. When that does not happen and lovers stray, the partner probably experiences another emotion: jealousy.

Jealousy in love

Love makes us feel valued by someone else, and we feel jealous when we fear that he or she does not value us. (On a technical point of definition, one is jealous of what is one's own, but envious of that which is other people's. Thus one is jealous – or possessive – of one's own partner, but envious of – covetous of – someone else's.) Positive emotions are often reported in a way that suggests they make us feel competent whilst negative ones are explained in terms of inadequacy (Davitz, 1964) – that is, inadequacy relative to other people and their feelings for us. The negative emotions in relationships (like jealousy) are often unpleasant precisely because they affect our self-esteem or our sense of competence as a social performer or partner (Bringle, 1991). They are also complex blends of feelings, thoughts and behaviours (in the case of jealousy these are often treated by researchers as if they are coping behaviours) and some researchers (Pfeiffer & Wong, 1989) have recently begun to assess jealousy as a multidimensional construct. This breaks jealousy down into three elementary components: cognitive, emotional and behavioural. The authors' own multidimensional jealousy scale includes questions about these three categories. For example, how often have the following thoughts occurred to you? (. . . I suspect that X is secretly seeing someone of the opposite sex; . . . I am worried that someone of the opposite sex is trying to seduce X); how would you react emotionally to the following situations? (. . . X is flirting with someone of the opposite sex; . . . X hugs and kisses someone of the opposite sex), and how often do you engage in the following behaviours? (. . . I look through X's drawers, handbag or pockets; . . . I question X about his or her telephone calls).

BOX 2.3 Jealousy and envy

Smith (1991) notes that envy is very often characterized by a sense of injustice that partly 'legitimates' the feeling.

Hupka (1991) argues that jealousy is at least in part a human creation based on the social structures in which human activity is organized (see text here on social rules for expressing jealousy).

Clanton & Kosins (1991) also note that jealousy is a sign that something is wrong with the relationship rather than with just one of the partners.

Hansen (1991) points out that jealousy also has implications for family structure and family stress and is not truly an individual emotion, at least in its consequences.

According to research, men feel jealous when they feel inadequate but women feel jealous when they feel dependent on a relationship (and believe that it is better than any other relationship possibilities presently open to them). Men are more likely to react to jealousy with anger and women with depression (Hansen, 1991).

Obviously, it is a powerful emotion, but what exactly is jealousy? Buunk & Bringle (1987) define it broadly as 'an aversive emotional reaction caused by an extra-dyadic [e.g. extramarital] relationship of one's current or former intimate partner – a relationship that is real, imagined, likely to occur, or has occurred in the past'. In other words, it is a negative feeling that we get when our partner 'steps out' of the relationship – or when we 'think' he or she might.

This definition is broad and allows for considerable personal differences in jealous reactions. Look, for instance, at the phrase 'likely to occur'. People will differ in beliefs about the likelihood of a partner getting into an 'extra-dyadic relationship'. Such beliefs and judgements will depend on a whole mix of possible influences (e.g. our feelings about the partner's attractiveness, knowledge of the partner's behaviour, age and availability of alternative partners, partner's trustworthiness – even our own personality, possessiveness and ability to trust others).

Buunk & Bringle's (1987) work is based on sexual affairs, but most of us have felt jealous when we see partners just showing an interest in other people (or having an interest shown in them by others). In some cases people also report feeling jealous not about a real partner but about a desired one. One sign of increased desire for involvement with someone is precisely when we start to get upset that he or she is going out with someone else.

Since we can feel jealous about different sorts of relationship and since the different relationships have varying levels of importance to us, it is possible that they are afflicted by different sorts of jealousy. What we need to understand is what exactly makes us feel one sort rather than another. Is it entirely personal, or are we influenced by social rules about how we 'should' experience jealousy? Let us look first at types of jealousy and then at the point about rules.

Types of jealousy

Perhaps, like love, there are different types of jealousy. Mazur (1977) distinguished five types: possessive, exclusive, competitive, egotistical, and fearful.

Possessive

A possessive jealousy is a response to perceived violation of 'property rights'. We feel this type of jealousy about things or status or even other people if we think that they belong to us or are our property. For instance, we sometimes feel possessive jealousy if our partner acts in an independent way.

Exclusive

An exclusive jealousy is a response to occasions when we are omitted from a loved one's important experiences or when we are not allowed to share a loved one's private world. For instance, if our partner wants to go camping in the mountains to commune with nature and specifically forbids us to accompany him or her, then we might feel a twinge of exclusive jealousy.

Competitive

A competitive jealousy with our partner is our reaction to a feeling of inadequacy and an attempt to restore the balance. In this case, we may feel competitive jealousy if our partner is actually better than we are at something where we ourselves wish to excel.

Egotistical

Egotistical jealousy is the feeling that our way is the only way and an inability to expand our ego awareness or role flexibility. It consists of difficulty in altering our perspective or accepting the need to change ourselves or our routine ways of behaving. In short, it is a desire to stay as we are, being uninfluenced to adapt to other people's wishes or needs.

Fearful

A fearful jealousy is a reaction to the threat of loneliness or rejection. This type is felt when we are rejected and left alone by our partner, whether or not that partner runs off with someone else.

The blend of jealous feelings experienced

Is jealousy identified with any particular visible display of behaviours? No, but different instances of jealousy do all seem to have one underlying theme, namely loss of control (or believed loss of control) over our partner's feelings for us. This results in a general sense of hurt or anger (Ellis & Weinstein, 1986), but this sense is 'blended' in different ways by different persons on different occasions. As Ellis & Weinstein (1986) argue, this is partly because the expression and communication of emotion are mediated by symbols that have meaning to the person feeling the emotion. Thus there is no direct and agreed way for people to express or feel jealousy, but each person does it according to their own system of meaning. Different people refer to quite markedly different blends of feelings that, for them, make up jealousy. A common core of hurt, anger and fear is frequently described, but even then the exact recipe for the pain of jealousy is variable (Ellis & Weinstein, 1986). Sharpsteen (1991) in fact proposes that jealousy is a blended emotion based on knowledge, but sharing features similar to those in other emotions like anger and fear.

We might feel hurt and angry on some occasions, whereas in other circumstances we would feel only mildly aroused. For instance, we may feel a mild type of excitement if we know that our partner is just teasing us with the prospect of entering another relationship (indeed, we may now recognize it as Ludus love), but we would probably feel both hurt and angry if we found out that the partner really had another relationship.

Our blend of feelings is provided partly by the context and by particular interpretations or symbolic meanings that we give to the acts that 'cause' jealousy on a given occasion. These will probably direct a person's attention to specific parts of the whole jealousy-evoking event (e.g. to a sense of feeling helpless or to angry words). Contexts vary as a result of the degree of 'attachment' or relationship intimacy between the relevant parties (Ellis & Weinstein, 1986). They vary according to the 'valued resources' that flow through and are controlled by that attachment (i.e. whether the relationship runs through our life fabric or is marginal and peripheral to it); and to the perceived degree of 'intrusion' into that attachment by the third person (whether he or she really threatens it or just slightly unsettles it). This latter is important because no one expects a relationship with someone else to exclude all outsiders in all respects all of the time. We recognize that our partner will need and want other friends too: we cannot have the partner all to ourselves.

Rather, we feel jealous when a third party threatens an area that is seen as central to our attachment to a partner (e.g. we would feel jealous if someone else looked like becoming our best friend's best friend), or else when feelings of discontent are brought about by another's evident superiority (Smith, 1991).

In our society, we usually have labels – 'friendship', 'marriage' and 'engagement' – that help us to mark out our relationships and warn outsiders that our partner is central to our attachment in this way. The labels indicate where the limits of the attachment lie, and the community helps in various ways to enforce the relationship. So to announce an engagement or a marriage is to use a tie sign to tell the community to act as an extra guardian against intrusion or trespass on the relationship by outsiders.

Rules about jealousy

Feelings are shaped partly as a result of social context and partly as a result of general social rules about the appropriateness of expressing certain emotions about relationships (Jellison, 1984). We may feel outrage as well as jealousy if someone infringes cultural rules, for example by committing adultery with our spouse. In Victorian times, husbands were often encouraged to go and shoot their wife's lover(s) and in some countries the claim to have felt overwhelming jealousy is a permissible legal argument against severe sentences in 'crimes of passion'. However, if the relationship between sexual partners has not been formally agreed by society (e.g. if we are living together but are not married) then no rules govern the expression of feelings about the same sexual transgression. We may feel jealous but get no social support for feeling outraged.

Further, personal experience of our partner and the ways our lives are intertwined by routines together provide a basis for interpreting the meaning of certain behaviours that may affect our reactions. For instance, if we both agree that flirting with other people is an acceptable behaviour then we should not feel jealous when we catch a partner doing it (Bringle & Boebinger, 1990). In open marriages, for instance, partners feel jealous of their partner only when his or her behaviour violates the agreed rules about sexual conduct in the relationship and not just because the behaviour occurred (Buunk, 1980). 'Swingers' note that it is acceptable for their partner to have sex with another person so long as he or she does not 'get emotionally involved'. Such swingers would not feel jealous because the partner had extramarital sex – they would feel jealous only if the partner became emotionally involved.

Such rules stabilize the relationship and act as guides for feelings about the partner's behaviour in it (Hochschild, 1979). They can even specify when a society expects a person to be jealous and in what circumstances (Davis, 1936). For example, Trobriand Islandsmen used to be expected to 'offer' their wives to a visitor and were specifically forbidden to feel jealous if the visitor accepted (Malinowski, 1929). In our own ways, we often attempt to suppress and control jealousy, partly because it may be socially disapproved, partly because we may feel that it reveals too much of a dependency on the relationship, and partly because it creates an unpleasant degree of restrictive possessiveness of the partner.

An emotion like jealousy can be experienced in everyday life, then, in a social context that defines the appropriateness even of strong emotions. With jealousy, it seems that loss of control or of social 'face' is one important element in the emotion. Jealousy is an appropriate emotion to feel when our social status, self-esteem, or control over a relationship is threatened

To put it slightly differently, but only slightly, jealousy is a response to an imagined loss of influence over a routine part of life, namely over the feelings of another person towards ourselves (Radecki Bush et al., 1988). When we imagine that we have lost influence over another person's feelings for us or when we are given evidence that they do not care, we experience jealousy. Such a reaction can take the form specifically of a sensed threat to security, even when a person is *imagining* the situation (Radecki Bush et al., 1988). The more we took loving feelings for granted and the more extensively they are threatened, the more jealousy we feel unless, of course, we were in Manic love and experienced a strong sense of threat and dependency. Another source of jealousy is when there is a threat to some attribute or accomplishment that we feel is particularly relevant to our own self-image or self-definition (Salovey & Rodin, 1989).

Jealousy is another topic area where work on relationships is developing and concepts are getting narrowed down and refined (Salovey, 1991). It is another area where I feel that future research can develop our understanding of the communicative element and the interactive nature of human relationships. The traditional split of psychological experience into A (Affect), B (Behaviour), and C (Cognition) is latent in the work on jealousy, but the B part seems to treat Behaviour as something that the subject just does *to* the world before moving on to something entirely new.

Look again at the Behaviour elements of jealousy in the Pfeiffer & Wong (1989) questionnaire, and think how many are simply modelled on the notion of one agent active in an inert and unresponsive scene. The questions assume that the actor does something *to* a passive environment (e.g. 'I would look through X's drawers, handbag or pockets') rather than *with* it. Only two questions in the full questionnaire reflect the idea that the person is an *inter*actor with the other person and might ask questions or engage in interactive debate. But even here the focus is on 'questions I would ask X' (e.g. I [would] question X about his whereabouts) rather than 'interactive discussions I would enter with X' or 'long-term changes that I would make to my own behaviour or to interaction in the dyad'. Once again the emphasis is on one person's action rather than two persons' interaction. In short, the idea of 'Behaviour' in the A–B–C trichotomy (Affect, Behaviour, Cognition) that underlies much traditional social psychological and social scientific thinking about human relationships is that 'I do something *to* X'.

I believe instead that we need to add a D (for Dyadic, i.e. interactive or communicative or interpersonal) to the ABC. B is not just an individual action that happens in the head or in the heart or to the external world but is most often an interpersonal *Dyadic* activity with communicative consequences and interactive implications. Researchers need to pay attention to the D (for Dyadic) and communicative elements of jealousy. How do people's communications change when they are jealous? Does the style or the content, or both, change in systematic ways? How does that influence the relationship in which the jealousy is experienced? What do subjects talk about when they are jealous? To what degree do they talk in different manners and styles, avoid eye contact, leak emotion, or adopt a hectoring, inquisitive style? How do partners react when confronted with jealous D-behaviour in *inter*action (rather than jealous B-Behaviours in the form of individual action exerted upon an inert receiver)? In other words, jealousy research typically stops the film at the point where the subject feels the jealousy. For me, the most interesting questions for future research concern the continuation of the film beyond that, to the point where the relationship interactions are moulded or altered or affected by it.

Embarrassment and shyness

Embarrassment

D (for Dyadic, interpersonal, communicative or interactive) behaviour is a key element of another 'relational emotion', namely embarrassment, to which I now turn. Embarrassment can result in individuals feeling A(ffect, about themselves or the relationship), changing B(ehaviour towards others) or having different C(ognitions about themselves or others or the relationship). Yet it does not stop with those things: it also moulds and alters the subsequent relationship in the D(yad).

To understand more fully, let us imagine the following scene. You are talking to your favourite professor about a great idea you had concerning the class and as you get excited about the idea you spill coffee all down your leg. Do you think that you would feel good or bad about it (A)? Would you be more likely to laugh or not (B)? Would you think that you had made a good or a bad impression (C)? But don't you think that it might also affect future interaction in the D(yad), becoming a thing that is studiously never mentioned, or else a reference point of some kind that might be used as a teasing example in your future relationship? Also consider this. If you observed that same thing happening to your enemy, would the feelings be the same? If you observed this in a comedy on television or in a clown's act in a circus, what, if anything, do you think you would feel?

Loss of face or centre of attention?

One obvious element in the preceding scenario is that you look awkward, incompetent and clumsy, which is opposite to how you were trying to look in front of someone you liked. Embarrassment follows from the discrepancy between the self-image a person wants to project (how you want to appear) and the self-image that gets projected in the event (how you actually appear).

In one definition, embarrassment is the unexpected and unqualified discrediting of a central assumption in an interaction (Gross & Stone, 1964). Thus, in the example, if you are trying to seem intelligent, cool, competent and commanding, you undermined the assumption of competence quite thoroughly by spilling the coffee. You would consequently feel embarrassed since you have 'lost face' by acting inconsistently with your image. Such loss of face, however, has to be 'undesired'. Suppose that instead of doing this for real, you were in a drama class and had been play-acting the whole scene or had been doing it for real but were trying to get sympathy. In these cases you would not feel embarrassed at all. You would not have acted inconsistently with the image you wanted to project and the 'discrediting' would not be undesired. The above definition, then, emphasizes a kind of unintended personal diminishment as the cause of embarrassment.

A different approach to embarrassment suggests that it arises when a person is made the unwanted centre of attention rather than from a feeling of personal diminishment (Semin & Manstead, 1982). According to this view, a person's self-image is unaffected by the incident and the embarrassment comes, instead, from the heightened sense of self-attention, that is from being 'thrown unexpectedly into the spotlight'.

Social anxiety

This is another component of embarrassment (and also of shyness). Social anxiety depends on evaluation ('anxiety resulting from the prospect or presence of personal evaluation in real or imagined social situations': Schlenker & Leary, 1982, p. 642). When the evaluation comes as a result of unintentional and undesired social predicaments or transgressions, as in spilling the coffee, then it is embarrassing. The key element, however, is that the person is concerned with the 'public image and reactions from real or imagined others to inappropriate behaviour' (Edelmann, 1985, p. 196). The idea implicit in Schlenker & Leary's definition is that the evaluation of self is either negative or undesirable, and Edelmann makes that explicit.

Embarrassment is not a simple, single event but a sequence of events. Edelmann (1988) uses 'self theory' to explain how it works and why it is so painful to us. Self theories tell us that we have a private self (those aspects of our self that cannot be seen or observed directly by other people, such as our private thoughts) and a public self (the extremely visible and observable aspects, such as physical appearance and the ways we behave).

An undesired discrepancy between our behaviour and our internal standard for that behaviour leads to the focus of attention falling on to the public self. The embarrassed person quickly becomes concerned about public identity and feels negative. This negative feeling sets off a chain of expressive or communicative behaviours (like blushing, looking down at the floor, becoming agitated) that get labelled and felt as embarrassment. Both the person involved (and, usually, the others present) also then begin a series of behaviours to distract everyone and cover the embarrassment. This is partly what

I mean by the D(yadic) element because it involves both parties conjointly, but I am also indicating the long-term effects on the dyad's relationship that are caused by such isolated incidents.

There is a range of Dyadic strategies to deal with embarrassment this way. For example, minimizing the importance of the incident or the failure to carry it out successfully ('Don't worry, it doesn't matter; the coffee is less important than your contribution to my course'); referring to mitigating circumstances ('It's difficult to balance a coffee cup on the arm of that wobbly chair'); or referring to one's own experience of similar predicaments ('Oh! don't feel bad about that; I've done things like that myself when I get excited by an idea!'). Other tactics for the Dyad to restore the status quo are for the person to apologize (usually countered by the other person saying that there's no need to since it doesn't really matter anyway) and 'jokework', that is, the use of humour and laughter in an attempt to minimize the incident. All these methods are Dyadic efforts to restore the transgressor's public image or indicate that negative evaluations have not really been made and that they will not seriously impact on the dyadic relationship in the long run.

Cupach et al. (1986) have gone further with this idea and explored the ways in which subjects *cope* with embarrassing predicaments, given that a person has got into one. They usefully distinguish between two sorts of embarrassing predicament: *loss of poise*, which demonstrates loss of control over one's own behaviour or the environment (for instance tripping up on stage, or spilling a food tray in a restaurant), and *loss of identity*, where the person fails to complete an identity role (e.g. having eaten a meal in a restaurant, finding that one does not have the means to continue the customer role by paying for the food). Cupach et al. (1986) found that females regarded deferential communicative strategies, such as excuses or apologies, as more appropriate than did males, but that both sexes actually used the same strategies to about the same degree.

A key feature of embarrassment, then, seems to be anxiety about our self-image caused by heightened self-attention. Here, 'self-image' means not only 'what I think about myself' but 'what I think other people think about myself'. If I feel that their estimation of me is lowered then I feel anxious about my worth and value to other people. This threat can be minimized by the onlookers working on the relationship by stressing that their response to the person and their long-term relationship with him or her are not spoiled by the embarrassing transgression. The sooner that dyadic routine can be restored, the more quickly the embarrassment goes away.

Shyness and social anxiety

Shyness is rather similar to embarrassment in some ways but is an affective-behavioural syndrome consisting of social anxiety and inhibition. Everyone feels shy from time to time, but some people are likely to feel more shy than others (Buss, 1980; Cheek & Busch, 1981). Shyness is caused by an anticipation of a discrepancy between a person's desired self-image and his or her way of projecting the self-image so that the actual projection is expected to fall short of the desired one. Shyness is embarrassment in advance, created by the belief that our real self will not be able to match up to the image we want to project.

Some 41 percent of people believe that they are shy and up to 24 percent think that it is a serious enough problem for them to do something about it (Pilkonis, 1977). If you are not shy yourself, then two out of the next four people you meet will be and one of them will feel that it requires seeking professional help.

There is one key feature to shyness and it revolves around problems with interpersonal communication (Kelly, 1982). A central problem for many shy people is their unwillingness to communicate (i.e. 'reticence'), characterized by avoidance of, and ineptitude at, social interaction and performance in public or at the centre of attention in a social encounter. Is the cause deficient communication skills; or anxiety about communication (so-called 'communication apprehension'); or simple avoidance of communication? In other words, is it because the person generally dislikes communication; or becomes paralysingly anxious about it; or just cannot do it well behaviourally? In practical terms there are few differences between the results of these three possible causes (Kelly, 1982), although the first two seem to be attitudinal or cognitive causes whilst the last is a behavioural or communicative problem. Programmes that improve (behavioural) performance actually reduce anxiety too, so we cannot distinguish the behavioural and the attitudinal components readily. What is readily distinguishable is that part of shyness is the experience of dyadic communicative difficulties and that part of it is the communicative difficulties themselves.

The remaining problem for shy people is that reticence is evaluated by outsiders as if the shy person feels negative towards people rather than being shy about them (Burgoon & Koper, 1984). When strangers are asked to assess videotapes of reticent persons talking to other people, the strangers rate the reticents quite negatively. They see reticents as expressing too little intimacy/ similarity, being detached and uninvolved in the interaction, and showing too much submissiveness and emotional negativity. They also rated reticents as not credible or somewhat 'shifty'. When the shy persons' friends saw the same videotapes, however, they usually rated the behaviour as more positive. In other words, shy persons' behaviour appears negative to strangers, but their friends become used to it. Once shy people get friends they are seen positively; the problem is that their behaviour is such that strangers probably would not want to become their friends in the first place.

Leary & Dobbins (1983) show that there are quite severe relational consequences of shyness, in that surveyed persons who were highly shy had had fewer sexual experiences, less sexual intercourse, and a smaller number of sexual partners than people who were not very shy. Dating, a usual preliminary to sexual encounters, is a situation that gets rated as highly anxiety-provoking by between 37 percent and 50 percent of men and 21 percent to 50 percent of women, in any case. Presumably, the very shy are at a considerable disadvantage in dating; their shyness effectively cuts them off from normal social life.

If we can define the precise nature of the problem then help can be prescribed. There are different elements to shyness. Some stem from anxiety about communication ('communication apprehension') and some from reticence or lack of skill in performing communication adequately. In the latter category are a speech impediment or a belief that we have nothing to say that would interest people, or an awkwardness and inability to converse easily (Kelly, 1982). The end result is the same – the person does not communicate – but the reasons are different.

Tragically, the anxious person might be a perfectly competent communicator if the anxiety could be overcome. Many such people are perfectly good communicators when they are relaxed in the company of friends, but the unskilled person would perform badly even when not anxious (Leary et al., 1987). The anxious, or 'privately shy', person typically focusses on the subjective discomfort and fear of negative evaluation whilst the 'publicly shy' person thinks of the behavioural inadequacies as the main problem.

If the problem is identified as anxiety then a cognitive therapy would help, and if it is lack of skill that causes the shyness, a social skills training programme might be the solution.

Cognitive therapy

Cognitive therapy (Beck, 1976) is based on changing a person's beliefs. If someone believes that he or she is unattractive or awkward (even when no one else agrees) then that will influence his or her attitudes towards encounters with other people. If such persons are challenged to provide evidence of their beliefs about themselves and to give instances of their own awkwardness, it often becomes clear that they have double standards for their own and for other people's behaviour. Usually, they are highly critical of themselves and their own performance, but overlook examples of other people doing exactly the same. By confronting them with their misperceptions, cognitive therapy reshapes their false beliefs and so reduces their anxieties.

Social skills training

Social skills training programmes are effective in alleviating shyness that results from communicative inadequacies (Kelly, 1984). The bases, usually, are that shy people lack conversational skills, do not ask the right questions, cannot offer social invitations effectively, or do not talk openly and easily about themselves (Duck, 1991). By training such people through direct instruction, through modelling or example, through coaching, and through feedback of videotaped conversations with new partners, it is possible to increase their conversational effectiveness and help them to overcome the skill deficits that led to their reticence (Kelly, 1984).

Shyness is shown to relate to loneliness in new situations (Cheek & Busch, 1981). Shy students entering college are significantly more lonely than non-shy students, although both groups become less lonely in time. Shy students improve their situation more dramatically than do the non-shy ones but, obviously, they have more room to do so (Cheek & Busch, 1981). Unfortunately, even after such improvements, the shy students are still much more lonely than the non-shy ones.

It does seem as if something about shyness fundamentally affects a person's system of social communication with other people and as if that serves unintentionally to keep others away. Communication problems contribute to the difficulties of the shy person and help to ensure that they stay lonely. It may work the other way around, such that social isolation contributes to communication difficulties, for instance through lack of practice (Zakahi & Duran, 1982). One particularly important problem is that shy or communicatively incompetent persons become used to not being intimate or open with others. They thus 'learn' to give out signals in their routine social behaviour that are interpreted as meaning that they are not interested in relationships with other people (Zakahi & Duran,

1985). Clearly, a state like shyness is built into a person's routine ways of handling life, other people and new situations, and is the habitual style of behaviour in such new situations. So shy persons contribute nonverbally to their own social rejection and hence to their future loneliness.

Loneliness

Loneliness is more common than we may believe, is not confined to a group of odd or abnormal people, is associated with both unhappiness and illness, and can be cured. People who are lonely do not necessarily have fewer relationships or daily interactions than other people have, but they are often less satisfied with the ones they do have (Larson et al., 1982). Satisfactory interactions – especially cross-sex interactions – are associated, on the other hand, with better feelings about health (Wheeler et al., 1983).

Who becomes lonely?

Who becomes lonely? We all do. Roughly 26 percent of a large sample reported feeling 'very lonely within the past few weeks' (Bradburn, 1969), and almost everyone experiences intense loneliness at some time or another (Peplau & Perlman, 1982), although men are rejected more often than women if they admit to loneliness (Borys & Perlman, 1984). We often think of loneliness as more rampant in elderly rather than younger populations, but research casts doubt on this (Schultz & Moore, 1988) and actually shows that loneliness is higher in high-school students than in the elderly. For elderly people what is important is the availability of a close confidant (Peplau et al., 1982) and whether the person has been used to being single through life (Shanas et al., 1968). In one study, contrary to popular myth, only 15 percent of old people reported that they felt lonely quite often (Tunstall, 1967).

There are some situations where everyone becomes lonely, and we can distinguish *trait loneliness* (a stable and persistent pattern of feeling lonely – definitely a feature of the person; he or she invariably takes the feeling into new situations) and *state loneliness* (a transient, temporary feeling of loneliness – probably resulting from the situation or a move to a new environment rather than to the specific person; everyone might feel lonely in such circumstances). When people move to college they all tend to experience loneliness but some cope better with it than others. Interestingly, males who are lonely tend to form a more negative view of themselves than do females, since they attribute it to personal failure rather than to forces over which they have no control (Schultz & Moore, 1988).

What is loneliness?

Clearly, loneliness is not necessarily the same as being alone (DeJong-Gierveld, 1989). We can be lonely in a crowd and can be perfectly happy on our own sometimes in the 'bliss of solitude'. The crucial feature of loneliness, according to Perlman & Peplau (1981), is a discrepancy between what we're doing and what we expect or hope to do. To put it more precisely, loneliness results from 'a discrepancy between one's desired and achieved levels of social relations' (Perlman & Peplau, 1981, p. 32). If we desire a small number of friends (say one or two) and that is what we have, then we will be happy and not lonely. If, on the other hand, we desire fifteen friends and have only fourteen, then we shall feel lonely.

To assess loneliness, we must look at the person's desired or needed levels of social contact rather than at just the levels of social contact that he or she actually achieves. Our expectations, desires and needs can fluctuate from time to time independently of our actual levels of social contact. For example, when we are under some sort of stress we might want company, but when we are working on a difficult task we would rather be alone and would find company annoying. The Perlman-Peplau model is also perfectly comfortable with the finding that our experience of loneliness can vary according to internal factors like feelings or beliefs even when our number of friends or social contacts stays objectively the same. In other words, even when our contacts stay the same and our number of friends is constant, we could still feel lonely on some days and not others or in some circumstances and not others, depending on our present desire for company or solitude. For example, people feel more lonely just after they have been beaten at racquet ball (Perlman & Serbin, 1984), whilst teenagers experience more loneliness at weekends (Larson et al., 1982) not because they have fewer contacts then but because they expect to have more.

Expectations about relationships and about loneliness will be influenced by personality, beliefs about attractiveness, and whether one tends to take credit for social successes in meeting new people or blame for failures to make friends.

We learned in the preceding section that shy people habitually fear making new friends and may be anxious in ways that could affect their adequacy in carrying out new encounters. Those who usually assume that social failures are their own fault ('because of the person I am and the problems I always have') are likely to overlook other obvious factors that could account for loneliness – such as 'circumstances' or 'moving to a new neighbourhood'. They will probably blame their isolation in the new circumstances on their habitual and personal difficulties even when no one else would make that inference. Accordingly, they are much more likely than everyone else to feel negative about themselves and personally hopeless. Trait lonely people (i.e. the long-term lonely) are found to have exactly the characteristics that make it more likely that they will blame themselves in this way. They have a low opinion of themselves, see themselves in negative terms, dislike talking about their feelings, and are low in intimate behaviours (Jones et al., 1981; Solano et al., 1982).

Later work (e.g. Marangoni & Ickes, 1989; Rook, 1988) has urged researchers to differentiate loneliness, emphasizing variations in the duration of loneliness, and different levels of motivation, such as social anxiety, or interpersonally deficient causes of loneliness, such as social skill problems. As Solano & Koester (1989) show, the anxiety component may be more powerful than any other component, such as social skill deficits. Several other theorists (e.g. Vaux, 1988) have also distinguished different sorts of loneliness. *Social loneliness* is a deficiency in the social network (i.e. a small number of contacts) perhaps due to a change in circumstances such as moving to a new town; *emotional loneliness* is a deficit in close attachments, especially romantic ones. In the case of social loneliness, the numbers of relationships are low, but in the case of emotional loneliness the quality is low (especially of certain types of relationship). The possibility obviously exists that these forms of loneliness result from different sorts of deficits in the person involved. Mikulincer & Segal (1990) break the experience of loneliness down into psychological components: cognitive (what you think about loneliness and other people in general); emotional (what you feel about loneliness and other people); motivational (how concerned you are to do anything about loneliness when it happens); behavioural (what you actually do about it). There are also those researchers who distinguish the situations of loneliness and differentiate it in respect of different relationships. Some people find it quite easy to be amiable to everyone but find close intimacy difficult for various reasons, like past experiences or personality structure

(Duck, 1991). Others feel shy in company, except in the company of one specific person, such as their romantic partner.

Lonely people may have several deficits rather than just one. They may have poor social skills (see Chapter 1 and the next section), they may be poor at perceiving others' needs in conversation or social situations, or they may be poor at adopting the roles necessary in interaction. Wittenberg & Reis (1986) explored all three possibilities and found that they all contributed to loneliness (hardly surprising if you imagine what a person with all these deficits would be like to talk to!). However, those subjects who were assertive and responsive to others were best able to avoid loneliness. Spitzberg & Canary (1985) found that although lonely subjects were less competent at communication than other subjects, they also tended to recognize this. Interestingly, they also devalued and criticized the social skills *of their partners*. Despite this, Vitkus & Horowitz (1987) showed that lonely people were just as good at adopting roles given them by the experimenter as were any other subjects. Perhaps if lonely people are given roles to adopt then they can fulfil them, but in everyday life they do not do so because, as Spitzberg & Canary show, they devalue the whole social performance. Thus they do not feel like getting involved in it by playing the appropriate roles well for themselves.

What do lonely people do?

Lonely people do habitually report quite consistent feelings (Rubenstein & Shaver, 1982). These are: *desperation* (being panicked and feeling helpless); *depression* (feeling sad and worthless); *impatient boredom* (restlessness and boredom simultaneously); *self-deprecation* ('What's wrong with me?' and 'Why am I so useless?'). Chronically lonely males have characteristic sets of beliefs about themselves and other people that lead them to act in an aggressive and hostile way (Check et al., 1985). Lonely males are more punitive than non-lonely males are, particularly towards female partners who make errors on a learning task that the male is 'supervising'. Many violent males, particularly rapists, are found to score highly on loneliness scales and to have been socially isolated well before they committed their violent assaults (Howells, 1981).

Chronically lonely persons tend to be self-absorbed, nonresponsive, negativistic and ineffective in their interactions with strangers (Jones et al., 1985). They spend more time alone, particularly at weekends, and are less involved with voluntary organizations, dating, relatives and neighbours or social activities generally (Jones et al., 1985). They sometimes show 'sad passivity', which involves overeating, oversleeping, watching television, crying, drinking alcohol, or taking tranquillizers (Rubenstein & Shaver, 1982). They also watch more TV than average, especially news broadcasts (Rubin et al., 1985), which might suggest that their loneliness is associated with a sense of lack of stimulation. Also found in this study, though, is that lonely people tend to 'interact' with a favourite local news anchor, often talking to the newscaster or commenting aloud on the reader's appearance and performance!

Other typical styles of coping with loneliness are to engage in 'busy-busy' activity, solitary hobbies, jogging alone, or taking vigorous exercise. Other people react to loneliness by self-indulgent actions, particularly buying themselves 'toys' like microcomputers and remote-control miniaturized stereo systems, or just generally running riot with their credit cards. When we get lonely we often turn into 'big spenders' in an effort to make ourselves feel better about ourselves. More useful are coping strategies that involve visiting other people, writing to friends, calling them (briefly!) on the phone, or just attempting to increase social contact.

The key feature is the belief system that we hold about the causes of our loneliness and about our ability to control it. If we believe that it will go away as long as we take positive action, then we are more likely to attempt to socialize. If we believe that it is somehow 'our fault' – and a permanent feature or, at least, a stable feature of our lives at that – then we are more likely to become depressed. Several studies show that it is possible to reduce loneliness by giving the person a sense of control over it. Thus, for instance, Shulz (1976) found that old people who were allowed to schedule visits from volunteer workers felt less lonely than those whose schedule was fixed for them by someone else – even though the total number and length of the visits was the same for both sets of people.

When you are forced to be alone

The sense of control is probably one reason why not all 'being alone' is loneliness, as the Perlman-Peplau model makes clear. If our desired level of social contact is low for some deliberately controlled reason (e.g. if we are feeling creative and want to write a novel) then low levels of social contact will be highly enjoyable and high levels may be unattractive to us.

The problems arise when someone is forced to be alone willy-nilly.

For instance, students typically report feeling lonely soon after they arrive in their new university at the start of their freshman year. Friends rather than dates or lovers are the best buffer against loneliness in those circumstances (DeJong-Gierveld, 1989).

The loneliness of the college freshman

What happens, then, when new students go to college? Shaver et al. (1985) looked at ways of predicting which students would stay lonely and which would develop fuller networks in the new environment and so cope with loneliness. Their results show that the transition to college was particularly stressful for males, whose loneliness increased four times more than females'. Also, males' dating frequency declined more than females'. The latter may have resulted from freshman males having a smaller pool of dates available to them since there is a cultural norm that encourages females (but not males) to date older as well as same-aged members of the opposite sex and to decline requests for dates from younger males.

Old relationships back home decline both in number and in perceived quality, whereas new ones do not quickly reach the satisfaction levels of pre-college ones. The transition to college causes the end of almost half (46 percent) of the pre-college romantic relationships and also produces strain in the other 54 percent, which were rated much less positively after the transition than before it.

On the more positive side, the students were quick to establish new groups of casual acquaintances, but experienced considerable uncertainty about them. Their feelings about family and kin became more positive, and they experienced less conflict with parents even though they did not see them as often – or perhaps because of it. Seemingly, though, this was a subjective change rather than a real or objective one, since there obviously was little interaction going on with the family that could improve; the students just felt better about their family.

Curing chronic loneliness

Loneliness causes loneliness. That is, people who are lonely may, like shy persons, communicate in such a way that other people do not feel inclined to relate to them or might disregard them and find them unattractive (Spitzberg & Canary, 1985). Whole programmes of research are now geared up to identifying the interpersonal skills (or rather the lack of skills) of the chronically lonely in an attempt to understand the most effective ways of helping them (Jones et al., 1985).

The basic argument here is that lonely people, like shy people, lack certain skills in communication and social behaviour, such as assertiveness, or else they are higher in shyness and self-consciousness (Jones et al., 1981) and experience inhibited sociability (e.g. difficulty making friends). Lonely people in a laboratory setting select less effective power strategies and are generally less effective in meeting new people (Perlman et al., 1978). Lonely students are below average at sharing their opinions on personal topics. (Hansson & Jones, 1981). Jones et al. (1984, p. 146) conclude provocatively that 'the interpersonal behaviours often associated with loneliness may actually reduce the likelihood that the lonely person will be able, without intervention, to restore mutually satisfying relationships with others'.

A number of successful programmes for testing chronic loneliness have been developed recently to help people to cope with loneliness, prevent the more serious consequences like depression and suicide, and help them to create broader and more satisfying networks – as well as preventing people from becoming lonely in the first place (Rook, 1988). In essence there are four approaches:

1 Cognitive treatment, aimed at changing lonely people's expectations that they will be rejected in social encounters (similar to the one used on shy people in the preceding section);

2 Social skills training, aimed at improving people's ability to be effective in encounters with other people;

3 Group therapy, aimed at increasing sensitivity to other people;

4 Community-based approaches, aimed at increasing people's opportunities for interaction.

The community-based approaches are not much use to people with underlying social skill deficits since 'Go out and meet more people' really just amounts to 'Go out and be rejected by more people' unless the underlying problem is solved first (Duck, 1991).

In one social skills training programme, Jones et al. (1982) trained some very lonely males to increase their attention to their partner in a conversation (e.g. by asking questions about the partner, continuing, rather than changing, the topic of conversation, showing interest in partner's views). Training involved exposure to audiotapes of 'good' and 'bad' conversations in which the instructor pointed out places where attention to the partner would have been particularly appropriate. In a similar programme, Gallup (1980) trained lonely people in other interactional skills (e.g. paraphrasing partner's comments; summarizing their statements; giving positive evaluations). In both programmes, lonely people became more skilful in conversation and reported subsequent increases in sociability, reductions in loneliness, and reduced feelings of shyness.

Cognitive treatments, on the other hand, aim to restructure the way in which lonely people think about themselves and the interpersonal events in which they participate. Individuals who are lonely usually are high in social anxiety, just as shy people are, and they feel that they are being judged or ridiculed by other people. Treatments such as Young's (1982) cognitive therapy are intended to change these attitudes and to encourage the person to engage in activities with other people, including open disclosure of his or her feelings and emotions.

One method of effecting such change is to challenge the person to produce evidence that other people are ridiculing or judging him or her. Examples of other people making errors are then discussed and comparisons made of the subject's reactions to them. Often it can be shown that the lonely person has a higher standard for his or her own behaviour than for other people's. Another means of changing the unhelpful beliefs is to videotape lonely persons in an interaction. Frequently, they are surprised to see how relaxed they look from the outside even when they feel anxious inside.

It is encouraging that such therapies are being developed. Loneliness is something that we all experience from time to time and that we all try to avoid or correct. It is thus a common human concern for which social science can by systematic study provide some answers and correctives. It is a good instance of the fact that relational problems affect our lives fundamentally by getting incorporated into our routine ways of interacting. We should also note that since relational problems lead to pronounced loss of concentration, one of the most dangerous people in the world is a lonely air traffic controller.

Summary

The four emotions that we have looked at here (love, jealousy, embarrassment/shyness and loneliness) have a number of features:

1 They occur in relationship to other people, involve expressive and communicative behaviour, and are closely connected to the notion of worth and competence in relationships. Each in its own way is a form of expression that communicates our assumed value and worth to other people.

2 These emotions do not need specific external events to spark them off but can all be rekindled just by thought and by fantasy or imagination about social encounters, past, present or future. They can be experienced in the absence of other people but are 'about' them.

3 They are sometimes experienced as just hot surges of emotion, but are more often enduring emotional states reported in dispositional *language* (I am in love; I am a shy person) or seen to have possible long-term effects on relationships. They can become ways of social life, enshrined in ways of communicating and expressing ourselves through behaviour, or can have long-term effects on the dyad in the relationship.

4 They are structured into or impact upon social routines and everyday behaviours. That we feel jealous or shy or lonely or in love influences the way we *communicate with other people* in the long term, as well as in the short term. It can affect how we look at them, how we speak to them, and how we deal with them, as well as how we choose to relate to them. In short, emotions have dyadic, communicative effects also.

5 The isolating feelings (shyness, loneliness) can be treated by training programmes that affect the person's communicative behaviour, as well as other people's responses and hence the lonely or shy person's feelings about their own worth.

In short, I have been making the case that *social emotions* are essentially dyadic, communicative and relational ones.

Further reading

Daly, J.A. & McCroskey, J.C., (eds) (1984) *Avoiding Communication*. Sage: Beverly Hills.

Edelmann, R. (1988) *Embarrassment*. Wiley: Chichester.

Leary, M. (1984) *Understanding Social Anxiety*. Sage: Beverly Hills.

Peplau, L.A. & Perlman, D. (1982) *Loneliness: A Sourcebook of Current Theory, Research and Therapy*. Wiley-Interscience: New York.

Salovey, P. (ed) (1991) *The Psychology of Jealousy and Envy*. Guilford: New York.

CHAPTER 3

Interaction and Daily Life
in Long-term Relationships

When we are asked what matters to us most in life and gives it its fullest purpose, the majority of people give one simple answer: relationships (Klinger, 1977). Relationships are obvious sources of joy and happiness – we like being with friends, we enjoy the company of others, being in love is wonderful. On the other hand, they can be hell when they go wrong and cause pain, as we saw in chapter 2 in discussing jealousy. Chapter 2 also showed us that specific emotions about, or experiences in, relationships have very powerful effects on people and their daily lives. The present chapter extends that idea by showing the important role of relationships as a whole, particularly change in relationships, not only on social life but also on our 'sense of being' or sense of self-esteem.

BOX 3.1 Points to think about
- *Why do we like some people and not others?*
- *Are dating agencies right to try to fix up partners who 'match' on attitudes and personality?*
- *How do relationships start? How do they develop and what promotes their growth?*
- *We like some people enough to try to start up a friendship with them but why does it not always work?*
- *How should people get out of painful or unsatisfactory relationships?*
- *What are the best ways to put things right for people who want to repair their relationships?*

Relationships with other people are obviously important in childhood and may even lay the bases for self-esteem, for ability to relate to others, and for deviant personality (Duck, 1991). They are also implicated in the effectiveness of physicians (patients recover faster in the hands of friendly and liked physicians: Hays &

DiMatteo, 1984), in the quicker recovery of patients who have lots of friends (Reis, 1984), in successful careers at work (Dillard & Miller, 1988), and in general as protection from the pains, stresses and hassles of life (Hobfoll & Stokes, 1988). The relationship between teacher and pupil affects the rate of learning (Menges, 1969); medical knowledge is transmitted as much by personal relationships between doctors as it is by advertisers' mailings (Menzel & Katz, 1957) and the fashionability of scientific ideas is influenced as much by the relationships of scientists as by the merit or originality of the ideas themselves (Innes, 1980). We had better hope that the latter does not happen too often.

There is, of course, also a negative side to relationships. Poor relationships are associated with criminality, violence and aggression, neurosis and depression, illness, shyness, drug and alcohol problems, marital difficulties, divorce, spouse and child abuse and 'granny battering' (Duck, 1991). They also create demands on us to provide help, comfort and resources to others (Schwarzer & Leppin, 1991). Friendships and kin relationships oblige us to be available to others when they are in difficulties, especially in times of illness and stress (Wiseman, 1986). Not everyone finds it enjoyable to listen to others' painful self-disclosures, however, or to histories of personal problems, or recitals of symptoms of disease (Giles, 1989). Furthermore, not all of us are able to produce the resources necessary to be helpful when comfort is needed (Burleson, 1990), so we could feel bad because we cannot fulfil the role of 'friend' well by helping to cheer up the other person (Barbee, 1990). The phenomenon of 'care-giver burnout' is now widely known and researched (Millei et al., 1988) and it is found that mental health service professionals and counsellors experience exhaustion from all their caring for others (La Gaipa, 1990).

Considering what we may be letting ourselves in for, there might be a case for never getting into relationships at all! But we do, all the same, because they provide so many rewards and create so much 'meaning' for us in life. The costs are readily discounted and we enter relationships in the hope of the benefits. How do relationships start and develop, and what are their ramifications?

Starting relationships

In everyday life we are enormously influenced by first impressions. Job applications, interviews, and the whole course of a relationship can be 'set' by the first few moments. In everyday life, we make many snap judgements about people and form instant likes and dislikes. We all know that we can create 'irrational' first impressions, sudden lusts and likings, and intense hatreds for strangers. We can like the manner of a person we do not know and can form instant dislikes of someone who has not even uttered a word to us. So, paradoxically, the study of initial responses to strangers makes sense as a starting point for understanding long-term human relationships; it is the point when relationships most often start or fail to start. We may decide (not) to date someone whose appearance does (not) appeal to us, and so we may (fail to) embark on a relationship that could have changed our lives (Rodin, 1982). Indeed there is evidence that in as short a space of time as 30 seconds, partners can usually decide that a date is going to be a success or failure (Cortez et al. 1988).

Aside from appearance, what makes us attracted (and attractive) to other people? Common sense will answer 'You were attracted because you have similar attitudes and personalities'. That is a reasonable proposition, but how does it stand up to investigation?

Laboratory investigation of attraction

If we find that friends have similar attitudes, we may congratulate ourselves that we found an answer to the question until we realize that we have not shown whether similarity causes liking or liking causes similarity. (After all, we do try to discuss things with friends and persuade our friends to adopt our ideas and become more like us, don't we?) The aim is to find a way to alter similarity levels between people and then see what it does to their attraction for one another.

The problem was cleverly solved by Tony Smith (1957; 1960), whose solution was subsequently taken up and adapted by Donn Byrne (1961 and see Box 3.3). Byrne gave full credit to Smith in his early papers, but later Byrne's own approach became the focus of a certain amount of criticism, from which Byrne shielded Smith. The essence of the solution involves experiments on attraction to strangers, in which subjects filled out an attitude questionnaire and then were given another scale completed (allegedly) by a stranger. Byrne then assessed subjects' responses to the stranger (who was actually non-existent, i.e. bogus or hypothetical, in honour of whom the method was called 'the bogus stranger method', although the experimental subjects did not *know* that the stranger was fictitious).

BOX 3.2 Exercise on relationships

- *Think for a moment about the people with whom you are particularly friendly. What do you like about them and how did the relationship get started? How does the relationship with each person differ from those that you have with the others? Write out 2 short lists (say 10 items each) giving: (a) the features of the other person that you like (7 items) and those that you dislike (3 items) (b) the sort of activities that you perform or topics you talk about almost exclusively with friends (7 items) and those that you do with other people too, but that are 'better' with friends (3 items).*
- *Think for a moment about an attractive person you have seen but not really met – one you would like to start a relationship with if you were completely free to do so. Write 2 short lists (10 items each) giving: (a) what you find attractive about them (7 items) and what you find unattractive about them (3 items) (b) 7 things you would do or talk about with them if you got to know them and 3 items you would definitely not talk about or do.*
- *Compare your various lists and try to work out the important differences between them, if any. Consider the differences involved in 'relating' to strangers and friends, and think what it is that changes when strangers gradually turn into acquaintances and friends.*
- *Take a look at the chapter by Rodin (1982) that outlines the bases for comparison between such lists.*

The subjects would be presented with the information allegedly provided by this stranger, and they would then be asked what they thought of him or her. Byrne carefully arranged the information so that the stranger's attitude scale matched up with the subject's own to a precise degree (say 80 percent or 65 percent or 20 percent).

Byrne's work, also known as 'the attraction paradigm' (or 'the paradigm that would not die': Bochner, 1991), assumed that attitude similarity is an example of 'reinforcement' or reward – something attractive, desirable and positive that we like to experience. The important point is that it is *reinforcement* that we like and attitude similarity is usually reinforcing. Note that Byrne does not say that attitude similarity is always reinforcing or attractive (sometimes it may be boring to meet someone whose attitudes are absolutely the same as ours). But usually, Byrne says, attitude similarity will be reinforcing, and so we find it attractive.

When all we know about someone is his or her sex and a sample of his or her attitudes, then we will like that person in proportion to the amount of reinforcing similarity between us; the more similar, the more we like him or her. If we know a little more about the person then the picture becomes more complicated: for instance, it matters whether we have a positive view of him or her (e.g. that we have not found out that the person is a thief or a homicidal maniac or mentally ill – unless we are too). It also matters whether the similar attitudes are important to us, whether the reasons given for holding them are similar to ours, and whether we believe the strangers are stating their true opinions. In brief, as the picture becomes more complicated, so the plain and simple commonsense rule that 'similarity is attractive' turns out to be more and more inadequate and in need of refinement. In investigating this area, Byrne (1971) and colleagues established an enormous amount of detail about this particular phenomenon, assuming the truth of the basic assumptions.

We usually like people whose attitudes are similar to our own, so long as we like ourselves and the other people are normal, sensible people stating their true opinion. This fact is the basis of the method used by dating agencies who match partners up by selecting people with similar attitudes and beliefs – though the strangers there are real, not bogus. Byrne often tested the validity of his work outside the 'laboratory'. He found that bank managers give bigger loans to people with similar attitudes, for instance, that jurors are more likely to be lenient to defendants with attitudes like theirs, and that similarity of attitudes can overcome the prejudices of racial bigots so that prejudiced whites actually express liking for blacks who have similar attitudes (Byrne, 1971).

Laboratory-based, experimental, manipulated studies of liking may not penetrate real liking. In life we rarely gain such unambiguous access to someone else's attitudes. When was the last time a stranger came up to you and gave you a written list of his or her attitudes? Sometimes we have to be 'detectives'; we know that people often conceal their true attitudes and we have to uncover them through communication. For instance, they may conceal their true attitudes from us to get something from us or to ingratiate themselves. Also, sometimes people withhold their 'true' attitudes for other reasons, such as desire to create a positive impression or fear of how their 'true confession' might be received by us. We know that we behave in these concealing ways ourselves.

Social processes operate to ensure that initial encounters (and even later ones) are not always open, frank exchanges of unambiguous information. For these reasons, we have to work at uncovering the

BOX 3.3 Byrne's work

We prefer strangers who are reinforcing for us and this often takes the form of their being attitudinally similar to ourselves (Byrne, 1961). We like strangers who agree with us.

The amount of liking is directly predictable from the proportion of similar attitudes and hence from the reinforcement derived; the more the reinforcement, the greater the liking (Byrne & Nelson, 1965).

Some attitudes are difficult for us to check and validate or gain evidence for. The more difficult it is to validate an attitude, the more we appreciate it when someone shares that attitude with us (Byrne et al., 1966). Uncommon similarity (i.e. similarity on attitudes that are not widely held) is especially attractive (Lea & Duck, 1982).

'Coke dates' arranged on the basis of attitude similarity are more successful and partners can remember more about one another several months later (Byrne et al., 1970).

Similarity to unreinforcing strangers (e.g. mentally disturbed persons) is not attractive (Byrne & Lamberth, 1971); reinforcement matters more than similarity.

Attitudinal similarity affects electrical skin conductance but not heart rate. Disagreement makes us more aroused than agreement, but both are arousing (Clore & Gormly, 1974).

The inferences we draw from similarity may be what makes it attractive. Duck (1975a) reports that the underlying extent of similarity mattered; that is, it is more attractive to be similar to someone who gives the same reasons as yours for holding the attitude than it is to be similar to someone who holds the attitude for different reasons. When we find attitude similarity attractive, it may be because we assume that the person will share many other underlying values with us and will be generally rewarding.

People will actually return to a laboratory to work with an attitudinally similar stranger (Gormly & Gormly, 1981).

true picture; and some of us will be more proficient than others. Thus my argument here (also adopted by Bochner, 1991) is that the business of initial attraction is not just one of *matching* our attitudes or characteristics with someone else's but of *communicating* about them.

This opens up the possibility that aside from individual differences in the detecting skills of 'normal adults', it is likely that young children will be less good at interpreting people's attitudes, as will be some psychologically disturbed patients. These extreme examples merely make the point that differences in detecting skills can exist. Perhaps the shy and lonely 'normal adults' are at the poor end of the scale when it comes to determining whether someone has similar attitudes, and so they get off to a bad start with strangers. The effects of 'detective work' are likely to be less important than those of other conversational skills.

When strangers are introduced – even in the laboratory – to have a conversation, the effects of attitude similarity 'wash out' (Sunnafrank & Miller, 1981). Similar subjects do not like one another any more than do dissimilar ones after they have had a brief interaction. Dissimilar partners who are able to interact also like their partner more than do dissimilar ones who do not interact. Interaction has a positive effect on liking, and it modifies the effect of dissimilarity on its own. When communication exceeds a 'one-off conversation' and is extended over time and to explicit discussion of attitudinal issues, again it is the dissimilar stranger who gets a better rating (Sunnafrank, 1991).

Attitudes, attraction and relationships

Researchers of initial attraction are usually well aware that they are studying a small part of a broader set of issues (e.g. Clore & Byrne, 1974). Often they are both startled and hurt by critics who effectively say 'This work on strangers is silly because it tells us nothing about marriage'. Work on obstetrics tells us little about senility, but that is not a reason for not doing it. Many real-life examples make initial attraction an obvious and important area of concern. What we must bear in mind, however, is that of course not all attractions lead to relationships (Byrne, 1971).

'Attraction does not mean relationship'

There are a myriad of reasons why we do not set up relationships with every attractive person we meet, the most significant being lack of a wish to do so (e.g. already married or engaged, going steady, not enough time, too many commitments); inappropriateness (e.g. differences in status, circumstances not conducive); or, perhaps more poignant, incompetence. Many people who report being lonely or shy feel unable to carry out their wishes to set up desired relationships. Occasionally I get letters about this, saying things like 'I am a 25-year-old male and have this inability to converse, communicate, or form any sort of relationship with the opposite sex. It is a long-standing problem. Girls do seem attracted to me but as soon as it gets on to speaking, conversing, etc. it goes no further' (actual letter). Obviously, we might begin by looking at the social skills of such persons (see Chapter 1), but the commonness of the problem is significant. It is the most frequent problem dealt with by the various counselling services on university campuses. If you can't deal with strangers you won't get friends.

Attraction to strangers is the starting point for all relationships that do eventually start. Researchers need to know why we select between strangers, why we prefer some to others, and what happens once we move on from our initial attraction. A problem with laboratory work on attraction is that it 'freezes' situations out of context: subjects go to a room for an experiment, meet a stranger (or don't meet a bogus one), and then go home. This might lead us to think of all interactions as frozen and context-free – like separate snapshots rather than single still frames from a continuous movie. Life is not made up of such separate snapshots, but is continuous and much more like a movie. In life, one meeting with a person often leads to another. When we know that fact, it probably affects what we do and how we treat those strangers whom we may see again and get to know better. So we must expect that our reasons for initial attraction are not necessarily those that influence long-term development of relationships or help us to stay in relationships. Why should they be? Perhaps as Bochner (1991, p. 487) argues, 'Whether individuals actually have similar or dissimilar attitudes is not as important as the assumption shared by most individuals that they should have something important in common with the other (e.g. attitudes) if they are to form a relationship.'

Acquaintance is made up of several different elements, dimensions and stages, each with its own influences as things proceed (Van Lear & Trujillo, 1986). Acquaintance is thus a process (Duck, 1990b). Long-term acquaintance is probably not simply caused by, say, physical attraction even if that is what grabs our interest initially. The development of relationships is not simply caused by initial attractions. Relationships do not work like electric motors, which just start and run whenever we press the right switch. That simile, surprisingly, is widely held ('we just clicked'), even though it is an inadequate idea. Of course we have to do something communicatively in the long term to make relationships work: we do not just 'sit there looking pretty' in the hope that the rest is automatic. Relationships do not develop only because two people start out with 'compatible personalities'. But rather than dismissing the impact that attitudes and personality may have on relationships, we need to understand their role in our lives, just as Byrne (1971) and Clore & Byrne (1974) urge us to.

Attitudes and personality as elements of relationships

Sometimes we act as if two people *are* similar and that's that. It is not so simple: even if two people are similar, they must communicate that similarity to one another before it can have an effect. Bochner (1991, p. 487) claims that 'one of the main functions of communication in early and perhaps even in later encounters is to foster perceptions of attitude and personality similarity and also to create the impression of being an interesting and stimulating person.'

What do we have to *do* to find out that we are similar to someone else? Does it take time and might it not be quite difficult in reality? Most of us have thought that we were similar to someone else and then found out that we were not as alike as we first thought. That two people are similar to one another is a 'cognitive' fact; that they learn that they are similar is a 'communicative' fact. To discover that we are similar to someone else we have to communicate effectively, draw the right conclusions, manipulate and process the information correctly, and recognize what it means when we see it. Byrne's work shows us what happens when the information is already easily available, but what are the real-life processes by which we make it available? How do we bring out the similarity in the course of normal social life? Byrne tells us about the cognitive stimuli that may be attractive, but not about the communicative and interpersonal processes by which they are pulled into the open in interpersonal interaction. One-sided attractions do not explain relationships; acquaintance is a two-sided venture in which both persons take an active role. They communicate. They adapt.

One major area of adaptation and communication in the development of relationships concerns nonverbal behaviour and the 'microstructure of interaction' (Cappella, 1988). Each person's nonverbal behaviour changes in response to changes in the other person's behaviour and the partners adapt to one another's communicative styles; they do not simply persist in behaving in their own style irrespective of the responses that they get.

In line with the argument I am developing here, Cappella (1988) argues that relationship formation is interactional; it is predictable not from the way in which two persons happen to 'click together' but from how they *make* the pieces click together. We never see the internal states or attitudes of other persons directly so we can only infer them from nonverbal and verbal behaviour. Because of this, the meshing of nonverbal behaviour will be crucial to this inference process and highly significant in acquaintance. The microstructure of interactions does change as relationships develop, so nonverbal behaviour does reflect and illustrate growth of relationships.

Revealing (and detecting) information in the acquaintance process

Precisely how and why do we go about choosing information about ourselves so that we can communicate it to other people who can use it? To answer this, let us look at the work of negotiating and creating a relationship out of all the information that partners manipulate in interactions.

Uncertainty reduction

Information from others usually helps us to reduce uncertainty about them and to form a clearer picture of them and their relationship to us (Berger, 1988). Sometimes, when we learn about another person's past relationships or attitudes or feelings for us, we become more certain about the future of our relationship and also feel we know the person better. New information, at times, does not 'fit', and we have to rethink what the other person is like or second-guess them (Planalp et al., 1988) – for instance when we learn that he or she has been 'cheating' or has a side to his or her character that we had not seen before. Those discoveries increase uncertainty for us.

Neither does all information from others come directly from their words or intentional communications over which they have direct control (as we saw in Chapter 1). Not all the information fits with our (initially sketchy) model of them. When we find surprises then we have to re-evaluate our beliefs about the others' personality and what they are really like. Basically, our aim in real-life acquaintance is to make a good 'model' of the other person and to assess its matching with our own personality (Duck, 1991). *Then* we have to make the relationship work.

Social life helps us in these tasks by reducing uncertainty for us in many subtle ways (Allan, 1989). For instance, other people's suitability for us is sometimes socially determined. We do not have the complete freedom of choice we like to believe we have. Research consistently shows that people choose partners who come from their own racial, religious, economic, intellectual and social background (Kerckhoff, 1974). One reason is communicative: it is easier to talk to people whose background helps them to understand and share the experiences we describe. Another reason is sociological: every relationship is conducted in a context of other relationships and social norms (Allan, 1989). Our family, for instance, often feels it has some right to approve our dating or marital partner, and families tend to prefer people who are from the same background as themselves. A third reason why 'like is attracted to like' is because we dislike uncertainty; every similarity between us and a partner reduces uncertainty (Berger & Bradac, 1982). We feel surer about a partner and of our relationship's future the more like us they are.

Gaining information progressively

We must not assume that uncertainty reduction is a culmination; we become acquainted by an extended process of uncertainty reduction that continually shifts its focus and moves on to new, unknown areas (Duck, 1988). When we understand a person at a superficial level, we look more deeply and broadly into other parts of his or her make-up. When we know someone's attitudes to sport, we may want to know more about his or her deep personal feelings about parenthood, for instance. We keep turning to new areas of his or her personality or value system. The process of getting to know someone is the process of reducing uncertainty in as many ways, as many places, and as many levels as we can. But it is also a process that continues for ever – unfinished business that proceeds right through our lives and the life of the relationship (Duck, 1990b), since each new day, every new meeting, and all meetings with the partner are fresh and informative. So we are continually exploring our partner as we see him or her in the unfolding circumstances of life. Van Lear & Trujillo (1986) propose that such needs create a four-stage model of acquaintance that starts with uncertainty (and the need to reduce it by gathering information about the partner), moves on to exploring affect and feeling, develops personal growth, and then turns to issues of interpersonal stability. In such a model, partners are developing more than just feelings and are eventually structuring an interpersonally stable relationship by attending to different issues in the course of the relationship's growing life.

Changing our focus to different matters as acquaintance progresses is generally called 'filtering' (Kerckhoff & Davis, 1962). We can see why: it is as if we have a sequence or series of filters or sieves and when a person passes through one they go on to the next. Our first 'filter' may be physical appearance. If we like the other person's looks then we will want to go on and see what his or her attitudes are like and whether we enjoy those. 'Attitudes' could then be the second filter, and so on. We assess our acquaintances within a progressive series of 'tests': those who pass one test go through to a deeper level of friendship – and on to the next test.

In my own model (Duck, 1973; Duck & Condra, 1989), such tests are subtler and subtler comparisons of one's own attitudes, beliefs and personality compatibility with the partner. We start out asking broad questions in a gross way ('Are they extroverts – or introvert like me?'), and become more and more fine in our 'tuning' as the relationship goes on. What specific values do they hold most dear and are they the same as mine? What little things upset them when they are in a bad mood? What 'personality buttons' can I press to cheer them up and what sort of comforting works best with them? What are their deep, deep, deep fears about themselves? We work through such filters because we wish to understand and create a thorough picture of the partner's mind and personality in as much detail as possible. The tests, or filters, help us to reduce uncertainty and draw our partner's personality in finer and finer detail as the relationship deepens and develops. Indeed, Duck & Craig (1978) found that, in the long-term development of relationships, such processes are precisely what occurs.

Filtering theories are more sophisticated than the 'switch on' models that suggest that relationships are caused by one simple feature, like attitude similarity or physical attractiveness. However, while filtering theories overemphasize thought and cognition, they really only propose a more sophisticated sequence of motors to be switched on. They say little about the other processes that go into developing a relationship, such as daily life conversations that influence people's feelings towards one another in interesting ways, such as the fact that Wednesdays have been found to produce more conflict in conversations than other days do (Duck et al., 1991b)! In focussing on tests, filters or permanent personality characteristics, researchers have underplayed the daily routines of life in relationships that involve action and talk (Hays, 1989; Duck et al., 1991a,b). Surprisingly, these routines fit in with a lot of the planning that we do!

Much research into other aspects of acquaintance shows that acquaintance is not an accident but often happens by design (Berger & Bell, 1988). Two important lines of work are: the ways in which we form and carry out the intention to become related; and the strategic use that we make of self-disclosure, that is, revealing personal information about ourselves as a sign of growing intimacy and trust of our partner. Work on the first of these has explored the fact that people plan to become related (Berger & Bell, 1988). (They form specific plans and communicative strategies to ask people out on dates, increase the intimacy of their relationship, propose sexual involvement and even plan to leave relationships, for example.) Work on the second of these has focussed on the information about oneself that is revealed in developing relationships ('self-disclosure') and, although it is open to the criticism that it focusses on a behaviour that is actually not all that common in everyday life (Duck et al., 1991a,b), it is an important mechanism when it does occur. 'Self-disclosure' usually occurs by words but occasionally by nonverbal means, as when we let someone sit closer or touch us more than before. We self-disclose when we tell someone how we have been upset by something recently or 'what I am most ashamed of about myself' or 'what I dislike most about my parents'. We self-disclose when we tell secrets or give other people access to private attitudes that we share with very few others. We can also self-disclose nonverbally by 'giving ourselves away', for instance bursting into tears unexpectedly or suddenly blushing.

In most social psychological work, self-disclosure refers to verbal intimacy, particularly the messages that are so disclosed. This work assumes that we can tell how intimate others are merely by examining the words they use, the topics they talk about, and the subjects they introduce to a conversation. Such topics have occasionally been listed and rated for intimacy level. For example, Davis & Sloan (1974) put 'How I react to others' praise and criticism of me' at the bottom of their list and 'My feelings about my sexual inadequacy' at the top of their list for very intimate topics.

Remembering the discussion in Chapter 1, you may find this a bit dissatisfying. In life, there are more indicators of intimacy than just words; nonverbal cues as well as the relationship between the partners help to define and communicate intimacy. For this reason, Montgomery (1981) talks of 'open communication' rather than just self-disclosure. She describes it as composed of five elements, some of which occur more often in some types of relationship whilst others appear more frequently in others. *Negative openness* covers openness in showing disagreement or negative feelings about a partner or situation. *Nonverbal openness* relates to a communicator's facial expressions, vocal tone, and bodily postures or movements (see Chapter 1). *Emotional openness* describes the ease with which someone's feelings or moods are expressed and his or her concealment of emotional states. *Receptive openness* is a person's indication of his or her willingness to listen to other people's personal information. *General-style openness* refers to the overall impression that someone creates.

Even if we look at just the content of speech we can split openness into different elements, of which topic intimacy is one (Montgomery, 1981). Intimacy of a topic is not the same as 'intimacy of topic in a relationship'. For instance, what is said about a topic can make it intimate or non-intimate and the target of the disclosure likewise. Thus, the question 'How is your sex life?' looks like a promisingly personal and intimate topic unless we reply 'pretty average', or if it is our physician who asks us about it. In short, even intimate-sounding topics can be discussed non-intimately, or in non-intimate contexts. Other factors that make for intimacy in conversation are, as we have learned before, verbal immediacy, nonverbal accompaniments and relational context. Openness, then, includes both verbal and nonverbal aspects of behaviour and deals as much with the function of a message as with its medium (Montgomery, 1984). When we look at open communication in its living context, we see clearly that content and topic intimacy alone simply do not discriminate between high and low open communicators.

How strategic are we in making acquaintances?

Has it struck you how passive much of the work assumes that we are? Do we actually try to make other people like us sometimes or do we just sit back, smile, flash a few attitudes around and hope that people will react positively? I believe we actually spend quite a lot of time trying to get other people to like and appreciate us and also to check out how we are doing. We become upset when we fail to create positive feelings in other people; it is a great source of personal distress and dissatisfaction. We must have strategies for making others appreciate us and an awareness of 'how we are doing'. Douglas (1987) explored the strategies that people use to discover whether another person is interested in developing a relationship ('affinity testing'). These are listed in BOX 3.4. In essence, people rarely ask directly whether someone is interested in a relationship or not (well, the person might say 'no' and that would be that!). There is a preference for indirect strategies that give us the information without us asking directly – which would put ourselves on the line.

If we are successful in initially attracting someone to us, what happens to deepen the relationship? Recall the earlier discussion of

BOX 3.4 Douglas on affinity testing

Confronting

Actions that required a partner to provide immediate and generally public evidence of his or her liking.

 1. *I asked her if she liked me.*
 2. *I asked her if I appealed to her.*
 3. *I put my arm around her. It made her say yes or no.*

Withdrawing

Actions that required a partner to sustain the interaction.

 4. *I just turned myself off and just sat there real sedate. I knew if he started jabbering (which he did) then he was interested.*
 5. *I would be silent sometimes to see if he would start the conversation again.*
 6. *We were at a disco and I said, 'Well, I'm leaving'. I wanted him to stop me. You know, to say, 'Are you leaving already?'*

Sustaining

Actions designed to maintain the interaction without affecting its apparent intimacy.

 7. *I kept asking questions. You know, like, 'Where was she from?' 'What music did she like?'*
 8. *I met this girl. I liked her. I asked all these questions. 'What do you do for a living?' 'Where do you live?'*
 9. *I tried to keep him talking. I asked him questions. I told him about me.*

Hazing

Actions that required a partner to provide a commodity or service to the actor at some cost to himself or herself.

 10. *I told him I lived 16 miles away. Sixteen miles from the church I mean. I wanted to see if he would try and back out.*
 11. *I told her I didn't have a ride. She said that was OK. She said she would take me. I told her where I lived; it took about an hour to get there. I told her she couldn't come into my house even if she gave me a ride. I knew that she liked me because she accepted the situation I put her in.*
 12. *I met this guy at a party. He asked me if I wanted to go see a movie. I said OK. When we got there, I told him I didn't want to see it. I wanted to go home. I didn't really. I wanted to see how much he would take.*

Diminishing Self

Actions that lowered the value of self; either directly by self-

deprecation or indirectly by identifying alternative reward sources for a partner.

13. I asked her if she wanted to talk to somebody else. You know, 'Was I keeping her from something?'
14. I told him I wasn't very interesting. Waiting for him to say 'Oh, no'.
15. There were these other guys there. I kept pointing them out to her.

Approaching
Actions that implied increased intimacy to which the only disconfirming partner response is compensatory activity.

16. I would touch his shoulder or move close to see if he would react by staying where he was or moving closer.
17. I moved closer. He didn't move away.
18. I moved closer to her. We were sitting in a bar. You know, at one of those benches. I wanted to see if she would move away.

Offering
Actions that generated conditions favourable for approach by a partner.

19. I waited for him to come out of the restroom. Everyone else had left by that time. If he wanted to ask me out, he could.
20. I helped him carry some things out to his car. I made it to where we were by ourselves so that if he was going to ask me for a date, we would be in a position where he could do it.
21. I knew we would have to play with someone close to us in line. So I stood in front of him. I wanted to see if he would pick me.

Networking
Actions that included third parties, either to acquire or transmit information.

22. I went over and asked his friends about him. I knew his friends would tell him about it. Then, if he came over to me again, I would know he liked me.
23. I told other people there I liked him. I knew it would get back to him. I knew other people would tell him. If he ignored it, I would know he wasn't interested.
24. There was one guy at a party. We chit-chatted and he looked pretty interesting. There were some of my friends there, so I left and, later, I asked them what he had said about me.

Source: Douglas (1987, pp. 7–8).

self-disclosure. Some self-disclosure is a sign of good mental health and influences the course of relationships: a certain amount of intimate disclosure is expected in our culture, as an indication that we genuinely trust another person. We are supposed to say a few disclosing and revealing things in order to 'open-out'. Women are particularly 'expected' to self-disclose and are often pressed into doing so if they do not do so voluntarily; 'closed' women are asked direct questions that make them open out (Miell, 1984).

Reciprocity of self-disclosure is also expected, at least in the early stages of relationships. If I self-disclose to you, you will self-disclose back. It confirms a desire to develop a relationship since you could have chosen not to reveal the information, especially if it is quite personal. Conversely, we could hold back a relationship, if we wanted, by just not revealing something personal to our partner even if our partner did so to us (Miell & Duck, 1986). Self-disclosure is used strategically both to develop relationships (Davis, 1978) and to hold them back or to shape the relationship into one form rather than another (e.g. to keep someone from getting too intimate, too fast, or to protect the relationship from straying on to taboo topics; Baxter & Wilmot, 1985; Miell, 1984, see BOX 3.5). It is also worth noting, however, that reciprocity of self-disclosure wears off as relationships mature. As Wright (1978) puts it, 'Apparently, in the more comfortable and less formal context of deeper friendship, the partners do not feel they owe it to one another, out of politeness or decency, to exchange trust for trust: the trust is already there.'

While self-disclosure is clearly important in developing relationships, Helgeson et al. (1987) show that intimacy and self-disclosure are not by any means the same thing, while Duck et al. (1991b) indicate that self-disclosure does not occur in everyday conversation to anything like the extent that would be predicted on the basis of laboratory study of the topic. Although self-disclosure does serve to develop relationships when it happens, there are other very important forces in relationships that, in everyday life, have more powerful effects and everyday chit-chat seems to be one of the most important and overlooked of these forces (Duck et al., 1991b).

Acquaintance is not entirely orderly, always 'cognitively driven', or utterly strategic. Many of us have sensed that we did not know how a relationship would develop; many have been in chaotic relationships; all have been in uncertain ones. Although some theorists represent acquaintance as rational, orderly and well-planned logical decision-making, we know that they are probably wrong if they think that acquaintance happens like that all the time.

BOX 3.5 Strategic self-disclosure

Partners use self-disclosure as a tool for the control of relationships. For instance, we will occasionally make a disclosure just so that we plunge our partner into a 'norm of reciprocity' requiring him or her to respond with something equally intimate and revealing (Miell, 1984; Miell & Duck, 1986).

Acquainting persons frequently use false disclosures to provoke an argument or debate (Miell, 1984). By doing this we find out what our partner really thinks (i.e. we induce partner to self-disclose by a devious means rather than by a direct question asking for partner's views).

Self-disclosure serves an important role in creating relationships and helps partners to construct a story of the origin of a relationship (Duck & Miell, 1984). Partners begin to construct 'relational disclosures' to make to outsiders to indicate depth of involvement.

Sprecher (1987) compared the effects of self-disclosure given and received, rather than treating self-disclosure as one global concept, as many previous researchers had done. Amounts of disclosure the person received from the partner were more predictive of the feelings that a person had about the relationship than was amount of disclosure given to the partner. Overall, however, the amount of disclosure in the relationship predicted whether the couple was still together in a four year follow-up!

There is a reverse side to this. There are 'taboo topics' that we recognize and respect (Baxter & Wilmot, 1985). Some themes are 'dangerous' ones to explore (e.g. partner's past relationships; the present state of our relationship). Lack of self-disclosure can sometimes be strategic and can help to preserve the relationship because it keeps us away from topics that can be inherently threatening.

Duck et al. (1991b) indicate that self-disclosure does not occur in everyday conversation to anything like the extent that is assumed by laboratory research and in everyday life there are important aspects of conversation other than self-disclosure that are influential on relationships (e.g. the mere occurrence of conversations even on trivial topics). Duck et al. (1991a) also found that persons in a conversation tend to see the conversation as less significant than do outside observers, or to draw a conclusion for the present argument, researchers are likely simply to have overestimated the impact of self-disclosure for a variety of reasons.

Establishing, developing and maintaining relationships

What is the psychological relationship between initial attraction and long-term liking? What are the processes by which we convert 'gut attraction' into a working relationship? Note also, of course, that most meetings with strangers do *not* develop into intimate relationships (Delia, 1980). (There are some very interesting questions to do with the ways in which we keep relationships at a distance, but researchers have not really addressed these yet.)

In life, my experience is that we plan to meet people and we share points of contact but also that predictable routines bring us together frequently with those we know well. If researchers study only meetings between interchangeable, anonymous strangers in contextually sanitized laboratory environments, we miss the point that our real-life encounters are only occasionally unforeseen, unexpected and accidental but can also be predictable, anticipated and (often) prearranged. Because meetings are like this, they come from somewhere and we have coded memories about the persons and the relationships in which they arise: stories about where the relationship came from, what it means to us, and where it is going. Miell (1987) has shown that a person's beliefs about the future of the relationship are very often influenced by the last three days of routine experience in the relationship more than by the whole history of its long-term idealized past, and Duck et al. (1991a) have shown that memory for past relational events is influenced very strongly by the *present* state of the relationship. This makes a lot of sense: when relationship problems occur, they occur in the present, the here-and-now, and all the fond memories of the distant past become degraded by the insistence of urgent present feelings. Such a view runs counter to that offered by theories that assume relationships are based on the exchange that has taken place in them in the past, or that commitment is an enduring thing based as much in the past as in the present.

Relationships are often buried in daily routines

Some theories (e.g. *Equity Theory*, Hatfield & Traupmann, 1981; *Exchange Theory*, Huesmann & Levinger, 1976) claim that relationships depend on the past, present or future levels of reward which we receive vis-à-vis our partner. I think this approach makes the fundamentally wrong assumption that we sustain our relationships by conscious (or even unconscious) acts of reinforcement, testing or strategic development once they are established. Instead, most of the time daily life is remarkably humdrum, routine, predictable. We take our long-term relationships for granted most of the time and assume that the partner we slept next to will wake up still feeling like a partner tomorrow. We do not go through a ritual each breakfast time where we treat each other like strangers and run through a whole range of rewarding techniques to re-establish the relationship and take it to where it was the day before: we behave that way only with friends we have not seen for ages.

The remarkable fact about daily life is that continuities exist and do not have to be worked for, once the relationship is defined and established (Duck, 1990b). Friendships can feel as if they exist and continue over years and miles without any contact except the occasional phone call, Christmas card or letter. Relationships have their permanence in the mind, on the basis of beliefs not just of rewards (Duck & Sants, 1983). They survive distance, climate, revolt, pestilence and Act of God, as long as we both *think* they have.

Relationships which have major effects on people are of this perpetual but dormant kind: parent–child relationships, marriages, friendships, collegial relationships at work. They are part of the unchallenged and comfortable predictability of lives made up of routine, regular conversation, expectation, and assumptions that most of tomorrow will be based on the foundations of today.

These predictabilities help to explain why breakdown, development and repair of relationships are disruptive. Distress at disruption and loss of relationships is often precisely because they are so humdrum that they become built into the other routines of our lives. These taken-for-granted routines build in ways that we do not always realize until they are removed. Their loss takes away unspoken and unrealized parts of ourselves.

However, relationships do not just pop out of strings of routines but from the way the partners *think* about those interactions (Duck, 1980) and *talk to one another* in and about them (Duck & Pond, 1989). Also, as Honeycutt et al. (1989) show, their development is partly a result of memory structures that people have. Events and experiences (and relationship development) are remembered in ways that may be helpful or functional without actually being 'accurate'. Rather than there really *being* stages for development of relationships, Honeycutt et al. focus on the *beliefs and memories for stages* that people have in terms of the themes that they expect, based on experience and 'out of relationship thinking' (Duck, 1980), daydream or fantasizing. The study thus emphasizes the role of *memory* for stages in the formation of relationships and neatly cuts through the problem of identifying *actual* stages that people go through in relationship development.

Do partners always agree about their relationship?

Discrepancies of interpretation, even between close partners, are an inevitable part of everyday social life (McCarthy, 1983). When researchers find such disagreements, it should surprise them less than it does. Our own and everyone else's cognitive processes are inaccessible to us; if we do not know what other people are thinking, we can depend only on guesswork and we often guess wrongly. Yet Hewes et al., (1985) show that people have pretty sophisticated knowledge about the likely sources of error in information that we have about other people and are able to correct for biases in 'second-guessing'. By talking to others in routine ways, we can assess their cognitive processes more and more accurately, but to do so we may have to work through disagreements during conversation. Secondly, we seldom discuss our views of relationship openly and explicitly with our partners except when we think something is wrong (Baxter & Wilmot, 1984). So we do not get much experience of seeing explicit agreement about our relationships, and the experiences we do get will emphasize the discords instead.

The problems with relationships are more likely to be visible, accessible and familiar than are the smooth parts. In particular, we misperceive other people's feelings in one important respect: we tend to be uncertain about partners' commitment to relationships and assume that they might change their mind – as if we are their friend for only as long as *they* think we are (Duck, 1991). More importantly, partners probably each see different events as crucial in the relationship, so there is no good reason to expect partners to be in total agreement about the nature or course of the relationship (McCarthy, 1983). What happens when disagreements are detected is that people talk them out, so once again in everyday life conversation is an important tool for developing and sustaining relationships. However, in real life, relationships take place in a context provided by other people. The presence of others (and what they know about the relationship) is what distinguishes between fixed and tentative relationships, between public and secret relationships, between cooperative and competitive, between open, trusting and closed, threatening relationships.

Does it matter what 'outsiders' think?

Much research shows that we are aware of outside influence on relationships (Milardo, 1988) and that outsiders can affect the course of a relationship. First, as we pull into one new relationship we correspondingly have a little less time for our old friendships (Milardo et al., 1983). New friendships disrupt old ones. Secondly, outsiders, in the shape of the 'surrounding culture', give us clues about the ways to conduct relationships. We try to hide affairs and hope that the newspapers do not find out about them but we are happy to publicize marriages in those self-same newspapers, for instance.

As partners become more involved in a courtship, so this adversely affects their relationships with friends (Milardo et al., 1983). Respondents in the later stages of courtship interact with fewer people, relative to persons in the earlier stages of courtship, and see them less often and for shorter periods of time. However, the most noticeable changes in rates of participation occur with intermediate friends rather than close ones. Changes in frequency and duration of interactions subsequently lead to a decrease in the size of network. In other words, as we see our date more, we see our casual friends (but not our close friends) less until they finally drop out of our network altogether, if the courtship progresses satisfactorily (Milardo et al., 1983). Courting partners are thus less of a substitute for close friends than for casual acquaintances. In brief, emotional commitment to one person affects the structure of the larger network to which we belong.

Every culture has certain views about the nature of relationships and the 'rules' for conducting them (see BOX 3.6 p. 91). Some of the preceding developments mean that the relationship begins to have meaning for other people, too, to become an 'organization' over and above the feelings that the partners have for one another (McCall, 1982). Whilst social psychologists explore the ways in which feelings for one another pull partners together, and communications scientists explore the ways in which those feelings are expressed and communicated, sociologists are interested in relationships as social units over and above the two members in them (McCall, 1982). In a sociological analysis of friendships, Allan (1989) points to the ways in which social life structures our choices of partners and creates patterns of activity that help us to express emotions, regulate our feelings in relationships and provide opportunities for relationships to take a particular form. Gender, class position, domestic relationships and existing friendships all pattern and constrain an individual's choices and limit freedom in various ways not considered by those psychologists, for example, who imagine that attraction and friendship choices are the simple result of emotion or of cognitive processes of information management.

Think also for a moment how often we have heard people say 'It was too intense' (i.e. the relationship was), 'It wasn't going anywhere' (i.e. the relationship wasn't), 'We have a nice relationship where we both feel relaxed', and the like. Sociologists have noticed that persons develop a sense of membership in 'a relationship' and that the formation of interpersonal liking bonds is not the complete story. 'Institutionalized social forms' of relationships affect our relating and acquainting too (e.g. we know what our culture thinks 'a friendship' is as distinct from an 'extramarital affair', and we know that professors and students are 'permitted' to have one form of relationship but not the other).

Each real-life form of a relationship creates some tension with the social blueprint, as it were, in that we may become aware of discrepancies between our own relationship and the cultural expectations for it ('I guess it wasn't a "perfect marriage"'). Third parties, particularly in-laws it seems, exert 'audience effects' on relationships by commenting on the partners' attempts to implement the social blueprint.

Wanting to enter into a relationship, therefore, means that we have to do more than just like our partner. There are factors, beyond the purely individual ones (e.g. the liking), which affect and exert influence on a relationship and the partners in it. There are cultural rules and scripts for relationships (Ginsburg, 1988) and our execution of the rules will affect the picture that people form not only of our skills as a relater but, to some extent, of our intentions during the early stages of relationships: for instance, if we break the rules we may seem too pushy or too shy. But the relationship also needs to be 'organized' so that we know who does what and who plays which roles in the couple (McCall, 1988).

Relationships, then, are not mere reactions to the qualities, properties or attributes of another person. Other influences such as time, viewpoint, strategy, the wider culture and skill are all relevant. Against this background, what do people actually do?

Making sense of relationships

I am convinced that a large number of the findings reviewed here point to one startlingly overlooked fact: sometimes people think about their relationships and sometimes they do not. We may think about it when we are face to face with our partner, but we also do it frequently when they are not there as when we daydream, fantasize, plan, plot and hope. We can plan the relationship; we can think back over encounters and try to work out what went wrong with them or what we can learn from them (Duck, 1980). We can learn about our partners by thinking things over in this way since we can easily pick up on some crucial point that may have escaped us before. This 'out-of-interaction' fantasy, or thought work, is a very important aspect of both the building and destroying of relationships. As Miell (1987) has shown, partners typically remember interactions in a way that influences their future behaviour in the relationship. As Duck et al. (1991) have shown, the present or recent experiences in a relationship also influence the way in which the past of the relationship is recalled. By thinking about and recalling interaction, we actually construct a context for its future and its past!

One essential feature of relating is the need to provide a 'story' about it, and, clearly, these stories could be readily made up in the course of such out-of-interaction thinking. Try keeping a diary of how you feel about your partner, then you'll know what I mean. You will also see how much a relationship is characterized by *variation* in thinking about the other person, not by the monotonous constancy of feelings that is often assumed by research based on ratings of commitment or liking. This kind of musing might also help us to create a sense of continuity, a sense that the relationship is a lasting venture, not a temporary phase. That sense of continuity, by means of humdrum routine, is what sustains our beliefs in the continuity of the relationships to which we belong. It is functional in that it preserves us from the need for continually re-establishing new relationships or continually re-enacting our existing ones on each new day.

Beliefs, routines and future projects are central to everyday life, but we are not always completely sensible, thoughtful people. I see myself making mistakes and wrong assumptions, being inconsistent, losing my temper, taking unreasonable dislikes to people, unfairly teasing people, feeling uncertain, embarrassed and ashamed occasionally. Yet it is all too easy to overlook these little foibles and assume that no one else does these things. It often

---

BOX 3.6 Rules and skills of relationships

There are 13 rules that apply particularly to friendship (Argyle &
Henderson, 1984). Examples are 'Show emotional support', 'Trust
and confide in the other', 'Don't criticize the friend in public',
'Don't nag', 'Respect privacy'. Although some 43 rules altogether
were expected by subjects to apply to friendship, most of them did
not apply very strongly.

There are cross-cultural differences in friendship rules, too, and
friendship is not the same the world over (Gudykunst & Nishida,
1986). Argyle & Henderson (1984) conclude that there are central
'friendship rules' whose breaking will dissolve the friendship, but
also that there are 'general rules' to distinguish friendship from other
relationships and 'quality rules' to differentiate ordinary friendship
from high-quality friendship.

Within a particular culture, we know the characteristics that
make up a friendship and that make it different from casual
acquaintance (Davis & Todd, 1985). For instance, enjoyment,
trust, mutual assistance, respect, understanding and intimacy are
all-important, defining features of friendship.

There are also skills of friendship based on the social skills we
learned in Chapter 1 (Duck, 1991). Better-adjusted people have
greater relational competence and a larger repertoire of social skills
that they use more appropriately than have poorly adjusted people
(Burns & Farina, 1984). They know the rules and they follow
them. Intriguingly, Burns & Farina (1984) show that such skills
run in families, and it looks as if we learn friendship skills from
our parents.

---

looks to me as if the rest of humanity is going around soberly and
seriously processing information in the manner of true scientists, in
rational, statistically defensible ways, reaching conclusions, being
competent, liking people who are well dressed, attitudinally
similar, and who order their arguments properly. Yet I know I am
often persuaded by people not for these reasons but because I
cannot be bothered to argue about some issues, do not think of the
effective debating point till I am half-way down the street, am in
a rush to do something more important to me, or simply do not
know enough about the topic to challenge them adequately.

As in the rest of life, so in relationships I think we can easily
misunderstand what really goes on. It does not feel to me as if the
world is full of relationships where perfect strangers grasp one
another's collars in breathless attempts to shake out the other

person's attitudes in a search for reinforcement. Neither do I see people in long-term relationships going round giving grades to partners for their every action and calculating whether the arithmetic works out well enough for them to stay in the relationship for the next ten minutes. Not every encounter is a surprise; not every person a blank slate upon which rapid calculations have to be performed. Not every member of the family has either just fallen in love with you or is about to file for divorce, is either a young child with a tendency to initiate violent acts or an elderly incontinent who feels lonely. Neither is precisely the same level of feeling felt towards each partner all the time irrespective of mood or circumstances (Barbee, 1990).

Relationships are a part of life, and everyday life is a part of all relationships. As those lives change through our ageing, so do the concerns we have and the things we do. As days go by, so our feelings and concerns are subject to change or variation. Our friendship needs vary through life as do our opportunities for getting them and our bases for seeking them (Dickens & Perlman, 1981). They also vary day by day in the face of circumstances (Bolger et al., 1989). In teenage years, the main search is for a group of friends and for sexual partners; later, most people become committed to one partner and their network of friends stabilizes for a while. If we marry the partner and have children, our friendship needs are affected by these circumstances and by career developments. When the children leave home, parents often become involved in the community more extensively and start up new friendships in the middle years of life, and so on. As life develops new demands and new routines so we change friendship 'work'. But also important, and very sadly overlooked, is the fact that our day-to-day experience of friendship and marriage is not all the same (Shotter, 1987). Instead, our feelings can go up and down as joys and resentments arise, recede and gain resolution. So the statements that we make about liking and loving are likely to be *summary statements* (see Chapter 2) that can be more or less accurate reflections of how we felt three days ago, just as any 'average summary' is a more or less accurate reflection of a specific case.

A consistent element of all lifelong routines consists of such trivial variation, and we apparently waste a lot of time doing seemingly unimportant things. For example, we spend much of our time talking to other people about commonly experienced events (Duck et al., 1991b; Duck & Rutt, 1988), gossiping, and giving views of one another (Emler & Fisher, 1982). For that reason, regular behavioural measures of friendship are better predictors of relationship growth than are monolithic cognitive structural ones (Hays, 1984). For instance, people do not sit down and check up all the time on whether their attitudes or personalities are similar – at least, not directly or explicitly. Frequently, they are being active together but in seemingly unimportant ways, and everyday talk is one such activity (Shea & Pearson, 1986).

People 'outside the laboratory' are not engaged in the kinds of activity that have often been supposed, and one major difference is that our encounters are not *only* unforeseen and fortuitous. They can also be pre-planned and foreseeable because they fit in with the other routines of everyday life such as living in a family or an institution where events have predictable sequences (e.g. meal times, habits, patterns).

Individual interactions in social relationships are not interchangeable, because of these chains of routine that keep us together. Routine makes us predictable for one another and defines some of the sorts of behaviour that will (not) occur between us (e.g. I won't sit and watch TV with my colleagues in the department but will do so with my family).

Routines are not only predictable but they tie people together behaviourally – ensuring that the relationship continues, as part of those other routines. For instance, we meet friends because we have arranged to do so, and these routines and appointments are not trivial and unimportant in developing relationships; they are the bases of the normal day (Duck et al., 1991b). When we meet one another we talk. This talk is not necessarily very significant in terms of its content, but it is nonetheless important for the relationship (See BOX 3.7)

Handling the break-up of relationships

So far I have focussed on the bright side of relationships but much talk and many routines are also directed towards the less appealing side of relationships: when they break up or need repair. The rosy picture of relational progress drawn so far is only part of the truth. Things often go wrong in relationships in all sorts of ways and cause a lot of pain when they do. How does it happen?

BOX 3.7 Social participation and everyday talk

Wheeler & Nezlek (1977) devised a method (called the 'Rochester Interaction Record') for recording people's daily social interactions. Essentially, the method is a structured diary that records, for instance, whom the subject met, where, for how long, what was talked about, and how the subject felt about the interaction.

They find that 56% of interactions that last more than 10 minutes are with persons of the same sex. The women subjects spend more time in interaction in the first part of their first university year than do men, but by the second part of the year this difference disappears. This may show that women adjust to the stress of their new arrival at university by seeking to involve themselves in social life.

Reis et al. (1980) show that physically attractive men have more social interaction than less attractive men. For women, there is no relationship between their physical attractiveness and their level of social participation, somewhat surprisingly. However, both attractive men and attractive women report greater satisfaction with their social interactions than do the less attractive persons.

Employing a new technique that adds assessment of communication *to the other elements of social participation, Duck et al. (1991b) have shown that the quality of women's communication is judged higher than men's in day-to-day interaction and that most regular day-to-day communications are low in self-disclosure and have low impact on the future of the relationship (except conversations of lovers). They also found that there is a tendency for conversation on Wednesdays to be more conflict-laden than conversation on other days of the week.*

When things go wrong

There are several parts to acquaintance, and so we should expect there to be several parts to the undoing of acquaintance during relational dissolution. This is partly because relationships exist in time and take time to fall apart, so that at different times different processes are taking a role in the dissolution. It is also because, like a motor car, a relationship can have accidents for many reasons, whether the 'driver's' fault, mechanical failure or the actions of other road users. Thus, in a relationship, one or both partners may be hopeless at relating, or the structure and mechanics of the relationship may be wrong, even though both partners are socially competent in other settings, or outside influences can upset it. All these possibilities have been explored. However, I am going to focus on my own approach to these issues and refer you elsewhere for details of the other work. One reason for doing this is that my own theory of relationship dissolution is closely tied to my theory of relational repair (Duck, 1984) as well as to my theory of the development of acquaintance (Duck, 1988) and so provides links between what has gone before here and what follows.

The essence of my theory of relational dissolution is that there are several different phases, each with a characteristic style and concern (Duck, 1982a). Thus, as shown in Figure 3.1, the first phase is a breakdown phase wherein partners (or one partner only) become(s) distressed at the way the relationship is conducted. This generates an *intrapsychic phase* characterized by a brooding focus on the relationship and on the partner. Nothing is said to the partner at this point: the agony is either private or shared only with a diary or with relatively anonymous other persons who will not tell the partner about the complaint. Just before exit from this phase, people move up the scale of confidants so that they start to complain to their close friends, but do not yet present the partner with the full extent of their distress or doubts about the future of the relationship.

Once we decide to do something about a relational problem we have to deal with the difficulties of facing up to the partner. Implicit – and probably wrongly implicit – in my 1982 model was the belief that partners would tell one another about their feelings and try to do something about them. Both Lee (1984) and Baxter (1984) show that people often leave relationships without telling their partner, or by fudging their exits. For instance, they may say: 'I'll call you' and then not do it; or 'Let's keep in touch' and never contact the partner; or 'Let's not be lovers but stay as friends' and then have hardly any contact in future (Metts et al., 1989). Given that my assumption is partly wrong, it nevertheless assumes that partners in formal relationships like marriage will have to face up to their partner, whilst partners in other relationships may or may not do so. The *dyadic phase* is the phase when partners try to confront and talk through their feelings about the relationship and decide how to sort out the future. Assuming that they decide to break up (and even my 1982 model was quite clear that they might decide not to do that), they then move rapidly to a *social phase* when they have to tell other people about their decision and enlist some support for their side of the debate. It is no good just leaving a relationship: we need other people to agree with our decision or to prop us up and support what we have done. Other people can support us in ways such as being sympathetic and generally understanding. More important, they can side with our version of events and our version of the partner's and

BREAKDOWN: Dissatisfaction with relationship

↓

Threshold: I can't stand this any more

↓

INTRA-PSYCHIC PHASE
Personal focus on partner's behaviour
Assess adequacy of partner's role performance
Depict and evaluate negative aspects of being in the relationship
Consider costs of withdrawal
Assess positive aspects of alternative relationships
Face 'express/repress dilemma'

↓

Threshold: I'd be justified in withdrawing

↓

DYADIC PHASE
Face 'confrontation/avoidance dilemma'
Confront partner
Negotiate in 'Our Relationship Talks'
Attempt repair and reconciliation?
Assess joint costs of withdrawal or reduced intimacy

↓

Threshold: I mean it

↓

SOCIAL PHASE
Negotiate post-dissolution state with partner
Initiate gossip/discussion in social network
Create publicly negotiable face-saving/blame-placing stories and
   accounts
Consider and face up to implied social network effects, if any
Call in intervention teams?

↓

Threshold: It's now inevitable

↓

GRAVE DRESSING PHASE
'Getting over' activity
Retrospection; reformulative post-mortem attribution
Public distribution of own version of break-up story

Figure 3.1: *A sketch of the main phases of dissolving personal relationships*
(Duck, 1982a)

Source: Reprinted from Duck, S.W. (1982) 'A topography of relationship disengagement and dissolution'. In Duck, S.W. (ed.) *Personal Relationships 4: Dissolving Personal Relationships.* Academic Press: London. Reproduced by permission.

the relationship's faults. ('I always thought he/she was no good', 'I could never understand how you two could get along – you never seemed right for each other'.) This is the *grave-dressing* phase: once the relationship is dead we have to bury it 'good and proper' – with a tombstone saying how it was born, what it was like, and why it died. We have to create an account of the relationship's history and, as it were, put that somewhere so that other people can see it and, we hope, accept it.

Those are the main elements of the approach, although it took thirty pages in the original to expound it properly. How does other work support (or not) this set of proposals? I have already noted that Lee (1984) and Baxter (1984) produced results that support it in some ways, but not in others. BOX 3.8 gives some detail of their (and other) work.

Gossip plays a key role in the social and grave-dressing phases: in a dissolving relationship, we actively seek the support of members of our social networks and do so by gossiping about our partners (La Gaipa, 1982). In some instances, we look for 'arbitrators' who will help to bring us back together with our partner. In other cases, we just want someone to back up and spread around our own version of the break-up and its causes. A crucial point made by La Gaipa (1982) is that every person who leaves a relationship has to leave with 'social credit' intact for future use: that is, we have to leave in such a way that we are not debarred from future relationships. We must leave with a reputation for having been let down or faced with unreasonable odds or an unreasonable partner. It is socially accept-able to say 'I left because we tried hard to make it work but it wouldn't'. It is socially unacceptable to leave a relationship with the cheery but unpalatable admission: 'Well basically I'm a jilt and I got bored dangling my partner on a string so I just broke the whole thing off when it suited me'. That statement could destroy one's future credit for new relationships.

Accounts often serve the purpose of beginning the 'getting over' activity essential to complete the dissolution. A large part of this involves selecting an account of dissolution that refers to a fault in the partner or relationship that pre-existed the split or was even present all along (Weber, 1983). This is the 'I always thought she/he was a bit of a risk to get involved with, but I did it anyway, more fool me' story that we have all used from time to time.

However, accounts also serve another purpose: the creation of a publicly acceptable story is essential to getting over the loss of a rela-tionship (McCall, 1982). It is insufficient having a story that we alone accept: others must also endorse it. As McCall astutely

BOX 3.8   Dissolution of relationships

*Lee (1984) reports on work examining a framework to explain the
sequences that we go through when we break off long-term romantic
relationships. He identifies 5 stages:*

D (Discovery of dissatisfaction)
E (Exposure of the dissatisfaction)
N (Negotiation about the problem)
R (Resolution of the issue)
T (Transformation of the relationship).

*Not all dissolutions involve the partners in explicit disclosure of
each of these stages. Sometimes people move to T without N (e.g.
they leave without making any attempt to put the relationship right).*

*How do partners disengage themselves from a relationship?
Baxter (1984) found that there are 6 distinct elements to a
disengagement:*

(1) onset of problem;
(2) decision to exit;
*(3) initiation of unilateral disengagement action (e.g. expressing the
    desire to get out);*
(4) initial reaction to broken-up-with party;
*(5) ambivalence and repair scenarios where partners try to reconcile
    but find they cannot;*
*(6) initiation of bilateral disengagement – when both partners
    accept that it's all over.*

*These stages are evident even in divorces. If partners are to have
an orderly divorce (i.e. one where we both successfully cut ourselves
off from not only our feelings about our partner but our attachment
to the routines of the marriage and also the feeling of being married)
then there is a need for 'lee-time' (Hagestad & Smyer, 1982). This
means that we need time to prepare ourselves for being divorced and
to get away from our old relationship. Mostly, the authors found,
it is the wife who takes charge of this process.*

*Metts et al. (1989) looked at the ways in which romantic couples
attempt to redefine their relationship as a friendship when they want
to break off the romance. Couples who were friends before the
romantic break-up were most likely to be able to accomplish the
redefinition of the relationship back to friendship, but the strategy
of break-up and reasons for ending had some effect. Those people
who felt exploited in the romance were the least likely to reformulate
the relationship as friendship and just broke it off altogether.*

> *Felmlee et al. (1990) conducted a longitudinal investigation of break-up of premarital relationships and found that predictors of break-up were: amount of time spent together (less time together predicted greater risk of break-up), dissimilarity in race, lack of support from social network, and length of the relationship at the time of the study.*
>
> *Cupach & Metts (1986) found differences between accounts of dissolution of different sorts of relationship, with accounts of marital dissolution being markedly more complex than accounts of premarital relationship dissolution. It seems that the strong enmeshment of lives in marriage (through daily routines of behaviour, such as meal-times, and extensive shared experience) has a strong effect on the ways in which the dissolution is reported (and experienced) over and above the emotions that are experienced, so that researchers need to be cautious in extending their work from one type of relationship to another.*

observes, part of the success of good counsellors consists in their ability to construct such stories for persons distressed about relational loss.

Putting it right

If two people wanted to put a relationship right, then they could decide to try and make it 'redevelop'; that is, they could assume that repairing a relationship is just like acquaintance, and go through the same processes. This means that we have to assume that break-up of relationships is the reverse of acquaintance, and to repair it all we have to do is 'rewind' it. This makes some sense: developing relationships grow in intimacy whereas breaking ones decline in intimacy, so perhaps we should just try to rewind the intimacy level.

In other ways, this idea does not work. For instance, in acquaintance we get to know more about a person and in breakdown we cannot get to know less. We probably just reinterpret what we already know and put it into a different framework, model or interpretation ('Yes, he's always been kind, but then he was always after something').

I think that we need to base our ideas about repair not on our model of acquaintance but on a model of breakdown of relationships

Dissolution States and Thresholds	Person's Concerns	Repair Focus
1. Breakdown: Dissatisfaction with relationship	Relationship process; emotional and/or physical satisfaction in relationship	Concerns over one's value as a partner; Relational process
Threshold: I can't stand this any more		
2. Intrapsychic Phase: Dissatisfaction with partner	Partner's 'faults and inadequacies'; alternative forms of relationship; relationships with alternative partners	Person's view of partner
Threshold: I'd be justified in withdrawing		
3. Dyadic Phase: Confrontation with partner	Reformulation of relationship: expression of conflict; clearing the air	Beliefs about optimal form of future relationship
Threshold: I mean it		
4. Social Phase: Publication of relationship distress	Gaining support and assistance from others; having own view of the problem ratified; obtaining intervention to rectify matters or end the relationship	*Either:* Hold partners together (Phase 1) *Or:* Save face
Threshold: It's now inevitable		
5. Grave-dressing Phase: Getting over it all and tidying up	Self-justification; marketing of one's own version of the break-up and its causes	

Figure 3.2: *A sketch of the main concerns at different phases of dissolution*

Source: Reprinted from Duck, S.W. (1984) 'A perspective on the repair of relationships: repair of what when? In Duck, S.W. (ed.) *Personal Relationships 5: Repairing Personal Relationships*. Academic Press: London. Reproduced by permission.

that is consistent with the principles governing formation of relation-ships in general. Research on relationships has begun to help us understand what precisely happens when things go wrong. By emphasizing processes of breakdown of relationships and processes of acquaintance, we have the chance now to see that there are also processes of repair. These address different aspects of relationships in trouble. This, I believe, also gives us the chance to be more helpful in putting things right. Bear in mind the theory just covered, as you look at Figure 3.2, and you will see that it is based on proposals made earlier. There are phases to repair of relationships and some styles work at some times and not at others (Duck, 1984).

If the relationship is at the intrapsychic phase of dissolution, for instance, repair should aim to re-establish liking for the partner rather than to correct behavioural faults in ourselves or our nonverbal behaviour. These latter may be more suitable if persons are in the breakdown phase. Liking for partner can be re-established or aided by means such as keeping a record, mental or physical, of the positive or pleasing behaviour of our partner rather than listing the negatives and dwelling on them in isolation (Bandura, 1977). Other methods involve redirection of attributions, that is, attempting to use more varied, and perhaps more favourable, explanations for the partner's behaviour – in brief, to make greater efforts to understand the reasons that our partner may give for what is happening in the relationship.

At other phases of dissolution, different strategies of repair are appropriate, according to this model. For instance, at the social phase, persons outside the relationship have to decide whether it is better to try to patch everything up or whether it may serve everyone's best interests to help the partners to get out of the relationship. Figure 3.2 indicates that the choice of strategies is between pressing the partners to stay together or helping them to save face by backing up their separate versions of the break-up. An extra possibility would be to create a story that is acceptable to both of them, such as 'It was an unworkable relationship . . . and it is nobody's fault'.

Essentially, this new model proposes only three things: relationships are made up of many parts and processes, some of which 'clock in' at some points in the relationship's life and some at others; relationships can go wrong in a variety of ways; repairing of disrupted relationships will be most effective when it addresses the concerns that are most important to us at the phase of dissolution of relationships which we have reached.

The ways we change our 'stories' about a relationship provide important psychological data, and they indicate the dynamic nature of the help that outsiders have to give to relationships in trouble. Different parts of the story need to be addressed at different phases of breakdown. Is one and the same kind of intervention appropriate at all stages of a relationship's decline? Probably not. It makes more sense to look for the relative appropriateness of different intervention techniques as those dynamics unfold.

There are few 'scripts' for handling break-up of relationships and many intriguing research questions surround the actual processes by which people extricate themselves (or can be helped to extricate themselves) from unwanted relationships. For example, Miller & Parks (1982) look at relationships dissolution as an influence process and show that different strategies for changing attitudes can help in dissolution. It is now a major aim in the personal relationships field to explain dissolution and repair of relationships.

Summary

This chapter has looked at personal relationships by exploring the ways in which they start between strangers and it has elaborated the processes (attitude similarity, uncertainty reduction and organization of routine behaviours) that are needed to develop relationships. It has stressed that this process is not a simple one of merely comparing attitudes and personality characteristics with those of other people, but is a social, dyadic and communicative process of discovery and bonding. It has emphasized the view that relationships are continually developing processes rather than static states begun and defined purely by partners' initial psychological make-up or reward levels. There is emphasis on the creation of relationships; the effects of time and process; the interaction of beliefs with social skills and behaviour; and the role of perspectives and influences from outside the relationship. Decline, dissolution and repair of relationships were considered in tandem with the role of everyday routines and everyday talk.

Now we can look at the family and at children's relationship, perhaps the two most important kinds of relationship in life for us all.

Further reading

Baxter, L.A. (1992) *Relationships and Culture*. Guilford: New York.

Bochner, A.P. (1991) 'The paradigm that would not die'. J. Anderson (ed.) *Communication Yearbook 14*. SAGE: Newbury Park.

Duck, S.W. (1988) *Relating to Others*. Open University Press: Milton Keynes; Dorsey/Brooks/Cole: Chicago and Monterey.

Duck, S.W. (1991) *Friends, For Life*, second edition. Harvester Wheatsheaf: Hemel Hempstead (Published in the USA as *Understanding Relationships*. Guilford: New York).

Hinde, R.A. (1979) *Towards Understanding Relationships*. Academic Press: London & New York.

Orbuch, T.L. (1991) *Relationship Loss*. Springer Verlag: New York.

CHAPTER 4

Relationships with Relations: Families and Socialization

What sort of picture comes to mind when you think of the typical family? Two youngish parents with 2.4 children driving in an average-sized car to an ordinary supermarket to buy their normal breakfast cereals, right? The advertisers love families. So do politicians. Even average people in ordinary families like typical families. There are many aspects to family functioning that fascinate researchers, too, and relationships in families – particularly as they form the basis for a child's beliefs about relationships with other people in general– raise a number of particularly interesting issues for us. There are also a host of interesting issues raised by gay and lesbian relationships (Kurdek, 1991a). In the present chapter I will confine myself to heterosexual relationships for the most part, drawing in research on gay and lesbian relationships when it is particularly informative or needs to be directly contrasted with the work on heterosexuals.

The nature of the family has been evolving through time, as most other social institutions do. Western marriages '[continue] to modify their structures and functions to accommodate changes in the larger society and its institutions' (Berardo, 1990, p. 809). The expressions of, and changes in, family forms do, however, create a few problems for their members and not all forms are ideally suited to their 'inhabitants'. It is important in considering this, to recall that kinship and membership of a family are biological and genetic relationships, but also social ones. It is the social aspect of family life that concerns us here. What is social life like in the family? Yours may or may not be typical.

Most families seem to be enjoyable and safe environments in which to live or grow up. Our adherence to the pastime of keeping family albums and family trees testifies to most people's wish to remain in a family and to see themselves as a part of it through their life. Yet there are other aspects to families, too. Outside of the armed forces, the family is the most physically violent group or

> **BOX 4.1 Points to think about**
>
> *How does the interaction of married partners influence the family that they create and how far does it depend on their courtship?*
>
> *Is it sensible to treat individuals for their problems or should we look deeper and explore their experiences in the family setting?*
>
> *How far do children's experiences with parental caretakers affect their future relationships?*
>
> *Are our later social lives predetermined by what happened in the family when we were kids, or do playground experiences at school matter also?*
>
> *Do some people stay disturbed because they stay in their family?*
>
> *Why are some children unpopular? Do they lack social skills and can that be corrected?*

institution that a typical person is likely to encounter (Straus, 1985). We are more likely to see, commit, or be a victim of violence within the family than in any other setting. We are more likely to be murdered, beaten or physically abused by our spouse, mother, father or siblings than by a random stranger (Straus, 1990; Straus & Gelles, 1986), and every year a large number of people are permanently relieved of the pressures of daily life by a family member's violent and fatal burst of rage (Eiskovits et al., 1991).

Despite the cosy family photographs in the album and all those family picnics and Christmas parties, there is also a dark side to families. Partly this is because we spend most of our time there, but it is also because of the intensities of emotion, both positive and negative, that are learned and experienced there. Also, as Berardo (1990) points out, the cosy glowing view of families, whether traditional or alternative, must be seen in the context of the *problems* that any style of family life has (some more than others, but all having some to an extent).

A recent paper (Martin & Bumpass, 1989) suggested that two-thirds of first marriages in the USA will end in divorce, with recently married cohorts predicted to have an eventually higher divorce rate than older cohorts (Kitson & Morgan, 1990). By the time they are eighteen years old, one out of every two children will experience some of their upbringing in a single-parent household (Glick, 1989). Furthermore, while the Victorian family was something of an emotional iceberg, the recent trend is towards families expected to be emotional refuges and strongholds. These shifting demands couple with new economic and social conditions to place new strains on the family as a unit. Spouses are now asked to be satisfying lovers, caring friends, and even mutual therapists in a society that forces the marriage bond to become the closest, deepest, most important and most enduring relationship in one's life. At first we might see this as a welcome development, but the increased importance has the paradoxical effect of making it more likely that the members of the family will fall short of the emotional demands placed upon them. Thus much recent research is focussing on the internal dynamics of 'the family' and how to improve them to meet the changing circumstances of social history. Such a refocussing has poured attention on the family in all its forms, for example when people begin to get interested in 'practising' it as adolescents (Miller & Moore, 1990), as it is brought into embryonic being by courtship (Surra, 1990), created in early marriage (Coombs, 1991) and sustained throughout the life course (Brubaker, 1990). The emphasis falls clearly on the *organization* of families and the ways in which emotional attachments to partners are worked out in couples' behaviour. In short, love is enough to draw people together, but they need coordinated behaviour to enmesh them and keep them together. Emotions won't do it on their own.

People who live continuously in proximity to one another will interrupt one another's goal attainments and get in each other's way frequently. We should be less surprised about the turmoils inherent in family life than we often are, especially if we see the significance of daily behaviour in the service of such goal attainments. Feminists have presented a radical critique of the family, which argues that, when it functions best, the family is the ultimate destroyer of people by social means (cf. Braverman, 1991). It draws people together through a sense of their own incompleteness, it impedes the deve-lopment of an individual's identity, it exerts too strong a social control over children, it indoctrinates family members with elaborate and unnecessary taboos. Other views are more accepting of the family and see it as a primary source of stability in society. It is true that many people find the family their greatest source of support in times of stress and their greatest comfort in life as a whole. However, the two views exist. Take a look at your own family album, and make your own choice.

Developing the bonds

From first date to marriage

Forget, for the purposes of this chapter, that marital relationships magically result from love. Here I will be pointing out how the relationship is built and made to work through everyday life behaviour – prompted by the impetus of emotion, sure enough, but certainly not as a simple consequence of it. The family usually starts with a marriage and a marriage usually begins through a courtship that is a social transition from 'being single' to 'being married' (Surra & Huston, 1987). In a sense, then, each nuclear family starts on the first date between the two partners who eventually marry, though obviously not all first dates have those consequences. From first dates to marriage is a long and sometimes rickety journey, however, clearly involving a lot of organization and work, communication, and the restructuring of the routines of personal life.

It may seem strange to start with courtship, but if we are interested in the effects of parental divorce upon the children, for instance, we need to know something about the causes of broken marriages since they may set the tone for communication in the family home – communication that the kids will see and experience. Some research is beginning to find that 'faulty' courtship predicts faulty marriages (Cate & Lloyd, 1988). It would be too simplistic to claim that all divorces are consequences of mistakes in courtship but a couple's courtship history and couple relational organization do have some relevance here (Huston, 1990).

If marriages are not made in heaven, how much of what kind of work do we have to do ourselves? Current research indicates that there are different routes, pathways or trajectories through courtship, and some of them seem to bind the couple together more effectively than do others. How do new couples organize their relationships and does it matter? Yes, particularly in long-term committed relationships, we are concerned with the ways in which partners make a good, working, living partnership – and their ability to do this in courtship is not only an indication of courtship progress but a measure of the success of the relationship (Cate & Lloyd, 1988).

You may have noticed that I headed this section 'Developing the bonds'. 'Bonds' is a metaphor that implies tying, connection – chains, even. When we talk of a 'couple' we are actually using a similar metaphor. How do people tie themselves to someone else through the restructuring of their daily routines and thus become part of one another's life? As I pointed out in Chapter 3, such routine connections are the basis of relationships that mere feelings for one another do not provide alone. There is even evidence that couples have to adjust their sleeping habits (Larson et al., 1991)! If people are classified according to their life preferences ('morning person' or 'night person') then couples with one night and one morning person have greater dissatisfaction with their relationship than do couples who match on sleeping habits.

So while feelings might start the courtship process, it is the weaving together of routines, the tango of conversation and the enmeshment of daily lives that are the creative parts of forming relationships. Initial selection of friends and marital partners may well be due simply to their attractive looks or nice qualities, but long-term acquaintance and courtship are much more complex interpersonal interactive processes.

How does courtship work?

Not all heterosexual courtships follow the same track, and important differences have been found between four basic types (Huston et al., 1981). The four distinct pathways to marriage are associated with a different pattern of partner involvement in one another's daily routines. BOX 4.2 gives details of the study and others in similar vein.

The simple feelings that partners have for one another are not necessarily a good predictor of their success at creating a sound relationship. Couples who are deeply in love may nevertheless fail to set up an effective relationship, may become frustrated at the length of time it takes to carry out courtship successfully, or may give up and either leave the relationship or marry anyway and just hope that it will all work out. Bonding takes place through time and affects the activities and routines with which the couple intertwine themselves. Those that lead to greatest satisfaction with the courtship are those in which the couple's daily lives become most fully entwined as the routines of their day get more closely interlocked (Suitor, 1991).

Working out such issues as 'who does what' will involve discussion, if not conflict, and there are good and bad kinds of conflict to have during courtship. Some conflict seems to help the relationship but some of it most decidedly does not (Lloyd & Catc, 1985). 'Good' conflicts which facilitate the courtship are those about negotiation of tasks or activities or roles in the relationship. Couples may expect to argue about who does what, who goes where how often, what I shall do for you if you do this for me, who decides

BOX 4.2 Pathways to marriage and the decision to wed

Huston et al. (1981) found 4 different pathways towards marriage. They report on the development of a premarital and marital activities checklist which assesses 3 basic domains of the relationship: affectional activities, leisure activities, and instrumental activities such as household chores. They also developed a graphing procedure by means of which they could track the paths taken by couples towards marriage: essentially they asked married couples to think back over their courtship and indicate the points where they noted changes in their confidence that they would eventually marry. The resulting graphs identify 4 courtship types:

1 Accelerated-arrested *begins with a high level of confidence in the probability of marriage, but slows down in its final progression to marital commitment.*
2 Accelerated *starts off more slowly than type 1, but proceeds smoothly and directly to certainty of eventual marriage.*
3 Intermediate *evolves quite slowly and gradually, with the most turbulence and difficulty occurring at the last stages.*
4 Prolonged *courtships develop slowly and uncertainly, with much turbulence and difficulty.*

Partners in the intermediate courtships are the most independent of one another, particularly as regards feelings and joint actions (i.e. the so-called affectional and instrumental domains). They show less affection and joint activity. Partners in prolonged courtships report less affectional activity and lower proportions of leisure activities done together. Accelerated courtships are characterized by close affiliations and high, strong levels of liking, but partners are not necessarily more cohesive or bonded together when it comes to activities and time shared with other people.

Couples in the different types of courtship give different styles of explanation for why the relationship developed at given turning points (or why they were seen to be turning points).

For committed relationships, partners give a higher percentage of explanations in dyadic rather than circumstantial terms (Surra, 1984), that is, they say they get together because they want to rather than because of circumstances, chance, or things over which they have no personal control. Surra et al. (1988) have also shown that partners who get committed rapidly tend to be those who explain commitment in terms of their own personal norms and standards, but dramatic upturns in commitment are explained in terms of

> dyadic *effects, such as joint realization of something about the rela-*
> *tionship and its meaning for each partner.*
>
> *Partners give more dyadic reasons for upturns in the probability*
> *of marriage ('we both were keener on it'), but more individual*
> *reasons for breaking off a relationship themselves ('I became bored';*
> *'my partner found someone else'), according to Lloyd & Cate*
> *(1985).*
>
> *Patterns of conflict and activity management in courtship predict*
> *stability in the marriage several years later (Kelly et al., 1985).*
> *Specifically, couples with high conflict in courtship do not seem to*
> *learn to handle it any better and continue to be highly conflictive*
> *in later marriage. But, as Zimmer (1986) indicates, the prospect of*
> *marriage causes strong anxieties about the stability and success of*
> *the marriage, with partners getting cold feet and going through a*
> *turbulent phase just at, or after, the point where they have decided*
> *to get married. Often couples doubt the possibility of being able to*
> *have both security and excitement in the same relationship.*

who does what, and the like. By sorting out these issues, even if it causes a few arguments at first, the couple is actually binding itself together more effectively as the two separate individuals start to function as a social unit. So those kinds of conflict (and their resolution) can be helpful. Those that are not helpful are the ones that centre on incongruent goals or inconsistency of desired outcome in the relationship. If we argue about the nature of the relationship (e.g. whether it is to be a marriage vs friendship) rather than who does what in it and how it should be organized, then we are in trouble.

If partners handle these aspects of their courtship successfully, they lay the foundations for handling them successfully in the later marriage where tasks and duties shift and new problems occur (e.g. during the transition to parenthood: Lips & Morrison, 1986). The effects of conflicts or unresolved negotiations at this stage do not always show up until later into the relationship (Markman et al., 1988). Even serious conflicts in a courtship do not necessarily prevent couples from carrying on and developing the relationship, but these conflicts predict dissatisfaction with the marriage five years later (Kelly et al., 1985). The important lessons for us, then, are to do with the manner of constructing properly interactive daily lives, communicating about the issues and routines there, and interactively conducting the relationship. These interpersonal communicative ventures are fundamentally more important than any simple, and essentially abstract, 'psychological structures'.

Managing sexual activity in courtship

One difficult aspect of courtship is the question of sexual behaviour. In this context, too, there are different paths to follow and Christopher & Cate (1985) identify four typical pathways towards sexual intimacy, as indicated in BOX 4.3.

Sexual behaviour can be a source of pleasure and mutual satisfaction in a couple, but it has to be 'managed'. Questions arise as to frequency, initiation, context, and type of sexual activity agreed or permitted in the relationship. How often should it occur? Should it grow only from mutual desire or may either partner initiate it? What styles and variations are acceptable? Who is allowed to say 'No' and what does that mean? Such matters are negotiable, and lots of conflict in the creation of a couple centres on these negotiations and behaviours (Christopher & Cate, 1985).

Couples often find that they are arguing about (or, at least, discussing) sexual matters as both the relationship and their expectations develop. Satisfaction with the level of sexual activity is usually closely matched with overall satisfaction in the relationship. Conversely, sexual dissatisfaction is a major source of unhappiness in marriage, leading to arguments and extramarital affairs (Buunk & Bringle, 1987). However, nothing is ever simple and couples therapists sometimes see couples who have a great sex life but who have little else in common. The important element in these cases, as in the sexually dissatisfied couples, is that the 'organization' of the couple or relationship is out of tune in some important dimension, possibly because the couple does not talk to one another often enough about their relationship (Acitelli, 1988).

Getting the relationship organized

Thus far, we have learned more about the relatively obvious points that: families, marriages and courtship have a history; the different parts of the history have to be established and organized by communication, agreement and negotiation; and they are quite likely to influence one another. The family, the marriage and the courtship involve at least two of the same persons. The different labels that are applied to that pair of people ('courtship', 'marriage') mean that only some parts of the relationship are new or different at each turning point. The partners are the same, though, and live life in many of the same old ways throughout. For this reason, many of the same sorts of issue and problem recur for the couple throughout that interconnected history from courtship to marriage (and, maybe, to divorce).

BOX 4.3 Pathways to sexual intimacy
(Christopher & Cate, 1985)
There are 4 different pathways to sexual intimacy through the stages of (a) first date, (b) casual dating, (c) considering becoming an exclusive couple, to (d) partners seeing themselves as an established couple:

- Rapid involvement. *Such couples begin their sexual interaction at a high level during the early stages of dating, often having intercourse on the first date.*
- Gradual involvement. *These couples are characterized by a slow incrementation of sexual activity from first date to the 'couple' stage with orgasmically oriented sexual interaction starting typically at the stage when the couple begins contemplating becoming 'a couple'.*
- Delayed involvement. *Such couples are characterized by a gradual incrementation that nonetheless starts from a level lower than that of gradually involved couples. Sexual intercourse is typically delayed until after the couple see themselves as 'a couple', at which time there is a dramatic rise in the average level of sexual involvement and in varieties of sexual activity.*
- Low involvement. *Such couples start at a minimal level of sexual involvement on first date, and, by the time they become 'a couple', they are still at a preorgasmic level of sexual intimacy.*

Rapidly involved couples report high conflict but also high levels of love at the early stages, and, for the other types, increases in sexual involvement are associated with increases in both conflict and love.

Christopher & Frandsen (1990) examined the different sexual influence strategies used by premarital partners and found four general strategies: antisocial acts *(ridicule, insult, guilt manipulation, threat, for instance);* emotional and physical closeness *(expressing love, claiming that relationship with the partner is special, flattery, hints, for instance);* logic and reason *(claiming to be knowledgeable about appropriate levels of sexual involvement; compromise on level, persuasive arguments, for instance);* pressure and manipulation *(using drugs or alcohol, manipulating mood, talking fast and telling white lies, for example). The authors suggested that the different strategies have different impacts on the development of relationships.*

Therefore, a marriage is influenced not only by the endogenous (or 'internal') factors (e.g. how the two partners progress in interactions, communicate, feel about one another at a given time) but by some exogenous (or 'external') factors that do not arise specifically in interactions (e.g. the relational history). There are other exogenous factors, such as societal views about the ideal forms of relationships. When partners are married, they become a socially recognized unit ('the couple'; 'the happy couple', even), and the rest of us often treat them as one 'entity' that is invited everywhere together (by only one invitation, as opposed to individually), expected to do things together, has the same address, television and social status.

Relationships become organized and take on many of the properties and qualities of other organizations, such as shared history, private jokes and languages, distribution of labour and a sense of belonging, as we saw in Chapter 3 (McCall, 1982). These are additional to the feelings that the partners have for one another, but they are just as important (Kirchler, 1988). Relationships can succeed or fail as much because they become disorganized as because the partners stop liking one another as people (Suitor, 1991). In perhaps unwitting ways, we have all heard people complain about relational organization, and it is not all about chores or division of labour. The relationship has to have an emotional organization too; for example, 'The relationship was too intense' or 'The relationship wasn't going anywhere' or 'We liked one another, but the relationship just didn't work out'.

The formation of the bonded unit, or married couple, has to be handled in its own right, and this often proves difficult. The couple's attempt to 'become a socially recognized unit' is not an automatic consequence of their liking, and they have to work at it and handle it. Even the honeymoon has this kind of role (Hagestad & Smyer, 1982): it helps the couple make the important transition between one couple type (engaged) and another (married). Immediately after being formally joined by the marriage, the couple go away from all the friends and relatives who knew them as 'unjoined' individuals. When they return, they return as a couple, and the honeymoon period has given everyone the chance to adjust to the transformation.

Equally, the transition to parenthood is an important time of adjustment for the married couple, both in attitude and in distribution of time, activities and the ways in which they view themselves and each other (Lips & Morrison, 1986). It is particularly associated with an increased focus on family issues, and I noticed that when they were expecting a first child, many of my friends developed an interest in tracing their family tree, just as I did in the same circumstances. One gets a sense of belonging to a larger historical enterprise. So the transition to parenthood is a developmental process not only in obvious ways in respect of the family organization but also in less obvious ways in respect of the parents themselves and their view of the world and themselves.

The ways in which the relationships is worked out and organized in transitions, such as courtship and parenthood, will eventually affect the way the marriage and the family work out.

The working family

Marriage: who does what?

Major factors that influence a couple's satisfaction are exogenous to the relationship, as noted earlier. They come from outside and are not part of its workings or of the feelings that the partners have for each other. Such factors could be, for instance, knowledge of the average statistics for frequency of sexual intercourse, which may affect the partners' views of whether they are behaving 'normally'. More important examples come from societal definitions of the 'proper' distribution of labour in marriage.

If a society generally believes that the 'good husband' carries out certain duties whilst the 'good wife' performs other quite distinct duties, then the couple who arrange things that way will feel that their marriage is ideal in this respect (Allan, 1989). But if the society generally expects both partners to share all duties equally, then the same couple (or one member of it) will feel aggrieved and dissatisfied. The difference in the two cases is not the actual work or duties carried out but the context of attitudes in which they are carried out (Allan, 1989). What counts as a perfectly acceptable distribution of labour in the 1990s bears no resemblance to that in the ideal marriage in the 1890s. Couples from the two times who felt perfectly contented would probably look on each other's marriages with disbelief and even shock.

Part of the feeling that a marriage is working well depends on what the partners expect, and expectations can come partly from the beliefs that society has about marriages (Sabatelli & Pearce, 1986). Partners can see how their marriage matches up to society's ideals for the relationship. If they see themselves carrying out their roles well, then they will be satisfied. Dissatisfaction can be created by partners' feelings that their relationship does not live up to the societal ideal (Storm, 1991). Most of us are guided in our feelings and behaviour by some such influences, but some people actually take the lead almost entirely from social norms. Norms show people where they stand and increase their satisfaction with the relationship since norms make it easier for people to know what is required of them.

Exogenous factors matter as much as the factors we usually assume to be significant (i.e. the endogenous or emotional factors), in marital satisfaction. The partners' feelings for one another, communication style and relative power are examples of endogenous factors. The three (feeling, style and power) really represent one and the same thing: expression of affection is done through communication, and power is a communicative concept, too. When we talk of power in a relationship, we are describing partly the way in which one person's communications affect the other person and partly the way in which that other person responds. As Kelvin (1977) points out, power does not 'reside in' a person: you do not have power unless someone else treats you as if you do. Power is thus a relational concept and depends on the acceptance of a person's power ploys by the person to whom they are directed. Even in the case of violent abuse, the abused partner, who may appear to have to accept whatever the abuser does, has the choice of leaving the relationship or accepting the abuse. In most cases this is not a very real choice and certainly not a simple one, but it is ultimately the circumstance upon which the abuser's power depends (Mayseless, 1991).

Communication and satisfaction

How does this all impact on a couple? When one person acts and the other responds in a couple, they have accommodated, or adapted, to one another. Dyads, or pairs of people, communicating to one another do accommodate in various ways (outlined in Chapter 1). Couples communicate in terms of their ability to resolve conflicts, express affection for one another, be open in self-disclosure of thoughts and feelings, and the like. Satisfaction is related to these communicational variables, and the primary predictor of marital satisfaction and dissatisfaction is the communication that occurs between partners. Most forms of communication between partners are reciprocal or couple-based, which, we have seen, is true of power. Acitelli (1988), as noted above, found that relationship talk influences couples' perceptions of, and feelings about, the relationship. In general, the more a couple talks about the relationship, the more satisfaction they feel about the relationship. It is, however, atypical for husbands to do much talking about the relationship, especially when it is going well.

Therefore, the communication style of the couple should be far more important for their satisfaction and success than, say, demographic background and the personality matching of the partners are. In any case, the social meaning of any personality characteristic comes from the way that 'personality' is operated by the communicative behaviour of the persons (Duck, 1977). For many years, sterile debates took place about the role of similarity or oppositeness (i.e. complementarity) of personality in predicting success of marriages. But these abstract personality variables do not predict marital happiness: happiness is predicted by the concrete ways in which personality variables manifest themselves in practice through communication. Recent research has focussed less on the original choice of partners and more on the processes by which partners *become* partners (Berardo, 1990).

The different styles of communication in marriage

Are there different types of communication in marriage? Fitzpatrick (1977; Dindia & Fitzpatrick, 1985; Fitzpatrick & Badzinski, 1985) has developed a typology of marriage based on differences in communicative style. In the typology, there are three basic definitions which apply to individuals and thence to couples: traditional, independent and separate.

In a *traditional* couple, communication is characterized by interdependence and expressiveness, and each person has conventional views about marriage and family life. Such persons seek regularity in their use of time, prefer stability to change, and confront rather than avoid conflicts, but they do so with some degree of social restraint. Such persons intertwine their life with their partner, release their emotions in limited ways, and are traditional in outlook.

Independent persons are only moderately interdependent in their marriage and have nonconventional views about marriage and family life, but, more so than Traditional persons, are very expressive in communications with their spouse. They share and confront conflicts, preferring to be frank, open and unrestrained by social factors, but they like to explore novelty and change in marriage.

BOX 4.4 **Marital satisfaction and communication**

Happy couples give more positive nonverbal cues than do unhappy couples (Rubin, 1977).

Distressed couples, relative to non-distressed ones, attribute their partner's behaviour to enduring, stable traits (Fincham & Bradbury, 1989).

Happy couples express more agreement and approval for the other person's ideas and suggestions (Birchler, 1972).

Alberts (1988) showed that adjusted couples were more likely than maladjusted ones to voice their complaints about the other person's behaviour, and to express positive affect when doing so. Maladjusted couples tended to voice personal character complaints, to display negative affect and to countercomplain when the partner voiced dissatisfaction.

Satisfied couples confirm and support one another whilst dissatisfied ones reject and disconfirm one another – not only in respect of verbal statements but even in their very existence, often making statements that seem to imply 'You are nothing to me'; 'You do not exist for me'; 'Your comments and opinions do not matter to me'; 'I don't care' (Watzlawick et al., 1967).

Happier couples talk more about their relationship, and couples with high satisfaction are ones where husbands tend to talk more about the relationship (Acitelli, 1988).

Happy couples are more willing to reach compromises on difficult decisions (Birchler, 1972).

Happy couples express agreement more often than they express disagreement with the spouse during problem-solving or conflict (Gottman, 1979; Riskin & Faunce, 1972).

Happy couples are more consistent in their displays of nonverbal affect (Noller, 1982).

Cupach & Comstock (1990) found that sexual satisfaction in marriage was strongly associated with satisfaction about sexual communication.

Distressed couples are more likely to reciprocate negative communications than are happy couples (Gottman et al., 1977), and happy couples are more likely to reciprocate positive communications than are unhappy couples (Gottman, 1989).

Separate persons are not particularly interdependent, have ambivalent views about marriage and family life and are not at all expressive in their communications with their spouse. They emphasize autonomy, differentiation of space, emotional distance and avoidance of conflict.

From these three basic definitions for married individuals, we can obviously make nine possible couple types (3 possible husband types x 3 possible wife types). In the three cases where husband and wife are both the same, Fitzpatrick speaks of the relationship as a pure type (traditional, independent, separate), and some 60 percent of couples are like this. The remaining 40 percent are distributed across the remaining six mixed types of relationship. The types have been found in work in the USA and also in Australia (Noller & Hiscox, 1989), although in the latter work the Traditional couples were renamed 'Connected', since the key element in their case seemed to be connectedness rather than any constellation of traditional beliefs about marriage, the distinguishing feature in the US samples (Fitzpatrick, 1988).

There are different relationships between communication styles, or patterns, and satisfaction with marriage, depending on the type of marriage – particularly in the pure types (Noller & Fitzpatrick, 1990). Independent couples are more likely to enjoy informational exchanges (self-disclosure, descriptions and discussion of conflict, etc.), and so they are more likely to be satisfied with an open, frank and direct marriage that would be a source of great dissatisfaction to a separate couple (Sillars et al., 1983). Separates are satisfied by denial of conflict or by refocussing on to other issues that serve to avoid conflict rather than to explore it. Thus conflict avoidance is more satisfying to separates than to independents. Satisfaction, then, is not necessarily created by any particular style of communication, per se: different couple types are satisfied with different types of communication style.

Satisfaction and behaviour

Relational behaviours predict satisfaction and create the inter-connectedness of different parts of the courtship/marital history of a couple. Even if disembodied personality variables are used to explain or predict satisfaction, the most recent thinking in marital relationships has now also come round to the view that personality works through its expressive and communicative functions (Fincham & Bradbury, 1989). Communicative and negotiative work is necessary to forge the bonds that turn pairs of 'starry-eyed' individuals into a satisfactory, socially recognized unit. Enduring aspects of the relationship are the expressive behaviours, and these continue through courtship to marriage – and into the family that follows. Kurdek (1989) reports, in a one-year follow-up study, that those couples who experience the greatest distress are those who prepare inadequately for the demands of married life and that an important factor influencing satisfaction is the way in which couples evaluate their interactions and communication.

A couple's communication influences their level of satisfaction and also affects the atmosphere in the rest of the family they have. If courting partners mesh their routine together, they improve the chance of working out ways to deal with new relational routines that become necessary (e.g. coping with the birth of children). Kelly et al. (1985) studied couples before marriage and then followed them up after their marriage to see whether features detected during courtship were predictive of marital stability, and, if so, which ones. Make your own predictions and then check them out below.

What is a good premarital predictor of marital stability? It is the ability to deal with conflict in the time before marriage (Kelly et al., 1985), which is a communicative factor rather than an individual one. On the other hand, ineffective nonverbal communication is associated with marital dissatisfaction (Pike & Sillars, 1985), and nonverbal cues provide a context for verbal communications. Nonverbal affective patterns (i.e. showing affection by smiling, touching, etc.) are more important than verbal disclosure and explicit verbal attempts to avoid conflict. Gottman (1991) has concluded that couples' interaction patterns early in the relationship predict problems later and this is evident even in videotapes where the sound has been turned off and when all you can observe is nonverbal communication!

Obviously, such work as the above helps marriage (and premarital) counsellors trying to prevent marital problems. Their effort is to try and create in courtship a stable basis for the subsequent marriage over and above the intention to increase the couple's satisfaction with their courtship. Some couples, for instance, volunteer for 'enrichment programmes' without feeling that their relationship is in serious difficulties; they merely want to get more out of it in the present or future (Ridley & Nelson, 1984). Nonetheless, Markman (1981) shows that the more positively couples rated each other's communication during negotiation exercises, the more satisfied they were with their relationship later on (both two and a half years and five years later on). This was so even when the degree of positivity/negativity of communications was not related to partner's satisfaction at the time when the assessments were initially made. In other words, partners' future satisfaction is

---

BOX 4.5 Couple behaviour and communication

Zietlow & Sillars (1988) compared the characteristics of communication in younger, middle-aged and older couples and found that retired couples tended to be the least analytic and least conflictive in their communications. Middle-aged couples were also non-conflictive on the whole but when they detected 'issues' they tended to analyse them hard. Young couples were much more analytic and confrontative but also used humour during conflict.

Pike & Sillars (1985) found that less satisfied couples had more negative reciprocity in their communication than did more satisfied couples, and that satisfied couples tended to avoid conflict rather than confront it. They also found that nonverbal behaviour seems to have a fairly generally accepted meaning but that the verbal communications of couples are more personalized in their meaning and interpretation.

In a general study of conflict strategies, Canary & Spitzberg (1989) found that there are distinct advantages to using 'integrative strategies' based on attempts to resolve conflict and to compromise, rather than blind assertion of one's own position.

Noller (e.g. Noller, 1982; Noller & Hiscox, 1989; Noller & Venardos, 1986) has consistently shown that unhappy couples (especially the husbands in such couples) tend to have poor reading of one another's NVC (see Chapter 1).

---

predictable from how they feel about present communication patterns, even though they do not notice this predictive relationship at the time (Gottman & Krokoff, in press).

So we could begin to see that families are made in marriages, marriages are made in courtships, and maybe courtships are made in activities, casual talk, communication and routines. What background do the partners' activities create for their future relationship as a family? Who 'does best' out of marriage, men or women?

Marriage as a background for the person's life

Men benefit more in the traditional marriage. Over sixty-five years ago, men reported being more satisfied with their marriage than their wives were, and women were more seriously disappointed (Hamilton, 1924). Marriage, or the status of 'being married', tends to be associated in men with decreased rates of suicide and a higher health status, even very recently (Glenn & Weaver, 1988; Kurdek, 1991b).

Although, compared to women, men are more liable to heart problems, ulcers and earlier death, the rates for married men are lower than those for single men and so are rates of depression, alcohol abuse and drug problems. We might immediately think of one criticism of these points: perhaps it is the healthier men who are able to attract spouses in the first place, so that figures are unfairly inflated. Maybe; but that idea is based on the same mistake the attraction literature made in assuming that the 'entry qualifications', such as personality profile, set the relationship for ever. As we saw in Chapter 3, it is unwise to ignore the behaviours of acquainting since these affect the relationships, too. Equally, we can expect the behaviours in marriage to be more important than the initial entry qualifications, like health and good looks. Maybe we have to be healthy to increase our chance of marrying, but good health does not guarantee that the marriage will 'work'.

Men suffer more severely from the consequences of death of the spouse or from disruption of their marriage by separation or divorce (Stroebe & Stroebe, 1983). Bereaved husbands suffer higher rates of sudden death and severe health difficulties following the death of their wife than women do after the death of their husband. The period of separation or divorce from a wife, children and family is particularly stressful for men (Kurdek, 1989) and a whole retinue of health problems ensues, ranging from tonsillitis to heart disease (Bloom et al., 1978). The existence of a marriage is good for men and its loss is bad for them.

Relationships with women actually correlate with good health (Reis, 1986) and the more women we meet in the day, the healthier we feel, although the most recent work (Duck et al., 1991b) suggests that the nature, features and quality of the *everyday talk* of women are the elements that create greater satisfaction with their interactions. It is understandable, then, that a husband gets benefits from marriage that the wife does not obtain within the marriage, but may obtain from talking to her female friends. Certainly, the wife does more of the work, with studies showing that the wife is often working while the husband is relaxing, but the husband is also relaxing when the wife relaxes (Clarke et al., 1985). More than this, the wife is likely to do an average of nine hours of work per week more than the husband (Rexroat & Shehan, 1987).

What can we deduce from those facts? Perhaps they show the deficiency of marriage for women; or, perhaps, they show the positive effects of marriage for men. At present one has to decide this issue for oneself. However, it points out that the emotional investments of family members in a marriage are unequal and so are the needs for each of the family members. In traditional marriages the 'resources' are often unfairly distributed, in that one partner (the husband) has more extensive control over them than does the other (the wife), and the wife is more likely to be expected to give up her 'self' to become part of the couple, including losing her career and her name, and moving with his job, so losing day-to-day contact with her friends (Suitor, 1991). We should bear this in mind whilst recalling that power is a relational construct that depends not just on control of resources but on control of information, communication style, and various 'couple variables' already discussed.

These differences in power, needs, investments and outcomes are important for the two adult members obviously, but are also relevant when we take a broader look at the family and include the children. Children have low power in families; they are subject to control by parents; yet their relationship with parents can act as a model for their own relationships with other people later in life.

Caretakers and children

There has been enough thinking about the impact of parental upbringing on 'life chances' for truisms to have reached the popular media as far back as the 1950s (e.g. 'Hey! I'm depraved on account I'm deprived' in *West Side Story*). Such truisms stem in part from the important pioneering work of Bowlby (1951), who claimed that an infant's relationship with the main caretaker, traditionally the mother, is predictive of later adolescent relational success. In brief, Bowlby's claim is that an infant separated from the mother developed psychological complexes that impaired subsequent relationships and could lead to delinquency in adolescence and adulthood.

It is accepted as common sense nowadays that the infant needs a steady relationship with loving, significant adults, even though Bowlby's work was revolutionary in its time. How often have we heard people say that their relationship with their parents is responsible for later life events? But do they mean to blame a relationship that happened before they could even speak? Do we really believe that people turn into delinquents just because their relationship with their mother was inadequate for four to six months?

This work has been seriously questioned (Rutter, 1972). One problem is that the 'maternal deprivation hypothesis' seems to assume that the most important events are those in the first twelve months of life and that everything that happens between the ages of one year and thirteen years does not have much effect. Instead, recent work urges us to look at the activities that occur during the rest of childhood, and the impact on the child's social life of its view of itself as a social being (Berndt & Ladd, 1989). Self-esteem influences our views of our attractiveness and so has a major effect on our relationships. So, let us take a good look at the experiences in the family which affect self-esteem and give us the basis for our relationship with other human beings.

The specific variable of parental style of control in a family not only can affect the child directly but can provide a model for the child's subsequent social relationships (Hinde, 1989). It lays out foundations for future relationships through its effect on the child's self-image. Fitzpatrick & Badzinski (1985) conclude that 'there is little doubt that making a child feel loved, supported and comfortable in the presence of a parent leads to the development of a large range of socially valued behaviours in the child'. As you may recall from Chapter 2, the same set of arguments is offered by Shaver & Hazan (1988).

There are essentially three styles in which parents treat children (Baumrind, 1972). The *authoritarian parents* try to control and evaluate the behaviour of a child using some absolute standards of behaviour. They stress obedience and punishment – often physical punishment but this also frequently takes the form of withdrawal of love or psychological blackmail. Secondly, *permissive parents* relate to the child's behaviour in nonpunitive and accepting ways, often consulting the child about its behaviour, offering rationales for the standards that are used, and relying on reason rather than punishment in child-rearing. Finally, an *authoritative style* is one based on direction of the child through reason but not on the basis of equality nor, necessarily, of acceptance of what the child is doing. Such a parent exercises firm control, but does so by verbal interchange and communication rather than physical force. This style of parenting is more successful in producing children who are independent, cooperative, friendly and achievement-oriented, and is generally the style recommended by family therapists.

These different styles affect the happiness and character development of the child and also provide different models for the child's own perception of the world and relationships between people. A child who is taught by example to be obedient to adults or authority figures is more likely to become authoritarian in relationships with superiors and inferiors (Adorno et al., 1950).

The different parental styles probably indicate differences in parental attitudes to one another also and are not simple products of parents' personalities. For example, reconsider Fitzpatrick's (1988) system of classifying married couples into traditionals, separates and independents, and note that as a classification system it contains some 'echoes' of the Baumrind model. This is so despite the fact that Fitzpatrick dealt with partners' communications with one another, whilst Baumrind looked at parents' communications with their children.

For a style to develop in a family, it has to be created, negotiated and shared. When the two parents have different approaches to child-rearing, we can expect to find problems for the child and the parents. For instance, a child is likely to become confused by inconsistencies (although this could itself be useful training for life, where inconsistencies are a far more frequent experience – in both ourselves and other people – than we might prefer to believe). Equally, two parents with different approaches are increasing the risks of their coming into conflict with one another, thus causing family distress which itself is likely to upset the child in question. Finally, inconsistencies of parental treatment between one child and another are sources of both family tension and personal anguish for that child who feels aggrieved or neglected.

An unsatisfactory, or dysfunctional, style of bonding in the family takes five forms:

1 The negative side of things is accentuated (i.e. there is a critical, punitive style focussing on poor performances rather than praising good ones).

2 The parents are poor observers of their children's behaviour and do not make good discriminations between different performances of the same acts (e.g. they may not notice slight improvements, may take little note of the amount of effort put into achieving the outcome, etc.).

3 The parents are highly inconsistent in their use of punishment, sometimes ignoring transgressions altogether but at other times inflicting dire retribution.

4 The parents establish low levels of positive contact; that is, they do not act particularly warmly or affectionately to the child in general and certainly do not go out of their way to do so.

5 The emphasis of their relationship to the child is on power, force and coercion. In this context, the model they present is one that tends to reward the child for being aggressive.

Such behaviours probably confuse the child and cause stress not least because of the child's lowly place in the scheme of things. Most of those dysfunctional behaviours have the obvious effect of devaluing the child, and, at early ages, it would be surprising if this did not lead to a paralysingly low self-esteem (Duck, 1991). If this occurs, we would be likely to find the child experiencing difficulties in other relationships because:

(a) the child has no reliable models of how to conduct good relationships;

(b) the child has a low opinion of his or her own social value to other people.

Problem children in nursery schools (aged 3–5 years), are of three basic types (Manning & Herrman, 1981):

Aggressive: such children present management problems for the teachers and are dominating, rough, defiant, and spontaneously violent;

Dependent: these children are anxious to please, are demanding of teachers, want everything done for them, and are timid with other children;

Withdrawn: these children do not enter games with the others but keep to themselves, often looking on longingly at the other children playing.

We cannot derive each of these styles directly from one particular parental style, but the possibility remains that some connection exists and, as we saw in Chapter 2, researchers such as Hazan & Shaver (1987) and Bartholomew (1990) have attempted to draw some parallels between childhood attachments and adult attachment styles, while Newcomb (1990) has extended similar notions to all forms of human attachment. As I have suggested, the dependent or withdrawn child may have developed low self-esteem coupled with fear of other people whilst an aggressive child may come from a home where aggression is rewarded or where parents are aggressive or abusive to one another and so act as models for the child's own style.

Of course one also needs to take into account the style not only of the parent but also of others in the family and also of the composition of the family itself. Rarely is there 'a family' that is a simple model and representation of all other families. A family is made up of many interacting and reacting systems and subsystems that do not interact in equivalent ways. For example one parent may prefer Child A and treat Child B less well; that difference in itself may influence the behaviour of each child as a growing individual and of each child towards the other. It may impact upon the development of each child's self-esteem as well as its interactions with the other parent. As another example, if one child in a family has a disability, then this may cause the parents to behave differently towards the other children in the family, and if the disability is severe the other children may get very little attention at all. Finally, parents are obviously not the only models for children; they are also exposed to the behaviours of grandparents, aunts and uncles, teachers and siblings, to say nothing of friends' parents and their friends themselves. A family is more than a pair of parents, and a child's world is increasingly made up of more than just the family anyway. Nonetheless, the family remains a major source of the child's learning about human relationships, both through its experiences in the family and its observation of the family.

Happy families?

How can we assess the quality of the family and its success?

We could ask whether the family accomplishes major family goals, whether the organization of the family violates societal principles, and whether the family contains a 'diseased' member. Riskin & Faunce (1972) once claimed that the least studied family unit is the family itself. Most work that claims to explore 'the family' actually explores particular dyads or pairs within the family, such as the marital pair, the mother–child pair, the father–child pair, or the sibling-pair (Fitzpatrick & Badzinski, 1985).

By considering the family all together, we can see the ways in which the parts influence one another. For example, we could bring families to the laboratory to discuss a problem or engage in a task that obliges them to interact whilst the experimenter records and then transcribes the interaction for later analysis (Yerby et al., 1990). As one instance of this, some clinical therapies have an exercise where the family gets together to work out a family tree or genogram and the therapist takes note of 'who knows what' as well as looking for recurring patterns in the family or in the respondents' descriptions of the family. For example, a person may be in a family where the 'father' is typically (i.e. in several generations has been) many more years older than the mother than is the norm, and the patients' brothers may all have married much younger women than usual.

When we look at families in this way, we usually find that abnormal children or adolescents (say, aggressive, delinquent or schizophrenic individuals) come from families in which positive, nurturant and encouraging or supportive behaviours are either less frequent than normal or else excessive and stifling, such that the child feels smothered and wants to do something to escape. For this reason, argumentative, noxious, negative, primitive or aggressive interactions are much more frequent in such families than are normal interactions (Fitzpatrick & Badzinski, 1985). This may occur because negative parents serve as poor models for their children, who may not only learn wrong behaviours from them but also develop many negative feelings towards them and towards other authority figures. More likely, children affect parents, too, so that disruptive children cause disruptive responses from parents.

Who causes an individual's problems?

'Individuals have problems and individuals should be treated for them' was, and in some places still is, the usual motto when a person developed aberrant behaviour, such as alcohol problems, drug abuse, depression or schizophrenia. That the person could be not only an individual but also a man or woman, a husband or wife, a sibling, a daughter or son tended to be given lesser importance.

In many cases, such a view may be quite right, and it would be correct to conclude that the social context for psychological problems is not necessarily important. If a person is depressed because he or she cannot establish relationships with other people, then his or her personal lack of social skills may be far more important than the family background (Duck, 1991) – although we may enquire whether the deficiency in such skills results from experiences within the family. What is needed in such cases could be simply an individualized training programme in social skills, focussing on the kinds of nonverbal and verbal communication that are covered in Chapter 1.

However, it is faulty to assume that a person's problems have an individualized locus without taking the necessary scientific steps to ensure that the social and domestic context is irrelevant (Feldman & Orford, 1980). A social context can 'cause' the problem (e.g. in a family where interaction is usually negative and causes much stress). On the other hand, it may just reinforce an existing problem (e.g. when one partner in a relationship is dependent on drugs or alcohol and members of the family are happiest, in some sense, when the person is calmed or stupefied by the substance).

Relationships and depression

Depression is a good example of an 'individual' problem that can have a basis in relationships. Relationships can both cause depression and reinforce it since other members of the family tend to treat the depressed member in a stilted, spurious or 'careful' way (Coyne, 1987), which in itself may reinforce the person's sense of insecurity and fragility. This can make depression become a self-perpetuating interpersonal system: all persons in the environment end up creating a system where feedback cannot be received or given properly. The depressed person keeps getting misleading feedback that says 'You're not normal', but no one does anything to help. The behaviour system thus only maintains the problem. Gotlib & Hooley (1988, p. 560) note that

> all is not well within the marital relationships of depressed persons. Their interactions are characterized by poor communication, negative affect, friction, tension, overt and covert hostility, and a tendency for positive verbal messages to be delivered with negative nonverbal affect. Moreover, disturbed marital relationships have been found not only to precede the onset of depressive episodes, but to be associated with the course of the depression and, in some cases, to persist following symptomatic recovery. . . . There is also evidence that depressed individuals interact more politely and positively with strangers than they do with their spouses, suggesting that their communication deficits may be particularly exacerbated when interacting with intimates.

– or that they have more control over their behaviour than they realize!

Once more, then, we are led back to the crucial point that *communication* (within families or friendships) is critical to the functioning of relationships and also of persons. To the extent that psychological variables influence individuals in relationships, they do so through communication about those variables, communication about everyday life, or communication styles that reflect those psychological characteristics.

Communication, as I have been discussing, is *essentially* a relational notion and we should note therefore that communication with specific individuals is not necessarily the same and does not necessarily provide the same resources as does communication with other specific individuals (Duck et al., 1991b). For example, combining what we learned above with what we learned in Chapter 3 about self-disclosure, we might expect that self-disclosure in specific relationships will help with depression. That is what has been found. A woman's characteristic pattern of social relationships could act to increase her vulnerability to depression (Brown & Harris, 1978). Absence of close confiding relationship with a husband or boyfriend is associated with higher risk of developing depression after a big loss or major disappointment. It looks as if a poor social relationship network – or, rather, absence of confiding relationships – is a major 'vulnerability factor'; it deprives people of the armour with which to defend themselves against severe blows or disappointments in life (Brown, 1984; O'Connor & Brown, 1984). In the absence of such blows and disappointments, the vulnerability is insignificant on its own; it is only when the person is 'stretched' and tested that the problem cannot be well handled.

An individual level of analysis is not necessarily wrong in all cases (e.g. some forms of depression result from metabolic disturbance in the person: Johnson, 1984). However, we must take account of human relational issues in the equation, particularly those that amount to concern over communication, especially when the nature of the problem creates relational consequences.

Family problems and family relationships

Family problems, communication problems, and interpersonal relationships usually go hand in hand (Burgess, 1981). The variables most associated with life-satisfaction are relational variables like marital happiness rather than, say, socioeconomic factors like income level. Equally and conversely, conflict and individual deviancy are directly 'traceable to contingency histories located within the family itself' (Burgess, 1981). In other words, we are happy when family relationships are going well, but we, and probably other people too, develop side-effects when things go wrong. Such side-effects can be as simple as stress or as complicated as physical and psychological conditions which appear to be totally unrelated to the family problem. Relational difficulties are suspected to underlie, for instance, anorexia nervosa, cancer, heart disease, and even sudden death (Lynch, 1987).

Let us, for the moment, look at a couple of detailed instances where family relationships appear to be influential in creation and extension of social problems (BOX 4.6 gives more instances). Such cases help us to see that when an individual has problems we should, at least, look at the domestic, social and relational context of that individual. We may find nothing, or we may see the root of the problem.

BOX 4.6 Family relationships and social, personal or physical problems

Some persons show depressive symptoms that are intended for a specific audience, that is, members in the family (McPartland & Hornstra, 1964). If someone withdraws, shows irritability and agitation in a family setting, it is difficult for the family members to ignore. It disrupts the social functioning of the family as the depressives' attempts to throw the burden of their problems on to other people become more strident and obscure.

Unhappily married people, relative to the divorced or happily married, showed more neurosis, depression, chronic illness and disability (Renne, 1971).

Men who felt unsupported by their wives were more likely to suffer physical and psychological disturbances after an involuntary job loss (Gore, 1978). Specifically, they showed changes in cholesterol, illness symptoms, and affectivity (or emotional instability).

Psychosomatic diabetic children have exaggerated 'turn-on' of free fatty acid (FFA) rates that relates to emotional arousal and the first step in the occurrence of a diabetic symptom pattern (Minuchin et al., 1978). The authors found these FFA turn-on rates are uniquely elicited within the family context and that they suffer an impaired turn-off ability following the child's participation in a family conflict.

Alcoholism, drug dependence, and relationships

How can alcoholism or drug abuse possibly have anything to do with the family? The heavy (problem) drinker is not merely an individual who happens to have impact on a family (i.e. it is not adequate simply to see the drinkers as 'the problem'). Although there are such impacts (e.g. on children of parents who drink excessively: Wilson & Orford, 1978), there are some problems with this kind of interpretation. For one, a large proportion of families are quite resistant to improvements in the family member with the problem (Orford, 1980). Spouses themselves sometimes break down when their partner's drinking problem is cured (Orford & O'Reilly, 1981). Also partners sometimes describe 'the other person when drunk' in terms more favourable than they describe 'the other person when sober' (Orford, 1976). In particular, wives often describe their 'drunk husbands' as more masculine and dominant (which they happen to regard as attractive characteristics) than they describe their 'sober husbands'. Orford et al. (1976) even found that unfavourable 'when sober' perceptions of a spouse were predictive of poor outcome for the drinking problem over the subsequent twelve months. If we prefer partners drunk it is unlikely we shall substantially support their attempts to stay sober. The feelings of one family member towards another who has a problem can help to sustain the problem and interfere with attempts to solve it.

What are the links between relational factors and 'individual problems' with drugs? Partners and children of opiate abusers are frequently called on to structure their lives in a way that, as it were, depends on the addiction of a family member. For example, the partner and children may spend the day routinely stealing money to pay for the drug. Such routines of life are important to us as frameworks in which to conduct ourselves. Suppose the addiction is treated. How does that alter the way in which the addict's partner and children need to spend their routine day, and does that change their attitudes to themselves? In a sense, they are no longer needed: their functions have become redundant. As we might predict, these people frequently resist the therapeutic exercise and lead the addict back to the addiction, thus restoring their routine usefulness (Lewis & McAvoy, 1984). In such cases, treatment for opiate abuse often includes treatment for the abuser's family. Treatments strive to provide some alternative structure and routine for the abuser's family so that the addict's return to normality does not simply empty their lives together (Lewis & McAvoy, 1984).

Breaking up

All through this I have written about distressed families that stay together nevertheless. Many couples, however, become divorced – in the USA something near 50 percent of all first marriages will end in divorce and that figure is slightly higher for second marriages. That means, conversely, that 50 percent of marriages endure through the years despite a multitude of factors that work against long-term marital satisfaction. But, just as I note at the start of the book that social scientists assume the positive and 'explain' the negative, so there has been less acknowledgement of this side of the question.

What 'causes' divorce? Answers range from demographic factors, like race and religion, to personality factors like achievement motivation and extroversion (see BOX 4.7), to interactional factors, to relational processes (see Orbuch, in press).

We must avoid treating divorce as an event for which a cause should be found. Rather, divorce is a transitional process not an event (Duck, in press), and researchers are now looking for those causal factors which combine to fuel the relentless, unforgiving development of that process. Divorcing takes so long because there is more to it than just 'falling out of love'.

There are at least three parts to marriage that have to be unpicked in divorcing (Hagestad & Smyer, 1982). As we saw in discussing courtship, partners have not only to love one another (one part) but to be successful in meshing their activities and daily routines together (second part). As their relationship becomes well bonded and the routines, work or division of labour in the relationship are sorted out, so the partners develop attachment to the role of spouse – the 'being a husband or a wife' (third part). These three things (love for partner, attachment to established routines, attachment to the marital role) all are built up in courtship and marriage. All have to be disassembled during divorcing. There are many types of divorce that are identified (Hagestad & Smyer, 1982). The first distinction is between orderly and disorderly divorce.

In orderly divorces, the partners detach themselves successfully not only from their feelings for one another but from their attachment to the role of 'husband' or 'wife', from their involvement in an established set of daily routines, and from the legal role. They have to decide that they do not love their partner, do not want to be 'a spouse', do not miss the routines of their daily life together, but do want to be legally divorced.

Disorderly divorces are those where at least one aspect of these disengagements is not successfully completed. For instance, one partner may stay in love with the 'ex', or may find it impossible to adjust to 'not being married'. Hagestad & Smyer (1982) list seven types of disorderly divorce. Given that in an orderly divorce the partners detach from all four of the elements noted above (attachment to partner, attachment to role, shared routine, and legal commitment), the disorderly divorces are made up from the seven remaining possible combinations of scores on the four elements. For example in the first type ('divorced in name only') the partners are legally divorced, but still emotionally involved, still invested in the spousal role, and still sharing routines, possibly even living together. Type 2 ('I wish it hadn't happened') is in evidence when partners' daily activities are disconnected from one another and they are legally divorced but one partner still feels love for the other and still connects with the spousal role. The partners in Type 3 ('I've got you under my skin') share no daily routines, no desire for the spousal

BOX 4.7   Some findings about marital breakdown

Marriage at a young age predicts a lower degree of marital happiness and adjustment (Bentler & Newcomb, 1978). It is also associated with a greater likelihood of divorce (Mott & Moore, 1979).

Individuals with gross psychiatric symptomatology have low marital adjustment and happiness, as do those with rigid defensive personalities (Murstein & Glaudin, 1968).

Men who see themselves as extroverted and invulnerable, with a high need for orderliness, more often are divorced than are men without those views (Bentler & Newcomb, 1978).

The more premarital sexual partners that a person has, the less marital happiness he or she is likely to report (Athanasiou & Sarkin, 1974). Premarital pregnancy is another predictor of low marital happiness (Furstenberg, 1979).

Heterogamy (i.e. unequal matching on age, race, religion, etc.) is strongly related to poorly adjusted and unhappy marriage (Newcomb & Bentler, 1981).

Couples who have cohabited before marriage report fewer barriers to terminating their marriage (Cole, 1976).

The presence of children consistently lowers the marital adjustment felt by both men and women (Renne, 1970).

There is a gradual decrease in happiness over the first 10 years of marriage (Rollins & Feldman, 1970) but it increases after the children leave home (Argyle & Henderson, 1984). This could result from the emerging effects of many of the preceding factors.

role as such and no legal connection, but all the same they are attached to their spouse. As one subject put it: 'If we ran into one another it used to just kill me. I used to take the long way home just so I wouldn't see him'. In Type 4 ('The common law arrangement') the partners do not want to be married, as such, and are legally divorced but do feel love for one another and desire to be connected in routine. These couples are essentially cohabiting after divorce instead of before marriage! The fifth type ('Why not be roommates') encompasses those who share their lives and like the marital status, even though they do not have a legal marital role but do not have any other emotional attachment to the partner. Type 6 ('Marriage has its advantages') includes people who think that the state of marriage is better than singlehood, even though they are not attached to their partner and do not share routines. Type 7 ('Business as usual') comprises couples who want to be legally divorced and do not love one another but continue, essentially for convenience, to stay in the same house and do the same sorts of things in daily life as they have always done.

Three points about divorce

First, divorce is a stressful process with both physical and psychological side-effects. It affects and disrupts the partners' daily lives, routines and sense of identity as well as just making them unhappy. Second, the divorce of two persons has consequences for many more people than just the two persons who are separating. It obviously affects the children of the marriage. Since we are looking at the family as a system, and the parents of the divorcing pair as well as their siblings, we should think about those effects. Third, and less obvious, to become divorced, couples have to separate – that is, to unmake, 'brick by brick', the relationship they have previously painstakingly put together. To do this they have to undo both the internal ties (e.g. affection) and the external binding (e.g. family and societal pressures and forces that may keep them together). Just as society creates exogenous influences on couples' courtships and marriages, so it creates barriers to the dissolution of marital relationships. Two obvious ones are that:

1 'Divorced' is a negatively valued state that people do not like to have to apply to themselves. One adjustment that divorcees have to make is to the sense of shame and failure that is often felt by the person or imposed by outsiders. In our society, it is believed that a divorce is a failed relationship (rather than, say, a courageous and honest response to an unworkable partnership).

2 Society is organized in a way that 'expects' people to belong to couples, so that it is actually regarded as embarrassing, say, to invite a single person to a dinner party without inviting another 'single' of the opposite sex to balance things. What may seem right to the hosts, however, can 'sometimes be embarrassing to the 'single' guests, who probably take mild offence at being crudely paired off like that.

Children and divorce

Divorce is an extended transition that inevitably 'affects the entire family system and the functioning and interactions of the members within that system' (Hetherington et al., 1982, p. 233). The outcome and experience of the divorce affect different members of the family differently, and the problems faced by the divorced parents are likely to be different – and to require different skills – from those faced by the children (Kitson & Morgan, 1990). There is no such thing as a victimless divorce (Hetherington et al., 1982) – that is, one where no member of the family reports any distress or exhibits disrupted behaviour.

Children in distressed families, particularly those that experience separation and divorce, develop certain personality styles or views of themselves and also manifest social-behaviour problems when interacting with other children (Amato, 1991). Children experiencing parental divorce tend to suffer from depression and psychological disturbance, such as excessive feelings of their own guilt – they particularly tend to assume that their parents' divorce is somehow their fault (Kitson & Morgan, 1990). Hetherington has also found that boys do better with their dads and girls do better with their mums, although if living with mum the boys adjust better than girls do to the stepfather (Hetherington, 1979).

In the first year, particularly, of the divorce, children from divorced families are more oppositional and obstructive, more aggressive, lacking in self-control, distractible, and demanding than are children from families that are still together. This is true even if the comparison (i.e. intact and undivorced) families are showing high rates of marital distress and discord. The divorce itself is a significant factor.

Being labelled 'the child of divorced parents' is something that children find difficult to cope with (Amato, 1991). For example, they may get a 'hard time' at school for 'having no mother or no father'. In an attempt to explore this issue, Gottlieb (1983) reports a programme in Canada designed to deal with the aftermath of parental divorce. By introducing children of divorced parents to one another, Gottlieb was able to establish support groups for them. The support group shows them they are not alone in their experience and helps them to share and develop ways of coping with their problems. This technique makes use of what we now have learned about children's friendships outside the family.

Outside influences

After it was realized that a mother's relationship to her infant in the first six months did not necessarily predetermine the rest of the child's social life, researchers looked first in two main directions: to adolescent gangs and to family life. For instance, work began to attend to fathers and show that a child could be securely attached to its mother but anxiously attached to its father (Park & Waters, 1988). Two other major areas also opened up: the impact of peer or sibling interactions (Schneider et al., 1989), and the relevance of style of fathering (Lewis & O'Brien, 1987). Researchers began to realize that brothers, sisters, fathers and friends – and childhood – had somehow been omitted from the earliest thoughts on this issue. In short, researchers began to ask many important questions about the relationships between relationships (Dunn, 1988) and the influence that children can have upon parents as well as vice versa (Mills & Grusec, 1988).

Are children essentially passive and receptive to various significant forces that stamp themselves on the developing person, or are children active persons who exert their own individual influences? Perhaps they are interactive. Perhaps the child is an active participant exerting influence and effects on others as much as being influenced and affected by them. Clearly the child perceives and, to some extent interprets, the parent's behaviour just as the parent interprets and supports the child's (Mills & Grusec, 1988). Thus the dominant view in developmental psychology now is that the parent–child relationship is an interactive and mutually influential one.

Our first interactions with our parents are a basic framework for understanding and evaluating our own personal worth. From this base, children work out their own value as a social object for other people; an understanding of the nature and structure of relationships between people; and the kinds of relationship that they are best at establishing with others. Such thoughts can be formed by influences as subtle as the mother's speech style. Garrard & Kyriacou (1985) found that mothers who use a language code based on awareness of others' feelings increase the child's social sensitivity, the ability to comprehend others' feelings in friendship, and the awareness of others' needs and goals in social settings. Putallaz et al. (1991) also note that mothers with predominantly anxious or lonely recollections of their own childhood took the most active part in their children's social development and actually had the most socially competent children. This exciting work suggests that the mothers' own social experience in childhood has a direct effect on the ways in which their own children are taught to approach social life.

Many influences on a child's willingness to relate to others are equally subtle – even, for instance, the age of the parents. As adults mature through their own life cycle, so their pattern of friendship alters in various ways (Dickens & Perlman, 1981). Homel et al. (1987), for instance, found that parents with stable and dependable friendships were more likely to have children whose self-rated happiness was high and who had better school adjustment as compared to parents without such networks. Parents' networks expand and contract as a result of the pressures on them from careers, family and age itself. At some ages (usually mid-20s to mid-30s), parents' own friends have young children and these, therefore, make good playmates for one another. If, however, a pair of parents are of unusual ages for parenthood (say they are much older than usual) then their friends may not have young children any more. There, a natural shortage of playmates exists for their own children, who may thus be exposed to fewer social experiences with other children.

Perhaps it is a small point then, but as a child develops, so do the parents and other members of the family system, who have their own life-tasks and concerns. Anderson (1985) shows that both mothers and fathers show sharp increases in role stress when their eldest child first enters school. For the average pair of parents, however, a child's entry to kindergarten or infant school presents them with a new range of friends themselves. Children's parents are sometimes enabled to become friends with one another just because the children meet at school and become friends. The parents' paths cross more frequently, and they begin to share common interests and concerns. Once again, we see that these 'events' have impact and direct effect on the communication patterns of the parents and the children.

This is an important change because very young children play with other children only if they are pointed at them. Obviously, they do not have the resources or mobility to go round choosing or visiting friends. They play with those who are 'put in front of them'. Yet, even at young ages, the child probably needs experience with other children. The smiling encouragement of caring parents is not enough; even when it paves the way, the way has to go somewhere.

Peer and family influences

If you were unpopular at school you are more likely to become an alcoholic, a depressive, a schizophrenic, a delinquent, a dishonourable dischargee from the army, or a psychotic (Duck, 1991). Who says that children's friendships with each other do not matter? Recognizing their importance, researchers have begun to explore the bases of children's friendships, the ways in which they change with age, the ways in which they go wrong, and the most effective means for putting them right. They have looked at the psychological structure of the individuals in relationships and at the dynamics of children's relational communication and behaviour. Also quite recently a great deal more emphasis is being placed on the whole context of the child's interactional experience, including the experience created in the family (Ladd, 1991). For example, Putallaz et al. (1991) show that children are likely to be influenced by their *mother's* recollections of her own childhood, which presumably affect the ways in which she prepares the children for the experiences of the playground at school. Also, Bhavnagri & Parke (1991) have explored the role of parents as direct facilitators of the child's social experience, in structuring their play and other interactions. So in the discussion that follows we should remember that the child does not lead an insulated life but is subject to many social influences upon interactive experience, over and above those that he or she creates personally.

Cognitive bases of children's friendships

It seems to make sense to ask whether children's friendships are based on their general mental development. In other words, is social development related to cognitive development? Children acquire moral reasoning and intellectually manipulated skills in a predominantly systematic and progressive fashion. Are their friendships based on similar principles? Is there a predictable sequence in children's approaches to friendship?

In a single sentence, children become less egocentric and instrumental in their friendships between the ages of zero and six, develop relationships based on cooperation during the ages five to ten, and begin to appreciate more fully the value of a friend's deep psychological qualities, like character, from about the age of nine. These developments and sophistications continue in adolescence (Duck, 1975b). To put it even more briefly, the focus shifts from 'Me and what you can do for me' to 'You and Me and what we can do together' to 'Us and how we can help one another to grow as people'. Figure 4.1 gives a comparison of two major approaches and shows the various labels that have been given to the stages behind my preceding short summaries.

Children initially (i.e. aged 3–7) define friends in terms of

Selman & Jaquette[a]			Bigelow & La Gaipa[b]		
Stage	Friendship awareness	Perspective-taking	Stage	Dimension	Grade at onset
0 (3–7)[c]	Momentary physical playmate	Undifferentiated; egocentric	I.	Situational	
				1. Common activities	2
				2. Evaluation	3
				3. Propinquity	3
1 (4–9)	One-way assistance	Subjective; differentiated	II.	Contractual	
				4. Admiration	4
2 (6–12)	Fair weather cooperation	Reciprocal; self-reflective	III.	Internal-psychological	
				5. Acceptance	4
				6. Loyalty and commitment	5
				7. Genuineness	6
				8. Common interests	7
				9. Intimacy potential	7
4 (12+)	Autonomous independence	In depth; societal			

[a] Adapted from Selman & Jacquette (1977) and Selman & Selman (1979).
[b] Adapted from Bigelow & La Gaipa (1975) and Bigelow (1977).
[c] The numbers in parentheses are rough guidelines of the age range in each stage.

Figure 4.1: *Two major theories of children's friendships*

Source: Dickens & Perlman (1981) in Duck & Gilmour (eds) (1981b, p. 96) *Personal Relationships 2: Developing Personal Relationships.* Academic Press: London. Reproduced by permission.

proximity and availability. Somewhere between the ages of four and nine children acquire an ability to differentiate another child's viewpoint from their own, but a friend is still valued for 'what he or she can do for *me*' rather than on any reciprocal basis. Between six and twelve ('fair weather' cooperation), children come to appreciate reciprocity in friendship and realize that the other person has rights, needs and wishes also. However, these are still seen as self-interested rather than mutual, and a child will satisfy a friend's needs only if it suits. From around nine, the child realizes that friendship is collaborative: mutual and common goals are important. Only around the age of twelve does complex appreciation of friendship appear and begin to take a more adult form, namely, recognizing that autonomy and independence can go together with friendship (e.g. the other person will need other friends and that fact does not threaten our friendship).

Do the stages of children's friendship development reflect the stages of adults' friendships or acquaintance (Duck et al., 1980)? There are many parallels. For instance, adults get to know one another first on the basis of physical cues, then behaviour, then attitudes and detailed structures of personality. In comparable fashion, children at younger ages form friendships on the basis of physical and outward signs, then in terms of (cooperative) behaviour and then, in adolescence, on the basis of character and personality.

Children's behaviour and friendship

Friendship is not all 'cognitive', as we found in adults: behaviour and communication have major parts to play, and both of these change as the child grows up. It is through behaviour, especially through reciprocity and cooperation, that children begin to learn about relationships (Youniss, 1980). In particular, they come to know about other people through social collaboration. Our knowledge of ourselves and of other people comes from an increasing understanding of social relationships built up from social interaction. Earlier I was claiming that a child establishes a level of self-esteem from early interaction with parents, and Youniss's (1980) more sophisticated view of the interactions of peers is entirely consistent with such a view.

The interaction of thought and behaviour is only one side of the coin: even if children do develop through stages at a reasonably steady rate, we need not assume that they all start with the same levels of abilities; some are tuned in to friendship and some are not.

Children scoring high in friendship motivation are different from other children in their detailed understanding of friendship (McAdams & Losoff, 1984). They also show very sociable behaviour (which is independently classified by teachers as 'friendly', 'affectionate', 'cooperative', 'sincere', 'happy' and 'mature'). Those with higher scores on motivation also have deeper friendships and they are very stable in best-friend choice.

BOX 4.8 Children's friendships

There is a relationship between a child's conception of friendship and behaviour with friends (Sants, 1984). Children with a highly developed friendship conception are more likely to ignore other children, to try to organize them or control them, and are more successful at doing so than are children with less developed concepts. 'Highs' are less likely to be the victims of all forms of negative behaviour. Sants also shows that level of friendship conceptions is positively related to IQ scores.

Girls and popular children of both sexes have a higher level of interpersonal understanding than do boys and unpopular children (Schofield & Kafer, 1985). However, the advances in ability to understand friendship are not uniform. Some aspects of friendship concepts seem to develop in different ways consistent with a gradual generalization of knowledge rather than with the idea of a strict sequence of stages. Most girls and all popular boys show a higher level of interpersonal understanding, and results of the study generally confirm the idea that the higher the level of a child's interpersonal understanding, the higher is his or her popularity.

On the opposite side of the popularity chart, we can distinguish between actively rejected children and those who are merely neglected; these are different sorts of unpopularity (Asher & Parker, 1989). Neglected kids are ignored whilst rejected kids are actively disliked and tend to get rejected in new groups too if they are placed in them without training. In particular, they are much more likely to complain of feeling lonely than are neglected children or those with low social status, and they are more 'at risk' for feelings of inadequacy and low self-esteem (Asher & Wheeler, 1985). What, then, differentiates them from other kids or, to put it another way, what do they do wrong?

Actively rejected children have unusual ways of explaining the causes of social events (Sobol & Earn, 1985). These differ from the explanations given by children who are merely isolated by neglect (i.e. nonparticipants who are not necessarily rejected) or controversial (i.e. frequently accepted by some peers but equally strongly rejected by other peers). Unpopular, rejected children see the world in more stable terms and, therefore, they see their rejection as quite likely to persist, more or less irrespective of what they do.

Self-esteem, acquired in interactions with parents, sets the scene for later feelings about friendship as represented in friendship motivation. This affects behaviour in social settings which interacts with beliefs about our popularity and acceptability to others. Together this affects our approach to explaining our social successes and failures.

How do we put it right?

The first question really is 'what are we trying to achieve when we try to 'cure' childhood unpopularity?' Is it adequate to assume that all we need to do is treat the unpopular child and implant some magical, 'spray' attractant, or should we take the whole children's group and deal with the complexities of their interconnections as a system? Is the child's problem possibly one of lack of general communicative competence or should we distinguish (Duck, 1989) social skill, general interpersonal competence in social or play settings, communicative competence in talking to other children, and relational competence (i.e. the specific competence of sustaining personal relationships)?

There are many different kinds of skill involved in successful relating in childhood, and hence there are many levels at which difficulties can arise (Furman, 1984). For instance, the child's behaviours may be inappropriate – in which case some form of social skills training may help – or the child's motivation for relationships may be low. Alternatively, the child may lack the relevant social knowledge about behavioural routine or the nature of relationships. The child may be deficient in internal feedback and poor at evaluating his or her own behaviour or general capabilities. The appropriate way to tackle the problem will depend first on correct identification of the underlying problem causing the behavioural inadequacies (Furman, 1984). By implication, no general style of approach will be universally effective.

Let us start by looking at the separate ideas suggested, before we look at the way that Furman integrates them. One approach we could use is based on 'targeting' the child who has social difficulties, then training the child in various skills that may otherwise be lacking. For instance, some children do not talk enough to their peers or do not engage in cooperative play or never take the initiative in entering games. Direct coaching of such children can be beneficial (Oden & Asher, 1977). In the Oden–Asher programme, children are trained for ten sessions in: participation in other children's play; cooperation and methods of collaborating rather than competing with others; communication skills of listening and talking; validation, support and nonverbal reinforcement by means such as looking, smiling and offering encouragement. We know from Chapter 1 what a stupendous impact such skills have on the flow of social behaviour and on our acceptability to other people. We also know that these skills are usually acquired at random, because efforts to train and guide children in them are so haphazard (Berndt, 1989). Paradoxically, governments spend vast amounts of money on teaching children academic skills, but ignore those relating skills which are just as important to adult happiness and success (Duck, 1991).

Such programmes of social skills training are obviously beneficial, but they may not be enough on their own. Even if the unpopular child is trained, the child's peers may not notice. The child's reputation for unpopularity may still exist in the minds of the child's classmates, and they may not notice the child's improved style of behaviour (Ladd, 1989). In that case, merely training the unpopular child may be ineffective if the classmates' behaviour is not affected, too. What is then required is a method that also involves the classmates (Walker & Hops, 1973). This method centres on reinforcing peers for interacting with isolated children: the peers are encouraged to approach and play with the previously rejected or ignored child, thus giving the child the experience of acceptance and joint play. In another instance, non-handicapped children were encouraged to play with handicapped children by the direct means of teaching them how (Guralnick, 1976). 'Normal' children can be taught to persist in engaging withdrawn children in play even if they had initially met with a cool and withdrawn reception (Strain et al., 1976). As Furman (1984, p. 115) concludes, 'peers can be effective therapeutic agents'.

Another strategy is to encourage mixed-age social interaction. An immature child given experience of play with younger kids can learn to take control, to have responsibility, and to direct the activities of others. Furman et al. (1979) successfully used such a technique to improve the interaction rates of withdrawn children. For later ages, however, the reverse strategy is proposed (Duck et al., 1980), namely, giving socially immature children the chance to observe

---

BOX 4.9 Social skills training for children

Rubin et al. (1989) emphasize the influence of a mother's beliefs about friendship as factors affecting the child's understanding of the nature of the relationship. Some mothers are strongly committed to helping their children develop an understanding of the social world and some believe that their help is not needed in such a venture.

LaGreca & Santogrossi (1980) identified children who are accepted by their peers and gave a group of them training in social skills whilst 2 other groups served as controls. Relative to these controls, the training group shows improvements in skill, knowledge, and performance in structured settings or initiations of play. However, on its own, the training does not increase popularity.

Gresham & Nagle (1980) extend such ideas to test out a training/coaching programme, a modelling programme (where unaccepted children watch skilled ones and are taught to identify key aspects of their performance), and a mixed coaching/modelling programme. All 3 methods improve the 'play with' sociometric/popularity ratings of the children.

Unaccepted children can be taught specific conversational skills, and they improve in ability to perform the skills until the follow-up four weeks later (Ladd, 1981). Popularity also increases for these children at that time.

Attili (1989) reports that children who are 'difficult' cause a depressed reaction from the mother, which itself feeds into the children's increased difficulty. Apparently the mother's attitude towards the children reflects upon the children's own feelings of emotional security and adversely affects the child's adaptation to school.

Siperstein & Gale (1983) specifically selected rejected children, rather than those who were ignored or unaccepted, as in the preceding examples. After coaching, such children increase in popularity and also show a decrease in the amount of self-isolation or bystander-onlooker 'hovering' behaviour outside groups of other children (when the child becomes an onlooker of a group he or she obviously wants to join but dares not do so).

---

older children's friendships so that they can use these as models. With aggressive children, this may have the additional effect of bringing them up against the dangers of using aggression against 'stronger opponents', so that they are encouraged to develop non-aggressive strategies for interaction.

In other cases, it is more suitable to train the child in techniques of entry to groups of other children. A particular characteristic of neglected and rejected children is that they 'hover' on the outside of groups as bystanders or onlookers and do not show effective means of getting themselves admitted to join in (Putallaz & Gottman, 1981).

For a child with problems that persist across situations, and who is obviously the major source of the difficulties, various techniques have been tried. Bierman & Furman (1982) attempted to coach such children in conversational skills by making videotapes about peer interaction and giving the children 'practice' in how to do it. Children are taught social skills based on reinforcements for increasing interaction, for talking to other children, and the like. But these forms of training are combined with group experiences where the skills are practised (under expert observation) in the environment where they will ultimately be used by the child alone. Such subject-oriented and peer-oriented combination programmes seem likely to prove effective in the long run (Furman, 1984; Schneider et al., 1989).

Summary

Complex interrelationships affect our social behaviour. Relationships, like people, have a history and have come from somewhere, often taking a long time to emerge and develop. A marriage can be affected by the style of the preceding courtship adopted by the partners; a family, as a whole, can be influenced by the kind of marital interaction of the two spouses in particular; the child at school can be affected by the quality of interaction in the family home. The learning that the child gathers about relationships from the family environment can carry over and influence the child's approach to or avoidance of other children.

A second, but somewhat underemphasized, theme in this chapter is that unhealthy family functioning can lead to unhealthy psychological functioning in individuals within the family. By extending this idea to relationships in general, the next chapter continues to apply relationship research to broader (and seemingly unrelated) social issues, such as health.

Further reading

Booth, A. (1991) *Contemporary Families: Looking Forward, Looking Back*. NCFR: Minneapolis.

Duck, S.W., Hay, D.F., Hobfoll, S.E., Ickes, W. & Montgomery, B. (1988) *Handbook of Personal Relationships*. Wiley: Chichester, UK.

Ladd, G.W. (ed.) (1991) Special issue on 'Family-peer relations during childhood: Pathways to competence and pathology?' *Journal of Social and Personal Relationships* (8), 307–14.

Schneider, B.H., Attili, G., Nadel, J. & Weissberg, R.P. (1989) *Social Competence in Developmental Perspective* (NATO ASI Series). Kluwer: Amsterdam.

CHAPTER 5

Influencing Strangers, Acquaintances and Friends

Social predicaments, like the poor, are always with us. When we go about our daily business, we are often confronted with unexpected situations that force us to deal with awkward strangers, usually to get them to stop some behaviour that is offensive to us – strangers who light a cigarette in a No Smoking area, who jump ahead of us in a queue, who irritate us in launderettes, or may even sexually harass us. On other occasions, the problem is to deal with people whom we know a little, but not very well, and ask them to do something for us that they may be inclined to resist. Our regular bus driver may have to be persuaded to accept and change a large banknote; we may have to ask our class instructor to extend the deadline for an assignment; a person in our large dormitory block may need to be asked to turn down the stereo system; we may want to ask a classmate to come out on a date with us. Sometimes we may even want to persuade a friend to do us a troublesome favour.

In each case, we need to persuade or encourage someone to do something that he or she may be reluctant to do or something where we cannot predict the response. They are instances of the everyday business of 'compliance', or getting people to do things for us. Of course, daily life brings us into contact with many different sorts of people, some of whom we know, and some of whom we do not. Some may even be enemies (Wiseman, 1989) with whom we are forced, by circumstances to interact.

How does this effort get affected by human relationships? In each of the cases of strangers, of acquaintances, and of friends, the issues are somewhat different. When dealing with strangers, we have to assume that they are average, sensible members of society about whom we know only what we can see; we have to assume that they will be influenced by the average things, such as power and likability, and that they have average attitudes. We react to them just as we would to any other strangers; they are contextless for us, and we have no knowledge of their personal characteristics. Since we have no relationship with them except as one anonymous human being to another anonymous human being, there is no special knowledge on which to draw.

By contrast, with acquaintances we attempt persuasion and compliance in a different context: we probably do want to emphasize that they know us a little and that they should consequently treat us as persons with individual characteristics. That they do know us means that we can claim special treatment: we are not 'just another person who wants something done in a hurry'. They have a minor obligation to treat us differently.

With friends, we use whatever special knowledge we have about them, but are probably concerned to preserve the relationship between us. However, friendship is a source of obligations, and part of the role of 'friend' is willing acceptance of chores, duties and favours that help the other persons. We do unwelcome or inconvenient things for them precisely because we are a good friend. Wiseman (1986) has pointed out that a part of the 'voluntary contract' of friendship involves us tacitly agreeing to support our friends in times of need, to offer them help even if it is personally inconvenient, to take time away from our own business in order to attend to *their* business, and to engage their demands upon our psychological and physical resources. Thus the context for influence is rather different in a friendship as compared to an acquaintanceship.

For these reasons, influencing strangers is different in some key ways from influencing friends and both are somewhat different from influence in the advertising market-place or the political campaign (although each situation has some thread of common elements).

In looking at persuasion and compliance, I shall avoid considering grand issues like political persuasion, voting behaviour, advertising effectiveness, the campaign for/against nuclear arms, or the general attempt to persuade people to give up smoking. When it comes down to it in everyday social life, we just want to get someone to change what they are doing (i.e. to comply with our desires) rather than to change their attitudes for ever on a key topic. Furthermore, since this is a supplementary text, I merely sketch out some approaches because I want to emphasize the role of social relationships in compliance rather than to repeat a review of attitude change research that can be read in any introductory text.

In keeping with my emphasis on daily life in this book, I happen to believe that large-scale decisions and attitudes occupy much less of people's time than the amount of work on attitude-change might lead us to imagine. I believe that people spend longer arguing about the best way to decorate the living room, the most desirable car to purchase, or where to go for a meal or a holiday than they do confronting partners about political issues or prejudice toward racial groups. I do not mean that the latter issues are not important; they are. However, to study them to the degree to which they are often studied in attitude-change texts is to seriously misrepresent the contours of social life and to fail to create a proper representation of human experience.

BOX 5.1 Points to think about
- What *general features of people* tend to make them more persuasive?
- What *overall techniques and strategies* tend to increase the effectiveness of persuasions in general?
- What *message structures* are most persuasive?
- How does the *relationship between persuader and target* affect persuasiveness? How does it modify the effects of any of the other things above?
- How easily can we employ this knowledge in the living reality of everyday social encounters?

Influencing strangers

In dealing with strangers, we usually lack knowledge about their particular characteristics. What we see is what we deal with. Accordingly, we are likely to pay attention to different aspects of the persuasive context from those we use when we deal with acquaintances or with friends. For instance, we may be concerned about other outside observers' views about the episode. If our behaviour towards a stranger causes a 'scene', we may be concerned about our appearance to any other people that are present; when dealing with friends, we probably have their feelings and interests in mind as much as our own. Consider this example.

Strangers on the train

At the time when I was beginning work on this book, I had to go to London for two days to record a television programme on 'social skills' with a man who specializes in assertiveness training. The journey back involved a three-hour train ride, which, on this occasion, took more than four hours because of poor weather. I always choose a No Smoking section, which is clearly marked with a red circular notice on every window, showing a cigarette crossed out, the words No Smoking, and a statement of the penalty for violating the rule. The carriage filled up with another thirty-one passengers, and off we went. I looked around at the strangers who were my fellow passengers. Directly opposite was a girl who looked as if she were a student and a young man who was stapling together leaflets about solvent abuse, warning teenagers about the social, health and legal disadvantages of glue sniffing. He soon started chatting to the student and it turned out that he was a vegetarian who jogged every day and helped to run a youth sports centre. I began to see why he had chosen a No Smoking section: he cared about health. Across the central corridor of the open-plan compartment was a table occupied by two large and hungry people who began tucking vigorously and, to my mind, unwisely into a selection of 'junk food' bags. I sat reading a paper about loneliness in college students whilst I listened to *The Lark Ascending* by Vaughan Williams on my personal stereo. I could keep an eye on things by 'looking out of the window' since it was a dark winter's evening and the carriage lights reflected the carriage events clearly. These cameos continued amiably enough along their own paths for some hour and a half, interspersed with announcements from the guard/conductor and bar steward.

Then one of the big eaters lit a cigarette.

I drew his attention to the fact that it was a No Smoking section and asked him to go to a different section of the train. He replied that someone further down the train was smoking but, as a computer manager from Manchester pointed out to him, that did not actually contradict my point that *he* was sitting in a No Smoking section. Out of the other thirty passengers just that one man joined in the argument and supported my request whilst the others looked on with a mixture of amusement and embarrassment.

What about these other passengers? The solvent/health man later left the section for a while and returned to place a pack of cigarettes and a lighter in front of him. He had said nothing, I assume, because he felt divided loyalties. On the one hand, he smoked, but on the other hand he recognized the need to consider other people's rights whilst doing so and had himself left the No Smoking carriage when he wanted to smoke. His behaviour did raise an interesting issue, though, since his other actions and statements pointed to a concern over health and a care for others; so why did he smoke? The student was a nonsmoker who said that she always chose nonsmoking compartments, so why did she say nothing?

When the smoker would neither put out his cigarette nor move there flashed across my mind one of the points from the television programme I had just finished recording: stick to your guns. However, it was with something of a sense of failure that I went looking for the guard/conductor who asked the man to move, which he then did.

What we had here is a 'social confrontation episode'. As Newell & Stutman (1988) point out, the key feature of such an episode is that one actor in the situation points out to another actor 'that his or her behaviour has violated a rule or expectation for appropriate conduct within the relationship or situation'. Key elements are: the legitimacy of the invoked rule; the legitimacy of any other rule that might supersede the first rule; whether or not the person actually performed the illegitimate behaviour; whether the behaviour actually amounts to a violation of the rule; whether or not the accused accepts responsibility. If we analyse the present problem and the ways in which it unfolded we can see that all of these elements were silent societal fellow travellers in that railway carriage on that dark and stormy night!

Some psychologists would point to the smoker's attitude structure: his beliefs about smoking, his beliefs about the legitimacy of his action, and, given that he could see others smoking, his consequent belief that he was being unfairly singled out. Some would argue that he felt his freedom was being constrained and so he reacted against the constraint. Others would look at the structure of my request and its evident ineffectiveness. Some would point to other relevant circumstances, such as the passivity of the others in the compartment. Some of these ideas have been applied generally to all persuasive contexts, but I think that some are more likely to be important in this setting and others elsewhere. Some matter in dealing with strangers and some do not; some are more important in dealing with friends, for instance.

Being noticed

When dealing with strangers, the first essential is to be noticed and have them pay attention to our request. To do this we have to present ourselves in a way that makes it clear that we have the right to have our request dealt with. By contrast, when dealing with friends, our right to be heard and noticed is built into our relationship: they heed us because they know us. With strangers, however, we might need to use some guile and devices.

Attention to a persuasive message is a critical factor for persuasion to occur (Hovland et al., 1953). People attend more closely to a credible source, that is, one that appears to justify our attention, one that has authority and can be trusted or believed. In the 1950s, when Hovland's studies were conducted, it was found, for instance, that Robert Oppenheimer, who headed the team that created the atom bomb, was believed more readily by a US audience than was *Pravda*, the Russian newspaper, whether or not the topic was nuclear bombs.

Source credibility is freely manipulated in advertisements. Advertisers like to say 'Doctors recommend' or 'As used in hospitals' as a way of tying their product to credible sources. When persons are shown recommending drugs or pharmaceuticals, they are frequently figures in white coats ('scientists') or smart business clothes ('executives') – with greying hair if they are male ('authority'). They usually wear glasses ('intelligent'), carry clipboards ('data'), are seen giving other people instructions ('power') against a background of test tubes ('science'), and they use fountain pens ('class'). The same person saying the same thing on a football field in sports gear would probably appear less credible even if the message, the facts, the words, the con, were all precisely the same. What we respond to are the cues in the context: all are cues carefully prepared to suggest credibility. Here credibility is produced by expertise (or, in the case of adverts, assumed expertise: after all, most viewers would realize that the 'expert' is not an expert but an actor playing that part – yet we still might believe what is said).

In dealings with strangers, source credibility is one of the most important factors. In the smoky warmth of my dark social predicament, I could claim such credibility in a number of doubtful ways ('Hey, I'm a brain surgeon/fighter pilot . . . please stop smoking') or in one of two other more effective ways. These are physical attractiveness and similarity: if we are attractive and are like the stranger in ways that are relevant to the message (e.g. if we wear sports gear when trying to persuade a sporting audience) then we are more likely to be persuasive, according to studies by McGinnis (1970) and by Berscheid (1966) respectively. We are not all physically attractive (although people who appear in adverts usually are – presumably because they are selected for the job as being more credible), but we can improve on Nature if it is important and we have the time and the forewarning to make those adjustments. If we are able or willing to do so, then we can also take some steps to become – or to seem – similar to the targets of our persuasion attempts. For instance, we dress up smartly for interviews with important people and take care over our appearance to impress people. We may also go to considerable lengths to agree with them and support their ideas (i.e. we ingratiate by appearing to be similar to them).

The findings on source credibility are helpful with strangers when we have time to prepare, but as researchers soon began to find, source credibility alone is not enough to explain persuasion nor is it always a helpful guide. We are quite often thrown into persuasive contexts quite unexpectedly by the unpredictable actions of other people, and we need to influence them then and there. 'Please serve me next, I was here before this person'; 'Please move your car, you're blocking my exit'; 'Please stop smoking, you're in a No Smoking section'; . . . 'Why don't you turn down your stereo, I'm trying to work'. Everyday life is not always conveniently arranged, yet we have to deal with the context in which we find ourselves. If we happen to be nicely turned out, and wearing spectacles then we may have influence but we may happen to be in running gear or a bathrobe or to have just (been) woken up. In any case, appearance alone does not guarantee persuasive success.

BOX 5.2 Source credibility

Credibility of a source affects a listener's likelihood of changing his or her attitudes (Hovland et al., 1953).

Expertise, trustworthiness, attractiveness, and similarity to the target are important elements of source credibility (Petty & Cacioppo, 1981).

A person is more credible when he or she argues against his or her best interests, perhaps because it is taken to indicate trustworthiness (Walster et al., 1966).

The racial origin of a communicator can influence the speaker's credibility especially for prejudiced audiences (Aronson & Golden, 1962).

A communicator who takes a predictable line (e.g. a fervent Catholic who speaks against pornography) is less persuasive than one who speaks in contrast to the direction one would expect to be taken (e.g. a fervent Catholic who speaks for the cathartic value of pornography: Eagly et al., 1978).

Knowing, liking, and being persuaded

Before we go further, think back to Chapter 3. What has a great deal of research found that physical attractiveness, similarity, trust and status, all 'produce' in observers? Liking. These results point out that we are persuaded by people whom we like or feel initially attracted to. My hunch is that the preceding effects are mediated by liking: the source credibility of strangers is based on cues that make us feel positive about them first.

When we deal with and are familiar with people we know, however, what about source credibility then? When friends and family want to influence us in those circumstances, credibility comes not from the usual cues of clothing and the rest, but from what we know about the person, his or her relevant competences, and how we feel about him or her. Since I know my brother is an expert economist, I am more likely to credit his statements on economics. Also I am more likely to credit the arguments of someone I love or have come to respect, even if he or she does not dress well and is not outwardly similar to me. Those I have come to know as irritatingly incompetent probably will not persuade me, however they dress up. Enemies whom I know will hardly ever be able to persuade me to do things, even if they sweeten the deal with gifts and promises (as Virgil, the Roman poet put it, 'I fear/distrust the Greeks even when they are bearing gifts').

Relative power positions are also well known in our everyday encounters and are significant in this context. Over a period of time, we get to know who has authority or credibility and who has not; which friend is the group leader or gives reliable advice; what student in class is bright and a good 'consultant' about classwork; which colleague is an authority or has a strong political base in the department.

Those real-life cues based on personal knowledge affect our perceptions of credibility in everyday life much more than the business clothes or the glasses. A friend is credible to me because I know and trust him or her, not because of the clothes. In everyday life, power, credibility and trust are based on vibrant, familiar relationships, not on the fripperies of the advertising image. When familiarity is lacking and we are with a stranger, a shopkeeper, a bus driver who will not give change for a large note, or a sexist waiter who gives the bill check to the man in the party when the woman booked the table, then we probably cannot rely on source credibility alone and need other strategies, like appearing friendly ('Hey pal') or choosing words carefully and taking great thought over the structure of our persuasive message, or appealing to bystanders for their help and intervention.

The apathetic context

Our predicaments in social life often involve us in taking a stand on some matter when other people are there to see, like other people standing in the line that someone tries to 'jump'. In the No Smoking compartment I found myself in that embarrassing public situation: my request to the smoker was uttered before an audience of other people who were also affected by the smoker's behaviour. No one else did anything and no one else (bar one) took my side. That means that there were twenty-eight people sitting around saying and doing nothing whilst the two-act melodrama went on their midst. In particular, it meant that the smoker was not being made to defend himself or being publicly 'boxed into a tight corner' by social pressure. This provided an important psychological context for my persuasive attempt. In terms of the Newell & Stutman (1988) analysis above, this apathetic context tacitly suggests the unimportance or illegitimacy of the invoked rule and my doomed efforts to enforce it.

Awareness of the reactions of strangers or friends, whether physically or only psychologically present, often guides our action and helps us to feel good or bad about the situation. We may well be guided in our actions and words by thoughts of 'What would the neighbours think?' or 'What do these other people think of all this?' These powerful relational and social concerns are extremely influential.

It is an important fact, not just a coincidence, that we live our lives as members of social and psychological communities which provide such contexts against which to evaluate our actions, thoughts and beliefs. We are strongly affected by the views and actions of relevant other people, and we habitually compare our behaviour, dress, attitudes and beliefs to other people's (Festinger, 1954). The essential argument of the 'social comparison theory' is that we are all inclined to assess ourselves against a relevant group of other persons to see if we compare equally, if not favourably, and we prefer to be liked and accepted rather than disliked and rejected. Have you had the experience of turning up to a party dressed in the 'wrong' kind of clothes? Then you have experienced the consequences of social comparison theory. Festinger argues that we compare our attitudes, opinions and emotions also: when we want to know if we are acting or thinking in an acceptable manner or making a sensible emotional response we compare ourselves with other people to see how they react. If they do as we do, then we are 'OK'.

Festinger's point is vital because it is such a common part of human life: we are *always* comparing ourselves to other people and we want to be accepted or acceptable. For instance, as students, we often want to know what sorts of exam/test/essay grades everyone else got, so that we can evaluate our own performance more thoroughly. Just knowing our own score may not be sufficiently reassuring. Whenever we feel the urge to compare our own jogging times, test grades, body weight or salary against average figures, we are experiencing the phenomenon of social comparison. It guides us as we attempt to find out if we are normal or right and can even be used as an argument in persuasion, as any parent of an adolescent knows: 'Can I stay at the party till 12.00? Everyone else is going to'.

If we look at what happened – or, rather, what did not happen – in the No Smoking section of the train, we can see social comparison at work, telling me I am in the wrong. For one, the smoker's first response was to indicate a comparison group elsewhere to 'make his behaviour right' (i.e. others were smoking in the train). Second, a more subtle comparison was that only one person was concerned about the smoking and no one else reacted. The smoker may look round and think, 'This smoke doesn't bother anyone else or they'd be reacting. I'm "doing OK". The guy here is overreacting'. I look round and think, 'I am upset by the smoking but no one else is saying anything. Perhaps my reaction is inappropriate'. Since people tend to assume that others are similar to them (Stotland et al., 1960), a nonreaction is equivalent to support for the status quo rather than for a new proposal. Through apathy, the others are supporting the 'smokus quo' rather than the proposal that it should stop. The message from the comparison group to me, then, is 'You care and we do not, so you are wrong'. In terms of the Newell & Stutman (1988) analysis, they essentially, but passively, deny that the smoker is violating a rule, or perhaps implicitly suggest that the rule written on the window (i.e. No Smoking) can be superseded by another rule (i.e. No Smoking Unless Other People Are Not Very Bothered By It).

How could I have reinterpreted their indifference so that it becomes supportive of me and provides me with a comparison group? A careful piece of oratory or a well-structured message directed at the apathetic bystanders might have energized a bit of support that could have changed the balance of opinion for comparison. The stratagem would be to make the other people feel good about themselves, and so to interpret their apathy as something positive and supportive of me. For instance, I could have tried suggesting that they were all too nice to speak up as I had done.

('These other people are too polite to say so but they are offended too.') If they are *really* apathetic, then they will not contradict and say 'No, I am not just being polite; I am really not offended', but they *might* and then my position would look a bit limp.

The dog owner's dilemma

Another useful incident showed me the power of comparison with other people's behaviour and also when fate can intervene to correct bystander apathy. I took Christina (then aged 9) and Jamie (then aged 4) to the children's playground where a special section for the under-fives is fenced off and has a sign: 'Dogs are not allowed in this area'. There were about twenty parents there, each with at least one child, when one turned up with two small children and a dog, which he brought in and allowed to run strenuously around. Apathetically, the rest looked from one to another, raised our eyebrows, muttered to one another in general terms about 'dogs' and made social comparisons: no one else reacted, so why should I be the first? We all did nothing, all expecting someone else to take the initiative, and all unwilling to risk the dog owner's reactions, since he had a cauliflower ear and a generally uninviting look about him. We were all transformed into nonapathetic good citizens, however, when the dog started to chase one of the children and several of us heroically united to draw the dog owner's attention to the sign. His response was one of those staggeringly brilliant real-life retorts (it is given below) that no one ever expects and no one can handle. The occurrence of the dog's extra contribution to the incident is what forced us from feeling good about ourselves in one way (tolerant, open-minded, unofficious) to doing it in another way (good citizens protecting children from danger). That was the crucial change that led to our intervention.

What did the dog owner say when we pointed his good eye at the notice? With marvellous aplomb, he said 'It's only a small dog; they don't count'. This points to something that is missing from the accounts of predicaments given so far: any reference to the fact that the *target* of our persuasion has a mind – in this case quite an inventive one. He probably felt about himself, as most people do, that he was a normal, rational human being, who is basically all right, acts in a reasonable way, and has an above-average sense of humour. How might this have affected his actions and accounted for his beliefs about the dog?

Balanced states

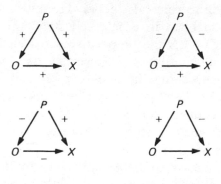

Unbalanced states

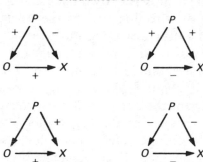

Figure 5.1: *Balanced states*

Balance and consistency

People seem to feel better about themselves when they act in a way which they feel is consistent (Heider, 1944; 1958). Note my careful wording of that statement: it does not state that we *are* consistent, but that we like to *think* we are. Consistency theorists suggest that we prefer consistency or 'balance' among our different attitudes. When we become aware of imbalance or inconsistency among them, then we shall be motivated to change something.

In Heider's model, there are usually two persons (P,O) and one object about which they have an attitude (X). P and O can feel + or − about each other and about X. Balance is the result if the signs all come out positive when multiplied algebraically (i.e. + + + or − − +), and imbalance is the result of negative product (i.e. + + −). So in our case, we have me (P), the dog owner (O) and the presence of the dog (X). Things would be imbalanced for me if I liked the dog owner (+); I disliked the dog's presence (−); and the dog owner liked the dog (+), that is, if the algebraic product of the +/−

signs comes out as negative overall. $(+)$ X $(+)$ X $(-)$ comes out negative, according to rules of algebra. However, I did not like the dog owner $(-)$, so I am in a balanced state: the overall algebraic product of $(-)$ X $(+)$ X $(-)$ is positive. So I shall not change my attitudes and I shall continue to believe that the dog should go. The dog owner is balanced too: he does not know or like me $(-)$; he knows that I dislike the dog $(-)$; but he thinks that the dog is nice and too small to count as a dog $(+)$. Once again, then, $(-)$ X $(-)$ X $(+)$ comes out positive, so he is balanced, and he will not move the dog from the area.

On this model, I have to create imbalance for the dog owner, so that he will be motivated to restore balance. I want to change his attitude to the dog's presence by this method, so I must create imbalance in him by affecting one of the other two items of the three. If he knows I dislike the dog but does not care, then he will not change, so I must make him care about my opinion. If I make him like me then he will feel imbalanced. I need to create the following thought system: I like P $(+)$; P does not like the dog being here $(-)$; I want the dog to stay $(+)$; this comes out negative overall $(+)$ X $(-)$ X $(+)$, so the dog owner would be imbalanced and would want to change something – for instance, his attitude towards the dog's presence. I should make him like me first; *then* tell him to take his terrier elsewhere.

Critics of consistency theories have noted that it's not so simple. How do I ensure that the attitude he changes is the one towards the dog's presence and not the positive attitude to me that I have induced him into having? Heider's theory, unfortunately, cannot predict which one of the two will be altered to restore balance (Newcomb, 1971). Since his new-found liking for me would have been a recent attitude whilst dog-loving is an old-established one, it's much more likely the dog owner would restore balance by changing from liking me to disliking me and would hang on to his belief that the dog can stay. One difficulty with Heider's approach here, then, is that the relationship between the two persons is as likely to be affected by the persuasion attempt as is the attitude I want to change.

In face-to-face attempts at influence, *either* the two parties do not know one another (so they will not care a great deal about their attitudes towards one another and are very likely to change those attitudes quite capriciously) *or* the two parties know one another well and will not want to bicker over a silly attitudinal disagreement, so they might agree to differ. In either case, the relevant attitude probably will not be altered, and balance theory has to be reconsidered or reformulated somewhat.

Dissonance

Another model, Festinger's (1957) dissonance theory, focusses on the attitudes of the target person (P) only (not those of P *and* those of O) and also admits P's behaviour into the equation. (Note: this is different from Festinger's social comparison theory.) In brief, it argues that a person will be motivated to restore balance (or, in Festinger's terms, to restore 'consonance') when the person holds two attitudes which lead to psychologically inconsistent conclusions or when the person's behaviour and attitude about it do not accord. Thus, if we disapprove of smoking but find that we have just lit a cigarette, we ought to experience dissonance.

Dissonance theory appears in all the psychology textbooks, although its original findings have hardly ever been unambiguously replicated (Stroebe, 1980). It is a striking theory and many of the results from studies into it are striking, too. People have lied for small amounts of money but not for large amounts (Dissonance: I lied; the money did not justify it; therefore, it was not a lie). They have bamboozled themselves (Dissonance: I find this group very boring; I went to a lot of trouble to join it; therefore, it is not a boring group).

Dissonance was probably felt by the solvent/health man in the No Smoking section. It takes two forms: I am a health enthusiast, but I smoke; I am a smoker, but I am sitting in a No Smoking section. We know how he resolved the second simple instance: he moved elsewhere when he wanted to smoke and thereby removed that particular bit of dissonance. As to the first case, it is much more interesting. It would have *created* or increased dissonance for the health enthusiast to support me (I am a smoker telling someone else to stop) *and* for him to support the smoker (I am a smoker advocating smoking in a No Smoking section when I care about other people's rights). Hence his silence.

How would dissonance work with the dog owner, though? To get him to change his behaviour, we have to create dissonance in him somehow. Our blatant attempt to do that ('You have a dog here' 'You're in an area where dogs are prohibited') failed. We could have tried to affect other attitudes of his. For example, there is the positive attitude that he probably holds about himself. We could have tried to make his positive view of himself inconsistent with his actions. (I once heard this used effectively on a plane: 'If you put your bag in that overhead rack it might fall on me and I know you'd feel bad about that. I'd prefer you not to feel bad so why don't you put it somewhere else?' It worked in that case.) We could have

pointed out what dissonance he would feel about himself, what a
jerk he would think he was, if a nice chap such as he did something
to upset a lot of other people, for instance, by letting his dog loose
in a children's play area. But, because he is a stranger to us, we do
not really know, just by looking at him, how much dissonance he
can tolerate. Maybe he has a high threshold and can easily withstand
it. Relevant to his tolerance here is the fact that, if he takes his dog
away, he would have to move himself and his children and all his
bags of shopping and the baby-stroller. If it comes to dissonance
versus inconvenience, he may choose to tolerate the dissonance. As
it turned out, in another brilliant stroke of ingenuity (proving that
he obviously got his cauliflower ear on a diplomatic mission somewhere), he picked up the dog and put it inside his coat, thus stop-
ping it running around (that keeps us happy), but not moving it
from the play area (that kept him happy).

The dog owner's behaviour (bringing in the dog, and letting it
loose) is what creates the difficulty and permits us to apply the principles of dissonance theory. What if he had not brought the dog in
before we spoke to him – that is, what if we said our piece after he
got his children out of the baby-stroller but before he let the dog
through the gate?

Behavioural intentions

A key element of a person's attitudes to anything is provided by
behavioural intentions (Fishbein & Ajzen, 1972). That is, the best
predictor of someone's eventual performance of an action is not that
person's expressed attitude to the act but his or her intention to
perform it. So the best place to exert persuasive pressure is on the
intention to perform the act rather than on the act itself. Once he
had let the dog in, he was committed and a whole range of new
psychological processes was triggered. Before he admits the dog, his
intention to do so has not been put into effect, and we could
influence his behaviour by influencing his intention.

Undoubtedly, our mistake was to wait until he had committed
himself to bring the dog in with him. By attempting to get him to
stop – rather than attempting to prevent him from starting – we
affected his sense of freedom, and we initiated *reactance* (Brehm,
1966; Brehm & Brehm, 1981). Reactance is a motivational state
brought about by the feeling that our freedom has been constrained.
When reactance is aroused, so the theory goes, we attempt to restore
our lost freedom, to restate our right to enjoy it, or to regain our

control over things. Research shows that reactance can lead people to do exactly the opposite of what they were requested to do – just to show that the persuader does not have control over them. 'This person told me to do X. Right, then, X is the last thing I'll do.' We have all seen other people do this, and, probably, we have all acted that way too. The dog owner was only being human: we should have acted sooner to prevent his reactance.

Problems with these ideas

In sum, then, even though I give these approaches sketchy coverage here because you can read them more fully in your main text, you can see that there are problems that have led to them being discarded. To use their principles, we must know in advance just what would be 'consistent' for the target, and, therefore, how to inject enough uncomfortable inconsistency into a personal situation for the person to be sufficiently disturbed to want to remove it. When dealing with strangers, this is precisely the kind of knowledge about them that we never have. On the other hand, if we know the other person well, we can take account of individual personal styles.

A second reason why consistency theories are problematic is because they misrepresent us. We are not actually consistent, but often wish we were or try to represent ourselves as if we were. People have all sorts of double standards and can happily do things that to an outside observer appear to be inconsistent or illogical. From the inside, however, the blinding logicality and consistency of our own actions is only too apparent ('Small dogs don't count, so I'm being consistent'). Consistency theories will, in my opinion, never be accurate predictors of all behaviour, but they will often predict the ways in which people will report behaving or would like to behave, or would like to see ourselves – rather than what we actually do. They are of little use when we meet strangers, except in extremely vague and general ways. We have to know people better before we know how to create specific feelings of inconsistency without having them simply decide to dislike and ignore us.

When we know people better and have more time then we can do things differently.

Dealing with friends and acquaintances

However casually we know acquaintances, we know them all the same and probably want to emphasize that knowledge in dealing with them or getting favours from them, since such knowledge carries an obligation to grant simple requests (Roloff et al., 1988). Also, we often have more time to get them to do things for us, so we can be a bit more strategic and longer-term in our persuasion. Several well-studied aspects of persuasion seem to fit in here, especially those dealing with more than one message from *us* (persuaders) to *them* (targets).

Techniques of persuasion

In any situation, the pattern of the messages that we choose is fundamental. Some message structures are more persuasive than others (Dillard, 1989). There is the 'foot-in-the-door' technique (i.e. asking for a small favour before asking for the big one), or the 'door-in-the-face' technique (i.e. asking for a big, unreasonable request, being refused, and then settling for a small request, which was actually the one you wanted all along). Thirdly, there is the 'low-ball' method, a technique that gets a person committed to something on the basis of false information (e.g. by quoting the costs as lower than they are). Once a person feels committed, he or she is likely to carry on with the behaviour even when hidden extras or increased costs are then revealed.

'Foot in the door'

Door-to-door sales people use a method of trying to put a foot in the door – literally or figuratively – and getting the prospective client to make a very small and harmless-looking commitment initially (e.g. a commitment to approving the format of a series of books). Once that is made, the commitment is increased gradually (e.g. to taking the first volume of the series on approval, then to agreeing to have a few volumes in the home to see how the set looks, and so on up to the original aim: paying for 26 volumes). The technique is based on small increments of commitment at each stage so that the client really feels that each step is a logical and hardly noticeable progression from the last step, until lo and behold, the client owns a fine, extremely expensive encyclopaedia.

Would you erect a large and unsightly billboard in your garden, even if it was for a good cause and encouraged careful driving? Not likely. In fact, only 16 percent of residents in Palo Alto, California, agreed when asked directly (Freedman & Fraser, 1976). Of those who were first asked to put a small sticker on road safety in a window of their home, however, 55 percent subsequently agreed to put up the large sign, too. Comparable results are found by several other researchers and DeJong's (1979) review of them concludes that the technique is effective as long as the initial request is small and when no compelling reasons, such as financial inducements, are offered for doing it.

One explanation is that the foot in the door works because the initial compliance allows the persons to feel good about themselves. Kraut (1973) finds that if people are 'labelled' positively when they give to one charity they give more to a second one also. The method of labelling is simple: 'You are really a generous person. I wish more people were as charitable as you'. For such an effect to work, however, the labelled action must be seen by the actor as resulting from 'internal' factors – those under the actor's own control – otherwise there is no credit for having acted that way. External causal factors – those not under the person's own control – often cause people to do things, so the positive label would probably not work if the actor felt that the actions were brought about by other than their personal free choice (Dillard et al., 1984).

Intelligent, generous and discerning readers like you who have made a thoughtful choice in buying this book will obviously find many ways of using this method in predicaments with strangers and friends. The technique is useful only if we have control over the circumstances or can choose the precise timing of the requests. Also, a useful relationship can be established even by some small expression of commitment to help and it can then be exploited. For instance, Cook (1977) notes that some seducers first attempt to get a partner to do a small favour for them before they make any explicit sexual 'move', and they take willingness as an encouraging sign. Then, they increase the scale of the requests and begin to steer to sexual themes.

'Door in the face'

Will persons who refuse a big demand be more likely to agree to a small one (the so-called door-in-the-face method)? In the original study of this possibility (Cialdini et al., 1975), subjects were first asked to serve as voluntary counsellors at a county juvenile detention centre for two years. Almost everyone turned this 'opportunity' down. When they were subsequently asked to agree to a much smaller request – that is, to chaperone some juveniles on a trip to the zoo – many did so.

The method seems to work if the initial request is almost ridiculously large, so that the person does not even entertain it as reasonable, and so does not feel negative about himself or herself when turning it down. It also works when the second request is made by the same person who makes the first one – possibly because we would feel bad about ourselves if we turn the same person down twice in a row. It would make us feel mean or unhelpful if we do this. The method is also more successful if the second, smaller request is related to the first, such as filling out a small insurance-company survey after declining to fill out a much longer one (Mowen & Cialdini, 1980).

'Low ball'

The low-ball technique (Cialdini et al., 1978) consists of raising the cost of doing something, once the target (client) agrees to do it in ignorance of the true full costs. For instance, if you consent to show up for an experiment you will be more likely to agree to come before dawn if I hold off on information about the time until after you agreed in principle to participate. This technique differs from the foot in the door only insofar as it involves initial commitment to the *same* behaviour that is ultimately requested, whilst foot in the door involves initial commitment to a different smaller request. It is useful in some circumstances (e.g. selling a car) and even more useful for prospective customers to be aware of. It really depends on there being little or no personal relationship between the people. It loses its effectiveness once we come to realise that someone might use it quite constantly. It is also an extremely offensive and exploitative approach, and will lose more friends than it will persuade. Save it for selling cars.

Reflections

There is one odd implication in the material reviewed so far. It mostly assumes that persuasiveness 'resides' in the external characteristics of the persuader (e.g. we are persuasive because we dress well or look good); in the internal psychological structure of the target (e.g. people generally change their attitudes in the direction of consistency); or in the broad relationship of parts of the message to other messages that have recently been sent and received (e.g. persuasion follows rejection of other persuasion attempts). The effects are largely assumed to be absolute. The strategies are presumed to work irrespective of personal circumstances or the situation or the relationship between participants.

Also, it assumes that our only goal is to persuade the other person, but in most predicaments we actually have multiple goals (Clark & Delia, 1979). For instance, we want to ensure no smoking in No Smoking areas, but we do not want to feel bad about it; we want to stop someone pushing ahead of us in line, but we do not want to look as if we are overreacting or officious; we want to get friends to do us a favour, but we certainly do not want to leave them feeling exploited. What is needed, then, is to recognize these multiple goals and explain the ways in which goals might affect the shape of requests that we make.

Was it something I said?

Let us assume that we all have a range of persuasive strategies to choose from in any set of circumstances (Miller & Boster, 1988; Miller & Parks, 1982). In that case, persuasion comes from the style of the communicator's message rather than the psychological characteristics of the target. This approach acknowledges that choices of message might depend on context, circumstances, or the relationship between us and the other person: we choose different methods in different encounters, with different people, or on different occasions with the same person. It sees persuasion as a 'homeless' concept growing from social relations or interactions.

Request strategies

Marwell & Schmitt generated a list of sixteen different strategies (Table 5.1), some of which are reward oriented (i.e. based on positive encouragements) whilst others are punishment oriented (i.e. based on negative features). Thus some strategies stress what the target will gain by complying, whilst others stress the pains that will be avoided by it. Miller & Parks (1982) further categorized them into those with communicator onus (e.g. 'Do this for me') and those with target or recipient onus (e.g. 'Do yourself a favour') – see Figure 5.1. So we can decide to emphasize either what *we* can do or what will happen to the *target* and either the rewarding or the punitive consequences.

Table 5.1 *Marwell and Schmitt's typology of 16 compliance-gaining strategies*

1. Promise	(If you comply, I will reward you.) You offer to release community property if your relational partner will agree to dissolution.
2. Threat	(If you do not comply, I will punish you.) You threaten to take all community property if your relational partner will not agree to dissolution.
3. Positive expertise	(If you comply, you will be rewarded because of 'the nature of things'.) You tell your relational partner that it will be a lot easier on both of you if he/she agrees to the dissolution.
4. Negative expertise	(If you do not comply, you will be punished because of 'the nature of things'.) You tell your relational partner that if he/she does not agree to the dissolution, it will be an extremely difficult emotional experience for both of you.
5. Pre-giving	(Actor rewards target before requesting compliance.) You finance a vacation for your relational partner to visit friends before telling him/her you wish to dissolve the relationship.
6. Aversive stimulation	(Actor continuously punishes target making cessation contingent on compliance.) You refuse to communicate with your relational partner until he/she agrees to discuss the possibility of dissolution.
7. Debt	(You owe me compliance because of past favours.) You point out to your relational partner that you have sacrificed to put him/her through college and that he/she owes it to you to let you live your life as you desire.
8. Liking	(Actor is friendly and helpful to get target in a 'good frame of mind' so that he/she will comply with the request.) You try to be friendly and pleasant as possible with your relational partner before bringing up the fact that you want to dissolve the relationship.
9. Moral appeal	(A moral person would comply.) You tell your relational partner that a moral person would let someone out of a relationship in which he/she no longer wished to participate.
10. Positive self-feeling	(You will feel better about yourself if you comply.) You tell your relational partner that he/she will feel better about him/herself if he/she lets you go.
11. Negative self-feeling	(You will feel worse about yourself if you do not comply.) You tell your relational partner that denying you your freedom will make him/her feel like a terrible person.
12. Positive altercasting	(A person with 'good' qualities would comply.) You tell your relational partner that because he/she is a mature, intelligent person, he/she will want you to do what is best for you.
13. Negative altercasting	(Only a person with 'bad' qualities would not comply.) You tell your relational partner that only someone who is cruel and childish would keep another in a relationship which the other desired to leave.
14. Altruism	(I need your compliance very badly, so do it for me.) You tell your relational partner that he/she must free you from the relationship to preserve your sanity.

15. Positive esteem	(People you value will think highly of you if comply.) You tell your relational partner that his/her friends and relatives will think highly of him/her for letting you go.
16. Negative esteem	(People you value will think worse of you if you do not comply.) You tell your relational partner that his/her friends and relatives will be ashamed of him/her if he/she tries to prevent you from leaving.

Source: Marwell & Schmitt (1967) 'Dimensions of compliance-gaining behaviour: an empirical analysis'. *Sociometry* (30), 357–8. Reproduced by permission.

The most commonly used strategy is liking, with altruism also being a high choice (see Table 5.1). On the whole, people seem to try to avoid punishing strategies when possible and to prefer reward-based ones (deTurck, 1985). We can see from Table 5.1 that the strategy I deduced from Heider's balance theory comes out as number 8 (liking) in the Marwell & Schmitt typology: it is essentially a preparatory strategy that gets the target/recipient in the right frame of mind for a persuasive communication that follows. The one from Festinger's dissonance theory seems to come out as number 15 (positive esteem) and is more direct.

Several attempts to reduce the typology to a more economical size have failed, but Hunter & Boster (1978) reckon that the strongest influence on the choice of strategy is whether the communicator perceives the goal to be to the benefit of the recipient or of the communicator. When the target/recipient is the beneficiary (e.g. when 'Don't drink too much' is the goal) then any strategy is likely to be used and persuaders will go to greater lengths to persuade the target (Boster & Stiff, 1984). When the communicator is the likely beneficiary (e.g. 'Do me this favour'), then the persuader typically does not exert such efforts, although this impressively altruistic model of human nature has been found not to work on every occasion (Clark, 1979).

Other work suggests that the list of strategies is not actually exhaustive (Burgoon et al., 1980) and that subjects can recognize others that are not in the list. For example, Wiseman & Schenk-Hamlin (1981) develop a typology in which two new strategies are 'direct request' (surprisingly absent from the more devious Marwell-Schmitt typology) and 'explanation' (when a straightforward, non-manipulative set of reasons for making the request is given). At the same time, some other strategies in the list appear to overlap conceptually. For example, positive altercasting ('A person with good

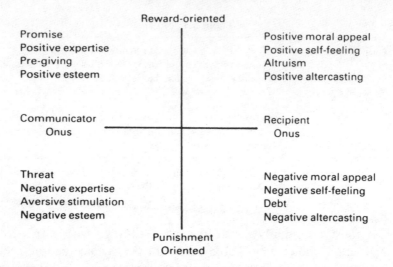

Figure 5.2: *Four-category typology of compliance-gaining message strategies*

Source: Miller & Parks (1982) Fig. 2, p. 151 in Duck (1982) *Personal Relationships 4: Dissolving Personal Relationships*. Academic Press: London. Reproduced by permission.

qualities would comply') achieves a similar result to that achieved by positive esteem ('People will think highly of you if you comply').

Forms of a request

What are the factors that particularly influence the form of a request? Two influences are variously called 'dominance and intimacy' (Cody et al., 1983), or 'status and familiarity' (Tracy et al., 1984). These define the amount of liking that exists between the two actors (or the degree to which they know one another) and their relative status (cf. Chapter 1 on the form of language as a result of the status and solidarity variables described by Brown, 1965). When we know, like, and have power over someone, we choose strategies not used with strangers. The third factor that influences choice of message type is, rather naturally and predictably, the size of the request or the amount of inconvenience or imposition that will result to the target of the request. The larger the request or favour is, the more the requester takes account of 'felicity conditions' and 'face wants' (Tracy et al., 1984).

'Felicity conditions' refer to two elements of messages: the speaker makes clear why the request is being made and hence establishes that there are legitimate needs for making it: the speaker enquires about the hearer's willingness to perform the requested act (in other words, the person establishes that he or she is making a request rather than giving an order or asking for fulfilment of an obligation).

'Face wants' refer to the concern that the speaker has for presenting a positive image of self and partner (Tracy et al., 1984). There are three elements to this:

1 Messages vary in the degree to which they acknowledge the hearer's desire to be liked and appreciated ('I really appreciate your help on this; you're very kind').

2 Messages vary in relation to the negative face wants of the hearer (i.e. the person's desires for autonomy, freedom of action and freedom from imposition). Speakers acknowledge this need by showing reluctance to impose on the hearer or by showing uncertainty in their request ('I hate to ask you this, but . . . Would it be at all possible for you to?').

3 Messages vary in the attention they give to the speaker's own positive face (e.g. when we ask to borrow money we might make it clear that we have saved some already, but not enough). Note that attention to face wants directly relates to something that we have found here to be vital – making the other person feel good about himself or herself – and that felicity conditions do so less directly but still could help do so.

Strategy selection

What strategies do we see ourselves having available to us and why do we make particular selections? Certain 'types' of person may habitually choose certain types of strategy. For instance, powerful people may regularly choose punitive strategies, explicitly or implicitly, and people who want to be seen as powerful may think that those strategies are the ones to use. Men and women may also choose typically different strategies; women are found to prefer to start with reward-based strategies, but their reaction to reluctance or noncompliance depends on the type and strength of the relationship between the two parties and the consequences for that (deTurck, 1985).

When persuading acquaintances (as distinct from friends), we do choose persuasive strategies that do not 'give us a bad time' if things go wrong (Miller, 1982). Our first thought is 'What are the consequences for me if I do not succeed here or things go wrong?' On the other hand, when attempting to persuade friends, we avoid strategies that the target cannot defend against without feeling obliged by friendship to do something for us that he or she would really much prefer not to (Miller, 1982). We ask 'What are the consequences for the friend and for our relationship if things go wrong?' Roloff et al. (1988) also show that the more intimate a person is with the target of the request, the less likely is any elaborate explanation of the request or any form of inducement. However, if the request is turned down, then intimates are more likely to come back with a less polite message than are people who are less intimate. The relationship between us and the target influences the strategies that we choose.

Everyday Influences on the Influence Process

One prominent influence on our behaviour in predicaments is the way that we feel about ourselves and our way of handling the situation. We all like to feel satisfied not only with the outcome of an attempt at persuasion but with the way that we dealt with the situation. If we are deciding about ways to tackle a predicament or to get another person to do as we want, then our relationship with him or her may affect this assessment of our satisfaction. Just think, if our neighbours turn their stereo up too loud, we *can* get the police, but it is not necessarily the best way from a social or personal point of view. Even if the other person is a stranger to us, our satisfaction with the outcome may depend not only on getting what we want but on doing it in a way that reflects well on our self-image and social presentation. In negotiations, for instance, it often helps to enter with a claim for slightly more than we actually want so that we have something to give away as a concession and with which to create a favourable image of our reasonableness as negotiators.

An important everyday fact, then, is the significance of the persuasion attempt in the here and now of the person's social life: persuasion has consequences for me now here. We often have to make persuasive attempts knowing that we must continue in the situation afterwards. If we try to get a neighbour to turn down the stereo, we may be making our future life less comfortable since the neighbour may become ill disposed towards other requests, may become 'difficult', or the like. Little persuasive attempts can, nevertheless, have large personal consequences. We would be making a big mistake if we regarded everyday compliance-gaining and persuasion as neatly packaged, done at a distance from insistently helpful friends and friendly advisers; or, if we saw 'compliance-doing' as a pure act of 'information processing' that is relatively rapid and based only on sensible principles.

A second point is that compliance-gaining in everyday life might take up a lot of time. It is not usually a simple, once-for-all event. The target is likely to resist us or challenge us, which will require us to take another shot. Furthermore, some compliance takes time to plan. Attempts to seduce a partner or have an essay grade changed can be thought about or planned in advance, can be modified, and can be thought about later, too, if they fail the first time. Also, as Christopher & Frandsen (1990) showed (see Chapter 4 here), individuals often use clusters of strategies in order to achieve such goals as premarital sexual intercourse.

For this reason, we do not try just one persuasive method, see if it works, and then go back to doing whatever we were doing. More often than not we persist, if the request matters to us. Not only do we persist in a particular encounter but we may persist over a longer timespan, say several encounters. Thus selection of strategies is, I think, a developmental procedure rather than an isolated, one-off choice. Often, we take time to think out alternative strategies and plan ahead. We may even be able to set up circumstances in a way that assists us (e.g. by getting the other person into a good mood first, before we try to influence him or her). We may even try to use deception, but even then, according to Neulip & Mattson (1990), the structure of messages is important. Deceptive persuasion contains higher percentages of rationales and explanations than honest persuasion does; instead it often involves messages with positive and negative sanctions built in!

It is in the unpredictable, spontaneous real-life circumstances, where such control or preparation is lacking, that persons are thrown back on general persuasive principles rather than personal knowledge. This is partly because events like queue-jumping 'just happen' and partly because the other actors in the events cut across our intentions and make their own independent attempts to have things go *their* way, too. Each person can react in an almost infinite number of ways to any behaviour, ploy or words of the other actor. When relationships or pre-organized conditions do not exist, the persuader is thrown back on personal resources, such as strategic style or communicative skills.

By contrast, when we are familiar with a target for our compliance-gaining efforts, our knowledge helps us to plan and gives us some awareness of likely consequences. For this reason, in everyday influence we do not need to be motivated (persuaded) in the usual ways to accept or yield to what we have been told, as we do in advertising and propaganda. In these two cases, for instance, people are depicted as needing to be motivated by fear (Janis &

Feshback, 1953) or by evidence that their behaviour does not match their stated opinions (Festinger, 1957) or by yielding a small, uncontentious point before being given the main issue (Freedman & Fraser, 1976; Cialdini et al., 1975).

When we look at the routine side of real life, though, we see that the 'motivation' is present and implicit in the situation or the role relationship between participants. When we have to get a parent to lend us the car, persuade someone to lend us a valuable book, or obtain an extension of a deadline for an assignment, there are inbuilt relational forces that affect not only the target of the persuasion but also the person attempting to achieve the outcome. For one thing, both parties have a view of themselves and their relationship – and probably wish to preserve it. Sometimes, we would rather give up on an argument than risk losing a friendship. For this reason, we shall most probably be unwilling to act in a way that threatens it, and they may make this fact a key element in their persuasion attempt. If we make a request that we recognize is too demanding, we accompany it by some relational preservative like an appeal to the person's good nature, an offer to restore the balance one day, a reminder of a past occasion when the positions were reversed, or a reference to our overwhelming need and the role requirements of friendship. In other circumstances when the relationship is more formal, such as between teacher and pupil, such relational references will refer to the demands of the *role* and the participants are unlikely to persuade by use of implied personal friendship.

Once we recognize that most persuasions occur in a context of living relationships, real social lives and our long-term goals or projects, not just our short-term persuasive objectives, we see that we need to look carefully into the impact of such contexts on our attempts to gain compliance.

Summary

We have looked at two real-life examples where one person chose to try to stop another person from doing something he wanted to do. I described, and tried to apply, a number of techniques that have been studied by social psychologists and communication scientists for many years. In real life, the relationship between the persuader and the target is vital, and there are a number of ways in which the social and relationship context for real-life decision-making could affect the ways in which we decide to attempt to persuade someone else. However small many of our persuasions are in real life, many of them can be drawn out and anxiety-provoking in ways not true of 'big' attitude change about, say, nuclear power. Our decision-making and persuasion in the context of our everyday life-concerns involve us in thinking about the consequences for our relationships with our partners, friends and colleagues as well as in assessing the merits or demerits of two sides of an argument or of two alternatives that lie open to us.

Further reading

Ajzen, I. (1988) *Attitudes, Personality and Behaviour*. Open University Press: Milton Keynes, UK.

Billig, M. (1987) *Arguing and Thinking: A Rhetorical Approach to Social Psychology*. Cambridge University Press: Cambridge.

Billig, M. (1991) *Ideology and Opinions: Studies in Rhetorical Psychology*. Sage: London.

Potter, J. & Wetherell, M. (1987) *Discourse and Social Psychology: Beyond Attitudes and Behaviour*. Sage: London.

CHAPTER 6

Staying Healthy . . . with a Little Help from Our Friends?

One aspect to everyday life seems, on the face of it, to have little to do with relationships, namely health. When one looks more closely, however, as research has recently begun to do, then health is shown to be significantly affected by personal and social relationships. Not only do relationships influence beliefs about what it is healthy to do and what not, but the numbers of friends that we have and even our relationship with our doctor influence our health status. If we have more friends, and we like our physician, then the chances are that we shall stay healthier.

BOX 6.1 Points to think about

How far is susceptibility to illness influenced by social psychological factors, personality factors, or behaviour style? Can we believe ourselves to death?

What psychological experiences make people decide that they are ill or ill enough to seek medical advice from friends or from professionals? How do psychological variables influence our judgements of our illness and our likely recovery rate?

How far does the relationship between doctor and patient influence the patient's recovery? Should we try harder to like the physician, and take fewer pills?

Can we preserve our health by altering our patterns of relationship with other people? Could our friendship keep us alive whilst loneliness kills?

Can the demands and obligations of friendship be so stressful that they can cause us strain?

Relational issues in sickness and in health

Take a good look or even just a quick look at the advertising around you, and you will see how much human effort is devoted to prolonging life, trying to stay young, and keeping healthy. Where fifteenth-century alchemists wasted their lives looking for chemical potions and elixirs to prolong life, we do the same thing in a different attitudinal framework: we eat fibre, jog, take up yoga, use dye to cover grey hair and skin creams to 'banish' wrinkles. The results are similar; only the attitudes and beliefs are different. Nowadays, we simply believe that many diseases are curable by 'science' rather than by 'witchcraft', although in some cases the 'healing factors' are not that different.

Most of us will die because of unhealthy lifestyles despite the fact that these are correctable through education (Rogers, 1983). The main causes of death and disease nowadays are not the old unhygienic infestations like cholera and typhoid but heart disease, cancer, sexually transmitted diseases (like AIDS), and liver disease. Each of these is related to our own personal choices about diet, smoking, sexual behaviours and alcohol. Other health risks in our society are also results of the way we choose to live: dangerous driving, crime, obesity, lack of proper exercise, stress, dangerous sports and loneliness. We may feel better when we are in love or surrounded by friends; we may become discouraged when we feel lonely; but there could be more to it than mere feelings. Do human relationships actually affect our physical well-being and medical status? Some researchers claim that loneliness kills, that divorcing creates physical illness, and that some interpersonal styles of behaviour (e.g. personality, coping style and self-esteem) can make us more or less prone to heart failure (Lynch, 1987).

The sick role and the social side of illness

We may think we go to the doctor just because we are ill, but the true picture is somewhat more complex. Reporting of illness is not based on absolutes: for example, we are not just either sick or well. We are often somewhere in between. The health–illness continuum is a continuum, not a dichotomy of absolute health versus absolute illness (Shuval, 1981). Why do we move along the health–illness continuum, and why, when and how do we decide we are ill enough to need help?

We do not report that we are sick every time we have germs,

viruses or physical trauma; it also depends on how we feel about the experience. Recovery from illness is more than just a physical matter, since medical intervention focussing only on germs does not always cure people as fast as it should. Also relevant are the 'hope factor' and the 'will to live'. In addition, reporting sick is at least partly influenced by a whole host of seemingly impertinent matters such as personality, way of life or personal beliefs. These in their turn are influenced by the beliefs that exist in the surrounding culture.

The decision that one is sick will depend on psychological factors based on the perception of symptoms and what they mean. Some people report sensations and symptoms which are caused by psychological sources, but which lead to physical symptoms (Skelton & Pennebaker, 1982). Extreme examples are hysterical 'glove anaesthesia' (when the patient reports loss of sensation in the hand) or various forms of panic attack which lead to asthmatic shortness of breath. Some symptoms are not reported and seem not to occur in some cultures; for instance, Mead (1950) reports that women in the Arapesh tribe show no signs of morning sickness during pregnancy. Finally, wounded soldiers' reports of pain are often unrelated to the extent of their wounds. In the heat of battle, perception of pain apparently can be depressed (Beecher, 1959).

Clearly, there are individual, cultural and circumstantial influences on the perception of pain and the reporting of symptoms. These raise the possibility that illness can have personal or social functions as well as medical ones, for example making someone out to be a martyr or getting someone out of a difficult assignment. (For instance my wife has noticed that I get migraines most often when I am driving somewhere to perform a task I'd prefer not to be doing!) This is not saying that illness has *only* social functions or *always* has social functions, but we should at least explore such functions when they can be legitimately suspected. Equally, illness can result from social events or experiences, which, again, is not saying that it always does. We need to look, then, at the social consequences of becoming ill or defining oneself as sick.

Deciding what the symptoms mean

Some symptoms in themselves mean little (indeed physicians tend to look for clusters of symptoms rather than single ones anyway). Accordingly we have to decide for ourselves whether they might indicate illness – and, if so, whether it is appropriate to consult a doctor. Loss of appetite, for instance, can mean nothing significant at all or it may be a sign of illness. It is, in any case, a *general* symptom of many different kinds of ailment, so we might decide that it tells us something important or that it does not, depending on our psychological attitudes to life at the time. A hypochondriac may decide that loss of appetite portends a serious illness and ought to be checked out; other persons may not notice or be influenced by their loss of appetite. (They might even be glad – if they are trying to lose weight.)

Since many pains are ambiguous, transitory, or due to any one of many possible root causes, they have to be interpreted. Jones (1982) points out that pain initiates a search for causes, and people will pin the explanation on any cause that seems both plausible and salient, even if it is actually incorrect. If a recent event seems likely to have caused the symptoms (e.g. a sudden severe headache following a blow to the head), then we are likely to attribute the effect to that cause even if, for example, the real cause is a spontaneous brain tumour.

By contrast, psychological state can contribute to the occurrence of certain symptoms (Mechanic, 1980); for instance, an extremely anxious person might develop ulcers or headaches. Indirectly, also, anxiety may cause us to change our habits: negative attitudes may make us careless or prepared to act in a self-destructive manner, for instance by drinking excessively, eating irregularly and driving dangerously (Kelley & Rolker-Dolinsky, 1987). Furthermore, a person can develop symptoms as a result of changes in daily routines or habits, and these can in turn come from psychological changes going on inside. For instance, if we become extremely anxious about life, we may start drinking or smoking and so develop liver or lung ailments.

Psychological variables can also affect health by increasing arousal or raising the level of body monitoring (i.e. by increasing our attention to physical symptoms). Various psychological states increase arousal and can create false symptoms, such as sleeplessness or headaches or tension that are really the by-products of increased arousal – a purely psychological change – although we usually fail to see it that way (Mechanic, 1980). We usually feel physiologically aroused, notice that we are sleeping less, have headaches and the like, then we think that there must be a cause for it: we must be ill.

'Being ill' can itself become closely tied up with our view of ourselves, since it excuses us from poor performance: 'What can you expect? I'm sick'. Also, it may become structured into our daily routines rather like the routines of heroin addicts' families (Lewis & McAvoy, 1984), who come to structure their lives around the addict, the addiction and the behaviour that is necessary to sustain it (such as theft and prostitution). Also someone may be easier to deal with when they are 'ill', so the family is happy for them to stay defined that way, or encourages them to see themselves as 'ill'. At least, if they are in bed they are doing no harm.

This all goes to show that illness is not simply a physically created state, but one where psychological factors intertwine with physical factors. Even illnesses which are reported fairly commonly could nevertheless indicate that in the person doing the reporting there is a psychological change taking place rather than a physical problem. We can conclude, then, that there is a close relationship between psychological state and the meaning of symptoms to the person who decides to report sick.

Deciding to report sick

There is more to becoming ill than merely feeling a twinge of pain in the stomach. We decide we are sick when we personally: feel that our physical state deserves attention; are not satisfied with other possible explanations; are willing to accept the consequences of being confirmed sick; and believe that some treatment would be more useful and effective than no treatment. These are psychological factors that link up with our views of ourselves, with our attitudes to pain, physicians and sickness, and with our personal beliefs about illness. If we believe that illness is a punishment for sin then we may be less likely to admit to illness than if we think it is a reward for doing good or if we assume it is caused by an invasion of viruses over which we have no legitimate control.

Equally relevant is our trust in the physician and the treatment. This trust will depend on our beliefs about physicians in general, the way we are handled in the consultation, whether the physician's breath smells of alcohol, and our own personal model of illness. People nowadays accept antibiotics whereas in previous times they may have believed in the efficacy of boiled newts' tongues, crocodile dung, and the sweat of pregnant women – treatments which were more often effective than we would suppose (DiMatteo & Friedman, 1982).

Neither the decision to report sick nor the confidence in the effectiveness of treatment is based on absolute factors. An individual's personal beliefs and those of friends or cultures at large will also give meaning to pain and illness. Each society takes its own view of why and how people get sick and what they should do to put it right. Which of the following explains why we get sick? God is punishing us for some sinfulness; our body contains too much blood and needs leeching; a demon has crept into our body; we caught a virus; we failed to make a sacrifice to the health god; we ate the wrong diet; we have bad attitudes towards our comrades; we did not get a regular health checkup; we do not exercise enough; we smoke; a witch stuck a pin into a model of our body; we are lonely; we have just moved house, lost our job, become divorced, and run into debt; an enemy gave us the Evil Eye; it was something we ate last night; we should have washed our hands. Not only have all of these views been held by some culture or another at some point in the past, but most of them are still believed by some group or another today. Our choice between them can be seen as partly influenced by culture.

Obviously, such beliefs affect what we do to be cured, whether we blame ourselves for our illness, and how our friends and relatives react to our predicament. For instance, if I regard illness as a punishment for sin then I shall remain silent about the pains in my chest so that my family does not suspect me of being evil. If, on the other hand, I believe the pains are caused by a witch then I shall call a priest to pray with me – and my friends will not think me odd. If I think the pains are 'a heart attack' I shall call an ambulance, which will probably race to the scene while other car drivers get out of its way, unthinkingly and willingly accepting that the ambulance is justified in making itself heard and disrupting traffic.

Over and above such background cultural factors, there are seven individual factors that influence psychological attitudes towards reporting of illness (Mechanic, 1974).

1 Number and persistence of symptoms;
2 Individual abilities to recognize and discriminate symptoms;
3 Individual judgements of their seriousness;
4 The extent of consequent social or physical disability;
5 Cultural or personal attitudes to stoicism and endurance of pain;
6 Amount of medical information available to the person;
7 Availability of help set against perceived costs, whether social or financial.

Whilst these are all individual judgmental influences, they all relate to one crucial point: an individual's (un)willingness to accept the sick role.

The sick role and the social consequences of illness

Being ill is a social as well as a purely physical condition and makes the individual enter the 'sick role'. To do this, a person must be legitimized by an accepted authority, such as a physician, or in the case of a child, by a parent (Parsons, 1951). Secondly, the illness must normally be beyond the person's responsibility to control (e.g. someone who is staggering and disoriented by reason of intoxication is not 'sick' whereas someone showing similar symptoms as a result of concussion truly is 'sick'). Thirdly, whilst the sick role legitimately excuses us from certain regular obligations like work, it brings others. A person is obliged to 'get well soon' or to act out the role in a socially acceptable way by, for example, 'bearing pain with cheerfulness and fortitude', being uncomplaining about discomfort, and appearing to be brave in the face of impending death. People who do this satisfactorily have it mentioned in their obituaries, whilst those who fail to do so do not have their reactions described at all. You will never see an obituary that says 'When he was told that he was dying he just broke down and cried like a real wimp' (although that might be an understandable reaction in the circumstances).

Illness has three further aspects to it (DiMatteo & Friedman, 1982), all with social psychological overtones: destructive, liberating and occupational.

First, illness is usually *destructive*: it causes physical deterioration, pains, disability and discomfort. This can cause anguish to loved ones, who see a father, mother, partner, child or friend deteriorating before their eyes. Insofar as the patient is aware of these feelings or reactions, then psychological pain, including feelings of guilt, can also afflict the patient. Equally, the patient has feelings about the destructive side of illness and is called on to cope not only with the pain itself but with its social management (e.g. not 'letting it show' to visitors).

A further social psychological consequence of the destructive side of illness is the direct effect on status and general 'social credit'. Many illnesses cause disfigurement or socially unacceptable sights, sounds and smells. These social stigmata must be endured by the patient along with the pain and they affect others' willingness to be involved socially with the patient (Lyons et al., 1990). Some illnesses disrupt social behaviour and cause inept actions like involuntary trembling, unexpected extensions of limbs, lolling of the head and tongue, dribbling, or disturbed eye movements. These, too, are stigmata that make it difficult for outsiders to interact with the patient in normal social ways and thus add to the burdens that the patient must endure (Lyons et al., 1990).

Some medication treats the illness but causes side-effects with nasty social consequences like drowsiness or inability to concentrate (e.g. some antipsychotic drugs cause stiffness in the limbs and occasional uncontrollable drooling). Alternatively, some treatments restrict patients' social calendars or require them to withdraw from social contact to carry out medical procedures (e.g. going to lie down for dialysis on a kidney machine or going to a private room for regular insulin injections for diabetes mellitus).

These aspects of illness make extra social demands on the patient, over and above the need to cope with physical discomfort. As such they afflict the person's ability to carry out and enjoy normal social relationships.

Secondly, illness can also serve a liberating social function. It frees people from dull routine, legitimizes their noncompletion of assignments, and releases them from exams, duties, tasks and obligations (Parsons, 1951). Social, intellectual and task-related failures can be excused by reference to sickness ('I wasn't concentrating: I have a headache'). These excuses are not damaging to the individual's social persona (or 'image'): the persons are 'off the hook', it is not their fault, they should not blame themselves, they do not lose their 'social credit'. They can blame the illness; the person is out of sorts and not fully responsible.

Thirdly, illness can become an occupation that takes over a person's life like a full-time job. The person may need to restructure daily routines like feeding and toilet needs in significantly restrictive ways or go to bed much earlier than usual, cut down on social time, and make much less effort to go out and see people. Although such things are caused by the illness, they nevertheless afflict the person's social life and relationships.

The sick role and failure

In the light of such points, perhaps illness is a mechanism for coping with failure (Shuval et al., 1973). Since illness gives us an appropriate, legitimate and accepted excuse to tell our friends why we are unable to perform roles, fulfil tasks or take on responsibility, some people might become ill or report or 'play up' an illness whenever they come up against evaluation, or when they are afraid of it. In brief, illness helps people to avoid evaluative situations, particularly ones which are important to them. Snyder & Smith (1982) suggest that illness operates as a 'self-handicapping strategy', as they call it, and so people exaggerate reports of illness (and may actually feel more ill) when they are faced with an esteem-threatening event. This is also known more dramatically as 'academic wooden leg'. ('What can you expect from someone with a wooden leg?'; it's borrowed from Berne, 1964, *Games People Play*). Such people might feel they have developed some serious illness just before class tests, for instance, if it really matters to them to get a high grade and they are worried that they are not going to make it. One 'way out' of the problem is to claim an illness which is absolutely debilitating and gives the perfect excuse not to sit the exam or be tested. How could we possibly do well in that exam if we have glandular fever and laryngitis?

Ultimately, the idea of self-handicapping goes back to Adler's explanation that people would report symptoms as self-protecting devices: what they protect is self-esteem. The symptoms provide reasons for failure that are an alternative to self-blame. We do not have to blame ourselves for being unable to do something; instead, we can blame the illness. It's the illness's fault that we cannot perform well in the exam, rather than because of our own incompetence. By developing these self-handicapping strategies (or rather, these pre-emptive self-serving attributions), people could avoid evaluations altogether. A second point is that if we are ill then we get a lot of attention from people and that bolsters our self-esteem. If we are feeling particularly down-at-heel, an apparent illness will evoke sympathy that picks up our self-esteem also. For instance, I know of a case where a girl developed hysterical paralysis of the leg that was so convincing (both to herself and to the physicians) that her leg was going to be amputated; but referral to a psychiatrist led to her admission to a special-care facility for adolescents, instead. At this time, her leg was useless and her muscles had atrophied from lack of use. She had had two operations, to no avail. After several months of therapy, she began to walk again. During psychotherapy it emerged that she had very low self-esteem and felt that she had never been any good at anything. If her leg had been amputated as she had wished, that would have given her a lifelong excuse for being unable to do certain things.

None of this is to say that people never get ill in the physical sense or that symptoms are nothing but self-protective strategies, but there are some cases where self-protection could be one of the major social roles of illness. If this is so, then manipulation of health and illness must take this into account to some extent.

Patient and physician

Visiting the physician: why and when?

Even if we decide that we are sick, there is another step to be taken also – the step of getting help. What influences whether and when we go to the doctor? We go to the doctor not just because we feel sick, but only when we feel that our physical state is serious enough to interfere with our life and so deserves special attention (Zola, 1972). We thus have a considerable amount of personal leeway surrounding the decision whether our physical state does interfere enough to deserve attention. It also depends on what is going on in our life at the time that could become disrupted. If we were going to be married tomorrow, we might well decide to postpone a visit to the physician to get on with everything else. If we have nothing much planned, then we may need less of 'an illness' to make us feel that we should see a doctor.

A second factor that influences the decision is a person's friend-ship status (Reis, 1990). People with supportive, closely knit networks of friends go to the doctor at an earlier point in the illness, presumably because they have been told by their friends that they do not look too well, and it's about time they did something and took professional advice (Hays & DiMatteo, 1984). On the other hand, people with no groups of friends, or with only small social networks, go to the doctor more often when there is nothing wrong with them – either because they have no access to preliminary lay advice that would tell them there is no real problem or because doctors have a caring role and they are seeking out someone to care. They may even hope to meet other people to talk to in the doctor's waiting room – an occurrence that is not as rare as you might think (Duck, 1991).

A third condition to be met before people will decide that they are ill enough to go to see the doctor concerns attitudes to physicians. Some people feel hostile towards or afraid of doctors (Hays & DiMatteo, 1984), do not believe that doctors actually cure people ('They don't really know what they are doing for lots of serious long-term illness; half of it is guesswork'). Others apparently fear the wait-ing room as a source of vicarious infection ('I knew a woman once who went to the doctor with a stiff leg and came out with bone cancer').

Lastly, people go to the doctors if they do not regard illness as a personal defeat or if it hurts so much that they must confront their inability to cope (Zola, 1972). Some people dislike classing themselves in the sick role because they regard themselves as having failed in some way. They may feel they are seeking attention they do not deserve or are being soft and needing support when they should be less dependent on other people.

Does it hurt enough to be worth a consultation?

What determines a person's timing of the decision that the pain is significant enough for help to be sought? DiMatteo & Friedman (1982) note that more deaths from myocardial infarctions (heart attacks) occur at times when it is socially inconvenient to interpret one's chest pains as a sign of heart problems rather than indigestion or strained muscles. That is, at weekends, when doctors are off duty, patients do not wish to call them out on a possible fool's errand – but by the time the patient acknowledges the true seriousness of his or her condition, it may be too late.

Other social psychological influences affect the decision to seek help at a particular time (Zola, 1972):

1 Some interpersonal crisis calls attention to the symptoms and makes the person dwell on them. For instance, a person may suddenly become aware of feeling faint during an argument or may experience difficulty breathing during a quarrel.

2 Some interference occurs to valued (social) activity. For instance, the person may not be able to join in a walking jaunt with friends because of breathlessness.

3 Symptoms are sanctioned by outsiders, who, for example, may remark that the person looks ill. If friends say that the person looks ill when the person also feels ill then that proves that the problem must show. It is not all just a figment of the imagination.

4 Symptoms are perceived as threatening; for instance when the pain becomes so severe that the person cannot move around properly.

5 Symptoms are perceived as similar to those suffered by other people of the patient's acquaintance. 'My uncle had just that sort of minor pain in the morning but by six o'clock that night he was dead'.

One might also expect that a strong social influence on such timing is provided by the social desirability of the illness and its treatment. We can readily admit to some diseases, but not others. People are more likely to hope that embarrassing symptoms will just clear up themselves, so that the sufferers will not have to go to a crowded drugstore and ask an attractive young assistant for some personally embarrassing medication, like delousing powder.

Doctor–patient relationships

Do we get better just because we like our doctor? Willingness to report sick is affected by confidence in and liking for the physician and so, more surprisingly, is recovery (Hays & DiMatteo, 1984). The doctor–patient relationship is one of the factors which affects psychological state, which in turn affects interpretation of symptoms, and whether we maintain the prescribed medication.

Faith in the physician has *some* curative effect. In the past, doctors frequently bled, purged, sweated or fumigated patients, attached leeches to them, and gave them all manner of strange concoctions, poultices and elixirs. It is less a miracle that anyone survived, than that doctors were allowed to continue to practise (which seems to have been what they were doing in more than one sense). Yet people had faith in these cures and frequently recovered, though one cannot be entirely sure that the threat of further treatment was not what brought it about.

Types of physician–patient relationships

Researchers have begun to understand a little more clearly the means by which physician–patient relationships can contribute to healing. Patients respond not only to their medical treatment but to their social treatment – the ways in which they are treated as human beings. Nowadays, doctors get instruction on ways of relating to patients (Pendleton & Hasler, 1983) and how to conduct medical interviews (Putnam et al., 1988). Bedside manner can influence the outcome of treatment: the more the patient feels like an individual and is treated as a person, rather than just as a collection of symptoms, the sooner he or she recovers (for example, physicians' elicitation of patients' descriptions of their symptoms and physicians' explanations for the symptoms in clinical interviews can be improved by training so that they reduce blood pressure in hypertensive patients: Orth et al., 1987). Obviously, when treated personally we feel less humiliated by the degrading aspects of treatment (e.g. being stripped and prodded, having to cough, spit and excrete or produce personal specimens while the nurse smiles encouragingly from the corner).

Being respected as a person can make us feel more important and want to recover, because we are being attended by someone who cares about us personally. It also, incidentally, makes the doctor feel better personally (because he or she feels more skilful, more personable, more important), feel more positive about the job, and more satisfied with doing it (Hays & DiMatteo, 1984). So one hidden consequence of this relational factor is that it makes doctors do a better job because they begin to feel better about what they are doing. The other hidden consequence is that patients who feel understood tend to communicate more effectively about their symptoms and so receive better treatment (Pettegrew & Turkat, 1986). As the authors conclude, patient–physician communication is not only instrumental but also relational, and style is as relevant as content.

There are three kinds of possible relationship between a physician and a patient (Szasz & Hollander, 1956):

1 *Activity-passivity*, when an active physician treats a passive and accepting patient. This is clearly a desirable model when, for instance, the patient is flat out comatose, but in other settings it implies an authority structure that would be uncomfortable for most people, since we regard our bodies as something in which we, too, have a 'voting' interest.

2 *Guidance-cooperation*, when an expert physician offers advice that a willing patient is expected to follow. This is entirely suitable when advice on, say, acute infections is offered by the doctor and the patient follows it. In other circumstances, however, it implies that the patient somehow has a duty to the doctor rather than vice versa.

3 *Mutual participation*, when physician and patient are mutually interdependent and where 'power' is more evenly distributed. The mutual-participation model is somewhat rare, even though patients prefer it and claim that they benefit from relationships where they are treated more personally and 'equally'. Physicians with a 'personal' approach to patients are liked more, trusted more, and have their advice followed more consistently by patients (Geersten et al., 1973). Since the patients in the study were suffering from arthritis, a crippling and extremely painful disease of the joints, the results are powerful. We would commonly expect that such people would be less affected by the physicians' styles and more influenced by the effectiveness of treatment. However, these two variables clearly interrelate: the social psychological and communicative elements matter, too.

A patient's perception of the doctor's social and medical skills affects confidence also. For instance, Parker (1960) shows that authoritarian medical *students* were disliked and disparaged, whilst authoritarian *consultants*, who are supposed to be expert, are indulged when they act masterfully and were both liked and trusted.

Unfortunately, where respect for a consultant's skills degenerates into fear, there are some serious effects on health. Jarvinaan (1955), working with people in coronary intensive care units, found that the most likely time for patients to have spontaneous relapses or a fatal heart attack was ten minutes before the doctors were due on their rounds to come and visit their patients. Evidently, stress was a cause of this, and the patients felt so belittled (in the 1955 pre-bedside-manner days) by the way they were treated by these eminent surgeons with all their students looking on, and poking them around, that they just decided they would shuffle off this mortal coil (Hamlet, 1597).

What can be done to improve the physician–patient relationship? If you cast your mind back to the materials on nonverbal and verbal interaction in chapter 1, you should get some ideas. For instance, we could devote special care to the physician's nonverbal style in the initial consultation when patients' expectations are set and when initial diagnosis is made. We could also look at the patients' nonmedical needs and the ways in which the physician could be helped to anticipate and deal with them.

BOX 6.2 An exercise on physician–patient relationships
Think back over the materials you have encountered in the book thus far. What measures could we take of the quality of the physician–patient relationship?

What aspects of the physician's – and, if it comes to that, of the patient's – behaviour should we, as social scientists, expect to be relevant to the relationship?

Write a brief list of the components that you would expect to be most suitable for attention.

Think for a moment about the recommendations you would make if you were appointed to initiate a programme of training for medical students to improve their rapport with patients.

The text gives you some answers.

Communication in the doctor–patient relationship

The central problem in doctor–patient relationships is communication. To make a diagnosis, the doctor needs to obtain all the relevant information, but has a much clearer idea of what would be relevant than the patient does. The skill is to obtain the details, bearing in mind that the patient may be medically unsophisticated and unaware of whether some piece of information is relevant to a diagnosis. If you are breathless, does it matter that you also have swollen ankles, for instance? A doctor would know that these together indicate heart disease and circulatory problems, but the patient may not.

Traditionally, then, the doctor takes control of the interactions and asks questions that will lead to the most helpful information. We have seen (Chapter 1) that the full relational system of communication has both verbal and nonverbal components. Both, therefore, are involved in doctor–patient communication. We have also seen that encoding (conveying what you feel) and decoding (working out what the other person feels) are important. Let us now look at these in the particular medical context that concerns us here.

Encoding One special difficulty for physicians is that they are bright people selected and trained for several years in a highly specialized and technical system of description about a common and familiar object: the human body, in its various appealing or grotesque manifestations. The patient, on the other hand, is concerned about a personal complaint and its cure, but is not necessarily intellectually curious about the why, the how and the wherefore. The patient comes to a consultation wanting, and perhaps needing, reassurance, and 'information'. (Indeed a major part of the physician's role is to explain the meaning of illness and to encourage appropriate preventive and curative measures which the patient must follow properly to do any good.) Most of us know little or nothing about what our liver does, have no idea why we have a spleen, and could not say where our pancreas is, let alone our ischial tuberosity or gluteus maximus, but we all have one (and, in some cases, two) of these. Sometimes we know we do not know, sometimes we think we do but are wrong, sometimes we have an idea that is partly right.

Most often patients are anxious enough to want reassurance but cannot understand what is said to them to provide it. Patients persistently request detailed explanations of what is happening to them, yet they do so unsystematically, tending to be passive and general (Boreham & Gibson, 1978). They ask for 'information' but are unclear about the areas of concern: what do they really want to know? In any case, patients mostly fail to comprehend what is said to them even when the 'information' is provided. Part of the problem is that medicine is so complex that most of us have very simple models of illness. We just are not aware of the mechanisms through which we could catch typhoid or do not have the faintest idea how gastroenteritis develops.

A further problem is that patients need to receive descriptions in common language whereas physicians tend to use 'medspeak' (Christy, 1979) and speak in jargon even when talking to patients who are relatively unsophisticated in medical knowledge. A doctor who knows the details of biochemistry must find it difficult to talk in terms of everyday examples that the rest of us can understand: doctors are taught to doctor not to teach. Words taken for granted by doctors will go 'over the heads' of most people: we may know what 'a diagnosis' is, but fewer know what 'a prognosis' means and can only ask 'How long have I got?'

Since medspeak is technical jargon, it is a high form of code (see Chapter 1) with many specialized terms, complex structure, and formality. It instantly freezes out informality and leaves little room for the friendly banter that may relax the patient enough to talk in detail about the symptoms. Patients are aware of very few central rules in the doctor–patient relationship, but two which stand out are: make sure that you are clean; and speak the truth (Argyle & Henderson, 1984). Since both emphasize the extreme power difference in the relationship, they, too, are likely to stand in the way of a friendly encounter – if that is what the patient truly desires.

The risks are that such rules and complex talk will alienate the patient and that they will increase the risk of misunderstanding. In tragic confirmation of this Boyd et al. (1974) found that more than 60 percent of patients misunderstood their physician's instructions about the method of taking their medication, even when they were interviewed soon after leaving the consultation. (I have always wanted to know if Boyd et al. ever did a follow-up, and, if so, how many subjects survived to take part in it.)

The best way that the physician can improve things is to provide the low code social form of discourse that the patient would like: the informal chatty style of language that we normally use to friends. Patients would rather have reassuring communication than emotionally neutral communications or humorous ones (Linn & DiMatteo, 1983). The second component is that the patient expects more general issues to be covered than simply those that relate directly to the illness. For instance, patients are more satisfied when psychosocial consequences of the ailment are specifically mentioned and addressed (Lau et al., 1982). In particular, how will it affect relationships with the family or the ability to socialize? It also seems likely to me that a preferred style would be one that emphasizes personal recollection of the patient's human individuality rather than simply the patient's medical history. Whether he had secretly written it on to my medical notes I do not know, but the doctor I best remember from my teenage years always ended each consultation with a question about my progress in my Classical Greek class at school. Whilst I forget why I went to see him, I remember this personal treatment and felt more confident about his medical skills than I did with another local doctor who not only forgot my name (a name like Duck?) but thought I was someone else. I'm just glad he didn't give me that person's medication instead of my own. It may be that their skills were equivalent but I, as a patient, find myself not believing that they could be.

Decoding Patients have a story to tell and often want to tell it in their own words. So the other side to the verbal interaction in a physician–patient interaction is decoding. Whilst a physician may need to ask some prompting 'closed questions' which produce 'yes/no' answers, 'Hearing the patient's true message is the . . . [essential feature] of a great physician' (Pickering, 1978, p. 554). (Interestingly, the original quotation has the Latin words *sine qua non*, where I put 'essential feature', and this tells us something about physicians' language codes – even when they are thinking about patients!) Attentive listening to a person's real meaning rather than the words themselves is an essential part of decoding messages (see Chapter 2), so it is not a surprise to find that patients prefer physicians who have an attentive listening style (Stone, 1979). Such attention can help the physician to learn more about the patient's psychological state (e.g. whether the person seems anxious, upset, depressed, obsessive, tense). Also, it may uncover something of the patient's psychosocial characteristics (e.g. value system, beliefs, norms, behavioural preferences and lifestyle) without the physician needing to ask intrusive questions about it. Such information may help the physician to work out whether the patient will take the tablets or whether the other family members will help. The physician may get family members to help the patient keep to a difficult drug prescription or dietary regimen.

Whilst the verbal part of interaction is significant, we know from Chapter 1 that the nonverbal component is more so (Walker & Trimboli, 1989). Predictably (from Chapter 1), both nonverbal encoding and nonverbal decoding will exert strenuous influence on the patient and physician. The whole range of nonverbal cues has effects on the physician's perception of the patient, and vice versa, as BOX 6.3 shows.

Naturally, patients are particularly sensitive to the effect that their condition has on other people, too. It is, therefore, crucial that the physician does not 'leak', through nonverbal channels, any sense of disgust, pity, revulsion, anxiety or lack of optimism (Friedman, 1982). Interestingly, Milmoe et al. (1967) show that a physician's effectiveness in referring alcoholics for further treatment is negatively correlated with the amount of anger present in the voice whilst talking about alcoholism. Physicians who 'leaked' their

---

BOX 6.3 Nonverbal cues in physician–patient relationships

Physicians who adopt a closed-arm position are interpreted as cold, rejecting and inaccessible, whilst moderately open positions convey acceptance (Smith-Hanen, 1977).

Physicians and counsellors who establish eye contact during a pleasant, accepting interaction make patients feel more positive about the encounter (LaCrosse, 1975).

Affiliative nonverbal behaviours, such as smiles, nods, and a 20-degree forward lean, increase the patient's perceptions of a physician's warmth, interest, concern – and attractiveness (LaCrosse, 1975).

Touch can have reassuring effects on patients, making them feel more relaxed, more comforted, more supported and more cared-for (Montagu, 1978).

Touch can exert a general enhancing effect on the perceived competence and effectiveness of health professionals (Blondis & Jackson, 1977).

Contact (e.g. in taking a patient's pulse) can influence patients' heart rate and cardiac rhythm, as well as reduce the frequency of ectopic beats – i.e. those that occur irregularly or out of place (Lynch et al., 1974).

Street & Buller (1988) showed that physicians use less touch with less anxious patients, however, and also use less dominant style with patients over 30 years of age than they do with younger ones.

---

distaste for alcoholism by seeming angry with the patient had the effect of discouraging patients from actually taking the further treatment that was advised.

On the other hand, patients frequently leak their true state of anxiety about an ailment through body posture, voice tone or (ir)regularity of speech and can also indicate fear or (dis)trust of physicians by the manner in which they regulate distance in the interaction (Hays & DiMatteo, 1984). A physician who attends carefully to the nonverbal cues which accompany the verbal messages will gain extra information about the patient's state of health and also about the patient's beliefs about that state, all of which may be useful in diagnosis.

The relational art of medicine

Doctor–patient communication is an extremely powerful influence on patients' satisfaction, so it is unsurprising that a number of

programmes are started with the intention of training medical
students in the 'art' of medicine, which has as one large component
the art of relating. Usually, these consist of training in nonverbal or
verbal communication skills (Engler et al., 1981). Typically, they
show that the student's interviewing, empathy and general handling
of patients improve. Results are not all positive (Farsad et al., 1978)
and may not have long-lasting effects even when they are positive.
We also do not really know whether such training leads to better
physicians or to more satisfied patients (which may or may not be
effectively the same thing). Nevertheless, it would be unusual for a
social scientist to conclude that the outlook for such work is not
promising, and I will not so conclude. If improvements in communication continue, then it seems likely that such training benefits both
the patients (who feel happier with their treatment) and the physicians (who feel happier with patients' responses and with their own
performance as experts). The main questions are whether there is
long-term maintenance of the skills and whether we can increase the
proportions of physicians who can sustain them.

Social networks and health

Can our friendships and social networks keep us alive? A 'social
network' is the group of persons with whom a person is involved
(usually friends); 'social support' refers to the help that they provide
or are felt to provide. There are major questions here of whether
and how the existence of a large social support network can 'buffer'
people against stress, affect our vulnerability to illness, and increase
our chances of recovery (Sarason et al., 1990; Duck, with Silver,
1990a). What matters most, the number or quality of supports
(Cobb & Jones, 1984)? What happens when the network is
disrupted? Is loss of relationships stressful and/or life-threatening
and if so, how (Reis, 1984)? If I expect support from someone and
he or she lets me down, will that make me ill (Melamed & Brenner,
1990)?

To suggest that our health might be influenced by our membership of a group and by the practices that are common in that group
is not a new idea. One early example of research on epidemiology
is based precisely on this idea. The British researcher Snow (1854)
showed that cholera was developed by villagers sharing one particular well more frequently than by others using a different source
of water. He also showed that Scots who put water in their whisky

were more likely to contract some diseases than was a group of people who drank whisky neat or who boiled their water to make tea instead.

The identification of such demographic or lifestyle features as correlates of disease remains one of the primary steps that researchers take. By such means, for instance, it is established that disadvantaged children tend to be born to young mothers who have not used antenatal services and who are more likely to be smokers (DHSS, 1976). Also the first step in understanding AIDS in the early 1980s was to discover the characteristics, lifestyles and relational histories of those who contracted it.

In a fundamental and exciting extension of this logic, some researchers have tried to identify specific features of a person's particular groups of friends and family or lifestyle that may relate to the diseases he or she contracts. Other researchers have looked at the relationship styles of the individual. For instance, Morgan (1990) is interested in such questions as how deeply a person is involved in a network of friends, how that feels, and what expectations are held in respect of friends and kin. Such research issues are generally described as concerned with 'social support'. Clearly there are major overlaps between the work on the resources that friends provide, on the one hand, and the work on the dynamics of personal relationships on the other. Surprisingly, it is only recently that there have been any explicit and wholehearted attempts to tie the two literatures together (Duck, with Silver, 1990b).

In their classic study, Brown & Harris (1978) show that the presence of a close, confiding relationship with a husband or boyfriend significantly reduced the risk of women developing depression after a major loss or disappointment. Brown & Harris argue that long-term feelings of self-worth or self-esteem are especially significant, that these are provided by important close relationships, and that, to a major extent, these feelings could stave off psychiatric disorder in a crisis. One problem here is that the existence of strong close relationships with very small numbers of friends might be concealed in studies that check just on the numbers of friends that we claim to have (Hobfoll, 1984). If I do a study that seems to show that people are better off with large numbers of friends, I may miss the point that large numbers are made up of several sets of small numbers and the level of intimacy in these small groups – rather than the total number of bodies in our network – may be the key issue. There is certainly evidence that intimate relationships with a small number of persons are what really counts (O'Connor & Brown, 1984). What may be important is that a minimum level of close relationships is maintained. In other words, within a large group of friends is at least one subset of one or two very close relationships with one or two special friends. Alternatively, regular conversations with specific friends provide the *sense* of support that is important (Leatham & Duck, 1990). Certainly there are features of the transactions of pairs of friends that are significant (Cutrona et al., 1990), such as comforting one another (Burleson, 1990), or cheering one another up (Barbee, 1990).

So, in broad terms, those are some ideas that drive research on social support: rephrased, the idea is 'can the existence, the transactions, and the reliability of close personal relationships prevent illness, promote recovery from illness, and help people to cope with stress?' People tend to suffer stress and illness when their relationships become disturbed (BOX 6.4). Also, the presence of strong, close relationships preserves people from the worst effects of stress (see BOX 6.5), whether the presence is just felt to be available or is actually enacted.

Obviously, there are two separate ideas here – both widely accepted. One tells us that disruption to relationships leads to ill-health; the other, that presence of good relationships leads to well-being. We have to be careful to distinguish these two thoughts, since they are not making quite the same point. If a researcher carried out a study showing that disrupted relationships 'cause' illness, that does not prove that good relations 'cause' health; it may be that good relations do nothing, they are just taken for granted. On the other hand, good ones could promote good health whilst bad ones could cause stress – because they bring rejection and also the need to restructure our lives to find alternative partners and establish new routines. Disruption to a relationship exposes one hidden benefit of being in a stable partnership, namely, that it has provided a division of labour in coping with life's problems. The dissolution of a relationship (Chapters 3 and 4) requires the person to take on extra and undivided responsibility for the labours of life. An important stressful consequence of relational loss, then, is loss of help with physical chores, as well as loss of emotional support, regular interaction, common understanding or view of the world, and all the daily conversations that make up relationships.

The social network and social support

When we talk of social support provided by friends and kin, do we mean physical support (e.g. help with car maintenance) or emotional

---

BOX 6.4 Health consequences of relational disruption

Widowed men have a higher mortality, rate of mental disorder, and tendency to suicide than have widowed women or married persons (Berardo, 1970).

Widows have a higher rate of health complaints during the year following bereavement than do a group of matched control subjects (Maddison & Viola, 1968).

Lonely people are more likely to suffer from depression, to have general medical complaints, and to attempt suicide (Lynch, 1987).

Men who are in the process of separation or divorce are much more likely to suffer from stress-related illness (Bloom et al., 1978).

Dissatisfied marital partners are more likely to suffer depression (Weiss & Aved, 1978).

Taken generally, several sets of results indicate that persons in disturbed relationships have higher incidences of low self-esteem; depression; headaches; tonsillitis; tuberculosis; coronaries; sleep disorders; alcoholism; drug dependence; cancer; and admissions to mental hospitals (Duck, 1991).

There is a markedly increased risk of separated men being the victim of a homicidal assault (Bloom et al., 1978).

Several sorts of physical symptoms follow closely on a sense of failure in relationships (Schmale, 1958).

Disruption of relationships late in life is particularly troublesome (Hansson et al., 1990), and instances of interpersonal betrayal in the social networks of older adults are surprisingly high, with some 19% of all elderly adults having been betrayed or seriously let down during a time of vulnerability (including being psychologically or physically abused).

---

support (e.g. advice about a particularly troublesome problem) or just plain old regular human contact? Which matters most, help with routine, help in times of crisis, reassurance of worth, or some generalized support, based on a feeling of common understanding of the world and how to deal with it? Hobfoll (1988) has argued that stress (the flipside of support in some ways) is occasioned by the loss or threatened loss of resources, whether personal, physical or psychological. Persons feel stress when the resources are expended or seem in their own judgement to be likely to be expended. Naturally, people try to preserve their resources or exchange them for others and so keep the general level high. Thus both stress and support are strongly related to personal and environmental factors as well as to the social network and what it can provide.

There are three important sorts of social support that are essential but are not related to physical provision of support. These are:

1 *Emotional support* i.e. provision of information that one is loved and cared for. This could be achieved by direct statements to that effect or could be indicated indirectly by, for example, buying flowers, arranging to spend time together, remembering birthdays, taking an interest in the other's welfare, and promoting that person's best interests.

2 *Esteem support* i.e. provision of information that one is valued and esteemed. This could be achieved by direct statements to that effect or could be indicated indirectly, for example by requests for advice, by treating the person's opinion as important, by allowing oneself to be guided by that person.

3 *Network support* i.e. provision of information that one belongs to a network of mutual obligations.

Support can be measured by looking at three elements (Cobb & Jones, 1984): the supportive behaviour that people actually provide; the properties of the network (i.e. whether it is close and cohesive or spread out); or by the way that a person feels about it (the subjective sense of social support). What would be helpful to know is how people actually get their friends to give them support (Gottlieb, 1985) and how support varies in quality and type as the relationship develops. Recent work (Barbee, 1990; Burleson, 1990; Cutrona et al., 1990; Leatham & Duck, 1990) indicates the importance of interpersonal transactions, particularly those involving talk and everyday conversation in this context. It is through the transactions of daily life, grounded as they are in conversational interaction, that individuals gain the sense of others 'being there' for them, and can also see the degree to which others can offer them assistance or can develop their ability to cope. As Leatham & Duck (1990) point out, such senses do not arise only when stress occurs, but are part of the ever-present results of dealing with friends in everyday life.

However, there are two other points that need to be acknowledged. They show the way in which this research field will grow during the time when you readers may be the ones developing the research for yourself. Hobfoll's (1988) point is that we must see support in context – or, in Hobfoll's terminology, we must look at the 'ecological congruence' of support and how it matches up to what is needed. A given resource or piece of support is not necessarily appropriate merely because researchers label it as a resource. What may be supportive for a woman in labour may not work in bereavement or unemployment. The resources, then, are only truly supportive relative to the needs of the person in question

– they must be ecologically congruent with his or her needs and requirements. Vaux (1990) further emphasizes the processes of actively developing the support network. Clearly, then, the work we need in future will identify the needs-in-context before it tells us about the support-in-context.

Equally, Sarason et al. (1990) emphasize the impact of the nature of the relationship in which the social support occurs and such a point has also been doggedly made by Gottlieb (1985; 1990). Gottlieb indicates the significance of rephrasing the question about social support. He suggests that we need to ask 'Is social support a property of a person or a property of personal relationships?' In other words, is the important aspect of social support the way I feel about it or what I actually get from my network, through transactions and interaction with the people who are my sources of support? Gottlieb makes it very plain that these interactions are what counts and that the actual marshalling of support is a major part of the whole business of social support.

As people get to know one another they feel more supported, but they are probably actually getting more help and support, too, although they may also be getting more obligations that can be a bind (Rook & Pietromonaco, 1987). As a relationship develops, so the partners get more from the relationship, and the course of the relationship's development is going to be affected by the amount of support (both felt support and actual support) obtained at various stressful times. For Gottlieb (1985), the key issue is the way in which particular episodes of socially supportive action create in the person the sense of being socially supported. What are the dynamics, what happens, what do people do when they support one another, and how is it recognized and acknowledged by the recipient? Clearly, argues Gottlieb (1985), the actual wresting of supportive behaviour from the environment is more important than just the sense of support. Coping depends both on the manifestation of support and on the belief that others would provide it if asked, and on the ability to obtain it when it is needed, not just on one aspect alone. As far as the perspective taken in this book goes, these beliefs and supports are *generated* by daily transactions in the routine social life of human relationships and then are *activated* by a person's needs or stressors in the context of what is going on in that relationship at the time (Leatham & Duck, 1990).

BOX 6.5 Social support and (the moderation of) stress or illness

Persons who were not socially isolated had much reduced incidence (i.e. about half the risk) of mortality, in a 9-year follow-up study in Alameda County (Berkman & Syme, 1979).

Positive self-concept and good social support have a combined effect in preventing a state of depression and of anxiety during an acute crisis (Hobfoll & Walfisch, 1984).

Social support is negatively related to the incidence of psychiatric symptoms, and absence of social support is a better predictor of disorders than is incidence of stressful events (Lin et al., 1979; Silberfeld, 1978).

Support from co-workers tends to buffer the stress of the job (La Rocco et al., 1980).

Women who have a close relationship with their husband are less likely to suffer postpartum depression (Paykel et al., 1980).

Those persons who have a high quality of family relationships tend to report fewer general psychiatric symptoms (Dean et al., 1981) and also fewer neurotic symptoms, such as depression and anxiety (Barrera, 1981).

By contrast, Hobfoll & London (1985) show that close networks can increase stress for Israeli women in time of severe pressure such as the mobilization of their husbands for war, since the networks served to transmit rumours and news of disasters.

Rook & Pietromonaco (1987) point out that although friendship has its good side and provides help with life stresses and tasks, companionship and intimacy and various other resources that prompt healthy behaviour, there is also a negative side. Help is sometimes offered in ineffective ways, it can be offered when it is not wanted or can be intrusive or excessive, and it can lead to unwanted interactions.

Ruehlman & Wolchik (1988) showed that interference with a person's personal projects was found to be extremely stressful and that support with such projects was significantly related to well-being.

Rook (1990) argues that our understanding of social support and the effects of human relationships on health will be gained from greater attention to the problematic exchanges that occur within informal social networks.

Barrera & Baca (1990) explored the reasons that make people satisfied with the support they receive and found that network

> *orientation, or the tendency to be open about receiving aid and to value interpersonal support, predicted distress.*
>
> *Lehman & Hemphill (1990) found that patients with multiple sclerosis valued the expression of love and concern rather than specific advice about the best ways to cope, or even attempts to minimize the seriousness of the disease. They also attributed the cause of the unhelpful attempts at support to kindly motives even though these were not a lot of use.*

Stress, daily life, and heart disease

Stress affects everyone in life and is often caused by worry about everyday life occurrences. However, some specific events, particularly, go with stress and disease. The most impactful of these clearly all refer to human relationships (such as death of a spouse or a child, getting married or divorced, moving to a new work environment or birth of a child: Holmes & Rahe, 1967), and there are now 'life event scales' which assess and assign scores to these and other events. The scores are determined by allotted points. You get a certain number of points for the death of a relative (63), for moving house (20), for going to college (20), for changing jobs (36), and so on. (You even score 12 if it is Christmas, but since quarrels and even murders increase in the family at that time, maybe it's not surprising: Duck, 1991). As your score increases – particularly if it does so sharply – there is a much greater risk of you suffering stress and/or severe illness. Usually these are stress-related illnesses or problems, but all sorts of illness (e.g. hypertension and diabetes) start happening when life-event scores build up (Wyler et al., 1971).

What is the explanatory link between life events and stress? Two aspects of life events are quite significant to the individual, so which of them matters most? Many life events are *undesirable* (e.g. being fired, death of a relative) but they also have a second element, which is *change*, just the fact that something has altered, for example moving to a different home or adopting a new job (and so a new work routine) or entering a new relationship.

What matters most, then, the undesirability of the event or the fact of the change? Rather surprisingly, Dohrenwend (1973) finds that change per se is the stressor, and not undesirability. It is not just the negative aspect of the change that is important, it is the fact that it is a change at all, particularly if the change requires major psychological readjustment or major reformulation of identity – such as is involved in becoming a widow(er). Obviously, these occurrences affect self-image as well as the routines of life. If we move to a new place, meet many new people and have to begin 'getting acquainted' again, or if we lose a relative who was very close to us or was part of our identity structure, we now have to rethink ourselves, as it were. Such changes to self-image require major psychological re-adjustment towards social restructuring and that is what is most difficult to cope with.

Two psychological reactions are relevant here. Firstly, a person's belief in self-efficacy (Bandura, 1977) – that is, a learned capacity and belief in our own control over the environment and our ability to deal with and cope with events. If we believe we can handle the problem, we shall not be overwhelmed by it. A person's beliefs in this regard could be area-specific: I may have great confidence in my self-efficacy as a lecturer but less in my ability to cope with insurance sellers, for instance. Whilst a lecture class of 2500 students may hold no terrors for me, the prospect of a brief meeting to discuss life assurance could frighten me to death.

Secondly, a general psychological reaction to stress is observed by Selye (1956) in the 'general adaptation syndrome'. According to this model, there are three stages to reactions to stress (which Selye regarded as a physical reaction to a noxious or unpleasant stimulus):

1 *Alarm reaction*: 'a generalized call to arms of the defensive forces in the organism'.

2 *Resistance (sustained)*: a kind of emergency reaction in which the body sustains alertness to danger and preparedness to deal with it.

3 *Exhaustion*: the defences become depleted through being 'stretched' for too long.

Other work (see Innes, 1981) indicates that these patterns are dangerous over a prolonged period since they simultaneously aggravate the body's inflammatory reaction to nasty stimuli whilst reducing resistance to them. In other words, risk is increased at exactly the same time as ability to cope is reduced.

Despite the previous findings, there is little agreement about the nature of stress. DiMatteo & Friedman (1982) define it as 'the state of an organism when reacting to new circumstances' (Note: 'state', 'reacting', 'new', 'circumstances'), whilst Selye (1956) defines it as the 'physical reaction to noxious stimuli' (Note: 'physical', 'noxious', 'stimuli'). From the foregoing, it may be clear that the definition of DiMatteo & Friedman takes account of the Dohren-wend findings that change per se rather than noxiousness can be stressful. The essential point seems to be that any unexpected and massive readjustment of life patterns causes stress at a psychological level, although noxious stimuli have an effect also, particularly at a physiological level. The real life question for research has concerned the means by which life events cause enough stress to cause illness, and there are three models proposed (DiMatteo & Friedman, 1982):

1 Life events call upon a person's coping style, which is found deficient. This leads to unhealthy or odd behaviour that causes a negative social reaction from others ('What's the matter with her? She's behaving strangely') which leads to a definition of illness ('She must be sick') and acceptance of the sick role. There is no organic disease here. What happens is that disturbed behaviour (drowsiness, hostility, weeping) leads people to assume that the person must be ill.

2 Life events call upon a person's coping style, which leads them to unhealthy styles of behaviour (alcohol abuse, nervous smoking, self-mutilation, fast driving) and these lead to organic disease (cirrhosis, lung cancer, heart disease, physical injury), which then leads directly to illness and the sick role. In this case, there is an organic disease that results but it results indirectly rather than directly from the need to cope. Those who cope by drinking or smoking lead themselves to the illnesses caused by those particular actions rather than to simple illnesses resulting 'directly from' stress.

3 Life events overpower a person's coping style and cause physiological stress (high blood pressure) that leads to organic trauma (stroke, heart attack). In this case, there is a direct link between the life events and the illness, mediated by physiological reactions, such as shock.

These interesting proposals make it clear that there can be several kinds of stress, of reactions to stress and of mediating agents, the most important of which is coping style and personality. Physiological, social and environmental stress can all be distinguished, and we should recognize that a person's social behaviour, social status and human relationships can expose them to these risks to different degrees.

Death, dying and bereavement

In the last four centuries not only have the most frequent causes of death changed in relative proportions but there have also been alterations in our attitudes to death and the social psychological reactions to it.

Cultural beliefs about death

One of the earliest markers of social evolution of humankind is the
change in attitudes to the dead. When a culture begins to bury the
dead in ritualistic ways (e.g. with food and weapons), it marks the
beginning of a change in beliefs about the nature of death and
beyond. If we believe that people should be buried with weapons,
food and slaves, that they should be ceremonially dressed,
embalmed and lying outstretched, it is because we believe that the
weapons, food and slaves will be needed after death, that the dead
person will need to be ceremonially identifiable and, therefore,
needs badges of rank on the body, that the person will 'need' his
or her body in an undeteriorated state after death, and that death is
only like sleeping.

Any treatment of the dead in such careful ways also presumes a
set of beliefs about what happens after death, and also some
thoughts about the nature of death itself (e.g. that it is similar to a
journey from here to somewhere else, the nature of which can be
described, such as a Happy Hunting Ground or Paradise or Hades
which involves crossing several rivers, such as the rivers of hate and
forgetting). Early concepts of death usually regarded it as a journey
to another place rather similar to the life experienced before death.
So the dead person needed to have food and weapons (and even
servants!) buried with him or her for the journey to be made safely.

It was quite a bit later that people began to believe that obtaining
the full benefits of the afterlife depended on what we had done on
earth. The Egyptians were early believers in the idea that our heart
and soul would be weighed to judge our earthly life and we would
get eternal afterlife only if we had been good. It was not until
relatively late (i.e. Christian times) that the notion of transfiguration
(rather than simple continuance of previous bodily forms, ranks and
activities) entered into the system of beliefs.

In the fourteenth century, in many countries, the dead were
represented, if at all, in two forms, one as in life, one as in death:
on top of the tomb was a representation of them lying at length, in
full living dress; beneath this was a representation of their naked,
rotting body. In those times, the body of the person was buried not
in a coffin but in a winding-sheet, and the person was referred to
as still a member of the living community (e.g. the Catholic burial
service said 'we commit *your* body to the ground'). Later the dead
were represented at a transitory stage, kneeling in prayer in full
dress half-way between life and death. At roughly the same time,
coffins were introduced, and the person was regarded as gone from

the earthly community (therefore, 'we commit *his/her* body to the ground' was introduced to the burial service). Later still, the dead were represented only in the living form and statues now show them standing or sitting, in full dress, doing something that typified them when alive (e.g. delivering a speech, riding a horse).

In the early days, sudden death was greatly feared, since it deprived the person of time to prepare for it by prayer and by receiving religious sacraments. It was also true that most people saw death fairly often not only because of diseases, war and famine but because public executions and public torture were well-tried methods of social control and, let's face it, entertainment. Naturally, all these fears and experiences, as well as the beliefs in the surrounding culture, affected people's perceptions about their own death and those that they witnessed around them.

What now characterizes our attitudes to death? One general difference is perhaps that natural death is expected by most people, although we also hope for it to be swift. A fear nowadays is that rampant technology could keep us alive as a vegetable somewhere between death and semi-consciousness (Kastenbaum, 1982). Edgar Allen Poe's and the Victorians' writings about being buried alive reflected prevalent fears within their readers; common anxieties, nowadays, emerge from the same problem dressed up in concern over technical definitions of brain death and the use of life-support machines to sustain those who are incapable of independent life.

Along with such changes in central concerns come reduced tolerance for minor pains (the 'headache pill' society), a considerable amount of medical game-playing (since patients fear that doctors no longer tell the truth), and such pronouncements as 'the patient's bill of rights'. Death has become a social psychological, attitudinal experience as well as a physical cvent.

How do people cope, in a social psychological sense, with impending death? There are essentially three foci for their concern: (1) the pain, discomfort, disability and social stigma of a terminal illness (see above); (2) the reactions and emotions of others, particularly of close others or life partners; (3) the person's own reactions.

Kubler-Ross (1969) proposed that there were five stages of psychological adjustment to death:

1 *Denial* (it's a mistaken diagnosis).

2 *Anger* (why me?). This can lead to envy of those still fit, resentment against them, and even to surprising verbal attacks on helpers, nurses and friends.

3 *Bargaining* (dealing with fate for more time). Terminal patients often leave their body to medical science as part of an implicit

bargain with Death for more time, and with medical staff for better care that may help them stay alive longer.

4 *Depression*, sadness and crying.

5 *Acceptance*. This is often characterized by silence, withdrawal, and a marked detachment from other people.

Some criticize this neat system on the grounds that the terminally ill more probably oscillate between the stages, rather than move steadily to each next one. Others note that some patients show all the stages at once or that the stages occur and recur. Whether or not these criticisms are valid, it makes sense to attend to the psychological dimension to dying and to concern ourselves with the psychological treatment of such patients as well as with their medical treatment.

The timing of death

There is some evidence that the timing of dying is influenced by psychological factors, such as whether the person gives up and whether significant dates are approaching. For instance, Jewish populations show a marked 'death dip' (a significant decrease in death rate) during the time prior to their solemn holy day, Yom Kippur – the Day of Atonement (Phillips, 1970; 1972). Other research shows that birthdays and anniversaries exert effects on death of widowed spouses (Bornstein & Clayton, 1972), who tend to die on days close to dates that had significance in the marriage. A personal observation of my own focusses on the number of people who die just after they have completed a major task or survived some major stress. When I point this out to friends and colleagues, the usual explanation is that people energize themselves to stay the course through the stress and so exhaust themselves. I call this the 'foot off the gas pedal theory of death'. However, cars do not stop just because you stop pressing the accelerator; they stop when you press the brake. It makes me wonder if there is not some over-reaction by a close-down mechanism which would have been just right if the stress still remained, but overacts once the stress has lessened (the 'foot on the brake pedal theory').

Reactions to the death of a close partner have recently begun to interest social scientists working on relationships. 'Death of a spouse' carries the highest risk on the life event scales, and bereavement brings with it a considerable need for large-scale readjustment to the routines of life. Adults responding to bereavement typically show stress and health problems over an extended period of time

(Greenblatt, 1978). They also show a sequence of reactions comparable to but not identical with the responses of patients to their terminal diagnosis: first, exhaustion and hollowness, characterized by a sense of emptiness, stress and overwhelming responsibility; second, a preoccupation with the image of the deceased, even extending to hallucinations or imagining that the person is still alive, has been seen in the street, and the like; third, guilt or a sense of things unsaid, feelings left unexpressed, time together unspent; fourth, hostility to others, or the 'leave me alone' reaction; fifth, changes to daily activity. The fifth reaction can be healthy or unhealthy depending on the nature and extent of the change, of course. Greenblatt's (1978) point, however, is that the psychological reaction to grief is a process that extends over time and is essential to the bereaved person, who naturally enough needs to reconstruct his or her life and identity. In many ways, the reactions of the grieving spouse mark out readjustments and changes to identity as the person comes to grips with the new demands upon them that stem from loss of partner and makes decisions about the parts, mannerisms, styles or traits of the lost person they wish to retain in their active life, perhaps by imitation.

Conclusions and summary

We began by thinking about eternal youth and ended on death! Throughout, however, we have seen some important and mounting evidence that social relationships influence or are relevant in many aspects of health, illness and recovery. Some factors are quite obvious, some are not, but they run the whole range from attitudinal influences derived from the surrounding community to personal beliefs derived from interpersonal experiences and even influences coming from the network of other people to which we belong and the friendships that we have. Further, social scientists contribute positively to preventive medicine and attempts to persuade us all to lead more healthy lives (Rogers, 1983). Whilst it is clearly not yet time for us to cry 'This person is sick. Send for the relationships expert', a number of major features of health and illness are relational in nature and will obviously receive deeper exploration in future.

Further reading

Duck, S.W. (ed., with R.C. Silver) (1990) *Personal Relationships and Social Support*. Sage: London.

Friedman, H.S. & DiMatteo, M.R. (1982) *Interpersonal Issues in Health Care*. Academic Press: New York.

Hays, R. & DiMatteo, M.R. (1984) 'Towards a more therapeutic physician–patient relationship'. In S.W. Duck (ed.) *Personal Relationships 5: Repairing Personal Relationships*. Academic Press: London.

Pendleton, D. & Hasler, I. (1983) *Doctor–Patient Communication*. Academic Press: London.

Sarason, B.R., Sarason, I.G. & Pierce, G.R. (1990) *Social Support: A Transactional View*. Wiley: New York.

CHAPTER 7

Human Relationships Take the Witness-Stand

Some previous chapters have dealt with courtship but this one deals just with court! At first sight, the workings of the law and the workings of relationships have little in common. Relationships are personal and the law is public. The law basically expects us to treat all others equally without fear or favour, while relationships demand our exclusive interest in specific others to whom we are committed through thick and thin, and to whom we give special privileges, information, services and favours.

Relationships and the law

Even given the belief in equality and impartiality, the law does recognize relationships in various ways (for instance, in giving parents certain rights over the future of their own children but not other people's; allowing tax breaks to couples who are 'married' but not to couples who are not; limiting the extent to which spouses can be forced to testify against one another: Rubin, 1987).

The law has also recently begun to get interested in whether cohabitors are, to all intents and purposes, rather like spouses as far as the rights to property are concerned after a relationship break-up. In the Lee Marvin 'palimony' trial, the case reportedly involved questions about the measurement of love and the extent to which there are different types of love (see Rubin, 1979 and Chapter 2 here).

The law even extends its interest to NVC (cf Chapter 1) where, in a recent case of *Pennzoil* vs *Texaco*, the jury apparently placed great weight on the fact that an 'agreement in principle' was sealed by a handshake between the parties (Rubin, pers. comm.). Also there is increasing evidence (Blanck et al., 1990) that trial judges' NVC can have unwanted effects on the outcome of a trial, such that

appellate courts have cautioned repeatedly that juries in criminal trials accord
even the most subtle behaviours of judges great weight and deference. One judge
concluded that juries 'can easily be influenced by the slightest suggestion coming
from the court, whether it be a nod of the head, a smile, a frown, or a spoken
word'. (Blanck et al., 1990, p. 653)

Clearly the law also has a role in the very existence of certain types
of relationship, whether these be contractual partnerships or the
more routine pairings of life. Marriage, after all, results *only* after a
legally recognized ceremony and so does divorce, if you call that a
ceremony.

Consider other connections between law and relationship processes. Now that we've looked at interpersonal persuasion in everyday life, what about special persuasive circumstances, like trials? We
know the importance of relationships in social behaviour, so we can
expect that the topics covered so far (NVC, language, space-usage,
liking/disliking, interpersonal persuasion, etc.) are relevant even to
the courtroom and help us to increase our understanding of what
goes on there. My purpose here is not to give an exhaustive review
of work on law and social behaviour, but to apply the earlier
material on human relationships to supplement the work on interpersonal persuasion which is available in the mainstream texts by
showing the relational underpinnings of such work. I also seek to
raise some issues about the role of relationship processes in such
occurrences as courtroom cross-examination or jury decision-
making.

There are many questions about the legal process that interest
social scientists and several have a relational substructure that is
presently implicit. Rubin (1990:2) points out his excitement as a
social scientist learning to practise law and

being struck by the central importance of psychological assumptions, not only
with regard to such psycho-legal staples as insanity and criminal intent, but also
with regard to such commonplace questions as what constitutes 'acceptance' of
an offer (in contract law), what makes a payment to a former employee a 'gift'
(in tax law), and what sort of behaviour is 'negligent' (in the law of torts).

Social science has become increasingly interested in the law in the
last two decades. For instance, one field of research looks at the
language used in court and we have already seen how language and
relationships influence one another, convey information about liking
and trust, or indicate power differences, such as we considered in
Chapters 1, 3 and 4. We are ready, then, to explore the ways in

which lawyers use such things as linguistic or relational 'tricks'. We can also think about the persuasion that goes on in court, and will revisit some of what was learned in Chapter 1 on relational language forms and styles. Another area of research concerns the influence of the personally attractive or unattractive characteristics of the defendant upon the outcomes of trials and whether good looks lead to good verdicts – or to put it another way, whether the fair get greater fairness! We will thus revive some of the issues about attraction to others (dealt with in Chapters 2 and 3). Does physical attractiveness improve your chances of getting a verdict of Not Guilty? We are ready to look at that one in terms of the influence of liking on social judgements. A final set of issues concerns the ways in which jurors, as a group, reach their decisions. Given the mission of this book, we could ask a relatively new question about the relational under-pinnings of jury decisions: are powerful members of smaller juries more likely to establish the kinds of influence that comes from liking than they are in larger groups? We could also look at the ways in which personal contact between jurors influences the manner in which decisions are reached and whether the jurors are likely to consider the detail of evidence in an *interpersonal and relational* context. For example, are the personal dynamics between jurors any more or less influential than the facts of the case? Are jurors likely to be swayed by the evidence or also by the personalities of the other jurors *discussing* that evidence? I will propose that relational principles and a knowledge of relationship processes help us here.

These three ways in which I shall take a look at the court and its activities (language; physical characteristics of defendant; intragroup relationships) are all closely related to the issues we have been dealing with so far and help to make the case that research on relationships can illuminate questions explored by other social scientists.

We can begin to look at these matters by going to the very roots of legality and looking at the ways in which the law makes assumptions about law-abidingness.

Assumptions of the law vs results of empirical studies

Do lawyers' assumptions about human nature – or lawyers' models of human beings – match up with research on daily relational interactions? For example, take the law's somewhat ethereal model concepts like the 'reasonable person'. Juries are often instructed that

---

BOX 7.1   Points to think about

*How do our common assumptions about, and everyday experiences
of, everyday behaviour and mundane reality match up with the
law's assumptions about criminal acts and social responsibility?*

Do attraction, relationships and relational behaviour affect trials?

*Do those features of everyday life that affect relationships also
affect outcomes in a special environment like a court?*

*Do interpersonal persuasive strategies, such as those encountered
in the preceding chapter, upset 'blind justice'?*

*How do issues of interpersonal influence relate to the processes in
a legal trial?*

*How do a defendant's (or a witness's) nonverbal characteristics,
looks and personality affect the credibility of their testimony?*

What is the role of language style in courtroom relationships?

*How do interpersonal relationships influence jury decision-
making?*

---

the conduct of a 'reasonable person' is not the same as what jurors
would do in the circumstance, nor even what the average person
would do in similar circumstances, but what this 'reasonable person'
would do, having account of all the facts. You, or the average
person, for example might react angrily to an insult and strike out,
but a reasonable person might not. This makes the concept essentially non-empirical: in other words, it asks juries to think
hypothetically and to detach themselves from their daily experience.
This would be like asking you to imagine what the perfect student
might be like on Mars: you'd have a few ideas culled from your
experiences here on Earth, but you might find it hard to imagine
what difference it might make being green and with your eyes on
stalks.

Particularly relevant to us in such a hypothetical environment is
the question of whether people ('reasonable people') take account of
their social and personal relationships in deciding (not) to report a
crime, if that report will adversely affect their friendships, marriages
or social relationships. Do you think you would find it harder to
report a crime committed by your enemy than by your father, for
example? As Rubin (1987) indicates, children are expected, in most
circumstances, to testify against their fathers if called upon to do so
and can be punished for not doing so. Did you expect that?

Crime and crime reporting

If we can assume some effect of 'who you know', can we expect an effect of 'what you know' from daily life? Do everyday folk take the same view of the nature of criminality as the law does? Obviously, people's attitudes to crime, to criminals, or attitudes to criminal acts will depend on what they think criminal acts are. Is it a crime to assist a suicide? Is it a crime not to prevent one (without actually assisting), for example? If people don't think something is a crime or if they happen to believe that a given law is unwise (as, say, many people believed that the laws prohibiting alcohol in the USA in the 1920s were) then they are less likely to report those whom they see breaking it. If you think that what has happened doesn't amount to a criminal offence, or you are not aware that there is a crime involved, then you won't report it. If you are ignorant of what the law says in a particular case, then you wouldn't go and report to anybody that someone has broken the law.

Clearly, then, beliefs about criminal offences will influence our behaviour in dealing with them. That is the assumption of social psychologists; what the law actually says, however, is that every citizen has to be presumed to know what the law is and ignorance of the law is no defence. You may not escape punishment by claiming to be unaware that your action was against the law. As far as the legal machine is concerned you are supposed to know what is against the law and you are supposed not to do it. Of course, this assumption is partly expedient. If anyone could claim ignorance of the law then we'd all be able to get off the charges for each first offence against a particular law. As John Selden put it in 1689 'Ignorance of the Law excuses no man [*sic*]: not that all men know the law, but because 'tis an excuse every man will plead and no-one can tell how to confute him.'

The law also assumes that you should be concerned to uphold the law, which is a different point – a lot of people know what the law is and don't try to uphold it. You are subject to prosecution for your own violations, of course, and should not aid and abet others, nor conspire with them when they commit crimes, even if they are your friends. The law also assumes that you must act in a socially responsible manner even if it is not in your best interests personally. For instance, even if it puts you physically at risk you may still be required (in the UK at least) to assist the police if they ask you to help or commandeer your vehicle to pursue a fugitive.

There are some crimes which are completely defined by the fact that you have failed to carry out this duty. For instance, harbouring criminals is an offence, which simply means that you are not living up to the duty of reporting on people that you know are criminals, even if they are your relatives or friends. Secondly, being an accessory after the fact (in other words, you weren't involved in the crime itself, but you helped somebody after they had done it) is another crime essentially against this duty to assist. The final example, an obvious one – receiving stolen goods – means that you weren't actually involved in the theft but you accepted goods knowing or believing that they were stolen and didn't report the fact or give them back. All of these imply a duty not only not to commit a crime but also to report one if you observe it being committed by anyone else or come to know that it has been committed. Interestingly, all of these crimes arise from the results of human relationships with the 'real' criminal, or else to your decision to do something that, in other circumstances, would be regarded as friendly (such as helping somebody, giving aid and comfort, taking care of their property for them). Nevertheless, the law assumes that people will subordinate these relational imperatives when they hear the call of the legal requirement.

BOX 7.2 Shoplifting: when is a crime not a crime?

People generally fail to report shoplifting, particularly when there is a readily identifiable victim, like a large corporation which, they feel could absorb the costs of minor thefts (Gelfand et al., 1973).

Persons from small-town or rural areas are more likely to report shoplifters than are persons from large cities (Gelfand et al., 1973).

The more valuable the item stolen, the more likely it is that the shoplifter will be reported (Hindelang, 1974).

There is no clear sex difference. Whilst Dertke et al. (1974) found that more females than males reported a shoplifter, Gelfand et al. (1973) found the opposite, and several studies find no effects (e.g. Bickman & Green, 1977).

If a person is made responsible for the items stolen (e.g. 'Please watch my bags while I go to the ticket counter'), then that person is more likely to pursue and stop the thief (Moriarty, 1975).

What people actually do however, is nothing like that at all: individuals very often fail to take socially responsible action when a crime occurs. Studies have shown that many crimes are not reported to the police by either the victim(s) or witness(es) (see BOX 7.2). An interesting example of such findings emerged from a study by Himmelfarb (1980), who found that subjects not only discouraged others from reporting non-serious crimes but actually rated others *negatively* if they did report. People not only fail to do what they are supposed to do; they positively discourage others from doing it either!

In everyday life you have human relationships with the people you live or associate with, and the social and relational consequences are likely to be a disincentive to reporting a crime. In short, considerations are not limited to those assumed by the legal ideal; we obviously consider the social consequences too, and assess whether we are going to be subjected to rejection by friends, social disapproval, unpopularity in the neighbourhood, or exclusion – and whether it matters to us. For most of us, close relationships may matter more than the carriage of justice: thus the decision whether or not to report a crime is at least complicated by human relationships. Our willingness to act as good citizens is affected by social pressures and social effects or the fact that we all live in personal communities where specific loyalty to personal friends may be counted higher than some generalized duty as a citizen.

Does our attitude to crimes depend on what we've been told? Does our range of knowledge and information about crime influence our willingness to report offences? In other words, does education about crime work? Klentz & Beaman (1981) conducted a campuswide leaflet campaign about shoplifting, stressing the importance of reporting thieves, and giving information on the action that should be carried out. The subjects were then placed in a position to observe someone (an experimental confederate) steal a combination lock from the university bookstore. (This kind of shoplifting is not only fairly common but is very often used as the 'crime' studied in this kind of research since it is easily staged – with agreement from the bookstore, of course – and minimizes the risk of the confederate being bravely tackled and beaten up by overenthusiastic subjects.)

The campaign made little difference: overall it didn't make subjects report shoplifting significantly more than control groups did. However, information given in a lecture format did do so, although the information was the same and consisted of one of (or a combination of) two sorts of facts. First of all it is important to indicate how and why to report shoplifters: what you have to do, why you have to do it, how important it is, what procedures you should go through, who is the resource person to speak to, what is the phone number of Campus Security, and so on. In short, people need information about the mechanics of reporting crime. Secondly and most important, it is helpful to offer information about why people often *don't* report. Reports of such research findings evidently make subjects feel that they understand why other people do not report – so they avoid falling into the psychological traps themselves. Essentially this comes down to saying that attitudes towards crime and information about attitudes towards crime (our own attitudes plus what we know about other people's attitudes) will influence behaviour in reporting shoplifters rather more than will some generalized duty to report.

However, that particular study seems to stack the cards a little, given the short time that elapsed between lecture and experience of the shoplifting. Indeed some 22 percent of subjects reported being suspicious that they witnessed shoplifting so soon after reading or hearing about it. When the responses of naive subjects were compared with those of subjects who were told that a crime was staged, there was a difference in witnesses' beliefs and suspicions (Murray & Wells, 1982). People who were not told that the crime was staged were less accurate in identifying the perpetrator in a line-up. So next time you are wrongly accused, make a point of telling witnesses the whole thing was being acted out for TV!

Does it depend on the ambiguities in the situation? All the above questions arise when the crime is unambiguous and obvious (although around 60 percent of people still don't report it). In real life our Honest But Naive Citizen has to make the extra decision about whether or not a crime has occurred before he or she goes on to decide whether or not to report it. What happens then?

When there is ambiguity about an occurrence (it may be a crime, it may not) we tend to rationalize it as 'not a crime'. A particularly striking study of this, which also indicates the subtle role of relationships in the legal arena, staged an assault in an elevator, using a man and a woman confederate (Shotland & Straw, 1976). Whenever the elevator stopped where there were people outside, the woman would scream and the man would appear to be assaulting her. What would *you* do if you saw this happen? What the subjects did, by and large, was nothing. Most people outside the elevator wouldn't do anything at all if the woman just shouted for the man to leave her alone. A more effective strategy was to shout 'I don't know you.' People intervened if the woman made it clear that the assaulter was a stranger – otherwise they apparently assumed that the combatants *did* know one another. Common assumptions were that it was a marital tiff or an argument between boyfriend and girlfriend, that it was none of the bystanders' business to intervene. Apparently people think it is 'OK' for men to beat up their wives or girlfriends, but it is not all right for them to beat up women that they don't know! So not only does a presumed human relationship between two persons influence observers' likelihood of protecting one of them from assault, the relationship creates evident dangers also.

Two points to think about, by the way, are: first of all, people often don't intervene in cases where violence is taking place because they are afraid that the violence will turn on them. However, in this example that doesn't explain why there was a difference between cases where the woman said she didn't know the man and where she said nothing about their relationship: it would have been equally 'dangerous' for people to intervene in either case and yet they intervened in one and not the other. Secondly, as a matter of fact, the police are very reluctant to intervene in domestic struggles precisely because both partners will often join together to turn on the police and the police officers end up getting attacked by both people rather than succeeding in separating them.

So we learn from this that relationships affect the ways in which the 'insiders' expect to be treated and the ways in which 'outsiders' deal with ambiguous events. We all seem to operate on the rule that what two related people do to one another is pretty much their business and we should leave them to get on with it. Fortunately for battered wives and the rest, the law takes a more sensible attitude about this than most of the rest of us do when left to our own devices. (Yet remember from Chapter 4 that the family is still a very dangerous place to spend your time: Straus, 1985!)

Having shown how the existence of human relationships between people complicates their decisions and operation on legal/criminal issues, let us now go into the courtroom and see how human relationships research illuminates that august institution.

Trial by jury: interpersonal influence in the legal process

First I want to make a short but relevant digression about the law. Although we tend to take the English and American legal systems for granted there are in fact many different systems which are used to try people, some of which are to establish guilt or innocence and some of which serve other social functions (Cooke, 1990). In France, for example, the evidence is sifted in advance of the trial by an examining magistrate. He or she has powers to call witnesses to give evidence, to recall them to give evidence again, to cross-examine them, to examine them in private if desired, or in places other than a courtroom, and has various other powers, too. By the time the

French 'trial proper' occurs the assumption that the person is guilty unless proved innocent is actually more sensible than it sounds to those of us familiar with the opposite assumption.

Equally, the Soviet system is intended to have an educative function (Berman, 1977), to develop correct thinking in the criminal who is on trial and to reinforce good citizenship in the non-criminal observer of the trial. In Soviet trials the establishment of guilt or innocence is not the only point: their point is also to illustrate what was wrong with the logic or state of mind of the felon at the time of the offence, and to encourage public repentance – over and above the imposition of punishment for the offence (Berman, 1977). So in Soviet law the function is also persuasive: to change attitudes and reinforce, amongst non-offenders, belief in the basic wisdom and goals of Soviet society. For this reason the Soviet law has a 'nurturing role' of guiding, training and improving the logic of the criminal and so the felon's expression of shame and repentance is a major feature of a trial.

By contrast with these systems, the English and American legal systems are most concerned with the establishment, *during the trial*, of guilt or innocence, and punishment of the guilty. Although some decisions about guilt or innocence take place before the trial (e.g. the decision by a client and the lawyers over the plea to be entered – guilty or not guilty) and may even involve the lawyers from both sides (e.g. plea bargaining), guilt or innocence is primarily established solely and exclusively in the court during a trial – and the trial is held in a courtroom, not at the scene of the crime. Although this system may strike us as perfectly natural, because we are familiar with it, it has a strange and unusual feature: what happens in court is the only thing that counts. In essence, one side presents an argument and the other side tries to cut it down, based on the *credibility* of witnesses, on the *plausibility* of evidence, on the *likelihood* that X or Y 'fact' was true at the time of the crime – in short, on the *persuasiveness* of one side against the other.

Such trials have their origin way back in English history, after the Norman conquest, when guilt or innocence were established on the basis of a test or trial. The assumption was that a decision could be referred to God, who would indicate what the truth was. Accordingly the ordeals were 'attended with elaborate religious ceremony, which accounts for the credence placed in their efficacy' (Walker & Walker, 1972, p. 15). The test or trial was put into one of several forms, such as a trial of strength or trial by ordeal. One method ('trial by ordeal') involved making the accused person hold a red-hot bar of metal or put a hand in boiling water for a given length of time. The hand was then bandaged up and left for some days. If after that time it had come out in a blister or the hand had not healed, this was taken to mean that God was indicating that the person was guilty; if the hand didn't come out in the blister, it meant that he or she was innocent (or dead from the wound!). A similar idea worked for witches: trial by ordeal for alleged witches involved binding them hand and foot and putting them in a sack to be thrown in a river. If they floated, it meant that the water rejected them because of their guilt and if they sank it meant that they were innocent – but again, probably dead by the time anybody got to pull them out. So the guiding idea was to refer the issue of guilt or innocence to God, who would indicate the right verdict by means of a sign.

Other kinds of trial were 'trial of strength' or 'trial by combat' and in both cases this was originally reserved for the knightly class – people whose rank or nobility allowed them to carry weapons. The idea was that two opposing parties fought it out between themselves and the one who was left alive or still willing to continue at the end was presumed to have God and right on his (in those days) side and hence to be the innocent one. Not unnaturally, several alternative forms of trial were developed, one of which originally relied on human relationships quite explicitly. This one (the 'wager at law') involved the defendant producing a number of friends or acquaintances (generally twelve of them, so the size of your network was important then too!) who, amidst appropriate religious ceremony, would wager their immortal souls on an oath that the accused was innocent (Walker & Walker, 1972). In medieval times, when such oaths about eternal life would be taken quite as seriously as we would regard open-heart surgery without anaesthetic, it was doubtless difficult to obtain the necessary social support in cases where guilt was even possible let alone where it was probable or certain. However, the point is that it introduces the notion of convincing twelve acquaintances that you are innocent and is thus an ancient forerunner of the jury system (which, for those interested is actually derived from the old French word *juree/jurer*, from the Latin *jurare*, meaning 'to swear on oath'). It was also supposed to be done by twelve people (men, of course, in those days) who were of equal rank to the accused, were from the same community, and who therefore knew a little of the situation in which the accused might have been before the alleged crime. So in these times, relationships became the basis for our present-day legal system's trial by jury, though nowadays the jury is not on one side or the other; by contrast, it is strongly intended to be impartial and to *not* have any social or personal relationship with any party in the trial.

BOX 7.3 Images of the trial
Miller & Boster (1977) present three different images of the trial:

1 The trial as a rational, rule-governed event. *This is perhaps the most widely held view of the trial, much supported by TV melodramas in which clever attorneys argue rationally and skilfully against one another, the victor being the hero (who brings brilliant argument, new testimony or perspicacious deductions to bear). Unfortunately, as Miller & Boster indicate, lawyers often break the rules (e.g. by deliberately introducing inadmissible evidence that will affect the jury, knowing that, even if the judge directs them to ignore it, the jury probably can't).*

2 The trial as a test of credibility. *There is more on this in the text of the chapter, but essentially the model relies on the idea that the opposing sides are in a search for credibility rather than, necessarily, for the Truth.*

3 The trial as a conflict-resolving ritual. *In this model, trials are essentially social rituals that take the place of other ways of resolving conflict, like fighting or arm-wrestling. See the text of the chapter for an account of the evolution of trials that supports this notion to some extent.*

At first an accused person could not be compelled to submit to trial by jury without first consenting, but a refusal to plead was often taken as an admission of guilt and, in the case of a felony, the accused could be subjected to 'inducements' to plead, such as being crushed by lumps of iron (*'peine forte et dure'*) until either consent or death resulted. Nice people, our forebears! Actually this procedure was not formally abolished in the UK until 1772, when the courts decided simply to accept a refusal to plead as an admission of guilt.

If you had power in a society like that, what would you do? . . . Of course you would, and so did they: they allowed themselves 'understudies' to undergo the trial for them. In the case of trial by combat, many people in the knightly class preferred to delegate their possible death to someone else and employed champions to fight the trials of strength on their behalf. In the course of time these people eventually evolved into lawyers who spoke, rather than fought, on your behalf! Originally a counsel was allowed to speak on your behalf only on matters of law, not on issues of fact, and a person could not necessarily call witnesses or give evidence on his or her behalf. In those days also (i.e. fifteenth-century England until 1670 and a trial known to precedent as 'Bushell's case') a jury could be fined for reaching a verdict that the judge didn't agree with or considered perverse. (In recent times, judges agree with juries in 79 percent of cases anyway: Saks, pers. comm.) In a trial by combat you would obviously try and pick the physically strongest understudy: in the case of trial by our system you are inclined to pick somebody who is a good advocate or a good lawyer (if you can afford it).

The idea remains that you are represented by some kind of 'champion' and that the two sides of the case are put by these two adversaries (defence and prosecuting lawyers), which leads to it being called the 'adversarial system'. Some countries do not follow or adopt the adversarial system and in these cases the court or the judge does the examining of witnesses instead (Cooke, 1990). In the latter society, the judge or examiner asks the questions and interprets the answers, can ask whomever he or she wants whenever he or she wants and can call them back again. The adversarial system, where one side presents its case and is followed by the other side presenting its case, is a notable feature of the Anglo-Saxon system and the judge's roles of ensuring fair play and acting as a general guide to the jury are features of that. In this system, the pursuit of the 'whole truth' is not really the goal; rather (at least in criminal cases) it is a test of the prosecution evidence and an attempt to assess whether a case can be proven beyond reasonable doubt (Mortimer, 1983).

The system also has rules for excluding evidence that might be unsafe or unfair (such as hearsay, or confessions obtained by force), but human stereotypes and the effects of human relationships can probably never be completely excluded from any system that runs on human fuel.

Deciding the facts

There is one key reason why this background, whilst brief and a little superficial, is significant when we try to apply relational principles to the courtroom. In the system which has evolved in our particular society, (legal) truth is established on the basis of plausibility and credibility. The issue in such a trial is whether the witnesses are *believed* at the time – not whether their statements are 'objectively' accurate. Also, because of the emphasis on establishing guilt or innocence during the course of the trial in the courtroom, there are rarely attempts to assess whether the witnesses' claims are true by other means except than just asking them more questions. If I say that something is true then I could be challenged only by someone assessing whether my claims seem to make sense, by reference to their own internal logic, their agreement or conflict with common sense, how they match up with the statements of other witnesses or experts and their ability to withstand attempts to make them look wrong-footed or appear implausible. It is very rare for the court (for instance the judge) to examine a scene of crime and return to court saying 'Look, you've told us this is a six-inch line, and it's an eight-inch line; therefore, you are a liar'. Instead a lawyer will say 'You said it was a six-inch line, other witnesses have said that it was larger, and I put it to you that it is an eight-inch line'. The important psychological point is whether the person can be made to look as if they know what they are talking about. Thus the whole issue of the factors that make people seem credible to others (see Chapter 5) becomes relevant. As we have seen, relationship factors influence judgements of credibility and authority much more than has previously been realized.

One important point in criminal trials, then, is that juries – people – have to decide the facts of the case as presented in court, because the law assumes that the people on the jury go in with neutral and unfettered minds that they will use reasonably and rationally and independently of personal, relational or 'irrelevant' influences in the court or the jury-room. Lawyers, on the other hand, assume that jurors are cauldrons of biases and they have instigated considerable research into this (Saks, 1986). Such work does not justify the abolition of the jury, but does not really support the amount of effort that goes into selection of jury members either. What lawyers forget is that relationships, rather more than abstract attitudes, account for the lion's share of preferential bias in real life and these are to a large extent excluded by the provision that requires the jury to have no relationships with the parties to the case or with the lawyers. This is particularly important because the whole issue in a court is whether or not somebody is found guilty – yet guilt is determined in law, not just by what the accused persons actually did, but by what the jury *thinks* they did.

The jury may have to decide whether the defendant had the required intent at the time the crime was committed, or, if the person admits the intent, to decide whether it was criminal, and so the jury's biases and presuppositions could have life-or-death importance. Here the law uses the concept of *mens rea* (which is to say, a guilty mind). There is 'specific intent' (related to specific purposes) or 'general intent' (which may be relevant in cases of

negligence or recklessness). Your act will be defined as criminal only
if you had bad intentions or criminal motives (*mens rea*) when you
did what you did. If you had no *mens rea*, your act could have been
accidental – and the consequences for you are different. If you
happen to be cleaning a shotgun and you shoot somebody with it by
accident (i.e. without *mens rea*) that is probably manslaughter, but
not murder. If, on the other hand, you take a shotgun, deliberately
aim it at somebody knowing that it is loaded, and deliberately pull
the trigger intending to kill them, then you have *mens rea* – you have
a guilty mind or criminal intent. You are therefore guilty of murder,
a more serious offence than manslaughter, even if the effect for the
victim is the same in both cases.

What is important, as far as the law is concerned, is your state of
mind at the time when the trigger was pulled and this, of course,
is one thing that juries often have to make attributions and
inferences about (Sarat & Felstiner, 1988). One of their jobs is to
assess the defendant's likely state of mind at the time of the offence.
In looking at trials, then, it is important that we are more openly
aware of the prejudices and unfounded theories of personality that
may add to the other problems that afflict a jury. The point is quite
simply that the jury is made up of human beings, not legal ideals,
and human beings have various kinds of social psychological
processes built into them which don't function in ideal kinds of
ways. They are also open to persuasion by other members of the
jury group and, as we have seen in Chapter 5, human relationships
and self-image can matter as much as the pure evidence or logic.

We can find a lot in the courtroom to fascinate us, given all this!
For instance, thinking back over the reasons why we disregard or
dislike others or suspect deception (see Chapters 2 and 3), if
credibility is the issue, what do lawyers do to make witnesses look
stupid or unlikeable, or to create an atmosphere of disbelief and
suspicion of deception in their testimony or to impugn their motives
in giving it? What about the NVC that indicates lying, and what
about the fact that, as we saw in Chapter 1, most of us cannot identify when someone is really lying nearly half so well as we think we
can?

Bearing in mind what we have covered so far, there are several
different aspects of trials that we can now analyse from a relational
point of view, beginning with the physical environment of the courtroom, the way that it is set up, and how that affects relationships and
interactions there (cf. Chapter 1 on use of space). Then I will look
at the nature of the trial and 'consensual truth explanations', that is
to say, where truth is defined by what people say it is or what the

majority of people agree it is. As students of human relationships we should expect many 'irrelevant' factors to influence what they think – things like likeability and attractiveness of defendants, discrediting of key witnesses, similarity of jurors to defendants, and relational persuasion.

Order in the court

In Chapter 1 we saw how the organization of space in social settings will affect the ways in which people get treated, since it indicates something about the nature of the social and personal relationships between them. This is true of the ways we stand and the places we stand in, the amount of space we use, the horizontal distance between actors in social space and the vertical arrangement of space also – i.e. who is placed in a powerful, high-up place and who is low down.

What does a student who has read Chapter 1 immediately notice? The courtroom is an intriguing example of the arrangement of such social space and implicitly accords greater respect and importance to the statements made by certain actors in the scene. Judges always sit in the highest position; defendants usually sit in an exposed but fixed position (sometimes in a prisoner's dock); jurors sit together on one particular side of the judge, also in a special place – though of course they could probably hear equally well from any other position. The lawyers are placed centrally but are usually allowed to move around.

Furthermore, what can we make of the nature of the interactions which take place and the effects that this has on the presentation of testimony? The interactions in a courtroom are extremely formal and very much outside the range of most people's experience. Ordinary people are inclined to act in a stilted and self-conscious way, except on the TV courtroom dramas – but then, they're actors! Similarly, on graduation day, students are extremely careful about how they walk about the stage, pick up the degree certificate and walk back to their seat. You can see people getting anxious about whether they've bowed in the right place or to the right person and whether they should now step back and stand up straight or bow again . . . and so on. We all feel very much 'on stage' in these kinds of formal interaction. This will be particularly true in court since judges really do have power. There are various special sanctions and rules which apply in court (e.g. the power to deprive you of life, property, money, liberty and relationships, as in divorce or child custody cases).

The normal arrangement of a court, then, conveys messages about the relationships between the actors and shows who has authority and who does not. Witnesses are likely to be affected by that since they are most probably unfamiliar with the experience of being in court and with what goes on there. They might be overawed by the structure of the courtroom and the fact that there are rituals and unusual forms of speech, and by the fact that some of the people are wearing robes (and, in England, wigs). These solemn aspects are outside the routines of their common experience, so we might find that this affects the demeanour of witnesses in court. We might expect them to feel intimidated, awkward, put on the spot, embarrassed. We could predict that some witnesses will cope with the pressures more effectively than others (for example, those whose job involves them talking to large groups might be at an advantage as against those who are not used to doing so). It will not surprise us, then, to find that these predictions are, by and large, readily confirmed by experimental work (O'Barr, 1982).

One reason why the law regards trial by jury as a mainstay of the criminal legal system of Anglo-Saxon courts is precisely because it is felt that ordinary men and women are the best judges of other ordinary men and women in such surroundings. Lord Denning, formerly the Master of the Rolls (a 'top judge' of one branch of the British legal system), noted

> Trial by Jury has been the bulwark of our liberties too long for any of us to seek to alter it. Whenever a person is on trial for a serious crime or when, in a civil case, a person's honour or integrity is at stake, or when one or other party must be deliberately lying, then trial by Jury has no equal.

He thinks that juries are reasonably good at deciding whether people are telling the truth or not, whether they are distressed or intimidated, and whether they are showing themselves up in a fair light. We have already seen in Chapter 1 that this assessment may be somewhat optimistic, in that we are often bad at detecting deception (Stiff & Miller, 1984), and are more likely to be influenced by credibility than by real truth, and so on. But in practice juries get extended exposure to witnesses (who may often be examined for several hours) and their impressions are not the simple one-off impressions that we sometimes find in experimental studies of juries and witnesses.

Bearing false witness?

What types of evidence affect juries? We have already seen (Chapter 3) that a person's physical appearance affects our liking for him or her in predictable ways and that liking makes us less careful about fairness – we like to favour people whom we like. Does this happen in court, where we are supposed to be fair rather than favourable?

How we think criminals look

Most of us hold to current stereotypes defining 'the criminal'. We share a clear, but wrong, idea of what criminals are like and this tends to be a physical stereotype based on whether the person *looks* aggressive or wicked. If all criminals looked like criminals, of course, then every law officer's job would be a lot easier (which may be one of the many reasons why criminals used to be branded, in a prominent place, with a letter denoting the type of crime they had committed).

So far as the law is concerned a criminal is somebody who commits a crime. People in general assume that criminals are ugly, or have scarred faces and that people with scars are criminals! We can test this stereotype by finding out how people react to photographs of men with and without scars (Bull, 1977). In such an experiment a photograph of a man's face has the negative 'doctored up' so that it looks as if he has a scar down his cheek or some kind of stigma such as a strawberry birthmark. Some subjects are shown the clean original and some the doctored version. Do people respond differently to each photo? For example, one might ask 'Is this person a lifeboatman who goes out helping people, or is this person a criminal?' When the face has no scar on it then subjects assert that the person is a lifeboatman, and when the face has a scar on it they think he is a criminal. Evidently we expect that criminals look like criminals and that people who look like criminals *are* criminals. Esses & Webster (1988) also showed that sex offenders who are average looking or plain unattractive physically are more likely to be assessed as dangerous and so deserving of the unlimited sentences allotted to dangerous offenders under the Canadian Criminal Code.

One explanation for this is quite simply that circulated police descriptions tend to dwell on identifying or distinguishing marks. They invariably note that the person has a scar down his or her left cheek, for instance, so people get used to hearing these kind of physical deformities associated with criminals. It is then an understandable, if illogical, leap to assume that *all* criminals are like that.

Perhaps criminality does have a physical basis. For years psychologists, sociologists and criminologists have often asked whether there is, in fact, a criminal physical type. One of the first to do so was Lombroso (1918), who worked with Italian prison populations. He found that prisoners typically had sloping foreheads with narrow hairlines, big ears, eyes close together, large noses and big jaws. Try to conjure up a picture of such a person and quite frankly you can understand why they would turn to crime!

Even if there is not a criminal face or physique, maybe there is a genetic factor in criminality. For instance, there is some evidence (Prins, 1983) that more criminals have chromosomal disorders than do non-criminals. Another possibility is that people end up looking like criminals because they lead criminal lives or take to crime because of some physical capacity that suits them to it. For instance, someone who is a cat burglar and has to get through small windows is likely to be advantaged by being short and thin. To that extent their physique is likely to be related to the crimes they commit because their physical stature suits them to their crime. People who habitually engage in violence would probably be muscular because they use their muscles a lot, but they might have been on the receiving end of physical violence, too, so their face may indeed have been moved around a bit.

There is at least some relationship between physical appearance and crime, but to go as far as Lombroso did and claim that there is a criminal type just by looking at the structure of the face and head is risky. What is certainly true is that most of us act in a way that shows that we secretly share Lombroso's theory! While the law assumes that people are reasonable and unbiased, evidence from research suggests the opposite. People are biased; we make unfounded assumptions about criminals' appearance; we will unjustifiably be prejudiced against people who have physical deformities, and possibly will favour those who look attractive, just as in Chapter 3 we found that people do in forming the attractions that are the basis for long-term human relationships.

Attractiveness and justice

We know that we tend to favour persons that we like. Do juries do this and, if so, what makes them favour a defendant? Two relational cues that foster attraction are attitudes and physical attractiveness (see Chapter 3). Does research show that these are influential in the courtroom?

Attitude similarity often leads to attraction, so does that affect a

---

BOX 7.4 Eyewitnesses and distractors of eyewitnesses

Bell & Loftus (1988) tested subjects' reactions to conflicting eyewitness testimony and found that the degree of detail in the testimony of prosecution eyewitnesses influenced subjects' judgements of guilt and their recommendations about sentencing severity for the accused. Subjects inferred that a more detailed report was given by a person with a better memory for events.

Sanders & Chiu (1988) showed that witnesses rarely just make things up and that errors in recall are quite predictable, so that jurors are unlikely to be given false overall impressions when there is more than one eyewitness to an event.

Brigham & Cairns (1988) found that subjects who had been shown 'mug shots' of suspects before they identified suspects from a line-up were more likely to identify the wrong person if they had been encouraged to pick out a specific (incorrect) mug shot from the list as being that of the accused. In these circumstances subjects are more likely to stick with their original choice rather than to identify the suspect correctly when faced with the real live person.

Platz & Hosch (1988) indicate that subjects are reasonably good at identifying suspects from their own racial grouping and are likely to be poor at distinguishing suspects from other racial groups.

Maass & Kohnken (1989) showed that people faced with a person carrying a threatening weapon are likely to focus on the weapon rather than the face of the suspect and hence to be poor at identifying the suspect (but, interestingly, to be rather good at identifying hands!).

---

jury's reactions to a defendant? Although jurors have very little opportunity to learn a defendant's attitudes (since defendants often do not testify and, where they do, they are limited to what is 'relevant' to the law governing the crime), jurors tend to take the side of a person who seems to have attitudes similar to their own (Mitchell & Byrne, 1973). If the jurors think that the person on trial is similar to them, thinks the same way as them, has the same sorts of attitudes about life, the same sorts of values – well the person can't be all bad, so must be not guilty! Normally the defendant does not know how to adopt the attitudes of the jurors, although, by dressing smartly and trying to present a front, most defendants try to aspire to the ideals that our culture holds dear and so to look 'good' and law-abiding. It is one of the strengths of the jury system that defendants have no prior relationship with jurors, no knowledge of their attitudes, and little influence over the selection of jurors.

Obviously when defence lawyers challenge jurors and try to have them barred from sitting on a particular jury, it is often because they assume that the juror holds attitudes different from the defendant and so may be unfavourable to the defendant (Saks, 1986).

Do physically attractive people get a better deal in court than other people? We have some evidence from studies using fake jurors in simulated or 'pretend' trials. Physically attractive people were given lighter sentences in these simulated trials (Landy & Aronson, 1969). This was a general finding except when defendants had used their physical attractiveness in the commission of the crime, for instance if they were confidence tricksters. Where confidence tricksters had used their physical attractiveness to 'con' people, then subjects gave them harder sentences. It had always been assumed from the Landy & Aronson study that physically attractive subjects would get acquitted more often, but evidently this is not so. They were given lighter sentences by experimental subjects, but did not get acquitted more often (Stewart, 1980). So the findings about attractiveness are a bit uncertain – and we cannot necessarily assume that they would 'work' on real-life juries to the same degree.

How we think criminals behave in court

Just as we hold to a few assumptions about the ways in which criminals' faces look, so we are probably going to be influenced by their nonverbal behaviour in court – just as we are in everyday life anyway. It is odd, given the amount of social psychological work devoted to the study of nonverbal behaviour in everyday life settings (see Chapter 1), that only recently has any time been devoted to understanding the effects it has in court. A lawyer's facial expressions or eye contact with the witnesses and jurors, a witness's manner and nonverbal style, spatial behaviour, movement and vocal characteristics such as speech rate, pitch and inflection can all affect his or her credibility (Stiff & Miller, 1984). Presumably a witness's nonverbal behaviour therefore can affect the ways in which a jury assesses him or her and evaluates the testimony that he or she gives in the courtroom (Pryor & Buchanan, 1984). Accordingly, the courts take specific note of this and guidance to jurors often explicitly states (as in the following quotation from Florida) that 'In determining the believability of any witness, and the weight to be given to his or her testimony, you may properly consider the demeanour of the witness . . .'.

Remembering from Chapter 1 that Stiff & Miller (1984) found that observers were actually very bad at detecting deception in real-life contexts, what would you expect to find happening in a court? Looking at some specific behaviours that normally indicate nervousness, Pryor & Buchanan (1984) compared nervous and relaxed defendants. They used self-manipulation (nervous fidgeting), eye contact or lack of it, and speech errors or fluency as indices of nervousness in a defendant and then looked to see the effects on a jury's ratings of that person. In this study, the jurors were given a summary of the case and then saw a videotape of the defendant before receiving a judge's (standard) guidance on determination of the case. Some of the jurors saw a videotape where the defendant was very nervous; some saw the same defendant not looking nervous at all. This study was particularly interesting because it found that moderately nervous defendants were judged to be the most guilty! The calm and confident ones were thought to be most credible and least guilty. Interestingly, female jurors reported being more influenced by the nonverbal signals than males did, as we might predict; however, when Pryor & Buchanan looked at their actual scores, they found that the females had not in fact been influenced by it any more than the males had. This is quite surprising in view of the findings by Blanck et al. (1981) that females are invariably found to be superior in decoding NVC.

The sequence of events in the courtroom

In forming impressions of strangers or acquaintances, we know that certain information (e.g. about attitudes) carries especial weight and that it can be very important whether we hear a piece of information at an early point in an interaction or later. Indeed in Chapter 3 we spent some time considering 'filter theories' of relationship development and pointing out that information is more relevant to relationships at some particular points than at others.

Does it matter, researchers have asked, which case is presented first, defence or prosecution? It is almost inevitable that prosecution comes first (or how would we know what the defence is a defence against?). But what effect might this have? The prosecution has the first crack at defining the case, establishing the main points, indicating who is to be accused of what, what it means, what is the strength of the evidence, and so on.

In the area of formation of impressions about people, researchers have thoroughly explored the issue of primacy versus recency or, in other words, 'what matters most, what comes first (primacy) or what is most recently heard (recency)?' Kassin et al. (1990) found that the issue is not a simple one! Some subjects, specifically those with a high 'need for cognition' (i.e. a strong desire to understand things) are influenced more by arguments preceding the evidence (which therefore gives the evidence a structure that the subjects can follow) than by the evidence itself. Subjects with a low need for cognition, on the other hand, were influenced by arguments *following* the evidence (i.e. those arguments coming after they had made their own judgements of what was significant and what was not and needed to hear how to put it in context).

In a study of a related but different point, Pyszcynski & Wrightsman (1981) examined the way in which the prosecution made its opening statement and the subsequent effect that this had on a jury's thoughts. They showed, rather surprisingly, that lengthy prosecution opening statements are really the best bet for a prosecution. The longer the opening statement the better the cards are stacked their way.

The reasons for this are quite simple (assuming that there is no 'time out' between the statements). If the defence also makes a lengthy statement in reply then the jury will probably begin to nod off; if, alternatively, the defence subsequently makes a brief reply because it wants to avoid boring the jury, then the jury assumes it is because it has not really got a good defence. So it pays the prosecution to make as long an opening statement as possible – at least in an experimental setting. Conversely, if the prosecution makes a brief opening statement the jury tends to think that the prisoner is not guilty, whatever the defence does. The study thus suggests that it is in the best interests of the prosecution to make a lengthy opening statement.

The same primacy-recency effects influence reactions to individual pieces of testimony. What matters is the structure of the messages – as we found in Chapter 5, too. Paying attention to the strength with which people make their points at the beginning and ends of their statement, Pennington (1982) showed that if the strongest points come first then observers (jurors) are more likely to believe what you say. Therefore, if the prosecution puts its best evidence first rather than keeping it in the bag and bringing it out with a flourish at the end, they are more likely to get verdicts of guilty.

We have to be careful in interpreting such studies, though, since many of the effects are actually created in very brief manipulations in the laboratory. By contrast, in a full court hearing, much time is spent on those same details. Chapter 3 showed us that there can be important brief effects on initial attraction but that relationships themselves are not necessarily formed by them alone. In a full trial

– which could last weeks – the jury sees much longer samples of each participant's behaviour, and initial impressions can easily be overturned by later evidence (Sunnafrank & Miller, 1981).

As I have been arguing throughout this book, these differences depend on the one crucial factor in human relationship that psychology minimizes and communication studies allows to prevail, namely, whenever a witness gives evidence – not just at the start of their testimony – they *talk*! What have scientists learned about the effects of the kind of language in which testimony is delivered?

Mind your language in the courtroom

It is not enough to speak the truth in court: one has to seem to be the sort of person who can be believed and therefore evidence must be presented in a convincing way. One way is to speak in a way that helps one's credibility (Cooke, 1990). Sarat & Felstiner (1988) note that the language of motives in the law is different from that in normal social relationships. Clients going through divorce tend to reconstruct the past and explain their own behaviour as well as the actions of others. (cf. Chapter 3 and the discussion of Miell's, 1987, work.) However, lawyers tend to focus on the way the divorce process works and to explain the actions of spouses in terms not of the motive but of the process. So lawyers (and judges) come at issues of human relationships from a different angle from the one that their clients use and this is embodied, as is much else, in the linguistic differences and code uses that they manifest.

Legal language is different from ordinary language and confuses Ordinary Mortals pretty easily. We ordinary people say things in low code, as we saw in Chapter 1. Lawyers use forbiddingly technical high codes. Consider this example given by O'Barr (1982): where the normal person in the street would say 'Have an orange' as they give it to somebody, a lawyer might say:

> 'I hereby give and convey to you my estate and interest, right and title, claim and advantages of, and in, said orange, together with its rind, skin, juice, pulp, pips, all rights and advantages therein, together with full power to bite, suck, squeeze, crush or otherwise eat or consume the same or to give away the same, whether with or without its rind, skin, juice, pulp, pips, anything heretofore or hereafter to the contrary notwithstanding.'

The problem for an Ordinary Mortal in court is therefore, 'What do I do? Should I speak normally or am I expected to use high code?' The answer seems to be that many OMs fall into the trap of attempting to use high code – and do it badly. What effects might this have?

Think of the contrast between the Ordinary Mortals and the lawyers in court. We normally expect lawyers to use high code and would be surprised if they didn't. So we would expect lawyers to cry 'Objection!' when they disapprove of a style of question or answer. Clearly this is not the normal everyday way of indicating disagreement. We expect judges to say 'Sustained' or 'Overruled' in response, which nobody says anywhere else but in court. We also expect lawyers to use formal modes of language like 'if it please the court' and 'my learned friend' and 'your honour' and 'with your honour's permission'. But just imagine what would happen if ordinary witnesses from the public started doing things like that to one another, too. They'd be regarded as pompous, arrogant, weird, peculiar, discreditable and possibly even unreliable witnesses.

In attempting to use 'proper' speech styles, witnesses invariably adopt a 'hypercorrectness' that is far more formal than would be used in everyday discourse. This means that they misapply imperfectly learned rules of grammar, use vocabulary incorrectly and produce overly precise pronunciation (Labov, 1972). Such speakers consequently make errors and speak in an unnatural manner, which may give the jury the false impression that they do not know what they are talking about. As examples of hypercorrect style, compare 'I lapsed into a comatose state, was not cognizant of the environment and although in a somewhat less than dire condition, was not at that precise moment ambulatory' with 'I became dazed and unaware of what was going on. I was not badly hurt but could not walk for the time being' (Based on O'Barr, 1982, p. 84). A witness speaking in hypercorrect style is usually dismissed as being of low social stature (Hurwitz, 1953) or as attempting to ingratiate (Jones, 1964). Witnesses using the hypercorrect style are regarded as less convincing, less competent, less well qualified and less intelligent than other witnesses (O'Barr, 1982). Mock jurors (i.e. student subjects acting as jurors) award lower amounts of compensation to defendants speaking in hypercorrect style.

By contrast, expert witnesses and probably also police witnesses are not only permitted to use the high code forms in giving formal reports, they are expected to do so. By the same token they are practised at doing it, make fewer errors and appear to be in greater command of their evidence.

People who break grammatical and linguistic rules are interpreted negatively and their actions are given a diminished meaning. It is important to note that the consequences of breaking the rules will be more severe for witnesses and defendants than for experts or lawyers, since experts and persons with power are always permitted to deviate from rules that the rest of us must follow (Hollander, 1958). People who speak in a way that makes them 'poor witnesses' are believed less often, even when they are right. So what is it about a witness's relational or speech style that makes him or her a naturally poor witness? The most direct route to being disregarded is to claim, honestly, that you are uncertain about your testimony. If a witness says, 'Well, I couldn't tell if the car was travelling at 30 m.p.h. or 35 m.p.h., but it was somewhere around that, certainly not 40 m.p.h. but it may have been 33 m.p.h.' he or she may be telling the exact truth, but will be disregarded by the jury (O'Barr, 1982). Sadly, anyone who admits to being uncertain risks being seen as unreliable even though, in fact, they may be telling the absolute truth, namely that they really can't tell. Such honesty somehow robs them of source credibility.

Witnesses are also regarded as poor if they repeat themselves a lot. Witnesses who are constantly going over the same ground and making the same point tend to seem unsure of themselves – as if they have only one idea in their head, which sums up what they can contribute to the case.

Jurors also think of a witness as a discreditable 'poor witness' if the person overuses qualifiers and hedges (that is to say, 'sort of', 'you know', 'kind of' rather than just using the proper word on its own). Such speech is 'powerless', as we saw in Chapter 1, and uses repetition too, as well as imprecision in use of words. O'Barr (1982) reports a case where the outcome hinged on the fact that a woman was unable to make a judgement about how far her car had travelled after it had been involved in an accident, and instead of saying that she was unsure of the distance she said, 'I am poor with feet'. The jury presumably either didn't know what she was talking about or thought it such a funny way of putting it that she must be an idiot and an unreliable one at that. The appeal court, however, took the honest view that she was a reliable witness who was simply good at making herself look stupid! By contrast, witnesses who claim to be able to remember minor details in their testimony, such as the colour of a man's necktie, are seen to be more reliable even if that specific detail has no real bearing on the case (Bell & Loftus, 1989). It seems that reporting of details creates the impression of attentiveness *and accuracy*!

Poor witnesses also use fragmented styles of speech; that is to say, they break off in the middle of sentences, use ungrammatical forms and do not get to the end of the sentence. This sends a message that says 'I am uncertain about my testimony'. These examples of powerless speech styles not only convey lack of power, authority and influence, as was shown in Chapter 2, but in the particular case of a law court, they affect a jury's assessment of a witness's reliability.

Lawyers' linguistic liberties

Some discrediting of witnesses stems from their own natural (mis)use of language, but occasionally lawyers can lead them into traps. The breaking of the social or linguistic rules can be accidental or it can be brought about by a careful lawyer trying to discredit a witness. Lawyers ask questions and witnesses answer them, so the lawyers have a considerable amount of control over the style of answers that the witnesses will produce (Cooke, 1990), even if they can't always necessarily affect the content of the answers (though sometimes they can).

Lawyers can affect the impression that witnesses give – and can do this by affecting the linguistic style of the evidence, for instance by making the witnesses break rules and so discredit themselves. For example, a lawyer might want to upset the manner in which a person gives evidence or at least to control the manner of its presentation, and indeed are urged to do this in legal training texts (Evans, 1983). Consider this: one of the things that makes people sound as if they know what they are talking about is if they talk in complete sentences or paragraphs; i.e. a narrative form of report. Narrative testimony, where a witness gives continuous prose answers without being interrupted, gives a strong message: it says 'I am well informed, unrehearsed and knowledgeable' (O'Barr, 1982). The witness does not need to be prompted to give the answers, appears to be able to talk without having to think about it too much and so seems well informed and knowledgeable about the topic. Knowing this, a lawyer who wants to make an important witness look knowledgeable, well informed and unrehearsed can ask a question in a form that allows a narrative sort of answer, such as 'Can you tell us what happened in your own words; just spend as long as you like telling us what occurred'. By contrast, witnesses who seem to need controlling can look garrulous or foolish (for instance, the lawyer may say impatiently 'Just answer the question' – and that instantly makes the witness look evasive or too wordy). Equally, if it can be made to look as if they have to have information dragged out of them then they appear as if they have something to hide. If the lawyer's questions are carefully phrased to set off pat answers then witnesses can appear to be making rehearsed or prepared answers, and may seem uninformed or unsure of what they are saying.

The style of question gives the lawyers more control in other ways, too. The lawyer can cut down what a witness says so that he or she has less chance to introduce anything the lawyer would prefer them not to tell the court. TV courtroom dramas often show lawyers doing this. They stop witnesses when they are beginning to expand their testimony in undesirable directions: 'Just answer the question'; 'Please stick to the question asked'. All of these give the impression, if done in the right tone of voice, that the witness is being exasperating and could be unreliable. On the other hand, 'May it please the court to direct the witness to answer the question' offers the lawyer the chance to imply that the witness is concealing something. By such means, in other words by structuring and manipulating the form of discourse, a lawyer can exert some control over the manner in which the testimony comes out from the witness and thus can affect the credibility which the witness enjoys afterwards. Saks (pers. comm.) observes that lawyers invariably ask narrative questions on direct examination (of their own side's witnesses) and adopt the choppier question-and-answer style for cross-examination (of the other side's witnesses).

Another technique which is often used to discredit experts is to try and lead them to look pedantic and petty (Brodsky, 1977; see BOX 7.5 for some delightful examples). This is done by asking questions in a loose way that causes them to object to the form of the question or to say, 'Well I couldn't possibly answer a general question like that', or to answer it in such a way that they appear to be undecided (e.g. 'Well, it depends what you mean by "crossing the road"'). It is possible to phrase the questions so that somebody with expert knowledge could not possibly answer it without having to clarify what the question means (such questions might be things like 'What actually causes schizophrenia?', 'What exactly is mental illness'). But of course as soon as the experts start clarifying the question they make themselves look trivial, pedantic, nit-picking, hostile and antagonistic or hopelessly academic and out of touch with everyday life. They then are much less persuasive than people who appear to be friendly, knowledgeable and on your side. Obviously a lawyer wants to discredit the other side's expert witnesses and can use such tactics as asking detailed esoteric questions (for example asking an expert psychologist 'What is the reliability of the comprehension subtest of the Wechsler Adult Intelligence Scale-Revised?'). If the expert has to admit ignorance, then the 'expert' status is less credible to the jury.

BOX 7.5   Lawyers' linguistic liberties

Brodsky (1977) points out a number of techniques used by lawyers to discredit expert witnesses. Examples from his longer list are:

Infallibility *tests ('Do you know the scientific work of X & Y on this topic?' X and Y are, of course, especially chosen because they are incredibly obscure, but if the expert has to admit to ignorance of the work then he or she is made to look foolish and fallible.)*

God only knows *('What is the cause of divorce?' The idea here is to trivialize the issue or to expose how little the profession truly knows about particular areas.)*

Historic hysteric gambit *('Wasn't Pasteur ridiculed by his contemporaries?' The point here is to suggest that scientific consensus can often be wrong despite the consensus, and the lawyer's clients could therefore be right even if the evidence of prevailing scientific fashion is against them.)*

Challenging *('Have other studies replicated your work and upheld its reliability and validity?' Again, the point is to challenge the authority of the work. Scientific work is very rarely replicated in all its details.)*

Cooke (1990) also notes that lawyers very often attempt to upset witnesses by jumping around from discussion of one piece of evidence to another until they are confused. Other attempts to discredit witnesses can involve the making of a prefatory statement before the question, such as 'We all know that women are worse drivers than men, in your opinion was the accused any worse than normal?' Such prejudicial comments must be objected to immediately before the question is answered. (Cooke also notes the importance of expert witnesses attending court in clothes that are evidence of expertise, such as dark, subdued clothing without distracting accessories.)

As discussed in Chapter 1, the *form* of a message is a way of communicating: the content is informative, but so too is the way in which it is put across. Because of that, variation in form conveys messages as well, as we saw in Chapter 1 in discussing 'switching'. If a lawyer makes a witness switch from non-narrative reporting into narrative then it begins to look as if the witness didn't know what they were talking about to start with but now they have got on to ground they do know well. Switching from one form to another is thus another way of conveying a message about knowledge, about certainty and about truth. So again, lawyers might be interested in encouraging variation in speech-form by witnesses (Suggs & Berman, 1979).

Language is used in court in a way that permits power and knowledge to be inferred. Language style in our courts is an important topic because our courts decide cases on the basis of credibility and plausibility and consensual truth; 'truth' is essentially what the jury decides it is. The jury may have heard half a dozen different versions of the same story and have to decide who is reliable and expert, which versions are true, what is consistent and what is not. The big questions of plausibility are based partly on the nature of evidence and partly on the credibility of the witnesses, which in turn derives in large part from speech style.

Sometimes, though, the lawyers may make a direct attempt to discredit a witness. What happens then? Lawyers assume that if you can discredit an opposition witness, it will also discredit the opposite side's case, but Hatvany & Strack (1980) suggest that things do not work in quite that simple boomerang way. Usually a discredited witness's testimony is ignored altogether, rather than it working in the opposite way to what the witness is saying. There is one exception: when the key witness's testimony was a character attack on the accused. If a key witness makes character attacks and is then discredited, the jury overcorrects for what the witness has said, and they are likely to think positive things about the accused person rather than negative. In most other cases the key witness is simply ignored if he or she has been discredited. Gibbs et al. (1989) found that expert witnesses are discredited most effectively by hostile attorneys using non-leading questions, who challenge on specifics.

What is quite clear from all of this is that the material discussed in Chapter 1 has direct bearing on a jury's beliefs about a particular witness as seen in the court during the trial. Presumably the jury takes these impressions with them into the jury-room where they decide the fate of the accused.

How do juries make decisions?

After members of the jury have heard the evidence in court without discussing it amongst themselves – i.e. after each of them has formed an independent judgement – they retire together to the jury-room and expose their views, their thinking, their judgements and their personalities to the other members of the jury. What goes on in the jury-room? What sort of impact will shy and lonely jurors make, for instance? Whose views will be given the most credence? What are the effects of having to present your thinking to a group of strangers and argue with them about your own personal judgements? How do interpersonal factors affect the decisions in a jury? Can likeability of jurors affect the weight given to their opinions by others? These questions are all, in one way or another, relational questions based on relational principles and processes. Let us now take relationships into the jury-room.

Actually, at the moment we can't know for sure how to answer these interesting questions (Blanck, 1987). Countries that have a jury system usually have strong laws to protect juries from direct interference, so researchers are not allowed to ask real juries about their decisions or their decision-making even though some countries (e.g. the USA) allow the press to talk to jurors after the verdict. The best that may be done is to have a substitute or simulated jury sitting in the same court pretending to be a real jury, and then take them off to a laboratory where they are asked to make a decision just as the true jury does. Sometimes it happens that the mock jury and the real one reach the same decision – but often it does not.

Another method involves rerunning the trial using transcripts and actors who pretend to be the real lawyers, judge, defendant and witnesses. However, it still is not quite the same. Though actors are very good at acting, they are not judges, and the mock jurors probably realize it. We cannot be certain whether mock jurors respond to something because they know that the experimenter is interested in it or because it really affects them. We must bear this in mind when we look at the research.

Are juries like other decision-making groups? Do they recall testimony accurately, stick to the correct issues, and reach verdicts felt by others (e.g. judges or trial lawyers) to have been the right one on the facts? For legal reasons, as we saw above, research cannot be conducted directly on real juries and simulated ones have to be used for studies on these issues. In some instances subjects are drawn from normal jury rosters and asked to listen to recordings of real trials. This work shows that higher-status members of (simulated) juries exerted more influence than other jurors on decisions (Strodtbeck et al., 1957). It also suggests that, as shown in Chapters 3 and 4, women are more willing to take on responsibility for relationships between people; in juries, just as elsewhere, they are more thoughtful about their reactions to the other jury members and spend longer making positive comments about other people and being more receptive and encouraging of their ideas than do the male members of the jury.

As we saw in Chapter 1, those who speak most often are usually held to be more expert. The research on human relationships shows that we are affected by those persons whom we like and we tend to be influenced by status. So it seems natural that, at least from some points of view, such persons will be most influential in a jury – even though the law assumes that all jurors are equal. What should matter, therefore, is what they say.

When we look at the specific content of speech in simulated jury discussions it is found that about 50 percent is devoted to expression of irrelevant material such as personal opinions about general matters (James, 1959). Only some 15 percent of talk is actually devoted to the testimony, whilst 25 percent is devoted to procedural issues in the jury itself (who should speak next, and so on). This could be used as evidence that juries are pretty ineffective and inattentive to the true needs of the court. On the other hand, it could be taken to make a much more interesting point, namely, that people in such a situation need to establish some familiarities with each other and to find out what sorts of people they all are before they get down to the business of making a complex decision about someone else's life. I have already pointed out many times that humans spend a good deal of their time talking to other human beings and we have learned how these trivial conversational discussions help to establish and bind relationships together as a basis for getting other life-activities coordinated. Establishing a 'trivial' but working relationship first is a good basis for discussing the later material, as we saw in the previous chapter – and these 'trivia' can help to establish the relationship first.

There are, in fact, four phases to group operation, of which the first (*Orientation*) is precisely this phase of getting to know one another (Fisher, 1970). However, two of the other three also have implicit relational purposes (the exception is *Conflict*, where each person states opinions unambiguously and strongly. This is the second phase, after Orientation). In the *Emergence* phase the general consensus begins to show through and so those in disagreement with it begin to make their points less strongly and more ambiguously so that they can be accepted as reasonable people and 'join the group again' (Fisher, 1970). Finally, the *Reinforcement* phase consists of an orgy of mutual backslapping, where everyone comments on the effectiveness of the group and generally fosters the view that a good decision was reached by a lot of nice people in a very nice and sensible way. This again serves relational goals and makes everyone feel good about the group – and about themselves, too, of course!

So some research that seems to show that juries are ineffective may on second thoughts suggest instead – or also – that jurors are merely ordinary human beings who want to establish good working relationships with one another, just like they do everywhere else.

An unnoticed point so far is that in giving opinions about other people (witnesses and defendants) the strangers on the jury are actually being encouraged to behave towards one another as friends do: they are self-disclosing about their personal opinions, their judgements and their value system (Chapter 3). They are giving away personal information about the ways in which they think and the attitudes they hold. . . . Remember that juries originated as groups of twelve members who were supposed to be friends or acquaintances of the accused and who were prepared to swear that he or she was innocent in the 'wager at law' described earlier. Times have changed but the relational underpinnings of jury work have not.

It may have struck you in reading the above, as it struck me in writing it, that a lot of work I have covered exhibits precisely the points that I dwelt on in the opening chapters of this book. It focusses on the individual characteristics of jurors rather than on how they get on with one another; it looks at how individual jurors form impressions of witnesses and defendants rather than on how they reach 'joint impressions' that represent a negotiated group view; it also regards jurors' relational needs and personal aims or projects as somehow irrelevant and irritating. I would propose, instead, that relational needs and personal aims are a central feature of the operation when a group of strangers gets together under the pressure of making difficult and responsible decisions – sometimes literally life-or-death decisions – about other human beings. Perhaps we should study more carefully the ways in which jurors establish personal relationships with one another under pressure; that influences their decisions, too.

Summary

Various aspects of legal procedure are centrally dependent on language and relationship processes between participants – even down to the level of whether the jury likes the defendant. You are now, therefore, in a position to judge which of the three models of the trial (see BOX 7.3 above) you think best fits in with the models of social behaviour offered in this book. I have argued that an important element in jury trials in the West is that they depend on plausibility and interpersonal persuasion – which, as we have seen, themselves depend quite importantly on the impressions that various people make on the jury and how much the jury likes them. A lot of the processes involved in jury decision-making also have a relational basis: some of the jurors' apparently irrelevant actions do establish relationships and some of their discussions make them act towards one another just as friends normally do.

Further reading

Ellison K.W. & Buckhout, R. (1981) *Psychology and Criminal Justice*. Harper & Row: New York.
Kassin, S.M. & Wrightsman, L. (1985) *The Psychology of Evidence and Trial Procedure*. Sage: Beverly Hills.
O'Barr, W.M. (1982) *Linguistic Evidence: Language, Power and Strategy in the Courtroom*. Academic Press: New York.
Sales, B.D. (1976) *Psychology in the Legal Process*. Halsted: New York.
Wrightsman, L. (1991) *Psychology and the Legal Process*, 2nd edn. Halsted: New York.

Afterword

This book grew out of my conviction that relationships are major concern in human lives but, more than that, they are major organizers of our social experience. It is, therefore, primarily a book showing how relationships intertwine with daily lives, our social behaviour, and personal experiences with other people. However, a second intention was to show the ways in which personal relationships affect the social behaviour that is studied in the 'vacuum' of the laboratory. Personal relationships, I contend, can modify general rules of behaviour in ways that present social scientific research does not acknowledge. However I may pressure people to buy soap powder, that is not how I influence a friend to take up my astrology classes. Whatever my general attitude to smoking, the way I handle a friend's lighting up in my house will differ from the methods that are appropriate for a stranger or for my boss or for the friend of one of my guests. There is a great power and social significance to the phrase 'Oh well, seeing as it's you . . .'. *Relationships are modifiers* and researchers need a better grasp of the ways in which generalized social behaviour – which is essentially what such researchers study – is tailored to relational circumstance.

These were my main reasons for showing the need to interweave work on relationships into the materials already available in social scientific texts. Another was to generate some thoughts for future research.

In writing the book, I have become aware of several promising issues that remain to be explored. How do everyday concerns, hopes, anxieties and plans about relationships affect other daily social behaviour? Why is there so little work on the dark side of relationships? For example where are the studies of effects of disliking or disappointment or remorse or regret on behaviour in interactions? Who studies boring communication or intentional social humiliation or bitchiness? There is much research on development of relationships but virtually none on the underdevelopment of relationships or the failure of relationships to develop. Why do our models of behaviour so often assume that we always know what we are doing, where we are going in relationships, and how our lives will develop when all around and within us we see instances of confusion and indecision? Despite their frequency in social life, there is no social psychology of flirtation, of forgiving, of regret, of remorse, of disappointment, of polite refusals, of impolite requests, or of 'needling' and bullying. Only recently has there been any investigation of the ways in which enemies are handled (Wiseman, 1989). Journal articles traditionally report that data from suspicious subjects are discarded, but, except on unexplored intuitive grounds, researchers do not actually know whether suspicion affects social behaviour, and, if so, how exactly it does so. How exactly do two people behave when they distrust one another, when they are enemies, or when they are 'falling out'? What precise differences are there in their interaction as compared to the interactions of friends? What variables differentiate the interactions of strangers from those of friends?

I hope that in presenting relationships as the organizing theme for this book I have stimulated present readers, from whom the future researchers in this field may ultimately come, to undertake to fill these gaps.

Appendix

To Help You and Your Instructor

Library and research skills

It can be frustrating to find that someone else has taken the only library copy of the book or article that was the basis of a class assignment, but with a little extra knowledge about some library techniques – and a bit of practice – you can get around the problem. The same techniques can help you to follow up on any topics in this book that you particularly want to pursue, and, as I mention earlier in the book, my students are all taught these methods to allow them to expand their abilities to 'read around' a favourite topic. It is to your advantage to have these skills available to you, so I want to round off by presenting them here and then building them into the exercises that will help you to apply the topics in the book to your life.

Many volumes in your library are there to help you to do your own research if you are particularly interested in a topic. The most useful are: *Current Contents*, *Psychological Abstracts*, and *Social Science Citation Index (SSCI)*.

Current Contents

Current Contents is published in sections and simply prints the contents pages of journals recently published. There are seven sections, and the one you need is for the social and behavioural sciences. By turning to the psychology or communication sections, you can see the titles of papers that you may be interested in for research. It also lists authors' addresses so that you can contact them and ask for a reprint of their article.
Useful for: showing you what has happened most recently.
Disadvantage: gives you only the title – and titles can often be misleading.

Psychological Abstracts

Psychological Abstracts deals with specific years or half-years and prints and catalogues the abstracts/summaries which appear at the start of most journal articles. It also lists the source (i.e. the journal that published it), the title, and authors' affiliations. It comes in two parts: index and catalogue. The index lists subjects and authors, and gives a code number for the relevant abstract; the catalogue lists the abstracts by code number. You start with the index to find the abstracts you need, then go to the appropriate catalogue section to find the abstracts. If they are of interest to you, you can find the original article in the journal where it was published.

Useful for: the list of keywords enables you to track down, say, all the articles on 'friendship in children' or 'prejudice' or 'self-esteem'. It is excellent for broadly encompassing a particular topic, and, because it prints the abstracts in full, it enables you quickly to find pertinent details of papers and so make a list of those that you should read in full.

Disadvantages: it is produced semiannually in volumes relating to a particular (half) year and so is not as up to date as *Current Contents*. It lists only those items published in a given year, without cross-reference.

(Social) Sciences Citation Index (SSCI)

SSCI is published in annual volumes, although sections covering parts of the current year are available separately. It gives: a list of keywords (permuterm subject index), a list of papers and authors consulted that year (source index), and a list of citations made to particular authors (citation index). (Always ensure that you are using the correct section.) The citation index is extremely useful. Suppose I want to find all the papers in 1983 that referred to S.E. Asch's classic study on conformity: I would look up Asch, S.E. in the citation index and there would be the list. This is useful because you can, for instance, trace the way in which a piece of classic work has been used in more recent work or criticized by subsequent researchers. Another advantage is that if someone has taken the very article that you wanted to read out of the library, then you can find others on the same topic that cite the article on loan. This is useful for essays and seminar classes because the more recent article may give you some good ideas about how to evaluate or criticize the set article.

Useful for: coming up to date on classic work; doing a broad review of related research; finding out the different lines that have been developed from one particular starting point; finding alternative reading sources.

Disadvantages: somewhat difficult to learn to use, but the effort really is worth it.

Exercises

As a part of your learning of the subject and as a test of your growing abilities, you might like to try the following exercises – or your instructor may assign them to you. Some questions are intended to encourage you to experience the materials and some are meant to stimulate you to use your growing knowledge to apply to practical issues – but they can make useful topics for small group discussion in class or with friends (instead of, or in addition to, the preceding purposes). All should help to illustrate the principles described in the book as they operate in real life – *your* real life.

Practising your library skills

Think of a topic that interests you and find out all you can about it using the preceding methods. Allow two hours to do this, pick one particular year, say 1989, for *Psychological Abstracts* and *SSCI* but carry through up to date with *Current Contents*.

Chapter 1: Verbal and nonverbal 'languages'

1 Sit next to someone who is reading a newspaper and begin to read it; *or*, Find a room or bus that is less than a quarter full and sit in the seat next to someone there whom you do not know; *or*, Hold a conversation with a friend whilst standing at the 'wrong' distance. Record your experiences for class discussion, especially noting the proxemic behaviour, the consequences of the encounter, and your own personal feelings during the 'breaking of the rules'.

2 Listen out for instances of speech that occur between pairs of men, pairs of women, and mixed-sex pairs. Consider the differences and similarities in the speech styles of men and women. Try to focus on the characteristics of the speech of each sex and see if you can detect a pattern of features. Does the pattern that you notice have

any dependency on the topics that are chosen for conversation? Compare these patterns with instances that you may see on TV in different types of programmes. Are there shifts in patterns as a function of the types of programmes that you select?

Chapter 2: Emotions

1 Pair up with another member of the class (or with an interested friend) for a couple of hours or so and keep a diary of your emotions and the partner's emotions. As an alternative or an addition, take it in turns to say 'If Peter calls, tell him I'm out', using different tones of voice to convey the widest range of emotions that you can. Do this without telling each other in advance which emotion you are encoding. Each of you should keep a list of emotions that are 'sent' and 'received' on each occasion and then compare notes to see if the 'decoder' received the message sent by the 'encoder' each time. At the end of the time check the two lists and discuss the extent to which they match up. Do you both communicate your emotions effectively in this setting? What problems do you experience in doing this exercise?

2 Find extra readings for chapter 2. Start with a book by Buss (1980) and find some people who have cited it. If you use the 1983 volume of *SSCI*, you should find 18 citations, of which Schlenker (1982) is one that you could profitably use.

Chapter 3: Long-term relationships

Think about the following four items and construct three arguments for and three arguments against the statement:

We have completely free choice over the friendships that we make.

Friendships should be arranged for us by our parents.

Friendships should be arranged for us by a national computer containing data on our personalities.

Friendships should be arranged randomly according to, say, birthdates, hair colour or IQ level. (Think up your own system for doing this.)

Discuss the results that you and your classmates come up with. As well as trying this in class discussion, you could try talking to your friends about it.

Chapter 4: The family

1 Look back at the exercise for Chapter 3. Repeat each step here, substituting the word 'marriage' for the word 'friendships'. Are cultures that arrange marriages really doing anything substantially different from what happens in cultures where love is the ostensible basis of the relationship?

2 Do you think it would reduce or increase the divorce rate if marriages were fixed up by:

Parents for their children,
Mutual friends,
Computers,
Chance.

3 Give three reasons for and three reasons against teaching 'relationships' in school. Should teachers be trained to identify unpopular children? What difficulties might there be with this notion? What did the unpopular children at your school do?

Chapter 5: Persuasion

1 Spend one day keeping a list of all the examples of persuasion or influence which you witness. At the end of the day, look at the list and work out what methods were used. Is there any relationship, do you think, between the strategy and the person's goals, the positivity/negativity of the request, the power differences between the persons involved, the closeness or distance of the relationship between the persons?

2 Persuade your instructor that you have prepared a good answer to the preceding exercise.

Chapter 6: Health

1 If an insurance company asked you for advice on social risk factors for their life assurance policies, what topics would you suggest they ask questions about on their proposal forms?

2 Look through the article by Kurdek (1991b) on the consequences of separation and divorce (use library skills to find it if you don't know the reference or haven't thought of checking this book's Reference Section!). When is the 'separating man' at greatest risk and at what point are women most vulnerable? How would you

suggest we monitor such risks and how could counsellors, friends or volunteer 'crisis' organizations help?

Chapter 7: Law

One exercise would be to go to the nearest law courts and watch a trial in progress to see if the participants use the techniques that are indicated in the text here. As an alternative or an addition, you could notice how people persuade one another in arguments and you could make a list of the techniques that are reflective of those listed here.

General

Look out for the ways in which the relationship between two persons affects the ways that they behave towards one another. How does it influence their spatial relationships, their verbal relationships, their nonverbal behaviour, their persuasive efforts, and their topics of conversation? Can you tell the relationship between two people from any of these forms of behaviour and if so, which? How do you know you are right?

References

Acitelli, L.K. (1988) 'When spouses talk to each other about their relationship'. *Journal of Social and Personal Relationships* (5), 185–99.

Adorno, T.W., Frenkel-Brunswick, E., Levinson, D. & Sanford, N. (1950) *The Authoritarian Personality*. Harper & Row: New York.

Ainsworth, M.D.S., Blehar, M.C., Waters, E. & Wall, S. (1978) *Patterns of Attachment: A Psychological Study of the Strange Situation*. LEA: Hillsdale, NJ.

Alberts, J.K. (1988) 'Analysis of couples' conversational complaints'. *Communication Monographs* (55), 184–97.

Allan, G. (1989) *Friendship*. Harvester-Wheatsheaf: Hemel Hempstead, UK.

Amato, P.R. (1991) 'The "child of divorce" as a person prototype: bias in the recall of information about children in divorced families'. *Journal of Marriage and the Family* (53), 59–70.

Anderson, S.A. (1985) 'Parental and marital role stress during the school entry transition'. *Journal of Social and Personal Relationships* (2), 59–80.

Argyle, M. (1967) *The Psychology of Interpersonal Behaviour*. Penguin Books: Harmondsworth, UK.

Argyle, M. (1975) *Bodily Communication*. Methuen: London.

Argyle, M. (1983) *The Psychology of Interpersonal Behaviour (4th Edn)*. Penguin Books: Harmondsworth, UK.

Argyle, M. (1987) *The Psychology of Happiness*. Penguin Books: Harmondsworth, UK.

Argyle, M., & Cook, M. (1976) *Gaze and Mutual Gaze*. Cambridge University Press: Cambridge, UK.

Argyle, M., & Dean, J. (1965) 'Eye contact, distance and affiliation'. *Sociometry* (28), 289–304.

Argyle, M., & Henderson, M. (1984) 'The rules of friendship'. *Journal of Social and Personal Relationships* (1), 211–37.

Argyle, M., Lalljee, M. & Cook, M. (1968) 'The effects of visibility on interaction in a dyad'. *Human Relations* (21), 3–17.

Argyle, M., Salter, V., Nicholson, H., Williams, M. & Burgess, P. (1970) 'The communication of inferior and superior attitudes by verbal and non-verbal signals'. *British Journal of Social and Clinical Psychology* (9), 222–31.

Aron, A., Dutton, D.G., Aron, E., & Iverson, A. (1989) 'Experiences of falling in love'. *Journal of Social and Personal Relationships* (6), 243–57.

Aronson, E., & Golden, B.W. (1962) 'The effect of relevant and irrelevant aspects of communicator credibility on attitude change'. *Journal of Personality* (30), 135–46.

Asher, S.R. & Parker, J.G. (1989) 'Significance of peer relationship problems in childhood'. In B.H. Schneider, G. Attili, J. Nadel & R. Weissberg (eds) *Social Competence in Developmental Perspective*. Kluwer: Amsterdam.

Asher, S.R., & Wheeler, V.A. (1985) 'Children's loneliness: a comparison of rejected and neglected peer status'. *Journal of Consulting and Clinical Psychology* (53), 500–5.

Athanasiou, R., & Sarkin, R. (1974) 'Premarital sexual behaviour and postmarital adjustment'. *Archives of Sexual Behavior* (3), 207–25.

Attili, G. (1989) 'Social competence versus emotional security: the link between home relationships and behavior problems in preschool'. In B.H. Schneider, G. Attili, J. Nadel & R.P. Weissberg (eds) *Social Competence in Developmental Perspective*. NATO ASI Series, Kluwer: Amsterdam.

Ayres, J. (1989) 'The impact of communication apprehension and interaction structure on initial interactions'. *Communication Monographs* (56), 75–88.

Bandura, A. (1977) *Social Learning Theory*. Prentice-Hall: Englewood Cliffs, NJ.

Barbee, A.P. (1990) 'Interactive coping: the cheering up process in close relationships'. In S.W. Duck (ed., with R.C. Silver) *Personal Relationships and Social Support*. Sage: London.

Barrera, M., Jr. (1981) 'Social support in the adjustment of pregnant adolescents: assessment issues'. In B.H. Gottlieb (ed.) *Social Networks and Social Support*. Sage: Beverly Hills, CA.

Barrera, M., Jr. & Baca, L. (1990) 'Recipient reactions to social support: contributions of enacted support, conflicted support and network orientation'. *Journal of Social and Personal Relationships* (7), 541–52.

Bartholomew, K. (1990) 'Avoidance of intimacy: an attachment perspective'. *Journal of Social and Personal Relationships* (7), 141–78.

Baumrind, D. (1972) 'Socialization and instrumental competence in young children'. In W.W. Hartup (ed.) *The Young Child: Reviews of Research, Vol. 2*. National Association for the Education of Young Children: Washington, DC.

Baxter, L.A. (1984) 'Trajectories of relationship disengagement'. *Journal of Social and Personal Relationships* (1), 29–48.

Baxter, L.A. & Wilmot, W.W. (1984) 'Secret tests: social strategies for acquiring information about the state of the relationship'. *Human Communication Research* (11), 171–202.

Baxter, L.A., & Wilmot, W.W. (1985) 'Taboo topics in close relationships'. *Journal of Social and Personal Relationships* (2), 253–69.

Beattie, G.W. (1981) 'A further investigation of the cognitive interference hypothesis of gaze patterns in interaction'. *British Journal of Social Psychology* (20), 243–8.

Beck, A.T. (1976) *Cognitive Therapy and the Emotional Disorders*. International Universities Press: Garden City, NY.

Beecher, H.K. (1959) *Measurement of Subjective Responses: Quantitative Effects of Drugs*. Oxford University Press: New York.

Beinstein Miller, J. (1989) 'Memories of peer relationships and styles of conflict management'. *Journal of Social and Personal Relationships* (6), 487–504.

Bell, B.E., & Loftus, E.F. (1988) 'Degree of detail of eyewitness testimony and mock juror judgements'. *Journal of Applied Social Psychology* (18), 1171–92.

Bell, B.E. & Loftus, E.F. (1989) 'Trivial persuasion in the courtroom: the power of (a few) minor details'. *Journal of Personality and Social Psychology* (56), 669–79.

Bentler, P.M. & Newcomb, M.D. (1978) 'Longitudinal study of marital success and failure'. *Journal of Consulting and Clinical Psychology* (46), 1053–70.

Berardo, F.M. (1970) 'Survivorship and social isolation: the case of the aged widower'. *Family Coordinator* (19), 11–25.

Berardo, F.M. (1990) 'Trends and directions in family research in the 1980s'. *Journal of Marriage and the Family* (52), 809–17.

Berger, C.R. (1988) 'Uncertainty and information exchange in developing relationships'. In S.W. Duck, D.F. Hay, S.E. Hobfoll, W. Ickes & B. Montgomery (eds) *Handbook of Personal Relationships* (pp. 239–56). Wiley: Chichester, UK.

Berger, C.R. & Bell, R.A. (1988) 'Plans and the initiation of social relationships'. *Human Communication Research* (15), 217–35.

Berger, C.R. & Bradac, J. (1982) *Language and Social Knowledge*. Arnold: London.

Berger, C.R., Karol, S.H. & Jordan, J.M. (1989) 'When a lot of knowledge is a dangerous thing: the debilitating effects of plan complexity on verbal fluency'. *Human Communication Research* (16), 91–119.

Berger, P. & Kellner, H. (1975) 'Marriage and the construction of reality'. In D. Brissett & C. Edgley (eds) *Life as Theatre*. Chicago: Aldine.

Berkman, L.F. & Syme, S.L. (1979) 'Social networks, host resistance and mortality: a nine-year follow-up of Alameda County residents'. *American Journal of Epidemiology* (109), 186–204.

Berman, H.J. (1977) 'The uses of the law to guide people to virtue: a comparison of Soviet and US perspectives'. In L.L. Tapp & F.J. Levine (eds) *Law, Justice and the Individual in Society*. Holt: New York.

Berndt, T.J. (1989) 'Contributions of Peer Relationships to Children's Development'. in T.J. Berndt & G.W. Ladd (eds) *Peer Relationships in Child Development*. Wiley: New York.

Berndt, T.J. & Ladd, G.W. (eds) (1989) *Peer Relationships in Child Development*, Wiley: New York.

Berne, E. (1964) *Games People Play*. Penguin Books: Harmondsworth, UK.

Berscheid, E. (1966) 'Opinion-change and communicator-communicatee similarity and dissimilarity'. *Journal of Personality and Social Psychology* (4), 67–80.

Berscheid, E. & Walster, E.H. (1974) 'A little bit about love'. In T.L. Huston (ed.) *Foundations of Interpersonal Attraction*. Academic Press: New York.

Bhavnagri, N. & Parke, R. (1991) 'Parents as direct facilitators of children's peer relationships: effects of age of child and sex of parent'. *Journal of Social and Personal Relationships* (8), 423–40.

Bickman, L. & Green, S.K. (1977) 'Situational cues and crime reporting: do signs make a difference?'. *Journal of Applied Social Psychology* (7), 1–18.

Bierce, A. (1985) *The Devil's Dictionary*. Fosdyke: New Cranton, PA.

Bierman, K.L. & Furman, W. (1982) 'The effects of social skills training and peer involvement on the social adjustment of pre-adolescents'. *Child Development* (53), 27–41.

Billig, M. (1987) *Arguing and Thinking: A Rhetorical Approach to Social Psychology*. Cambridge University Press: Cambridge, UK.

Birchler, G.R. (1972) 'Differential patterns of instrumental affiliative behavior as a function of degree of marital distress and level of intimacy'. PhD dissertation, University of Oregon.

Blanck, P.D. (1987) 'The "process" of field research in the courtroom: a descriptive analysis'. *Law and Human Behaviour* (11), 337–58.

Blanck, P.D., Rosenthal, R., Snodgrass, S.E., DePaulo, B.M. & Zuckerman, M. (1981) 'Sex difference in eavesdropping on nonverbal cues: developmental changes'. *Journal of Personality and Social Psychology* (41), 391–6.

Blanck, P.D., Rosenthal, R., Hart, A.J. & Bernieri, F. (1990) 'The measure of the judge: an empirically-based framework for exploring trial judges' behavior'. *Iowa Law Review* (75), 653–84.

Blondis, M.N. & Jackson, B.E. (1977) *Nonverbal Communication with Patients*. Wiley: New York.

Bloom, B., Asher, S.J. & White, S.W. (1978) 'Marital disruption as a stressor: a review and analysis'. *Psychological Bulletin* (85), 867–94.

Bochner, A.P. (1991) 'The paradigm that would not die'. In J. Anderson (ed.) *Communication Yearbook 14*. Sage: Newbury Park, CA.

Bolger, N., DeLongis, A., Kessler, R.C. & Schilling, E.A. (1989) 'Effects of daily stress on negative mood'. *Journal of Personality and Social Psychology* (51) 1320–34.

Boreham, P. & Gibson, D. (1978) 'The informative process in private medical consultations: a preliminary investigation'. *Social Science and Medicine* (12), 409–16.

Bornstein, P.E. & Clayton, P.J. (1972) 'The anniversary reaction'. *Diseases of the Nervous System* (33), 470–2.

Borys, S. & Perlman, D. (1984) 'Gender differences in loneliness'. *Personality and Social Psychology Bulletin* (11), 63–74.

Boster, F.J. & Stiff, J.B. (1984) 'Compliance-gaining message selection behavior'. *Human Communication Research* (10), 539–56.

Bourhis, R.Y. & Giles, H. (1977) 'The language of intergroup distinctiveness'. In H. Giles (ed.) *Language, Ethnicity and Intergroup Relations*. Academic Press: London.

Bowlby, J. (1951) *Maternal Care and Mental Health*. WHO: Geneva.

Boyd, J.R., Covington, T.R., Stanaszek, W.F. & Coussons, R.T. (1974) 'Drug-defaulting II: analysis of noncompliance patterns'. *American Journal of Hospital Pharmacy* (31), 485–91.

Bradburn, N. (1969) *The Structure of Psychological Well-being*. Aldine: Chicago.

Braverman, L. (1991) 'The dilemma of housework'. *Journal of Marriage and Family Therapy* (17), 25–8.

Brehm, J.W. (1966) *A Theory of Psychological Reactance*. Academic Press: New York.

Brehm, S. & Brehm, J.W. (1981) *Psychological Reactance: A Theory of Freedom and Control*. Academic Press: New York.

Brigham, J.L. & Cairns, D.L. (1988) 'The effect of mugshot inspection on eyewitness identification accuracy'. *Journal of Applied Social Psychology* (18), 1394–410.

Bringle, R.G. (1991) 'Psychosocial aspects of jealousy: a transactional model'. In P. Salovey (ed.) *The Psychology of Jealousy and Envy*. Guilford: New York.

Bringle, R.G. & Boebinger, K.L.G. (1990) 'Jealousy and the third person in the love triangle'. *Journal of Social and Personal Relationships* (7), 119–34.

Brodsky, S.L. (1977) 'The mental health professional on the witness stand: a survival guide'. In B.D. Sales (ed.) *Psychology in the Legal Process*. Halsted: New York.

Brown, G.W. (1984) 'Social support and psychiatric disorder'. Paper to Second International Conference on Personal Relationships, Madison, WI, July.

Brown, G.W. & Harris, T. (1978) *The Social Origins of Depression*. Tavistock: London.

Brown, R. (1965) *Social Psychology*. Free Press: New York.

Brubaker, T.H. (1990) 'Families in later life: a burgeoning research area'. *Journal of Marriage and the Family* (52) 959–82.

Bugental, D.E., Kaswan, J.E. & Love, L.R. (1970) 'Perception of contradictory meanings conveyed by verbal and nonverbal channels'. *Journal of Personality and Social Psychology* (16), 647–55.

Bull, R. (1977) 'The psychological significance of facial disfigurement'. Paper to International Conference on Love and Attraction. Swansea, Wales, September.

Burgess, R.L. (1981) 'Relationships in marriage and the family'. In S.W. Duck & R. Gilmour (ed) *Personal Relationships I: Studying Personal Relationships*. Academic Press: London & New York.

Burgoon, J.K. & Koper, R.J. (1984) 'Nonverbal and relational communication associated with reticence'. *Human Communication Research* (10), 601–26.

Burgoon, M., Dillard, J.P. & Doran, N.E. (1980) 'Situational determinants of message strategy selection: an exploratory analysis'. Unpublished manuscript, Michigan State University, East Lansing.

Burgoon, J.K., Coker, D.A. & Coker, R.A. (1986) 'Communicative effects of gaze behavior: a test of two contrasting explanations'. *Human Communication Research* (12), 495–524.

Burleson, B.R. (1990) 'Comforting as social support: relational consequences of supportive behaviors'. In S.W. Duck (ed. with R. Cohen Silver) *Personal Relationships and Social Support*. Sage: London.

Burns, G.L. & Farina, A. (1984) 'Social competence and adjustment'. *Journal of Social and Personal Relationships* (1), 99–114.

Buss, A.H. (1980) *Self-Consciousness and Social Anxiety*. Freeman: San Francisco.

Buunk, A. (1980) 'Sexually open marriages: ground rules for countering potential threats to marriage'. *Alternative Life Styles* (3), 312–28.

Buunk, A. & Bringle, R.G. (1987) 'Jealousy in love relationships'. In D. Perlman & S.W. Duck (eds) *Intimate Relationships*. Sage: Newbury Park, CA.

Byrne, D. (1961) 'Interpersonal attraction and attitude similarity'. *Journal of Abnormal and Social Psychology* (62), 713–15.

Byrne, D. (1971) *The Attraction Paradigm*. Academic Press: New York.

Byrne, D. & Lamberth, J. (1971) 'Cognitive and reinforcement theory as complementary approaches to the study of attraction'. In B.I. Murstein (ed.) *Theories of Attraction and Love*. Springer: New York.

Byrne, D. & Nelson, D. (1965) 'Attraction as a linear function of proportion of positive reinforcements'. *Journal of Personality and Social Psychology* (1), 659–63.

Byrne, D., Nelson, D. & Reeves, K. (1966) 'The effects of consensual validation and invalidation on attraction as a function of verifiability'. *Journal of Experimental Social Psychology* (2), 98–107.

Byrne, D., Ervin, C.R. & Lamberth, J. (1970) 'Continuity between the experimental study of attraction and real-life computer dating'. *Journal of Personality and Social Psychology* (16), 157–65.

Canary, D.J. & Spitzberg, B.H. (1989) 'A model of perceived competence of conflict strategies'. *Human Communication Research* (15), 630–49.

Cappella, J.N. (1988) 'Personal relationships, social relationships and patterns of interaction.' In S.W. Duck, D.F. Hay, S.E. Hobfoll, W. Ickes & B. Montgomery (eds) *Handbook of Personal Relationships* (pp. 325–42). Wiley: Chichester, UK.

Cappella, J.N. (1991) 'Mutual adaptation and relativity of measurement'. In B.M. Montgomery & S.W. Duck (eds) *Studying Interpersonal Interaction*. Guilford: New York.

Carr, S.E. & Dabbs, J.M., Jr. (1974) 'The effects of lighting, distance and intimacy of topic on verbal and visual behaviour'. *Sociometry* (37), 592–600.

Cate, R.M. & Lloyd, S.A. (1988) 'Courtship'. In S.W. Duck, D.F. Hay, S.E. Hobfoll, W. Ickes & B. Montgomery (eds) *Handbook of Personal Relationships*. Wiley: Chichester, UK.

Check, J.V.P, Perlman, D. & Malamuth, N.M. (1985) 'Loneliness and aggressive behaviour'. *Journal of Social and Personal Relationships* (2), 243–52.

Cheek, J.M. & Busch, C.M. (1981) 'The influence of shyness on loneliness in a new situation'. *Personality and Social Psychology Bulletin* (7), 572–7.

Cheyne, W.M. (1970) 'Stereotyped reactions of speakers with Scottish and English regional accents'. *British Journal of Social and Clinical Psychology*. (9), 77–9.

Christopher, F.S. & Cate, R.M. (1985) 'Premarital sexual pathways and relationship development'. *Journal of Social and Personal Relationships* (2), 271–88.

Christopher, F.S. & Frandsen, M.M. (1990) 'Strategies of influence in sex and dating'. *Journal of Social and Personal Relationships* (7), 89–105.

Christy, N.P. (1979) 'English is our second language'. *New England Journal of Medicine* (300), 979–81.

Cialdini, R.B., Vincent, J.E., Lewis, S.K., Catalan, J., Wheeler, D. & Darby, B.L. (1975) 'A reciprocal concessions procedure for inducing compliance: the door-in-the-face technique'. *Journal of Personality and Social Psychology* (21), 206–15.

Cialdini, R.B., Cacioppo, J.T., Bassett, R. & Miller, J.A. (1978) 'Lowball procedure for producing compliance: commitment then cost'. *Journal of Personality and Social Psychology* (36), 463–76.

Clanton, G. & Kosins, D.J. (1991) 'Developmental correlates of jealousy'. In P. Salovey (ed.) *The Psychology of Jealousy and Envy*. Guilford: New York.

Clark, R.A. (1979) 'The impact of selection of persuasive strategies on self interest and desired liking'. *Communication Monographs* (46), 257–73.

Clark, R.A. & Delia, J.G. (1979) 'Topoi and rhetorical competence'. *Quarterly Journal of Speech* (65), 187–206.

Clarke, D.D., Allen, C.M.B. & Dixon, S. (1985) 'The characteristic affective tone of seven classes of interpersonal relationships'. *Journal of Social and Personal Relationships* (2), 117–20.

Clore, G.L. (1977) 'Reinforcement and affect in attraction'. In S.W. Duck (ed.) *Theory and Practice in Interpersonal Attraction*. Academic Press: London.

Clore, G.L. & Byrne, D. (1974) 'A reinforcement affect model of attraction'. In T.L. Huston (ed.) *Foundations of Interpersonal Attraction*. Academic Press: New York.

Clore, G.L. & Gormly, J.B. (1974) 'Knowing, feeling and liking: a psycho-physiological study of attraction'. *Journal of Research in Personality* (8), 218–30.

Cobb, S. & Jones, J.M. (1984) 'Social support, support groups and marital relationships'. In S.W. Duck (ed.) *Personal Relationships 5: Repairing Personal Relationships*. Academic Press: London & New York.

Cody, M.J., Woelfel, M.L. & Jordan, W.J. (1983) 'Dimensions of compliance-gaining situations'. *Human Communication Research* (9), 99–113.

Coker, D.A. & Burgoon, J.K. (1987) 'The nature of conversational involvement and nonverbal encoding patterns'. *Human Communication Research* (13), 463–94.

Cole, C.A. (1976) 'A behavioral analysis of married and living together couples'. Unpublished PhD dissertation, University of Houston, TX.

Contarello, A. & Volpato, C. (1991) 'Images of friendship: literary depictions through the ages'. *Journal of Social and Personal Relationships* (8), 49–75.

Cook, M. (1968) 'Studies of orientation and proximity'. Unpublished manuscript. Oxford University, UK.

Cook. M. (1977) 'Social skills and attraction'. In S.W. Duck (ed.) *Theory and Practice in Interpersonal Attraction*. Academic Press: London & New York.

Cooke, D. (1990) 'Being an "expert" in court'. *The Psychologist* (May), 217–21.

Coombs, R.H. (1991) 'Marital status and personal well-being: a literature review'. *Family Relations* (40), 97–102.

Cortez, C.A., Duck, S.W. & Strejc, H. (1988) 'The heart is a lonely communicator: loneliness and dating patterns'. Paper presented to the Speech Communication Association, New Orleans, November.

Coyne, J.C. (1987) 'Depression, biology and marital therapy'. *Journal of Marriage and Family Therapy* (13), 393–407.

Cunningham, J.D. & Antill, J.K. (1981) 'Love in developing romantic relationships'. In S.W. Duck & R. Gilmour (eds) *Personal Relationships 2: Developing Personal Relationships*. Academic Press: London & New York.

Cupach, W.R. & Comstock, J. (1990) 'Satisfaction with sexual communication in marriage: links to sexual satisfaction and dyadic adjustment'. *Journal of Social and Personal Relationships* (7), 179–86.

Cupach, W.R. & Metts, S.M. (1986) 'Accounts of relational dissolution: a comparison of marital and non-marital relationships'. *Communication Monographs* (53), 311–34.

Cupach, W.R., Metts, S.M. & Hazelton, V. Jr. (1986) 'Coping with embarrassment: remedial strategies and their perceived utility'. *Journal of Language and Social Psychology* (5), 181–200.

Curran, J.P. (1977) 'Skills training as an approach to the treatment of heterosexual-social anxiety: a review'. *Psychological Bulletin* (84), 140–57.

Cutrona, C.E., Suhr, J. & McFarlane, R. (1990) 'Interpersonal transactions and the psychological sense of support'. In S.W. Duck (ed.) *Personal Relationships and Social Support*. Sage: London.

Daly, J.A., Vangelisti, A. & Daughton, S. (1987) 'The nature and correlates of conversational sensitivity'. *Human Communication Research* (14), 167–202.

Davis, J.D. (1978) 'When boy meets girl: sex roles and the negotiation of intimacy in an acquaintance exercise'. *Journal of Personality and Social Psychology* (36), 684–92.

Davis, J.D. & Sloan, M. (1974) 'The basis of interviewee matching of interviewer self disclosure'. *British Journal of Social and Clinical Psychology* (13), 359–67.

Davis, K. (1936) 'Jealousy and sexual property'. *Social Forces* (14), 395–405.

Davis, K.E. & Latty-Mann, H. (1987) 'Love styles and relationship quality: a contribution to validation'. *Journal of Social and Personal Relationships* (4), 409–28.

Davis, K.E. & Todd, M.J. (1985) 'Assessing friendship: prototypes, paradigm cases and relationship description'. In S.W. Duck & D. Perlman (eds) *Understanding Personal Relationships* (pp. 17–38). Sage: London.

Davitz, J.R. (1964) *The Communication of Emotional Meaning*. McGraw-Hill: New York.

Dean, A., Lin, N. & Ensel, W.M. (1981) 'The epidemiological significance of social support in depression'. In R. Simmons (ed.) *Research in Community and Mental Health*. JAI Press: New York.

DeJong, W. (1979) 'An examination of the self-perception mediation of the foot-in-the-door effect'. *Journal of Personality and Social Psychology* (37), 221–39.

DeJong-Gierveld, J. (1989) 'Personal relationships, social support and loneliness'. *Journal of Social and Personal Relationships* (6), 197–221.

Delia, J.G. (1980) 'Some tentative thoughts concerning the study of interpersonal relationships and their development'. *Western Journal of Speech Communication* (44), 97–103.

Department of Health and Social Security [DHSS] (1976) *Smoking and Pregnancy*. HMSO: London.

Dertke, M.C., Penner, L.A. & Ulrich, H. (1974) 'Observers' reporting of shoplifting as a function of thief race and sex'. *Journal of Social Psychology* (94), 213–21.

DeTurck, M.A. (1985) 'A transactional analysis of compliance-gaining behavior: the effects of noncompliance, relational contexts and actors' gender'. *Human Communication Research* (12), 54–78.

Dickens, W.J. & Perlman, D. (1981) 'Friendship over the life cycle'. In S.W. Duck & R. Gilmour (eds) *Personal Relationships 2: Developing Personal Relationships*. Academic Press: London.

Dillard, J.P. (1989) 'Types of influence goals in personal relationships'. *Journal of Social and Personal Relationships* (6), 293–308.

Dillard, J.P. & Miller, K.I. (1988) 'Intimate relationships in task environments'. In S.W. Duck, D.F. Hay, S.E. Hobfoll, W. Ickes & B. Montgomery (eds) *Handbook of Personal Relationships*. Wiley: Chichester, UK.

Dillard, J.P., Hunter, J.E. & Burgoon, M. (1984) 'Sequential-request persuasive strategies: meta-analysis of foot-in-the-door and door-in-the face'. *Human Communication Research* (10), 461–88.

DiMatteo, M.R. & Friedman, H.S. (1982) *Social Psychology and Medicine*. Oelgeschlager: Cambridge, MA.

Dindia, K. (1987) 'The effects of sex of subject and sex of partner on interruptions'. *Human Communication Research* (13), 345–71.

Dindia, K. & Fitzpatrick, M.A. (1985) 'Marital communication: three approaches compared'. In S.W. Duck & D. Perlman (eds) *Understanding Personal Relationships*. Sage: London.

Dohrenwend, B.S. (1973) 'Life events as stressors: a methodological inquiry'. *Journal of Health and Social Behavior* (14), 167–75.

Douglas, W. (1987) 'Affinity testing in initial interaction'. *Journal of Social and Personal Relationships* (4), 3–16.

Dovidio, J.F., Ellyson, S.L., Keting, C.F., Heltman, K. & Brown, C.E. (1988) 'The relationship of social power to visual displays of dominance between men and women'. *Journal of Personality and Social Psychology* (54), 232–42.

Duck, S.W. (1973) *Personal Relationships and Personal Constructs: A Study of Friendship Formation*. Wiley: Chichester, UK.

Duck, S.W. (1975a) 'Attitude similarity and interpersonal attraction: right answers and wrong reasons'. *British Journal of Social and Clinical Psychology* (14), 311–12.

Duck, S.W. (1975b) 'Personality similarity and friendship choices by adolescents'. *European Journal of Social Psychology* (5), 351–65.

Duck, S.W. (1977) *The Study of Acquaintance*. Gower Press: Farnborough, UK.

Duck, S.W. (1980) 'Personal relationships research in the 1980s: towards an understanding of complex human sociality'. *Western Journal of Speech Communication* (44), 114–19.

Duck, S.W. (1982a) 'A topography of relationship disengagement and dissolution'. In S.W. Duck (ed.) *Personal Relationships 4: Dissolving Personal Relationships*. London: Academic Press.

Duck, S.W. (1982b) *Personal Relationships 4: Dissolving Personal Relationships*. Academic Press: London & New York.

Duck, S.W. (1984) 'A perspective on the repair of personal relationships: repair of what, when?' In S.W. Duck (ed.) *Personal Relationships 5: Repairing Personal Relationships*. London: Academic Press.

Duck, S.W. (1988) *Relating to Others*. Open University Press: London: Dorsey/Brooks/Cole/Wadsworth: Monterey, CA.

Duck, S.W. (1989) 'Socially competent communication and relationship development'. In B.H. Schneider et al. (eds) *Social Competence in Developmental Perspective*. Kluwer: Amsterdam.

Duck, S.W. (1990a) (ed., with Cohen Silver, R.L.) *Personal Relationships and Social Support*. London: Sage.

Duck, S.W. (1990b) 'Relationships as unfinished business: out of the frying pan and into the 1990s'. *Journal of Social and Personal Relationships* (7), 5–28.

Duck, S.W. (1991) *Friends, for Life*. Harvester-Wheatsheaf: Hemel Hempstead, UK (published in USA as *Understanding Relationships*. Guilford: New York).

Duck, S.W. (in press) 'The role of theory in relationship loss'. In T.L. Orbuch (ed.) *Relationship Loss*. Springer Verlag: New York.

Duck, S.W. & Condra, M.B. (1989) 'To be or not to be: anticipation, persuasion and retrospection in personal relationships'. In R. Neimeyer & G. Neimeyer (eds) *Review of Personal Construct Theory*. JAI Press: Greenwich.

Duck, S.W. & Craig, G. (1978) 'Personality similarity and the development of friendship'. *British Journal of Sociology and Clinical Psychology* (17), 237–42.

Duck, S.W. & Miell, D.E. (1984) 'Towards an understanding of relationship development and breakdown'. In H. Tajfel, C. Fraser & J. Jaspars (eds) *The Social Dimension: European Perspectives on Social Psychology*. Cambridge University Press: Cambridge, UK.

Duck, S.W. & Pond, K. (1989) 'Friends, Romans, countrymen: lend me your retrospective data: rhetoric and reality in personal relationships'. In C. Hendrick (ed.) *Review of Social Psychology and Personality (10): Close Relationships* (pp. 3–27). Sage: Newbury Park, CA.

Duck, S.W. & Rutt, D. (1988) 'The experience of everyday relational conversations: are all communications created equal?'. Paper presented to the Annual Convention of the Speech Communication Association, New Orleans.

Duck, S.W. & Sants, H.K.A. (1983) 'On the origin of the specious: are personal relationships really interpersonal states?'. *Journal of Social and Clinical Psychology* (1), 27–41.

Duck, S.W., Miell, D.K. & Gaebler, H.C. (1980) 'Attraction and communication in children's interactions'. In H.C. Foot, A.J. Chapman & J.R. Smith (eds) *Friendship and Social Relations in Children*. Wiley: Chichester, UK.

Duck, S.W., Pond, K. & Leatham, G. (1991a) 'Remembering as a context for being in relationships: different perspectives on the same interaction'. Paper presented to the Third Conference of the International Network on Personal Relationships, Normal-Bloomington, IL, May.

Duck, S.W., Rutt, D.J., Hurst, M. & Strejc, H. (1991b) 'Some evident truths about communication in everyday relationships: all communication is not created equal'. *Human Communication Research*.

Dunkel-Schetter, C. & Skokan, L.A. (1990) 'Determinants of social support provision in personal relationships'. *Journal of Social and Personal Relationships* (7), 437–50.

Dunn, J. (1988) 'Relations among relationships'. In S.W. Duck, D.F. Hay, S.E. Hobfoll, W. Ickes & B. Montgomery (eds) *Handbook of Personal Relationships*. Wiley: Chichester, UK.

Eagly, A.H., Wood, W. & Chaiken S. (1978) 'Causal inferences about communications and their effect on opinion change'. *Journal of Personality and Social Psychology* (36), 424–35.

Edelmann, R.J. (1985) 'Social embarrassment: an analysis of the process'. *Journal of Social and Personal Relationships* (2), 195–213.

Edelmann, R.J. (1988) *Embarrassment*. Wiley: Chichester, UK.

Eiskovits, Z.C., Edelson, J.L., Guttmann, E. & Sela-Amit, M. (1991) 'Cognitive styles and socialized attitudes of men who batter'. *Family Relations* (40), 72–7.

Ellis, C. & Weinstein, E. (1986) 'Jealousy and the social psychology of emotional experience'. *Journal of Social and Personal Relationships* (3), 337–58.

Ellsworth, P.C., Carlsmith, J.M. & Henson, A. (1972) 'The stare as a stimulus to flight in human subjects: a series of field experiments'. *Journal of Personality and Social Psychology* (21), 302–11.

Emler, N. & Fisher, S. (1982) 'Gossip and social participation'. Paper to Annual Conference of Social Psychology Section, British Psychological Society, Oxford, September.

Engler, C.M., Saltzman, G.A., Walker, M.L. & Wolf, F.M. (1981) 'Medical student acquisition and retention of communication and interviewing skills'. *Journal of Medical Education* (56), 572–9.

Esses, V.M. & Webster, C.D. (1988) 'Physical attractiveness and the Canadian criminal code'. *Journal of Applied Social Psychology* (18), 1017–31.

Evans, K. (1983) *Advocacy at the Bar: A Beginner's Guide*. Financial Training Pubs: London.

Exline, R.V. (1971) 'Visual interaction: the glances of power and preference'. In J.K. Cole (ed.) *Nebraska Symposium on Motivation (Vol. 19)*. University of Nebraska Press: Lincoln.

Farsad, P., Galliguez, P., Chamberlain R. & Roghmann, K.J. (1978) 'Teaching interviewing skills to pediatric house officers'. *Pediatrics* (61), 384–8.

Feldman, P. & Orford, J. (1980) *Psychological Problems: The Social Context*. Wiley: Chichester, UK.

Felmlee, D., Sprecher, S. & Bassin, E. (1990) 'The dissolution of relationships: a hazard model'. *Social Psychology Quarterly* (53), 13–30.

Festinger, L. (1954) 'A theory of social comparison processes'. *Human Relations* (7), 117–40.

Festinger, L. (1957) *A Theory of Cognitive Dissonance*. Stanford University Press: Stanford, CA.

Fincham, F.D. & Bradbury, T. (1989) 'The impact of attributions in marriage: an individual difference analysis'. *Journal of Social and Personal Relationships* (6), 69–85.

Fishbein, M. & Ajzen, I. (1972) 'Attitudes and opinions'. *Annual Review of Psychology* (23), 487–544.

Fisher, B.A. (1970) 'Decision emergence: phases in group decision making'. *Speech Monographs* (37), 53–66.

Fitzpatrick, M.A. (1977) 'A typological approach to communication in relationships'. In B. Ruben (ed.) *Communication Yearbook I*. Transaction Press: New Jersey.

Fitzpatrick, M.A. (1988) *Between Husbands and Wives: Communication in Marriage*. Newbury Park: Sage.

Fitzpatrick, M.A. & Badzinski, D. (1985) 'All in the family'. In G.R. Miller & M.L. Knapp (eds) *Handbook of Interpersonal Communication*. Sage: Beverly Hills, CA.

Fransella, F. (1972) *Personal Change and Reconstruction*. Academic Press: London.

Freedman, J.L. & Fraser, S.C. (1976) 'Compliance without pressure: the foot-in-the-door technique'. *Journal of Personality and Social Psychology* (4), 195–202.

Friedman, K.S. (1982) 'Nonverbal communication in medical interaction'. In H.S. Friedman & M.R. DiMatteo (eds) *Interpersonal Issues in Health Care*. Academic Press: New York.

Furman, W. (1984) 'Enhancing children's peer relations and friendships'. In S.W. Duck (ed.) *Personal Relationships 5: Repairing Personal Relationships*. Academic Press: London & New York.

Furman, W., Rahe, D.F. & Hartup, W.W. (1979) 'Rehabilitation of socially withdrawn preschool children through mixed age and same age socialisation'. *Child Development* (50), 915–22.

Furstenberg, F.F. (1979) 'Premarital pregnancy and marital instability'. In G. Levinger & O.C. Moles (eds) *Divorce and Separation*. Basic Books: New York.

Gallup, C. (1980) 'A study to determine the effectiveness of a social skills training program in reducing the perceived loneliness of social isolation'. *Dissertation Abstracts* (41), 3424.

Garrard, G.G. & Kyriacou, C. (1985) 'Social sensitivity among young children'. *Journal of Social and Personal Relationships* (2), 123–36.

Geersten, K.R., Gray, R.M. & Ward, J.R. (1973) 'Patient non-compliance within the context of seeking medical care for arthritis'. *Journal of Chronic Diseases* (26), 689–98.

Gelfand, D.M., Hartmann, D.P., Walder, P. & Page, B. (1973) 'Who reports shoplifters? A field experimental study'. *Journal of Personality and Social Psychology* (25), 276–85.

Gibbs, M.S., Sigal, J., Adams, B. & Grossman, B. (1989) 'Cross examination of expert witnesses: do hostile tactics affect the impressions of a simulated jury?'. *Behavioral Science and the Law* (7), 275–81.

Giles, H. (1977) 'Social psychology and applied linguistics: towards an integrative approach'. *ITL: Review of Applied Linguistics* (33), 27–42.

Giles, H. (1978) 'Linguistic differentiation in ethnic groups'. In H. Tajfel (ed.) *Differentiation between Social Groups*. Academic Press: London.

Giles, H. (1989) 'Gosh, you don't look it: intergenerational communication in relationships'. Paper to the Second Conference of the International Network on Personal Relationships, Iowa City, May.

Giles, H. & Powesland, P.F. (1975) *Speech Style and Social Evaluation*. Academic Press: London.

Giles, H., Taylor, D.M. & Bourhis, R.Y. (1973) 'Towards a theory of interpersonal accommodation through language use'. *Language in Society* (2), 177–92.

Ginsburg, G.P. (1988) 'Rules, scripts and prototypes in personal relationships'. In S.W. Duck, D.F. Hay, S.E. Hobfoll, W. Ickes & B. Montgomery (eds) *Handbook of Personal Relationships*. Wiley: Chichester, UK.

Glenn, N.D. & Weaver, C.N. (1988) 'The changing relationship of marital status to reported happiness'. *Journal of Marriage and the Family* (50), 317–24.

Glick, P. (1989) 'Remarried families, stepfamilies and stepchildren: a brief demographic analysis'. *Family Relations* (38), 24–7.

Goffman, E. (1959) *Behaviour in Public Places*. Penguin Books. Harmondsworth, UK.

Gore, S. (1978) 'The effect of social support in moderating the health consequences of unemployment'. *Journal of Health and Social Behavior* (19), 157–65.

Gormly, J.B. & Gormly, A.V. (1981) 'See you later, alligator: goodbyes and farewells?'. *Language in Society* (17), 221–3.

Gotlib, I.H. & Hooley, J.M. (1988) 'Depression and marital distress: current and future directions'. In S.W. Duck, D.F. Hay, S.E. Hobfoll, W Ickes & B. Montgomery (eds) *Handbook of Personal Relationships*. Wiley: Chichester, UK.

Gottlieb, B.H. (1983) 'Social support as a focus for integrative research in psychology'. *American Psychologist* (38), 278–87.

Gottlieb, B.H. (1985) 'Social support and the study of personal relationships'. *Journal of Social and Personal Relationships* (2), 351–75.

Gottlieb, B.H. (1990) 'The contingent nature of social support'. In J. Eckenrode (ed.) *Social Context of Stress*. Plenum: New York.

Gottman, J.M. (1979) *Empirical Investigations of Marriage*. Academic Press: New York.

Gottman, J.M. (1989) 'The future of relationships'. Paper to Second Conference of the International Network on Personal Relationships, Iowa City, May.

Gottman, J.M. (1991) 'Predicting the longitudinal course of marriages'. *Journal of Marriage and Family Therapy* (17), 3–7.

Gottman, J.M. & Krokoff, L. (in press) 'The relationship between marital interaction and marital satisfaction: a longitudinal view'. *Journal of Consulting and Clinical Psychology*.

Gottman, J.M., Markman, H. & Notarius, C. (1977) 'The topography of marital conflict: a sequential analysis of verbal and nonverbal behavior'. *Journal of Marriage and the Family* (39), 461–78.

Greenblatt, M. (1978) 'The grieving spouse'. *American Journal of Psychiatry* (135), 43–7.

Greene, J.O., O'Hair, H.D., Cody, M.J. & Yen, C. (1985) 'Planning and control of behavior during deception'. *Human Communication Research* (11), 335–64.

Gresham, F.M. & Nagle, R.J. (1980) 'Social skills training of children: responsiveness to modeling and coaching as a function of peer orientation'. *Journal of Consulting and Clinical Psychology* (48), 718–29.

Gross, E. & Stone, G.P. (1964) 'Embarrassment and the analysis of role requirements'. *American Journal of Sociology* (70), 1–15.

Gudykunst, W. & Nishida, T. (1986) 'The influence of cultural variability on perceptions of communication behavior associated with relationship terms'. *Human Communication Research* (13), 147–66.

Guinan, P.J. & Scudder, J.N. (1989) 'Client-oriented interactional behaviors for professional-client settings'. *Human Communication Research* (15), 444–62.

Guralnick, M.J. (1976) 'The value of integrating handicapped and non-handicapped pre-school children'. *American Journal of Orthopsychiatry* (42), 236–45.

Hadar, U. (1989) 'Two types of gesture and their role in speech production', *Journal of Language and Social Psychology* (8), 221–8.

Hagestad, G.O. & Smyer, M.A. (1982) 'Dissolving longterm relationships: patterns of divorcing in middle age'. In S.W. Duck (ed.) *Personal Relationships 4: Dissolving Personal Relationships*. Academic Press: London.

Hall, E.T. (1966) *The Hidden Dimension*. Doubleday/Anchor: New York.

Hamilton, G.V. (1924) Reported in G. Hamilton (1948) *A Research in Marriage*. Lear: New York.

Hamlet, Prince (1597) 'Being and nothingness'. *Journal of Danish Dilemmas* (LVII) 223–411.

Hansen, G.L. (1991) 'Jealousy: its conceptualization, measurement and integration with family stress theory'. In P. Salovey (ed.) *The Psychology of Jealousy and Envy*. Guilford: New York.

Hansson, R.O. & Jones, W.H. (1981) 'Loneliness, cooperation and conformity among American undergraduates'. *Journal of Social Psychology* (115), 103–8.

Hansson, R.O., Jones, W.H. & Fletcher, W.L. (1990) 'Troubled relationships in later life: implications for support'. *Journal of Social and Personal Relationships* (7), 451–64.

Hatfield, E. & Traupmann, J. (1981) 'Intimate relationships: a perspective from equity theory'. In S.W. Duck & R. Gilmour (eds) *Personal Relationships 1: Studying Personal Relationships*. Academic Press: London.

Hatvany N. & Strack, F. (1980) 'Discrediting key witnesses'. *Journal of Applied Social Psychology* (10), 490–509.

Hays, R.B. (1984) 'The development and maintenance of friendship'. *Journal of Social and Personal Relationships* (1), 75–98.

Hays, R.B. (1989) 'The day-today functioning of close versus casual friendship'. *Journal of Social and Personal Relationships* (7), 21–37.

Hays, R. & DiMatteo, M.R. (1984) 'Towards a more therapeutic physician–patient relationship'. In S.W. Duck (ed.) *Personal Relationships 5: Repairing Personal Relationships*. Academic Press: London & New York.

Hazan, C. (1987) 'Love and work: an attachment theory perspective'. Ph D. thesis, University of Denver, CO.

Hazan, C. & Shaver, P.R. (1987) 'Romantic love conceptualised as an attachment process'. *Journal of Personality and Social Psychology* (52), 511–24

Heider, F. (1944) 'Social perception and phenomenal causality'. *Psychological Review* (51), 358–74.

Heider, F. (1958) *The Psychology of Interpersonal Relations*. Wiley: New York.

Helgeson, V.S., Shaver, P.R. & Dyer, M. (1987) 'Prototypes of intimacy and distance in same-sex and opposite-sex relationships'. *Journal of Social and Personal Relationships* (4), 195–233.

Hendrick, C. & Hendrick, S.S. (1988) 'Lovers wear rose colored glasses'. *Journal of Social and Personal Relationships* (5), 161–83.

Hendrick, C., Hendrick, S.S., Foote, F. & Slapion-Foote, M. (1984) 'Do men and women love differently?' *Journal of Social and Personal Relationships* (1), 177–96.

Hetherington, E.M. (1979) 'Divorce: a child's perspective'. *American Psychologist* (34), 851–8.

Hetherington, E.M., Cox, M. & Cox, R. (1982) 'Effects of divorce on parents and children'. In M. Lamb (ed.) *Nontraditional Families*. Erlbaum: Hillsdale, NJ.

Hewes, D.E., Graham, M.L., Doelger, J. & Pavitt, C. (1985) '"Second-guessing": message interpretation in social networks'. *Human Communication Research* (11), 299–334.

Himmelfarb, S. (1980) 'Reporting and non-reporting of observed crime: moral judgements of the act and the actor'. *Journal of Applied Social Psychology* (10), 56–70.

Hinde, R.A. (1989) 'Individual characteristics and relationships'. Paper to the Second Conference of the International Network on Personal Relationships, Iowa City, May.

Hindelang, M.J. (1974) 'Moral evaluation of illegal behavior'. *Social Problems* (21), 370–85.

Hobfoll, S.E. (1984) 'Limitations of social support in the stress process'. Paper presented at the NATO Advanced Study Seminar on Social Support, Bonas, France.

Hobfoll, S.E. (1988) 'Overview of community and clinical section'. In S.W. Duck, D.F. Hay, S.E. Hobfoll, W. Ickes & B. Montgomery (eds) *Handbook of Personal Relationships*. Wiley: Chichester, UK.

Hobfoll, S.E. & London, P. (1985) 'The relationship of self-concept and social support to emotional distress among women during war'. *Journal of Social and Clinical Psychology* (3), 231–48.

Hobfoll, S.E. & Stokes, J.P. (1988) 'The process and mechanics of social support'. In S.W. Duck, D.F. Hay, S.E. Hobfoll, W. Ickes & B. Montgomery (eds) *Handbook of Personal Relationships*. Wiley: New York.

Hobfoll, S.E. & Walfisch, S. (1984) 'Coping with a threat to life: a longitudinal study of self concept, social support and psychological distress'. *American Journal of Community Psychology* (12), 87–100.

Hochschild, A.R. (1979) 'Emotion work, feeling rules and social structure'. *American Journal of Sociology* (85), 551–75.

Hollander, E.P. (1958) 'Conformity, status and idiosyncrasy credit'. *Psychological Review* (65), 117–27.

Holmes, T.H. & Rahe, R.H. (1967) 'The social readjustment rating scale'. *Journal of Psychosomatic Research* (11), 213–18.

Homel, R., Burns, A. & Goodnow, J. (1987) 'Parental social networks and child development'. *Journal of Social and Personal Relationships* (4), 159–77.

Honeycutt, J.M., Cantrill, J.G. & Greene, R.W. (1989) 'Memory structures for relational escalation: a cognitive test of the sequencing of relational actions and stages'. *Human Communication Research* (16), 62–90.

Hopper, R., Knapp, M.L. & Scott, L. (1981) 'Couples' personal idioms: exploring intimate talk'. *Journal of Communication* (31), 23–33.

Hovland, C., Janis, I. & Kelley, H.H. (1953) *Communication and Persuasion.* Yale University Press: New Haven, CT.

Howells, K. (1981) 'Social relationships in violent offenders'. In S.W. Duck & R. Gilmour (eds) *Personal Relationships 3: Personal Relationships in Disorder.* Academic Press: London & New York.

Huesmann, L.R., & Levinger, G. (1976) 'Incremental exchange theory'. In L. Berkowitz & E.H. Walster (eds) *Advances in Experimental Social Psychology.* Academic Press: New York.

Hunter, J.E. & Boster, F.J. (1978) 'Situational differences in the selection of compliance-gaining messages'. Unpublished paper, Department of Communication, Arizona State University, Tempe.

Hupka, R. (1991) 'The motive for the arousal of romantic jealousy: its cultural origin'. In P. Salovey (ed.) *The Psychology of Jealousy and Envy.* Guilford: New York.

Hurwitz, J.I. (1953) *Group Dynamics: Research and Theory.* Bantam: New York.

Huston, T.L. (1990) 'The PAIRS data'. Paper to the Second Graduate Workshop of the International Network on Personal Relationships, Iowa City, May.

Huston, T.L., Surra, C., Fitzgerald, N. & Cate, R. (1981) 'From courtship to marriage: mate selection as an interpersonal process'. In S.W. Duck & R. Gilmour (eds) *Personal Relationships 2: Developing Personal Relationships.* Academic Press: London & New York.

Hyde, J.S. (1984) 'Children's understanding of sexist language'. *Developmental Psychology* (20), 697–706.

Innes, J.M. (1980) 'Fashions in social psychology'. In R. Gilmour & S.W. Duck (eds) *The Development of Social Psychology.* Academic Press: London.

Innes, J.M. (1981) 'Social psychological approaches to the study of the induction and alleviation of stress: influences of health and illness'. In G. Stephenson & J. Davis (eds) *Progress in Applied Social Psychology.* Wiley: Chichester, UK.

James, R.M. (1959) 'Status and competence of jurors'. *American Journal of Sociology* (64), 563–70.

Janis, I.L. & Feshback, S. (1953) 'Effects of fear-arousing communications'. *Journal of Abnormal and Social Psychology* (48), 78–92.

Jarvinaan, K.A.J. (1955) 'Can ward rounds be a danger to patients with myocardial infarction?'. *British Medical Journal* (1), 318–20.

Jellison, J. (1984) 'Social aspects of emotion'. Paper to International Conference on The Self, Cardiff, UK, July.

Johnson, F.N. (1984) *The Psychopharmacology of Lithium.* Macmillan: London.

Jones, E.E. (1964) *Ingratiation: A Social Psychological Analysis.* Appleton-Century-Crofts: New York.

Jones, R.A. (1982) 'Expectations and illness'. In H.S. Friedman & M.R. DiMatteo (eds) *Interpersonal Issues in Health Care.* Academic Press: London & New York.

Jones, W.H., Cavert, C.W., Snider, R.L. & Bruce, T. (1985) 'Relational stress: an analysis of situations and events associated with loneliness'. In S.W. Duck & D. Perlman (eds) *Understanding Personal Relationships.* Sage: London.

Jones, W.H., Freemon, J.E. & Goswick, R.A. (1981) 'The persistence of loneliness: self and other determinants'. *Journal of Personality* (49), 27–48.

Jones, W.H., Hobbs, S.A. & Hockenbury, D. (1982) 'Loneliness and social skill deficits'. *Journal of Personality and Social Psycholgoy* (42), 682–9.

Jones, W.H., Hansson, R.O. & Cutrona, C.E. (1984) 'Helping the lonely: issues of intervention with young and older adults'. In S.W. Duck (ed.) *Personal Relationships 5: Repairing Personal Relationships*. Academic Press: London.

Kane, J. (1971) 'Body buffer zones in Glaswegian prisoners'. Unpublished MA thesis, Glasgow University, Scotland.

Kassin, S.M., Reddy, M.E. & Tulloch, W.F. (1990) 'Juror interpretations of ambiguous evidence: the need for cognition, presentation order and persuasion'. *Law and Human Behavior* (14), 43–55.

Kastenbaum, R. (1982) 'Dying is healthy and death a bureaucrat: our fantasy machine is alive and well'. In H.S. Friedman & M.R. DiMatteo (eds) *Interpersonal Issues in Health Care*. Academic Press: New York.

Kelley, K. & Rolker-Dolinsky, B. (1987) 'The psychosexology of female initiation and dominance'. In D. Perlman & S.W. Duck (eds) *Intimate Relationships*. Sage: Beverly Hills, CA.

Kelly, C., Huston, T.L. & Cate, R.M. (1985) 'Premarital relationship correlates of the erosion of satisfaction in marriage'. *Journal of Social and Personal Relationships* (2), 167–78.

Kelly, L. (1982) 'A rose by any other name is still a rose: a comparative analysis of reticence, communication apprehension, unwillingness to communicate and shyness'. *Human Communication Research* (8), 99–113.

Kelly, L. (1984) 'Social skills training as a mode of treatment for social communication problems'. In J. Daly & J.C. McCroskey (eds) *Avoiding Communication: Shyness, Reticence and Communication Apprehension*. Sage: Beverly Hills, CA.

Kelvin, P. (1977) 'Predictability, power and vulnerability in interpersonal attraction'. In S.W. Duck (ed.) *Theory and Practice in Interpersonal Attraction*. Academic Press: London & New York.

Kemper, T.D. & Bologh, R.W. (1981) 'What do you get when you fall in love? Some health status effects'. *Sociology of Health and Illness* (3), 72–88.

Kendon, A. (1967) 'Some functions of gaze direction in social interaction'. *Acta Psychologica* (26), 22–63.

Kendon, A. & Ferber, A. (1973) 'A description of some human greetings'. In R.P. Michael & J.H. Crook (eds) *Comparative Ecology and Behavior of Primates*. Academic Press: New York.

Kephart, W.M. (1967) 'Some correlates of romantic love'. *Journal of Marriage and the Family* (29), 470–4.

Kerckhoff, A.C. (1974) 'The social context of interpersonal attraction'. In T.L. Huston (ed.) *Foundations of Interpersonal Attraction*. Academic Press: New York.

Kerckhoff, A.C. & Davis, K.E. (1962) 'Value consensus and need complementarity in mate selection'. *American Sociological Review* (27), 295–303.

Kirchler, E. (1988) 'Marital happiness and interaction in everyday surroundings: a time sample diary approach for couples'. *Journal of Social and Personal Relationships* (5), 375–82.

Kitson, G.C. & Morgan, L.A. (1990) 'The multiple consequences of divorce: a decade review'. *Journal of Marriage and the Family* (52), 913–24.

Klentz, B. & Beaman, A.L. (1981) 'The effects of type of information and method of dissemination on the reporting of shoplifters'. *Journal of Applied Social Psychology* (11), 64–82.

Klinger, E. (1977) *Meaning and Void; Inner Experience and the Incentives in Peoples' Lives*. University of Minnesota Press: Minneapolis.

Kovecses, Z. (1991) 'A linguist's quest for love'. *Journal of Social and Personal Relationships* (8), 77–98.

Kraut, R.E. (1973) 'Effects of social labelling on giving to charity'. *Journal of Experimental Social Psychology* (9), 551–62.

Kubler-Ross, E. (1969) *On Death and Dying*. Macmillan: New York.

Kurdek, L. (1989) 'Relationship quality in gay and lesbian cohabiting couples: a one year follow-up study'. *Journal of Social and Personal Relationships* (6), 39–59.

Kurdek, L. (1991a) 'The dissolution of gay and lesbian couples'. *Journal of Social and Personal Relationships* (8), 265–78.

Kurdek, L. (1991b) 'Divorce history, marital status, gender and well-being'. *Journal of Marriage and the Family* (53), 71–8.

Labov, W. (1972) 'Negative attraction and negative concord in English grammar'. *Language* (48), 773–818.

LaCrosse, M.B. (1975) 'Nonverbal behaviour and perceived counsellor attractiveness and persuasiveness'. *Journal of Counselling Psychology* (22), 563–6.

Ladd, G.W. (1981) 'Effectiveness of a social learning method for enhancing children's social interaction and peer acceptance'. *Child Development* (52), 171–8.

Ladd, G.W. (1989) 'Towards a further understanding of peer relationships and their contributions to child development'. In T.J. Berndt & G.W. Ladd (eds) *Peer Relationships in Child Development*. Wiley: New York.

Ladd, G.W. (1991) 'Family–peer relations during childhood: pathways to competence and pathology?'. *Journal of Social and Personal Relationships* (8), 307–14.

La Gaipa, J.J. (1982) 'Rituals of disengagement'. In S.W. Duck (ed.) *Personal Relationships 4: Dissolving Personal Relationships*. Academic Press, London.

La Gaipa, J.J. (1990) 'The negative effects of informal support systems'. In S.W. Duck (ed., with R.C. Silver) *Personal Relationships and Social Support*. Sage: London.

La Greca, A.M. & Santogrossi, D.A. (1980) 'Social skill training with elementary school students: a behavioral group approach'. *Journal of Consulting and Clinical Psychology* (48), 220–7.

Lakoff, R. (1973) 'Language and women's place'. *Language in Society* (2), 45–79.

Landy, D. & Aronson, E. (1969) 'The influence of the character of the criminal and his victim on the decisions of simulated jurors'. *Journal of Experimental Social Psychology* (5), 141–52.

LaRocco, J.M., House, J.S. & French, J.R.P., Jr. (1980) 'Social support, occupational stress and health'. *Journal of Health and Social Behavior* (21), 202–18

Larson, J.H., Crane, D.R. & Smith, C.W. (1991) 'Morning and night couples'. *Journal of Marriage and Family Therapy* (17), 53–66.

Larson, R., Csikszentmihalyi, M. & Graef, R. (1982) 'Time alone in daily experience'. In L.A. Peplau & D. Perlman (eds) *Loneliness: A Sourcebook of Current Theory, Research and Therapy*. Wiley-Interscience: New York.

Lau, R.R., Williams, S., Williams, L.C., Ware, J.E. & Brook, R.H. (1982) 'Psychosocial problems in chronically ill children: physician concern, parent satisfaction and the validity of medical diagnosis'. *Journal of Community Health* (7), 250–61.

Lea, M. & Duck, S.W. (1982) 'A model for the role of similarity of values in friendship development'. *British Journal of Social Psychology* (21), 301–10.

Leary, M.R. & Dobbins, S.E. (1983) 'Social anxiety, sexual behavior, and contraceptive use'. *Journal of Personality and Social Psychology* (47), 775–94.

Leary, M.R., Knight, P.D. & Johnson, K.A. (1987) 'Social anxiety and dyadic conversation: a verbal response analysis'. *Journal of Social and Clinical Psychology* (5), 34–50.

Leatham, G. & Duck, S.W. (1990) 'Conversations with friends and the dynamics of social support'. In S.W. Duck (ed.) *Personal Relationships and Social Support* (pp. 1–29). Sage: London.

Lee, J.A. (1973) *The Colors of Love: An Exploration of the Ways of Loving*. New Press: Ontario.

Lee, L. (1984) 'Sequences in separation: a framework for investigating the endings of personal (romantic) relationships'. *Journal of Social and Personal Relationships* (1), 49–74.

Lehman, D.R. & Hemphill, K.J. (1990) 'Recipients' perception of support attempts and attributions for support attempts that fail'. *Journal of Social and Personal Relationships* (7), 563–74.

Lewis, C.N. & O'Brien, M. (1987) *Fatherhood*. Sage: London.

Lewis, R.A. & McAvoy, P. (1984) 'Improving the quality of relationships: therapeutic interventions with opiate-abusing couples'. In S.W. Duck (ed.) *Personal Relationships 5: Repairing Personal Relationships*. Academic Press: London & New York.

Libet, J.M. & Lewisohn, P.M. (1973) 'Concept of social skill with special reference to the behavior of depressed persons'. *Journal of Consulting and Clinical Psychology* (40), 304–12.

Lin, N., Simeone, R.L., Ensel, W.M. & Kuo, W. (1979) 'Social support, stressful life events and illness: a model and an empirical test'. *Journal of Health and Social Behavior* (20), 108–19.

Linn, L.S. & DiMatteo, M.R. (1983) 'Humor and other communication: preferences in physician–patient encounters'. *Medical Care* (21), 1223–31.

Lips, H.M. & Morrison, A. (1986) 'Changes in the sense of family among couples having their first child'. *Journal of Social and Personal Relationships* (3), 393–400.

Lloyd, S.A. & Cate, R.M. (1985) 'The developmental course of conflict in dissolution of premarital relationships'. *Journal of Social and Personal Relationships* (2), 179–94.

Lombroso, C. (1918) *Criminal Anthropology (L'Uomo Criminale)*. Publicazione: Roma.

Lynch, J.J. (1987) *The Language of the Heart*. Basic Books: New York.

Lynch, J.J., Thomas, S.A., Mills, M.E., Malinow, K. & Katcher, A.H. (1974) 'The effects of human contact on cardiac arrythmia in coronary care patients'. *Journal of Nervous and Mental Diseases* (158), 88–99.

Lyons, R. et al. (1990) 'Personal relationship and disability'. Paper to International Conference on Personal Relationships, Oxford.

Maass, A. & Kohnken, G. (1989) 'Eyewitness identification: simulating the "weapon effect"'. *Law and Human Behavior* (13), 397–408.

Maddison, D. & Viola, A. (1968) 'The health of widows in the year after bereavement'. *Journal of Psychosomatic Research* (12), 297–306.

Malinowski, B. (1929) *The Sexual Life of Savages*. Harcourt Brace: New York.

Manning, M. & Herrman, J. (1981) 'The relationships of problem children in nursery schools'. In S.W. Duck & R. Gilmour (eds) *Personal Relationships 3: Personal Relationships in Disorder*. Academic Press: London & New York.

Marangoni, C. & Ickes, W. (1989) 'Loneliness: a theoretical review with implications for measurement'. *Journal of Social and Personal Relationships* (6), 93–128.

Markman, H.J. (1981) 'The prediction of marital distress: a five year follow-up'. *Journal of Consulting and Clinical Psychology* (49), 760–2.

Markman, H.J., Floyd, F., Stanley, S. & Storaasli, P. (1988) 'Prevention of marital distress: a longitudinal investigation'. *Journal of Counselling and Clinical Psychology* (56), 210–17.

Marshall, J. (1984) *Women Managers: Travellers in a Male World*. Wiley: Chichester, UK.

Marston, P.J., Hecht, M. & Robers, T. (1987) 'True love ways': the subjective experience and communication of romantic love'. *Journal of Social and Personal Relationships* (4), 387–407.

Martin, T.C. & Bumpass, L. (1989) 'Recent trends in marital disruption'. *Demography* (26), 37–51.

Marwell, G. & Schmitt, D.R. (1967) 'Dimensions of compliance-gaining behavior: an empirical analysis'. *Sociometry* (30), 350–64.

Maxwell, G.M. (1985) 'Behavior of lovers: measuring the closeness of relationships'. *Journal of Social and Personal Relationships* (2), 215–38.

Mayseless, O. (1991) 'Adult attachment patterns and courtship violence'. *Family Relations* (40), 21–8.

Mazur, R. (1977) 'Beyond jealousy and possessiveness'. In G. Clanton & L. Smith (eds) *Jealousy*. Prentice-Hall: Englewood Cliffs, NJ.

McAdams, D.P. & Losoff, M. (1984) 'Friendship motivation in fourth and sixth graders: a thematic analysis'. *Journal of Social and Personal Relationships* (1), 11–27.

McCall, G.J. (1982) 'Becoming unrelated: the management of bond dissolution'. In S.W. Duck (ed.) *Personal Relationships 4: Dissolving Personal Relationships*. Academic Press, London.

McCall, G. J. (1988) 'The organizational life cycle of relationships'. In S.W. Duck, D.F. Hay, S.E. Hobfoll, W.J. Ickes & B.M. Montgomery (eds) *Handbook of Personal Relationships* (pp. 467–86). Wiley: Chichester, UK.

McCarthy, B. (1983) 'Social cognition and personal relationships'. Paper to Lancaster University Relationships Research Group, November.

McGinnis, J. (1970) *The Selling of the President, 1968*. Pocket Books: New York.

McMillan, J.A., Clifton, A.K., McGrath, C. & Gale, W.S. (1977) 'Women's language: uncertainty or interpersonal sensitivity and emotionality? *Sex Roles* (3), 545–59.

McPartland, T.S. & Hornstra, R.K. (1964) 'The depressive datum'. *Comprehensive Psychiatry* (5), 253–61.

Mead, M. (1950) *Sex and Temperament in Three Primitive Societies*. Mentor: New York.

Mechanic, D. (1974) *Politics, Medicine and Social Science*. Wiley: New York.

Mechanic, D. (1980) 'The experience and reporting of common physical complaints'. *Journal of Health and Social Behavior* (21), 146–55.

Mehrabian, A. (1971) *Silent Messages*. Wadsworth: Belmont, CA.

Melamed, B.G. & Brenner, G.F. (1990) 'Social support and chronic stress: an interaction-based approach'. *Journal of Social and Clinical Psychology* (9), 104–17.

Menges, R.J. (1969) 'Student–instructor cognitive compatibility in the large lecture class'. *Journal of Personality* (37), 444–59.

Menzel, J. & Katz, D. (1957) 'Social relations and innovation in the medical profession: the epidemiology of a new drug'. In E. Maccoby (ed.) *Readings in Social Psychology*. Academic Press: New York.

Metts, S., Cupach, W. & Bejlovec, R.A. (1989) '"I love you too much to ever start liking you": redefining romantic relationships'. *Journal of Social and Personal Relationships* (6), 259–74.

Miell, D.E. (1984) 'Cognitive and communicative strategies in developing relationships'. Unpublished Ph.D. thesis, University of Lancaster, UK.

Miell, D.E. (1987) 'Remembering relationship development: constructing a context for interactions'. In R. Burnett, P. McGhee & D. Clarke (eds) *Accounting for Relationships*. Methuen: London.

Miell, D.E. & Duck, S.W. (1986) 'Strategies in developing friendship'. In V.J. Derlega & B.A. Winstead (eds) *Friendship and Social Interaction*. Springer Verlag: New York.

Mikulincer, M. & Segal, J. (1990) 'A multi-dimensional analysis of the experience of loneliness'. *Journal of Social and Personal Relationships* (7), 209–30.

Milardo, R.M. (1982) 'Friendship networks in developing relationships: converging and diverging social environments'. *Social Psychology Quarterly* (45), 163–71.

Milardo, R.M. (ed.) (1988) *Families and Social Networks*: Newbury Park, CA.

Milardo, R.M., Johnson, M.P. & Huston, T.L. (1983) 'Developing close relationships: changing patterns of interaction between pair members and social networks'. *Journal of Personality and Social Psychology* (44), 964–76.

Miller, B.C. & Moore, K.A. (1990) 'Adolescent sexual behavior, pregnancy and parenting: research through the 1980s'. *Journal of Marriage and the Family* (52), 1025–44.

Miller, G.R. & Boster, F.J. (1977) Three images of the trial: their implications for psychological research. In D.D. Sales (ed.) *Psychology in the Legal Process*. New York: Spectrum Publications.

Miller, G.R. & Boster, F.J. (1988) 'Persuasion in personal relationships'. In S.W. Duck, D.F. Hay, S.E. Hobfoll, W. Ickes & B. Montgomery (eds) *Handbook of Personal Relationships*. Wiley: Chichester, UK.

Miller, G.R. & Parks, M.R. (1982) 'Communication in dissolving relationships'. In S.W. Duck (ed.) *Personal Relationships 4: Dissolving Personal Relationships*. Academic Press, London.

Miller, K.I., Stiff, J.B. & Ellis, B.H. (1988) 'Communication and empathy as precursors to burnout among human service workers'. *Communication Monographs* (55) 250–65.

Miller, M.D. (1982) 'Friendship, power and the language of compliance gaining'. *Journal of Language and Social Behavior* (1), 111–22.

Mills, R.S.L. & Grusec, J. (1988) 'Socialization from the perspective of the parent-child relationship'. In S.W. Duck, D.F. Hay, S.E. Hobfoll, W. Ickes & B. Montgomery (eds) *Handbook of Personal Relationships*. Wiley: Chichester, UK.

Milmoe, S., Rosenthal, R., Blane, H.T., Chafetz, M.L. & Wolf, I. (1967) 'The doctor's voice: postdictors of successful referral of alcoholic patients'. *Journal of Abnormal Psychology* (72), 78–84.

Minuchin, S., Rosman, B.L. & Baker, L. (1978) *Psychosomatic Families: Anorexia Nervosa in Context*. Harvard University Press: Cambridge, MA.

Mitchell, H.E. & Byrne, D. (1973) 'The defendant's dilemma: effects of jurors' attitudes and authoritarianism on judicial decisions'. *Journal of Personality and Social Psychology* (25), 123–9.

Montagu, A. (1978) *Touching*. Harper & Row: New York.

Montgomery, B.M. (1981) 'Verbal immediacy as a behavioral indicator of open communication'. *Communication Quarterly* (30), 28–34.

Montgomery, B.M. (1984) 'Behavioral charcteristics predicting self and peer perception of open communication'. *Communication Quarterly* (32), 233–40.

Morgan, D.L. (1990) 'Combining the strengths of social networks, social support and personal relationships'. In S.W. Duck (ed., with R.C. Silver) *Personal Relationships and Social Support*. Sage: London.

Moriarty, T. (1975) 'Crime, commitment and the responsive bystander: two field experiments'. *Journal of Personality and Social Psychology* (31), 370–6.

Mortimer, J. (1983) *Clinging to the Wreckage*. Penguin Books: Harmondsworth, UK.

Morton, T.L., Alexander, I. & Altman, I. (1976) 'Communication and relationship definition'. In G.R. Miller (ed.) *Explorations in Interpersonal Communication*. Sage: Beverly Hills, CA.

Mott, F.L. & Moore, S.F. (1979) 'The causes of marital disruption among young American women: an interdisciplinary perspective'. *Journal of Marriage and the Family* (41), 335–65.

Mowen, J.C. & Cialdini, R.B. (1980) 'On implementing the door-in-the-face compliance technique in a business context'. *Journal of Marketing Research* (17), 253–8.

Muehlenhard, C.L., Koralewski, M.A., Andrews, S.L. & Burdick, C.A. (1986) 'Verbal and nonverbal cues that convey interest in dating: two studies'. *Behavior Therapy* (17), 404–19.

Mulac, A. (1989) 'Men's and women's talk in same-gender and mixed-gender dyads: power or polemic?'. *Journal of Language and Social Psychology* (8), 249–70.

Mulac, A., Studley, L.B., Wiemann, J.M. & Bradac, J. (1987) 'Male/female gaze in same-sex and mixed-sex dyads: gender-linked differences and mutual influence'. *Human Communication Research* (13), 323–43.

Mulac, A., Wiemann, J., Widenmann, S.J. & Gibson, T.W. (1988) 'Male/female language differences and effects in same-sex and mixed-sex dyads: the gender-linked language effect'. *Communication Monographs* (55), 314–35.

Murray, D.M. & Wells, G.L. (1982) 'Does the knowledge that a crime was staged affect eyewitness performance?'. *Journal of Applied Social Psychology* (12), 42–53.

Murstein, B.I. & Glaudin, V. (1968) 'The use of the MMPI in the determination of marital maladjustment'. *Journal of Marriage and the Family* (30), 651–5.

Neulip, J.W. & Mattson, M. (1990) 'The use of deception as a compliance gaining strategy'. *Human Communication Research* (16), 409–21.

Newcomb, M.D. (1990) 'Social support by many other names: towards a unified conceptualization'. *Journal of Social and Personal Relationships* (7), 479–94.

Newcomb, M.D. & Bentler, P.M. (1981) 'Marital breakdown'. In S.W. Duck & R. Gilmour (eds) *Personal Relationships 3: Personal Relationships in Disorder*. Academic Press: London & New York.

Newcomb, T.M. (1971) 'Dyadic balance as a source of clues about interpersonal attraction'. In B.I. Murstein (ed.) *Theories of Attraction and Love*. Springer: New York.

Newell, S. & Stutman, R.K. (1988) 'The social confrontation episode'. *Communication Monographs* (55), 266–85.

Noller, P. (1982) 'Channel consistency and inconsistency in the communication of married couples'. *Journal of Personality and Social Psychology* (43), 732–41.

Noller, P. & Fitzpatrick, M.A. (1990) 'Marital communication in the eighties'. *Journal of Marriage and the Family* (52), 832–43.

Noller, P. & Eallois, C. (1988) 'Understanding and misunderstanding in marriage: sex and marital adjustment differences in structured and free interaction'. In P. Noller & M.A. Fitzpatrick (eds) *Perspectives on Marital Interaction*. Multilingual Matters: Clevedon, UK & Philadelphia.

Noller, P. & Hiscox, H. (1989) 'Fitzpatrick's typology: an Australian replication'. *Journal of Social and Personal Relationships* (6), 87–91.

Noller, P. & Venardos, C. (1986) 'Communication awareness in married couples'. *Journal of Social and Personal Relationships* (3), 31–42.

O'Barr, W.M. (1982) *Linguistic Evidence*. Academic Press: New York.

O'Connor, P. & Brown, G.W. (1984) 'Supportive relationships: fact or fancy?'. *Journal of Social and Personal Relationships* (2), 159–76.

Oden, S. & Asher, S.R. (1977) 'Coaching children in social skills for friendship making'. *Child Development* (48), 495–506.

Orbuch, T.L. (ed.) (in press) *Relationship Loss*. Springer: New York.

Orford, J. (1976) 'A study of the personalities of excessive drinkers and their wives, using the approaches of Leary and Eysenck'. *Journal of Consulting and Clinical Psychology* (44), 534–45.

Orford, J. (1980) 'The domestic context'. In M.P. Feldman & J. Orford (eds) *Psychological Problems: The Social Context*. Wiley: Chichester, UK.

Orford, J. & O'Reilly, P. (1981) 'Disorders in the family'. In S.W. Duck & R. Gilmour (eds) *Personal Relationships 3: Personal Relationships in Disorder*. Academic Press: London & New York.

Orford, J., Oppenheimer, E., Egert, S., Hensman. C. & Guthrie, S. (1976) 'The cohesiveness of alcoholism-complicated marriages and its influence on treatment outcome'. *British Journal of Psychiatry* (128), 318–49.

Orth, J.E., Stiles, W.B., Scherwitz, L. Hennrikus, D. & Vallbona, C. (1987) 'Patient exposition and provider explanation in routine interviews and hypertensive patients' blood pressure control.' *Health Psychology* (6), 29–42.

Palmer, M.T. (1990) 'Controlling conversation: turns, topics and interpersonal control'. *Communication Monographs* (56), 1–18.

Park, K.A. & Waters, E. (1988) 'Traits and relationships in developmental perspective'. In S.W. Duck, D.G. Hay, S.E. Hobfoll, W. Ickes & B. Montgomery (eds) *Handbook of Personal Relationships*. Wiley: Chichester, UK.

Parker, S. (1960) 'The attitudes of medical students towards their patients: an exploratory study'. *Journal of Medical Education* (35), 849–55.

Parks, M.R. & Adelman, M. (1983) 'Communication networks and the development of romantic relationships: an expansion of uncertainty reduction theory'. *Human Communication Reserach* (10), 55–80.

Parsons, T. (1951) *The Social System*. Free Press: Glencoe, IL.

Patterson, M.L. (1988) 'Functions of nonverbal behavior in close relationships'. In S.W. Duck, D.F. Hay, S.E. Hobfoll, W. Ickes & B. Montgomery (eds) *Handbook of Personal Relationships*. Wiley: Chichester, UK.

Paykel, E.S., Emms, E.M., Fletcher, J. & Rassaby, E.S. (1980) 'Life events and social support in puerperal depression'. *British Journal of Psychiatry* (136), 339–46.

Pendleton, D. & Hasler, J. (1983) *Doctor–Patient Communication*. Academic Press: London.

Pennington, D.C. (1982) 'Witnesses and their testimony: effects of ordering on juror verdicts'. *Journal of Applied Social Psychology* (12), 318–33.

Peplau, L.A. & Perlman, D. (1982) 'Perspectives on loneliness'. In L.A. Peplau & D. Perlman (eds) *Loneliness: A Sourcebook of Theory, Research and Therapy*. Wiley-Interscience: New York.

Peplau, L.A., Miceli, M. & Morasch, B. (1982) 'Loneliness and self-evaluation'. In L.A. Peplau & D. Perlman (eds) *Loneliness: A Sourcebook of Theory, Research and Therapy*. Wiley-Interscience: New York.

Perlman, D. & Peplau, L.A. (1981) 'Toward a social psychology of loneliness'. In S.W. Duck & R. Gilmour (eds) *Personal Relationships 3: Personal Relationships in Disorder*. Academic Press: London & New York.

Perlman, D. & Serbin, R. (1984) 'A sports report: the effects of racquet matches on loneliness'. Paper to Second International Conference on Personal Relationships. Madison, WI, July.

Perlman, D., Gerson, A.C. & Spinner, B. (1978) 'Loneliness among senior citizens: an empirical report'. *Essence* (2), 239–48.

Pettegrew, L.S. & Turkat, I.D. (1986) 'How patients communicate about their illness'. *Human Communication Research* (12), 376–94.

Petty, R.E. & Cacioppo, J.T. (1981) *Attitudes and Persuasion: Classic and Contemporary Approaches*. W.C. Brown: Dubuque, IA.

Pfeiffer, S.M. & Wong, P.T.P. (1989) 'Multidimensional jealousy'. *Journal of Social and Personal Relationships* (6), 181–96.

Phillips, D.P. (1970) 'Dying as a form of social behavior'. PhD dissertation, Ann Arbor, MI.

Phillips, D.P. (1972) 'Deathday and birthday: an unexpected connection'. In J.M. Tanur (ed.) *Statistics: A Guide to the Unknown*. Holden Day: San Francisco.

Pickering, G. (1978) 'Medicine on the brink: the dilemma of a learned profession'. *Perspectives in Biology and Medicine*, Summer.

Pike, G. & Sillars, A. (1985) 'Reciprocity of marital communication'. *Journal of Social and Personal Relationships* (2), 303–24.

Pilkonis, P.A. (1977) 'The behavioral consequences of shyness'. *Journal of Personality* (45), 596–611.

Planalp, S., Rutherford, D.K. & Honeycutt, J.M. (1988) 'Events that increase uncertainty in personal relationships II: Replication and extension'. *Human Communication Research* (14), 516–47.

Platz, S.J. & Hosch, H.M. (1988) 'Cross-racial eyewitness identification: a field study'. *Journal of Applied Social Psychology* (18), 972–84.

Premo, B.E. & Stiles, W.B. (1983) 'Familiarity in verbal interactions of married couples versus strangers'. *Journal of Social and Clinical Psychology* (1), 209–30.

Prins, H. (1983) *Offenders, Deviants or Patients?* Tavistock: London.

Pryor, B. & Buchanan, R.W. (1984) 'The effects of a defendant's demeanor on prior perceptions of credibility and guilt'. *Journal of Communication* (34), 92–9.

Putallaz, M. & Gottman, J.M. (1981) 'Social skills and group acceptance'. In S.R. Asher & J.M. Gottman (eds) *The Development of Children's Friendship*. Cambridge University Press: Cambridge, UK.

Putallaz, M., Costanzo, P.R. & Smith, R.B. (1991) 'Maternal recollections of childhood peer relationships: implications for their children's social competence'. *Journal of Social and Personal Relationships* (8), 403–22.

Putnam, S.M., Stiles, W.B., Jacob, M.C. & James, J.A. (1988) 'Teaching the medical interview: an intervention study'. *Journal of General Internal Medicine* (3), 38–47.

Pyszcynski, T.A. & Wrightsman, L.S. (1981) 'The effects of opening statements on mock jurors' verdicts in a simulated criminal trial'. *Journal of Applied Social Psychology* (11), 301–13.

Rackham, N. & Morgan,T. (1977) *Behavior Analysis and Training*. McGraw-Hill: New York.

Radecki Bush, C., Bush, J.P. & Jennings, J. (1988) 'Effects of jealousy threats on relationship perceptions and emotions'. *Journal of Social and Personal Relationships* (5), 285–303.

Reis, H.T. (1984) 'Social interaction and well-being'. In S.W. Duck (ed.) *Personal Relationships 5: Repairing Personal Relationships*. Academic Press: London & New York.

Reis, H.T. (1986) 'Gender effects in social participation: intimacy, loneliness and the conduct of social interaction'. In R. Gilmour & S.W. Duck (eds) *The Emerging Field of Personal Relationships*. Erlbaum: Hillsdale, NJ.

Reis, H.T. (1990) 'The role of intimacy in interpersonal relations'. *Journal of Social and Clinical Psychology* (9), 15–30.

Reis, H.T., Nezlek, J. & Wheeler, L. (1980) 'Physical attractiveness and social interaction'. *Journal of Personality and Social Psychology* (38), 604–17.

Renne, K.S. (1970) 'Correlates of dissatisfaction in marriage'. *Journal of Marriage and the Family* (32), 54–67.

Renne, K.S. (1971) 'Health and marital experience in an urban population'. *Journal of Marriage and the Family* (33), 338–50.

Rexroat, C. & Shehan, C. (1987) 'The family life cycle and spouses' time in housework'. *Journal of Marriage and the Family* (49), 737–50.

Ridley, C.A. & Nelson, R.R. (1984) 'The behavioural effects of training premarital couples in mutual problem solving skills'. *Journal of Social and Personal Relationships* (2), 197–210.

Riskin, J. & Faunce, E.E. (1972) 'An evaluative review of family interaction research'. *Family Process* (11), 365–455.

Rodin, M. (1982) 'Nonengagement, failure to engage and disengagement'. In S.W. Duck (ed.) *Personal Relationships 4: Dissolving Personal Relationships* (pp. 31–50). Academic Press: London.

Rogers, R.W. (1983) 'Preventive health psychology: an interface of social and clinical psychology'. *Journal of Social and Clinical Psychology* (1), 120–7.

Rollins, B.C. & Feldman, H. (1970) 'Marital satisfaction over the lifecycle'. *Journal of Marriage and the Family* (32), 20–8.

Roloff, M.E., Janiszewski, C.A., McGrath, M.A., Burns, C.S. & Manrai, L.A. (1988) 'Acquiring resources from intimates: when obligation substitutes for persuasion'. *Human Communication Research* (14), 364–96.

Rook, K.S. (1988) 'Toward a more differentiated view of loneliness'. In S.W. Duck, D.F. Hay, S.E. Hobfoll, W. Ickes & B. Montgomery (eds) *Handbook of Personal Relationships*. Wiley: Chichester, UK.

Rook, K.S. (1990) 'Parallels in the study of social support and social strain'. *Journal of Social and Clinical Psychology* (9), 118–32.

Rook, K.S. & Pietromonaco, P. (1987) 'Close relationships: ties that heal or ties that bind?'. In W.H. Jones & D. Perlman (eds) *Advances in Personal Relationships*. JAI Press: Greenwich.

Rubenstein, C. & Shaver, P. (1982) 'The experience of loneliness'. In L.A. Peplau & D. Perlman (eds) *Loneliness: A Sourcebook of Theory, Research and Therapy.* Wiley-Interscience: New York.

Rubin, A.M., Perse, E.M. & Powell, R.A. (1985) 'Loneliness, parasocial interactions and local TV news viewing'. *Human Communication Research* (12), 155–80.

Rubin, K.H., Mills, R.S.L. & Rose-Krasnor, L. (1989) 'Maternal beliefs and children's competence'. In B.H. Schneider, G. Attili, J. Nadel & R.P. Weissberg (eds) *Social Competence in Developmental Perspective.* NATO ASI Series, Kluwer: Amsterdam.

Rubin, R.B. (1977) 'The role of context in information seeking and impression formation'. *Communication Monographs* (44), 81–90.

Rubin, Z. (1973) *Liking and Loving.* Holt, Rinehart & Winston: New York.

Rubin, Z. (1979) 'Los Angeles says it with love on a scale'. *Los Angeles Times*, 14 February 1979.

Rubin, Z. (1987) 'Parent–child loyalty and testimonial privilege'. *Harvard Law Review* (100), 910–29.

Rubin, Z. (1990) 'From love to law: a social psychologist's midlife passage'. *ISSPR Bullet* (March), 1–3.

Ruehlman, L.S. & Wolchik, S.A. (1988) 'Personal goals and interpersonal support and hindrance as factors in psychological distress and well-being'. *Journal of Personality and Social Psychology* (55), 293–301.

Rutter, M. (1972) *Maternal Deprivation Reassessed.* Penguin Books: Harmondsworth, UK.

Sabatelli, R. & Pearce, J. (1986) 'Exploring marital expectations'. *Journal of Social and Personal Relationships* (3), 307–22.

Saks, M.J. (1986) 'Blaming the jury'. *Georgetown Law Journal* (75), 693–711.

Salovey, P. (ed.) (1991) *The Psychology of Jealousy and Envy.* Guilford: New York.

Salovey, P. & Rodin, J. (1989) 'Envy and jealousy in close relationships'. In C. Hendrick (ed.) *Review of Social Psychology and Personality (10): Close Relationships.* Sage: Newbury Park, CA.

Sanders, G.G. & Chiu, W. (1988) 'Eyewitness errors in the recall of action'. *Journal of Applied Social Psychology* (18), 1241–59.

Sants, H.K.A. (1984) 'Conceptions of friendship, social behaviour and school achievement in six year old children'. *Journal of Social and Personal Relationships* (11), 293–309.

Sarason, B.R., Sarason, I.G. & Pierce, G.R. (1990) *Social Support: A Transactional View.* Wiley: New York.

Sarat, A. & Felstiner, W.L.F. (1988) 'Law and social relations: vocabularies of motive in lawyer/client interaction'. *Law and Society Review* (6), 737–69.

Schlenker, B.R. & Leary, M.R. (1982) 'Social anxiety and self-presentation: a conceptualisation and a model'. *Psychological Bulletin* (92), 641–69.

Schmale, A.H., Jr. (1958) 'The relationship of separation and depression to disease'. *Psychosomatic Medicine* (20), 259–75.

Schneider, B.H., Attili, G., Nadel, J. & Weissberg, R.P. (eds) (1989) *Social Competence in Development Perspective.* NATO ASI Series, Kluwer: Amsterdam.

Schofield, M.J. & Kafer, N.F. (1985) 'Children's understanding of friendship issues: development by stage or sequence?. *Journal of Social and Personal Relationships* (2), 151–66.

Schultz, N.R., Jr. & Moore, D. (1988) 'Loneliness: differences across three age levels'. *Journal of Social and Personal Relationships* (5), 275–84.

Schwarzer, R. & Leppin, A. (1991) 'Social support and health: a theoretical and empirical overview'. *Journal of Social and Personal Relationships* (8), 99–128.

Scotton, C.M. & Udry, W. (1977) 'Bilingual strategies – social functions of code switching'. *Linguistics* (193), 5–20.

Segrin, C. (1991) 'A meta-analytic review of social skill deficits'. *Communication Monographs* (57), 292–308.

Selden, J. (1689) *Table Talk*. Murray & Sons: London.

Selye, H. (1956) *The Stress of Life*. McGraw-Hill: New York.

Semin, G.R. & Manstead, A.S.R. (1982) 'The social implications of embarrassment displays and restitution behaviour'. *European Journal of Social Psychology* (12), 367–77.

Senchak, M. & Leonard, M. (1992) 'Attachment styles and marital adjustment among newly-wed couples'. *Journal of Social and Personal Relationships* (9).

Shanas, E., Townsend, P., Wedderburn, D., Friis, H., Milhoj, P. & Stehouwer, J. (1968) *Old People in Three Industrial Societies*. Atherton: New York.

Sharpsteen, D.J. (1991) 'The organization of jealousy knowledge: romantic jealousy as a blended emotion'. In P. Salovey (ed.) *The Psychology of Jealousy and Envy*. Guilford: New York.

Shaver, P.R. & Hazan, C. (1988) 'A biased overview of the study of love'. *Journal of Social and Personal Relationships* (5), 473–501.

Shaver, P.R., Furman, W. & Buhrmester, D. (1985) 'Transition to college: network changes, social skills and loneliness'. In S.W. Duck & D. Perlman (eds) *Understanding Personal Relationships*. Sage: London.

Shea, B.C. & Pearson, J.C. (1986) 'The effects of relationship type, partner intent, and gender on the selection of relationships maintenance strategies'. *Communication Monographs* (53), 352–64.

Shotland, R.L. & Straw, M.K. (1976) 'Bystander response to an assault: when a man attacks a woman'. *Journal of Personality and Social Psychology* (34), 990–9.

Shotter, J. (1987) 'Accounting for relationship growth'. In R. Burnett, P. McGhee & D. Clarke (eds) *Accounting for Relationships*. Methuen: London.

Shulz, R. (1976) 'Effects of control and predictability on the physical and psychological well-being of the institutionalized aged'. *Journal of Personality and Social Psychology* (33), 563–73.

Shuval, J.T. (1981) 'The contribution of psychological and social phenomena to an understanding of the aetiology of disease and illness'. *Social Science and Medicine* (15A), 337–42.

Shuval, J.T., Antonovsky, A. & Davies, A.M. (1973) 'Illness: a mechanism for coping with failure'. *Social Science and Medicine* (7), 259–65.

Silberfeld, M. (1978) 'Psychological symptoms and social supports'. *Social Psychiatry* (13), 11–17.

Sillars, A.L., Pike, G.R., Jones, T.S. & Redmon, D. (1983) 'Communication and conflict in marriage'. In R. Bostrom (ed.) *Communication Yearbook 7*. Sage: Beverly Hlls, CA.

Siperstein, G.N. & Gale, M.E. (1983) 'Improving peer relationships of "rejected children"'. Paper to Society for Research in Child Development, Detroit, MI.

Skelton, J.A. & Pennebaker, J.N. (1982) 'The psychology of physical symptoms and sensations'. In G.S. Sanders & J. Suls (eds) *The Social Psychology of Health and Illness*. Erlbaum: Hillsdale, NJ.

Smith, A.J. (1957) 'Similarity of values and its relation to acceptance and the projection of similarity'. *Journal of Psychology* (43), 251–60.

Smith, A.J. (1960) 'The attribution of similarity: the influence of success and failure'. *Journal of Abnormal and Social Psychology* (61), 419–23.

Smith, R.H. (1991) 'Envy and the sense of injustice'. In P. Salovey (ed.) *The Psychology of Jealousy and Envy*. Guilford: New York.

Smith-Hanen, S. (1977) 'Effects of nonverbal behaviors on judged level of counsellor warmth and empathy'. *Journal of Counselling Psychology* (24), 87–91.

Snow, J. (1854) 'On the mode of communication of cholera'. Reprinted in *Snow on Cholera* (1936), Commonwealth Fund: New York.

Snyder, C.R. & Smith, T.W. (1982) 'Symptoms as self-handicapping strategies: the virtues of old wine in a new bottle'. Unpub. manuscript.

Sobol, M.P. & Earn, B.M. (1985) 'What causes mean: an analysis of children's interpretations of the causes of social experience'. *Journal of Social and Personal Relationships* (2), 137–50.

Solano, C.H. & Koester, N.H. (1989) 'Loneliness and communication problems: subjective anxiety or objective skills?'. *Personality and Social Psychology Bulletin* (15), 126–33.

Solano, C., Batten, P.G. & Parish, E.A. (1982) 'Loneliness and patterns of self-disclosure'. *Journal of Personality and Social Psychology* (43), 524–31.

Sommer, R. (1969) *Personal Space: The Behavioral Basis of Design.* Prentice-Hall: Englewood Cliffs, NJ.

Spitzberg, B.H. & Canary, D. (1985) 'Loneliness and relationally competent communication'. *Journal of Social and Personal Relationships* (2), 387–402.

Spitzberg, B.H. & Cupach, W. (1985) *Interpersonal Communication Competence.* Sage: Newbury Park, CA.

Sprecher, S. (1987) 'The effects of self-disclosure given and received on affection for an intimate partner and stability of the relationship'. *Journal of Social and Personal Relationships* (4), 115–27.

Stang, D.J. (1973) 'Effect of interaction rate on ratings of leadership and liking'. *Journal of Personality and Social Psychology* (27), 405–8.

Stewart, J.E. (1980) 'Defendant's attractiveness as a factor in the outcome of criminal trials: an observational study'. *Journal of Applied Social Psychology* (10), 348–61.

Stiff, J.B. & Miller, G.R. (1984) 'Deceptive behaviors and behaviors which are interpreted as deceptive: an interactive approach to the study of deception'. Paper to International Communication Association, San Francisco, May.

Stone, A.C. (1979) 'Patient compliance and the role of the expert'. *Journal of Social Issues* (35), 34–59.

Storm, C.L. (1991) 'Placing gender at the heart of the MFT Masters program'. *Journal of Marriage and Family Therapy* (17), 45–52.

Stotland, E., Zander, A. & Natsoulas, T. (1960) 'Generalisation of interpersonal similarity'. *Journal of Abnormal and Social Psychology* (62), 250–6.

Strain, P.S., Shores, R.E. & Kerr, M.A. (1976) 'An experimental analysis of 'spillover' effects on the social interactions of behaviorally handicapped preschool children'. *Journal of Applied Behavior Analysis* (9), 31–40.

Straus, M.A. (1985) 'Family violence'. Paper to HDFR, University of Connecticut, Storrs, April.

Straus, M.A. (1990) 'Injury and frequency of assaults and the "representative sample fallacy" in measuring wife beating and child abuse'. In M.A. Straus & R.J. Gelles (eds) *Physical Violence in American Families: Risk Factors and Adaptations in 8145 Families.* Transaction books: New Brunswick, NJ.

Straus, M.A. & Gelles, R.J. (1986) 'Societal change and change in family violence from 1975 to 1985 as revealed in two national surveys'. *Journal of Marriage and the Family* (48), 465–79.

Street, R.L. Jr & Buller, D.B. (1988) 'Patients' characteristics affecting physician-patient nonverbal communication'. *Human Communication Research* (15), 60–90.

Strodtbeck, F.L., James R.M. & Hawkins, C. (1957) 'Social status in jury deliberations'. *American Sociological Review* (22), 713–19.

Stroebe, W. (1980) 'Process loss in social psychology: failure to exploit?'. In R. Gilmour & S.W. Duck (eds) *The Development of Social Psychology.* Academic Press: London.

Stroebe, W. & Stroebe, M. (1983) 'Who suffers more? Sex differences in health risk of the widowed'. *Psychological Bulletin* (93), 279–301.

Suggs, D. & Berman, L. (1979) 'The art and science of conducting the voir dire'. *Professional Psychology* (9), 367–88.

Suitor, J.J. (1991) 'Marital quality and satisfaction with the division of household labor across the family life cycle'. *Journal of Marriage and the Family* (53), 221–30.

Sunnafrank, M. (1991) 'Review of the attraction paradigm'. In J. Anderson (ed.) *Communication Yearbook 14*. Sage: Newbury Park, CA.

Sunnafrank, M. & Miller, G.R. (1981) 'The role of initial conversations in determining attraction to similar and dissimilar strangers'. *Human Communication Research* (8), 16–25.

Surra, C.A. (1984) 'Attributions about the decison to wed: variations by style of courtship'. Paper to Second International Conference on Personal Relationships, Madison, WI, July.

Surra, C.A. (1990) 'Research and theory on mate selection and premarital relationships in the 1980s'. *Journal of Marriage and the Family* (52), 844–65.

Surra, C.A. & Huston, T.L. (1987) 'Mate selection as a social transition'. In D. Perlman & S.W. Duck (eds) *Intimate Relationships*. Sage: Newbury Park, CA.

Surra, C.A., Arizzi, P. & Asmussen, L. (1988) 'The association between reasons for commitment and the development and outcome of marital relationships'. *Journal of Social and Personal Relationships* (5), 47–63.

Szasz, T.S. & Hollander, M.H. (1956) 'A contribution to the philosophy of medicine: the basic models of the doctor–patient relationships'. *Archives of Internal Medicine* (97), 585–92.

Tracy, K., Craig, R.T., Smith, M. & Spisak, F. (1984) 'The discourse of requests: assessment of a compliance-gaining approach'. *Human Communication Research* (10), 513–38.

Tunstall, J. (1967) *Old and Alone*. Humanities Press: New York.

Unger, R. (1986) 'Use of sex-discriminant terms'. Paper to Nags Head Conference, May.

Van Lear, C.A., Jr & Trujillo, N. (1986) 'On becoming acquainted: a longitudinal study of social judgement processes'. *Journal of Social and Personal Relationships* (3), 375–92.

Vaux, A. (1988) *Social Support: Theory, Research, and Intervention*. Praeger: New York.

Vaux, A. (1990) An ecological approach to understanding and facilitating social support'. *Journal of Social and Personal Relationships* (7), 507–18.

Vitkus, J. & Horowitz, L.M. (1987) 'Poor social performance of lonely people: lacking skills or adopting a role?'. *Journal of Personality and Social Psychology* (52), 1266–73.

Walker, M.B. & Trimboli, A. (1989) 'Communicating affect: the role of verbal and nonverbal content'. *Journal of Language and Social Psychology* (8), 229–48.

Walker, N.M. & Hops, H. (1973) 'The use of group and individual reinforcement contingencies in the modification of social withdrawal'. In L.A. Hanerlynck, L.C. Hardy & E.J. Mosh (eds) *Behavior Change: Methodology, Concept and Practice*. Research Press: Champaign, IL.

Walker, R.J. & Walker, M.G. (1972) *The English Legal System*. Butterworths: London.

Walster (Hatfield) E.H., & Walster, G.W. (1978) *A New Look at Love*. Addison Wesley: Reading, MA.

Walster (Hatfield) E.H., Aronson, V. & Abrahams, D. (1966) 'On increasing the persuasiveness of a low prestige communicator'. *Journal of Experimental Social Psychology* (2), 325–42.

Watson, O.M. & Graves, T.D. (1966) 'Quantitative research in proxemic behavior'. *American Anthropologist* (68), 971–85.

Watzlawick, P., Beavin, J. & Jackson, D. (1967) *Pragmatics of Human Communication: A Study of Interactional Patterns, Pathologies and Paradoxes*. Norton: New York.

Weber, A. (1983) 'The breakdown of relationships'. Paper presented to conference on Social Interaction and Relationships, Nags Head, North Carolina, May.

Weiss, R.L. & Aved, B.M. (1978) 'Marital satisfaction and depression as predictors of physical health status'. *Journal of Consulting and Clinical Psychology* (46), 1379–84.

Wheeler, L. & Nezlek, J. (1977) 'Sex difference in social participation'. *Journal of Personality and Social Psychology* (45), 943–53.

Wheeler, L., Reis, H.T. & Nezlek, J. (1983) 'Loneliness, social interaction, and sex roles'. *Journal of Personality and Social Psychology* (35), 742–54.

Wilkinson, J. & Canter, S. (1982) *Social Skills Training Manual*. Wiley: Chichester, UK.

Williams, E. (1974) 'An analysis of gaze in schizophrenia'. *British Journal of Social and Clinical Psychology* (13), 1–8.

Wilson, C. & Orford, J. (1978) 'Children of alcoholics: report of a preliminary study and comments on the literature'. *Journal of Studies on Alcohol* (39), 121–42.

Wiseman, J.P. (1986) 'Friendship: bonds and binds in a voluntary relationship'. *Journal of Social and Personal Relationships* (3), 191–211.

Wiseman, J.P. (1989) 'Enemies'. Paper to the Second Conference of the International Network on Personal Relationships. Iowa City, May

Wiseman, R.L. & Schenk-Hamlin, W. (1981) 'A multidimensional scaling validation of an inductively derived set of compliance-gaining strategies'. *Communication Monographs* (48), 251–70.

Wittenberg, M.T. & Reis, H.T. (1986) 'Loneliness, social skills, and social perception'. *Personality and Social Psychology Bulletin* (12), 121–30.

Wright, P.H. (1978) 'Toward a theory of friendship based on a conception of the self'. *Human Communication Research* (4), 196–207.

Wyler, A.R., Masuda, M. & Holmes, T.H. (1971) 'Magnitude of life events and seriousness of illness'. *Psychosomatic Medicine* (33), 115–22.

Yerby, J., Buerkel-Rothfuss, N. & Bochner, A.P. (1990) Understanding Family Communication. Gorsuch Scarisbrick: Scottsdale.

Young, J.E. (1982) 'Loneliness, depression and cognitive therapy: theory and application'. In L.A. Peplau & D. Perlman (eds) *Loneliness: a Current Sourcebook of Theory Research and Therapy*. Wiley-Interscience: New York.

Youniss, J. (1980) *Parents and Peers in Social Development*. University of Chicago Press: Chicago.

Zaidel, S.F. & Mehrabian, A. (1969) 'The ability to communicate and infer positive and negative attitudes facially and vocally'. *Journal of Experimental Research in Personality* (3), 233–41.

Zakahi, W.R. & Duran, R.L. (1982) 'All the lonely people: the relationship among loneliness, communicative competence and communication anxiety'. *Communication Quarterly* (30), 203–9.

Zakahi, W.R. & Duran, R.L. (1985) 'Loneliness, communicative competence and communication apprehension: extension and replication'. *Communication Quarterly* (33), 50–60.

Zietlow, P.H. & Sillars, A.L. (1988) 'Life-stage differences in communication during marital conflicts'. *Journal of Social and Personal Relationships* (5), 223–45.

Zimmer, T. (1986) 'Premarital anxieties'. *Journal of Social and Personal Relationships* (3), 149–60.

Zola, A.K. (1972) 'Studying the decison to see a doctor'. In Z.J. Lipowski (ed.) *Psychological Aspects of Physical Illness*. Karger: Basel.

Index of References

Acitelli, 1988 110, 114, 116
Adorno, et al., 1950 122
Ainsworth, et al., 1978 36
Ajzen, 1988 173
Alberts, 1988 116
Allan, 1989 76, 77, 89, 113
Amato, 1991 134
Anderson, 1985 136
Argyle, 1967; 1975; 1983 8, 12, 16
Argyle & Cook, 1976 9
Argyle & Dean, 1965 10
Argyle & Henderson, 1984 91, 132, 189
Argyle et al., 1968 26
Argyle et al., 1970 16
Aron et al., 1989 42, 43
Aronson & Golden, 1962 152
Asher & Parker, 1989 16, 140
Asher & Wheeler, 1985 140
Athanasiou & Sarkin, 1974 132
Attili, 1989 143
Ayres, 1989 19, 20

Bandura, 1977 101, 200
Barbee, 1990 68, 92, 194, 196
Barrera, 1981 198
Barrera & Baca, 1990 198
Bartholomew, 1990 36, 40, 124
Baumrind, 1972 122
Baxter, 1984 95, 97, 98
Baxter & Wilmot, 1984 15, 87
Baxter & Wilmot, 1985 83, 84
Beattie, 1981 13
Beck, 1976 56
Beecher, 1959 176
Beinstein Miller, 1989 37
Bell & Loftus, 1988 226
Bell & Loftus, 1989 232
Bentler & Newcomb, 1978 132
Berardo, 1970 195
Berardo, 1990 103, 104, 115
Berger, C. 1988 76
Berger, C. & Bell, 1988 78, 79
Berger, C. & Bradac, 1982 77
Berger, C. et al., 1989 20
Berger, P. & Kellner, 1975 1
Berkmn & Syme, 1979 198
Berman, 1977 216
Berndt, 1989 142
Berndt & Ladd, 1989 122
Berne, 1964 182
Berscheid, 1966 151
Berschied & Walster, 1974 37
Bhavnagri & Parke, 1991 137
Bickman & Green, 1977 212
Bierce, 1985 35
Bierman & Furman 1982 144
Billig, 1987 41, 173
Birchler, 1972 116
Blanck, 1987 237
Blanck et al., 1981 228
Blanck et al., 1990 207 208
Blondis & Jackson, 1977 191
Bloom et al., 1978 120, 195
Bochner, 1991 70, 72, 74, 75
Bolger et al., 1989 92
Boreham & Gibson, 1978 188
Bornsteiu & Clayton, 1972 204
Borys & Perlman, 1985 58
Boster & Stiff, 1984 167
Bourhis & Giles, 1977 28, 29
Bowlby, 1951 121
Boyd et al., 1974 189
Bradburn, 1969 58
Braverman, 1991 105

Brehm, 1966 160
Brehm & Brehm, 1981 160
Brigham & Carins, 1988 226
Bringle, 1991 45
Bringle & Boebinger, 1990 49
Brodsky, 1977 234, 235
Brown, G., 1984 128
Brown, G. & Harris, 1978 128, 193
Brown, R., 1965 22, 24, 168
Brubaker, 1990 105
Bugental et al., 1970 30
Bull, 1977 224
Burgess, 1981 128
Burgoon & Koper, 1984 55
Burgoon et al., 1980 167
Burgoon et al., 1986 12
Burleson, 1990 68, 194, 196
Burns & Farina, 1984 91
Buss, 1980 55
Buunk, 1980 49
Buunk & Bringle, 1987 46, 110
Byrne, 1961; 1971 69, 70, 71, 72, 73, 74
Byrne & Lamberth, 1971 72
Byrne & Nelson, 1965 72
Byrne et al., 1966 72
Byrne et al., 1970 72

Canary & Spitzberg, 1989 119
Cappella, 1988; 1991 12, 13, 75
Carr & Dabbs, 1974 10
Cate & Lloyd, 1988 106
Check et al., 1985 61
Cheek & Busch, 1981 55, 57
Cheyne, 1970 19
Christopher & Cate, 1985 110, 111
Christopher & Frandsen, 1990 111, 171
Christy, 1979 188
Cialdini et al., 1975 163
Cialdini et al., 1978 164, 172
Clanton & Kosins, 1991 45
Clark, 1979 167
Clark & Delia, 1979 165
Clarke et al., 1985 120
Clore, 1977 9
Clore & Byrne, 1974 73, 75
Clore & Gormly, 1974 72
Cobb & Jones, 1984 192, 196
Cody et al., 1983 168
Coker & Burgoon, 1987 12
Cole, 1976 132
Contarello & Volpato, 1991 34
Cook, 1968 11
Cook, 1977 163
Cooke, 1990 215, 219, 230, 233, 235
Coombs, 1991 105
Cortez et al., 1988 69
Coyne, 1987 127
Cunningham & Antill, 1981 40
Cupach & Comstock, 1990 116
Cupach & Metts, 1986 99
Cupach et al., 1986 54
Curran, 1977 17
Cutrona et al., 1990 194, 196

Daly et al., 1987 21
Davis, J.D., 1978 83
Davis, J.D. & Sloan, 1974 79
Davis, K., 1936 50
Davis, K.E. & Latty-Mann, 1987 37, 40
Davis, K.E. & Todd, 1985 91

Davitz, 1964 45
Dean et al., 1981 198
DeJong, 1979 163
DeJong-Gierveld, 1989 59, 63
Delia, 1980 85
Dept of Health & Social Security, 1976 193
Dertke et al., 1974 212
DeTurck, 1985 167, 169
Dickens & Perlman, 1981 92, 136, 138
Dillard, 1989 162
Dillard & Miller, 1988 68
Dillard et al., 1984 163
DiMatteo & Friedman, 1982 178, 180, 184, 200, 201
Dindia, 1987 26-27
Dindia & Fitzpatrick, 1985 115
Dohrenwend, 1973 199
Douglas, 1987 80, 81, 82
Dovidio et al., 1988 12
Duck, 1973; 1975a; 1975b; 1977 72, 98, 115, 137
Duck, 1980 86, 87, 90
Duck, 1982a, 1982b 95, 96
Duck, 1984 95, 100
Duck, 1988 77, 95
Duck, 1989 141
Duck, 1990a (with Silver) 192, 193
Duck, 1990b 74, 77, 86
Duck, 1991 13, 17, 33, 61, 64, 67, 68, 76, 78, 87, 91, 124, 126, 136, 142, 183, 195, 199
Duck, in press 131
Duck & Condra, 1989 78
Duck & Craig, 1978 78
Duck & Miell, 1984 84
Duck & Pond, 1989 86
Duck & Rutt, 1988 92
Duck & Sants, 1983 33, 86
Duck et al., 1980 139, 142
Duck, Pond & Leatham, 1991 79, 85, 90
Duck, Rutt, Hurst & Strejc, 1991 76, 78, 79, 83, 93, 94, 120, 127
Dunkel-Schetter & Skokan, 1990 17
Dunn, 1988 135

Eagly et al., 1978 152
Edelmann, 1985; 1988 13, 53
Eiskovits et al., 1991 105
Ellis & Weinstein, 1986 48
Ellsworth et al., 1972 9
Emler & Fisher, 1982 93
Engler et al., 1981 192
Esses & Webster, 1988 224
Evans, 1983 233
Exline, 1971 13

Farsad, et al., 1978 192
Feldman & Orford, 1980 126
Felmlee, et al., 1990 99
Festinger, 1954 154
Festinger, 1957 159, 172
Fincham & Bradbury, 1989 116, 117
Fishbein & Ajzen, 1972 160
Fisher, 1970 238
Fitzpatrick, 1977; 1988 115, 117, 123
Fitzpatrick & Badzinski, 1985 115, 122, 125, 126
Fransella, 1972 20
Freedman & Fraser, 1976 163, 172

Friedman, 1982 190
Furman, 1984 141, 142, 144
Furman et al., 1979 142
Furstenberg, 1979 132

Gallup, 1980 64
Garrard & Kyriacou, 1985 135
Geersten et al., 1973 186
Gelfand et al., 1973 212
Gibbs et al., 1989 236
Giles, 1977; 1989 28, 68
Giles & Powesland, 1975 18, 28, 29
Giles et al., 1973 29
Ginsberg, 1988 89
Glenn & Weaver, 1988 120
Glick, 1989 104
Goffman, 1959 42
Gore, 1978 129
Gormly & Gormly, 1981 72
Gotlib & Hooley, 1988 13, 17, 127
Gottlieb, 1983; 1985; 1990 134, 196, 197
Gottman, 1979; 1989; 1991 116, 118
Gottman & Krokoff, in press 119
Gottman et al., 1977 116
Greenblatt, 1978 205
Greene et al., 1985 14
Gresham & Nagle, 1980 143
Gross & Stone, 1964 52
Gudykunst & Nishida, 1986 91
Guinan & Scudder, 1989 22
Guralnick, 1976 142

Hadar, 1989 13, 29
Hagestad & Smyer, 1982 98, 112, 131-132
Hall, 1966 6
Hamilton, 1924 119
Hamlet, 1597 187
Hansen, 1991 45, 46
Hansson & Jones, 1981 64
Hansson et al., 1990 195
Hatfield & Traupmann, 1981 86
Hatvany & Strack, 1980 236
Hays, R.B., 1984; 1989 78, 93
Hays, R. & DiMatteo, 1984 16, 67-68, 183, 185, 186, 191
Hazan, 36
Hazan & Shaver, 1987 36, 40, 124
Heider, 1944; 1958 157
Helgeson et al., 1987 83
Hendrick & Hendrick, 1988 40, 44
Hendrick et al., 1984 39, 43
Hetherington, 1979 133
Hetherington et al., 1982 133, 134
Hewes et al., 1985 87
Himmelfarb, 1980 212
Hinde, 1989 122
Hindelang, 1974 212
Hobfoll, 1984; 1988 193, 195, 196
Hobfoll & London, 1985 198
Hobfoll & Stokes, 1988 68
Hobfoll & Walfisch, 1984 198
Hochschild, 1979 50
Hollander, 1958 232
Holmes & Rahe, 1967 199
Homel et al., 1987 136
Honeycutt et al., 1989 86
Hopper et al., 1981 27
Hovland et al., 1953 151, 152
Howells, 1981 16, 61
Huesmann & Levinger, 1976 86
Hunter & Boster, 1978 167
Hupka, 1991 45
Hurwitz et al., 1953 231
Huston, 1990 106
Huston et al., 1981 107, 108-109
Hyde, 1984 23

Innes, 1980; 1981 68, 200

James, 1959 238
Janis & Feshbach, 1953 171-172

Jarvinaan, 1955 186
Jellison, 1984 49
Johnson, 1984 128
Jones, E.E., 1964 231
Jones, R.A., 1982 177
Jones, W. et al., 1981 60, 64
Jones, W. et al., 1982 64
Jones, W. et al., 1984 13, 64
Jones, W. et al., 1985 61, 62, 64

Kane, 1971 11
Kassin et al., 1990 228
Kastenbaum, 1982 203
Kelley & Rolker-Dolinsky, 1987 177
Kelly, C. et al., 1985 109, 118
Kelly, L., 1982; 1984 55, 56, 57
Kelvin, 1977 114
Kemper & Bologh, 1981 44
Kendon, 1967 12, 13
Kendon & Ferber, 1973 13
Kephart, 1967 43
Kerckhoff, 1974 77
Kerckhoff & Davis, 1962 77
Kirchler, 1988 112
Kitson & Morgan, 1990 104-134
Klentz & Beaman, 1981 213
Klinger, 1977 67
Kovecses, 1991 35
Kraut, 1973 163
Kubler-Ross, 1969 203
Kurdek, 1989 120
Kurdek, 1991 103, 118

Labov, 1972 231
LaCrosse, 1975 191
Ladd, 1981; 1989; 1991 137, 142, 143
LaGaipa, 1982; 1990 68, 97
LaGreca & Santogrossi, 1980 143
Lakoff, 1973 26
Landy & Aronson, 1969 227
LaRocco et al., 1980 198
Larson et al., 1991 107
Larson et al., 1982 58, 59
Lau et al., 1982 189
Lea & Duck, 1982 72
Leary & Dobbins, 1983 56
Leary et al., 1987 56
Leatham & Duck, 1990 194, 196, 197
Lee, J., 1973 38, 39
Lee, L., 1984 95, 97, 98
Lehman & Hemphill, 1990 199
Lewis, C.N. & O'Brien, 1987 135
Lewis, R.A. & McAvoy, 1984 130, 177
Libet & Lewinsohn, 1973 16
Lin et al., 1979 198
Linn & DiMatteo, 1983 189
Lips & Morrison, 1986 109, 112
Lloyd & Cate, 1985 107, 109
Lombroso, 1918 225
Lynch, 1987 128, 175, 191, 195
Lynch et al., 1974 191
Lyons et al., 1990 180, 181

Maass & Kohnken, 1989 226
Maddison & Viola, 1968 195
Malinowski, 1929 50
Manning & Herrman, 1981 124
Marangoni & Ickes, 1989 60
Markman, 1981 118
Markman et al., 1988 109
Marshall, 1984 24
Marston et al., 1987 35, 40, 41, 43
Martin & Bumpass, 1989 104
Marwell & Schmitt, 1967 165, 166, 167
Maxwell, 1985 42
Mayseless, 1991 114
Mazur, 1977 46
McAdams & Losoff, 1984 140
McCall, 1982 88, 89, 97, 112
McCall, 1988 89

McCarthy, 1983 87
McGinnis, 1970 151
McMillan et al., 1977 26
McPartland & Hornstra, 1964 129
Mead, 1950 176
Mechanic, 1974; 1980 177, 179
Mehrabian, 1971 27
Melamed & Brenner, 1990 192
Menges, 1969 68
Menzel & Katz, 1957 68
Metts et al., 1989 95, 98
Miell, 1984; 1987 37, 83, 84, 85, 90, 230
Miell & Duck, 1986 83, 84
Mikulincer & Segal, 1990 60
Milardo, 1982; 1983 42, 88
Milardo et al., 1983 88
Miller, B.C. & Moore, 1990 105
Miller, G.R. & Boster, 1977; 1988 165, 218
Miller, G.R. & Parks, 1982 101, 165, 168
Miller, K.I. et al., 1988 68
Miller, M.D., 1982 169
Mills & Grusec, 1988 135
Milmoe et al., 1967 190
Minuchin et al., 1978 129
Mitchell & Byrne, 1973 226
Montagu, 1978 191
Montgomery, 1981; 1984 79, 80
Morgan, 1990 193
Moriarty, 1975 212
Mortimer, 1983 219
Morton et al., 1976 27
Mott & Moore, 1979 132
Mowen & Cialdini, 1980 164
Muehlenhard et al., 1986 17
Mulac, 1989 26
Mulac et al., 1987 13
Mulac et al., 1988 26
Murray & Wells, 1982 214
Murstein & Glaudin, 1968 132

Neulip & Mattson, 1990 171
Newcomb, M.D., 1990 36, 124
Newcomb, T.M., 1971 158
Newell & Stutman, 1988 150, 154, 155
Noller, 1982 116, 119
Noller & Fitzpatrick, 1990 117
Noller & Gallois, 1988 16
Noller & Hiscox, 1989 117, 119
Noller & Venardos, 1986 119

O'Barr, 1982 223, 230, 231, 232
O'Connor & Brown, 1984 128, 193
Oden & Asher, 1977 142
Orbuch, 1991 130
Orford, 1976; 1980 129
Orford & O'Reilly, 1981 16, 129
Orford et al., 1976 130
Orth et al., 1987 185

Palmer, 1990 19
Park & Waters, 1988 135
Parker, 1960 186
Parks & Adelman, 1983 42
Parsons, 1951 180, 181
Patterson, 1988 5, 11, 12, 15
Paykel et al., 1980 198
Pendleton & Hasler, 1983 185
Pennington, 1982 229
Peplau & Perlman, 1982 58
Peplau et al., 1982 58
Perlman & Peplau, 1981 59
Perlman & Serbin, 1984 59
Perlman et al., 1978 64
Pettegrew & Turkat, 1986 186
Petty & Cacioppo, 1981 152
Pfeiffer & Wong, 1989 45, 51
Phillips, 1970; 1972 204
Pickering, 1978 190
Pike & Sillars, 1985 118, 119
Pilkonis, 1977 55
Planalp et al., 1988 76

Platz & Hosch, 1988 226
Potter & Wetherell, 1987 173
Premo & Stiles, 1983 27
Prins, 1983 225
Pryor & Buchanan, 1984 227, 228
Puttalaz & Gottman, 1981 144
Puttalaz et al., 1991 37, 135, 137
Putnam et al., 1988 185
Pyszcynski & Wrightsman, 1981
    229

Rackham & Morgan, 1977 17
Radecki Bush et al., 1988 50
Reis, 1984; 1986; 1983 68, 192,
    183
Reis et al., 1980 94
Renne, 1970; 1971 129, 132
Rexroat & Shehan, 1987 120
Ridley & Nelson, 1984 118
Riskin & Faunce, 1972 116, 125
Rodin, 1982 69, 70
Rogers, 1983 175, 205
Rollins & Feldman, 1970 132
Roloff et al., 1988 162, 170
Rook, 1988; 1990 60, 64
Rook & Pietromonaco, 1987 197,
    198
Rubenstein & Shaver, 1982 61, 62
Rubin, A.M. et al., 1985 62
Rubin, K.H. et al., 1989 143
Rubin, R.B., 1977 116
Rubin, Z., 1973; 1979; 1987; 1990
    13, 42, 43, 207, 208, 210
Ruehlman & Wolchiki, 1988 198
Rutter, 1972 121

Sabatelli & Pearce, 1986 113
Saks, 1986 220, 227
Salovey, 1991 50
Salovey & Rodin, 1989 50
Sanders & Chiu, 1988 226
Sants, 1984 140
Sarason, B. et al., 1990 192, 197
Sarat & Felstiner, 1988 221, 230
Schlenker & Leary, 1982 53
Schmale, 1958 195
Schneider et al., 1989 135, 144
Schofield & Kafer, 1985 140
Schultz & Moore, 1988 58, 59
Schwarzer & Leppin, 1991 68

Scotton & Udry, 1977 29
Segrin, 1991 16
Selden, 1689 221
Selye, 1956 200
Semin & Manstead, 1982 53
Senchak & Leonard, 1992 36
Shanas et al., 1968 58
Sharpsteen, 1991 48
Shaver & Hazan, 1988 36, 37, 40,
    122
Shaver et al., 1985 63
Shea & Pearson, 1986 93
Shotland & Straw, 1976 214
Shotter, 1987 92
Shulz, 1976 62
Shuval, 1981 175
Shuval et al., 1973 181
Silberfeld, 1978 198
Sillars et al., 1983 117
Siperstein & Gale, 1983 143
Skelton & Pennebaker, 1982 176
Smith, A.J., 1957; 1960 69
Smith, R.H., 1991 45, 49
Smith-Hanen, 1977 191
Snow, 1854 192
Snyder & Smith, 1982 181
Sobol & Earn, 1985 140
Solano & Koester, 1989 60
Solano et al., 1982 60
Sommer, 1969 11
Spitzberg & Canary, 1985 15, 61,
    63
Spitzberg & Cupach, 1985 17
Sprecher, 1987 84
Stang, 1973 19
Stewart, 1980 227
Stiff & Miller, 1984 13, 14
Stiff & Miller, 1984 223, 227
Stone, 1979 190
Storm, 1991 114
Strain et al., 1977 142
Straus, 1985; 1990 104, 215
Straus & Gelles, 1986 104
Street & Buller, 1988 191
Strodtbeck et al., 1957 237
Stroebe, W., 1980 159
Stroebe, W. & Stroebe, M., 1983
    120
Suggs & Berman, 1979 236
Suitor, 1991 107, 112, 121

Sunnafrank, 1991 73
Sunnafrank & Miller, 1981 72, 230
Surra, 1984; 1990 105, 108
Surra & Huston, 1987 106
Surra et al., 1988 108–109
Szasz & Hollander, 1956 186

Tracy et al., 1984 168, 169
Tunstall, 1967 58

Unger, 1986 23

Van Lear & Trujillo, 1986 74, 77
Vaux, 1988; 1990 60, 197
Vitkus & Horowitz, 1987 16, 61

Walker, M.B. & Trimboli, 1989
    16, 30, 190
Walker, N.M. & Hops, 1973 142
Walker, R.J. & Walker, 1972 216,
    217
Walster (Hatfield) & Walster, 1978
    43
Walster (Hatfield) et al., 1966 152
Watson & Graves, 1966 11
Watzlawick et al., 1967 1, 116
Weber, 1983 97
Weiss & Aved, 1978 195
Wheeler & Nezlek, 1977 94
Wheeler et al., 1983 58
Wilkinson & Canter, 1982 17
Williams, 1974 16
Wilson & Orford, 1978 129
Wiseman, J.P., 1986; 1989 68, 146
Wiseman, R.L. & Schenk-Hamlin,
    1981 167
Wittenberg & Reis, 1986 61
Wright, 1978 83
Wyler et al., 1971 199

Yerby et al., 1990 125
Young, 1982 65
Youniss, 1980 51, 139

Zaidel & Mehrabian, 1969 29
Zakahi & Duran, 1982; 1985 57,
    58
Zietlow & Sillars, 1988 119
Zimmer, 1986 109
Zola, 1972 183, 184

Subject Index

Accent, 18, 19
Acquaintance, 74-75
Affinity, 81-82
Agape Love, 39-40
Alcoholism, 129-130
Attachment, 36ff
Attitudes, 69-71, 73f, 75
Attraction, 68ff, 73
Attractiveness, 225f
Authoritarian parents, 122
Authoritative parents, 122

Balance, 157-158
Bedside manner, 185
Behavioural intentions, 160-161
Body buffer zone, 11
Bogus stranger paradigm, 69f, 72
Bonding, 106f, 112
Breakdown of relationships, 94ff,
   98, 130, 132, 166-167, 195; See
   also Divorce
Burnout, 68
Byrne, 69f, 72

Children and friendship, 134-144
Children in marriage, 121
Children's behaviour, 123-124
Chilonas, 114
Communication, 1-240, 68, 69,
   71-76, 77ff, 187-188; In
   marriage, 114f, 116, 119
Competence, 21; See also Social
   Skills
Compliance, 166-167, 170-171
Conflict, 109; See also Breakdown
   of relationships
Courtship, 106f, 118; Predicting
   marital stability from, 118-119
Credibility, 151, 152, 220
Criminals, 224, 225, 227f
Current Contents, 243

Dating, 106f
Death, 201-205; Adjustment to,
   203-204; Timing of, 204-205
Deception, 13f, 223, 227f
Decoding, 5, 9, 190
Depression, 127-128, 193
Dissolution of relationships, 98,
   166-167
Dissonance, 159-160
Divorce, 104, 130-134; Children
   and, 133-134; Types of, 131-133
Doctor-patient relationships,
   185-186, 187, 188-189, 190-191
'Door in the face', 163-164

Embarrassment, 52f; Coping with,
   54
Emotion, 32-66
Encoding, 5, 188
Eros love, 38, 40, 41
Eye-witnesses, 223, 224-226

'Face', 52
Families, 103-133; Organization of,
   105, 110; Problems in, 128-133
Feelings, 32f
Filter theory, 77f, 228, 229
'Floortime', 19, 27
'Foot in the door', 162-163
Forms of speech, 21f, 230-233;

High form, 21f, 230-232, 233;
   Low form, 21f, 231-232; Men's
   vs Women's, 23; See also
   Powerless speech
Friendship, 33-34; And health, 183,
   192-199; Children's concepts of,
   122, 123, 124, 134, 137-141

Group decisions, 238-239

Illness, 177, 180f
Immediacy, 27-29
Inconsistency, 29-30
Independent marriage, 115-116

Jealousy, 45-51
Jury, 215f, 223, 237
Justice, 225f

Language, 230, 233, 234, 236; See
   also Forms of speech
Langue, 20
Larks, 149
Law, 207f, 220f
Lawyers, 215-223, 233-236
Loneliness, 58-65, 193, 198-199f;
   Coping with, 61; In freshmen,
   63; Types of, 60
Love, 34-44; Expression of, 41;
   Falling in, 42, 43, 44; Types of,
   37-41
'Low ball', 164
Ludus love, 38, 40, 41

Mania love, 39, 40
Marital breakdown, 132; See also
   Breakdown of relationships
Marital stability, 118
Marriage, 113f, 119f; Benefits of,
   119-120; Drawbacks of, 120-121;
   Types of, 115-117; See also
   Traditional marriage,
   Independent marriage, Separate
   marriage types
'Medspeak', 189
Memory, 37, 87
Mens rea, 220

NVC (Nonverbal Communication),
   1, 2ff, 5, 12ff, 17, 29f, 191f, 207,
   208, 221

Openness, 79-80
Outsiders, 88

Paralanguage, 18ff
Parental style, 122, 123
Parole, 20
Pathways to marriage, 108-109
Peers, 136f
Permissive parents, 122
Personality, 75f, 78
Persuasion, 146-173; Relational
   factors in, 146, 147, 148f, 162f,
   169, 170-172
Physical appearance, 224f, 225; See
   also Attractiveness
Physicians, 183f, 186
Power, 7, 26f
Powerless speech, 26-27, 233-234
Pragma love, 39, 40, 41
Primacy-recency, 229

Psychological Abstracts, 244
Psychology and sickness, 176, 180f,
   184

Rejected schoolchildren, 140
Relationships; And the law, 207f,
   208, 210, 211, 214; And
   medicine, 191; Dark side of, 241;
   Organization of, 89, 110f; Repair
   of, 99f; 'Stories' of, 90
Reporting crime, 211f, 214
Reporting sick, 178-179
Requests, 165f, 168-170
Routine, 78, 85, 86f, 90, 92, 94
Rules, 20-22, 91

Satisfaction, 114f, 116, 117
Secret tests, 13
Self-disclosure, 79, 83, 84
Self-esteem, 67-68
Self-handicapping, 182
Separate marriage, 116-117
Sex offenders, 224
Sex, 110f, 111, 116
Shoplifting, 212, 213, 214
Shyness, 55-58
Sick role, 175-182
Similarity, 153, 226
Similarity-reinforcement, 70f, 74
Social anxiety, 19, 55-58
Social comparison, 154-155
Social confrontation, 150, 154, 155
Social networks, 192-201
Social Sciences Citation Index,
   244-245
Social Skills, 16, 17, 21, 57, 91,
   126, 141-144; See also SST
Social support, 192-197, 198-199;
   Types of, 196
Sociological factors, 76-77,
   88-89
Space, 1-9, 222-223
Spatial metaphors, 4-5
Speech, 18-30, 190, 230f, 238;
   Content, 22-29; Dysfluency, 13,
   19, 20; Forms of, See Forms of
   speech; Interruption, 27; See also
   Powerless speech, Language
Speech accommodation, 28, 29
Spousal roles, 104-105, 107
SST (Social Skills Training), 10, 17,
   57
Starting relationships, 68ff; See also
   Attraction
Status, 22-27
Storge love, 38, 40
Strategy, 80-84
Stress, 199-201
Style switching, 28, 190, 230-236
Suspicion, 242
Swingers, 49
Symbolic decoration, 7-8

Talk, 93, 94, 120
Territory, 5-8
Traditional marriage, 115, 116
Trials: Nature of, 215f, 217, 218
Turn-taking, 11-12

Uncertainty, 77-80

Witnesses, 223, 231, 232, 235, 236

acq-1217